Advance Praise

"The authors demystify the complex process of building a corporate reputation in a comprehensive yet simplistic and easily understandable framework, drawing largely upon the journey of Indian corporates. The four critical factors for strategic structuring of reputation outlined in the book, viz., economic logic; goals and objectives; values, vision and mission and environment, appear analogous to the four movements of an orchestral symphony and align the theme of the book. A must-read for every organisation and leader targeting corporate excellence."

—N. K. Maini, Deputy Managing Director,
Small Industries Development Bank of India (SIDBI)

"A remarkably practical, lucid and well-researched book complete with examples, framework and strategies from corporations in India for building corporate reputation, invaluable for any corporate executive concerned with the subject of building corporate reputation."

—Dr Arvind N. Agrawal, Management Board Member, President,
Corporate Development and Human Resources, RPG Enterprises

"Decoding the DNA of the corporate reputation gene, more so in the Indian context, is a new path to discovery that the authors have commendably embarked upon. When corporates make larger societal value creation a core raison d'être and this commitment drives the enterprise mind, body and spirit, it can unleash a virtuous cycle of innovation and excellence for sustainable competitive advantage. Reputational assets are then a natural outcome."

—Nazeeb Arif, Vice President, Corporate Communications, ITC Ltd.

"Reputation of a corporate house cannot be built overnight. It takes years of sustained efforts to perpetually meet the expectations of various stakeholders, particularly customers, by instilling a deep-rooted culture of ethical business practices. Interestingly, like various other dimensions of a business, reputation can also be strategised, nurtured and developed for the gainful dividend. *Corporate Reputation Decoded* is an excellent practical handbook in this regard."

—Sudhir Vasudeva, Chairman and Managing Director,
Oil and Natural Gas Corporation Ltd. (ONGC)

Corporate Reputation Decoded

Corporate Reputation Decoded

Building, Managing and Strategising for Corporate Excellence

Asha Kaul
Avani Desai

SAGE | Response Business Books

www.sagepublications.com

Los Angeles • London • New Delhi • Singapore • Washington DC

First published in 2014 by

SAGE Response
B1/I-1 Mohan Cooperative Industrial Area
Mathura Road, New Delhi 110 044, India

SAGE Publications Inc
2455 Teller Road
Thousand Oaks, California 91320, USA

SAGE Publications Ltd
1 Oliver's Yard, 55 City Road
London EC1Y 1SP, United Kingdom

SAGE Publications Asia-Pacific Pte Ltd
3 Church Street
#10-04 Samsung Hub
Singapore 049483

Published by Vivek Mehra for SAGE Publications India Pvt Ltd, Phototypeset in 11/13pt Baskerville by Diligent Typesetter, Delhi and printed at Saurabh Printers Pvt Ltd, New Delhi.

Library of Congress Cataloging-in-Publication Data Available

ISBN: 978-81-321-1774-2 (PB)

The SAGE Team: Sachin Sharma, Alekha Chandra Jena, Rajib Chatterjee and Dally Verghese

To our families

Harsh, Anand, Rupa and Rohini   Akash and Vishwesh

Thank you for choosing a SAGE product! If you have any comment, observation or feedback, I would like to personally hear from you. Please write to me at <u>contactceo@sagepub.in</u>

—Vivek Mehra, Managing Director and CEO,
SAGE Publications India Pvt Ltd, New Delhi

Bulk Sales

SAGE India offers special discounts for purchase of books in bulk. We also make available special imprints and excerpts from our books on demand.

For orders and enquiries, write to us at

Marketing Department
SAGE Publications India Pvt Ltd
B1/I-1, Mohan Cooperative Industrial Area
Mathura Road, Post Bag 7
New Delhi 110044, India
E-mail us at <u>marketing@sagepub.in</u>

Get to know more about SAGE, be invited to SAGE events, get on our mailing list. Write today to <u>marketing@sagepub.in</u>

This book is also available as an e-book.

Contents

SECTION II
Building Corporate Reputation

SECTION III

Managing Corporate Reputation

SECTION IV

Strategising Corporate Reputation

List of Tables and Figures

TABLES

FIGURES

Preface

What is corporate reputation? Why is it important to understand, build, manage and strategise corporate reputation? What is the link between a stellar reputation and corporate excellence? Why has the term 'reputation' gained mammoth proportions? Can corporate reputation be decoded? These are some of the questions that are answered in this book, *Corporate Reputation Decoded: Building, Managing and Strategising for Corporate Excellence.*

Corporate reputation is a fairly new concept and discipline when compared to other management areas. Over the last few decades, researchers and academics have struggled to define this concept in terms of finance, accounting, marketing, etc. Gradually, with passage of time, the definitions have expanded beyond the narrow confines of management disciplines. Today, corporate reputation is viewed as a set of images created in the minds of stakeholders based on a company's products/services, financial performance, leadership, workplace culture, innovation, governance and employees. Would someone recommend your product? Have you been able to retain your employees? Would investors be willing to invest? These are some of the questions that stem from the aforementioned attributes of good corporate reputation. If the answer to all the above questions is yes, then the organisation has a stellar reputation!

Not all research is in agreement on the defining attributes of corporate reputation. There is an ongoing debate concerning determinants of corporate reputation that have been labelled as a set of tangibles or intangibles. However, what cannot be disputed is the fact that today a good corporate reputation has become synonymous with success and corporate excellence. Companies have begun to traverse that extra mile and build on existing competencies, engage with internal and external stakeholders, and align company values, philosophy, vision and mission to goals and targets. In this travail, the questions asked are: Has the journey begun? How much ground has been covered? How close is the desired destination? Answers to these questions often reflect the quantum of reputational capital amassed by the company in its journey of success. Greater the distance traversed, more the capital accumulated.

Much work has been done in the West on strategies adopted by companies to build corporate reputation. This book is the first of its kind that traces successes and failures of Indian companies, in the journey of building corporate reputation. The book deliberates on both, research conducted by academicians and practices followed by the corporate world in building a reputation par excellence. Additionally, it explores the company and leader perspectives in understanding and aligning stakeholders, building and managing relationships with them.

The increasing focus on corporate reputation in the Indian corporate scenario and enhanced number of corporate and marketing communication departments bear testimony to the relevance of the text. However, some of the questions that still need to be answered are: Do global practices hold in the Indian scenario? Can research done in the West be applied to Indian companies? Are strategies for building corporate reputation the same across the world? Can we build a universally and globally accepted model for corporate reputation? As we move in the domain of corporate reputation scholarship, we find that research findings in the West are equally applicable in the Indian context. Our proposed strategies, thus, have global underpinnings and major research significance for corporate reputation scholars, teachers and students. Additionally, the techniques proposed in the book for building corporate reputation are sure to be of interest to practitioners who can assess strategies followed by other companies for reputation enhancement. The reflection and implementation will be both an enriching and rewarding experience for the corporates.

STRUCTURE OF THE BOOK

Beginning with an overview of corporate reputation, the book leads the readers through the four phases of understanding, building, managing and strategising corporate reputation. The four phases are divided into four sections of the book.* The overview debates the relegation of corporate reputation to the category of a hammer or a tool. This chapter argues that reputation can be used as a hammer to negatively impact the top and bottom line, and also a tool or an enabler to positively influence the outcome of company actions and secure competitive advantage. The question is what strategies companies adopt to understand, build, manage and strategise corporate reputation so that it acts as a tool and not a hammer.

There is one chapter each in Sections I and IV. Sections II and III comprise four chapters each. *Waltzing with Stakeholders to Score on Corporate Reputation* in Section I, Understanding Corporate Reputation suggests ways for identifying and analysing stakeholders and argues the significance of aligning and leveraging their support for an enhanced reputational quotient. Methods for influencing, building and managing stakeholder relationships are posited.

The four chapters in Section II, Building Corporate Reputation discuss ways of building corporate reputation through advocacy of company values and philosophy embedded in corporate governance practices, leader behaviour, and relationships with investors and government. *Redeeming Corporate Trust and Reputation: A Systemic Look at Corporate Governance and Ethics* is the first chapter in this section. While providing an overview of corporate governance legislation in India, the chapter examines its relevance and advances a systemic perspective for understanding and implementing corporate governance, without diluting the centrality of leadership and values.

---

*Note: As all the sections and chapters in the book are designed to be standalone, there may be a few iterations that have deliberately been woven in the text to provide comprehensiveness and cohesion in the chapters.

The next chapter, *Orchestrating the Song and Dance of Reputation: The Role of Leaders* proceeds to understand how leaders craft their reputation and posits the critical link between leader and organisational reputation, examines the style most appropriate for building company reputation and suggests strategies for leader communication.

The significance of building relationship with investors is the focal point of Chapter 5, *Increasing Crescendo: Wooing Investors for Market Valuation and Visibility*. In this chapter, the benefits, structure and mechanics of investor relations together with communication strategies to woo investors are discussed. Additionally, techniques for drafting investor relation messages and connecting with the media for positive gains, despite challenges that crowd the reputational zone, are deliberated upon.

The most important entity in building corporate relationships is the government. How companies seek 'relational rent' and 'hedge risks' is addressed in Chapter 6, *Seeking Relational Rent and Hedging Risk: Building Reputation with the Government*. Often used terms as lobbying, corporate political ties and activities, public–private partnerships, tripartite partnerships and their significance in helping build relationships with bureaucrats, legislators and regulators are postulated.

It is easy to climb up the ladder of success but difficult to retain the position. How do companies manage their reputation? This is the underlying theme of Section III, Managing Corporate Reputation. Creating a social impact for stakeholders and communities in a company's area of operations has become a strategic imperative today. In Chapter 7, *Unleashing the Potential of Social Responsibility for Reputational Gain: Managing Social Impact*, reasons for higher firm performance due to societal investments are posited and communication strategies listed for projecting a positive image/reputation.

The media and social media have, today, changed the way the business functions and projects itself. Chapters 8 and 9, *Choreographing the Organisation–Media Tango: Managing Media Relations* and *Understanding the 'Tweet. Post. Call. Comment' Affair: Managing Reputation through Social Media*, discuss the criticality of managing relationships with the media and digital influencing. In the current situation of economic turbulence, it is important for organisations to understand and manage media relations. There is interdependence in the media–company relationship where none can survive without the other. What is framing, how does media employ it, and what counter strategies should/do companies use—are the central points of discussion in this chapter on managing media relations. The chapter on social media outlines the objectives of initiating a digital dialogue and strategies for the same. While assessing the return on investment (ROI) of social media, it proceeds to establish a link between social media and corporate reputation.

A company will face a crisis situation at some point in its life cycle that may create a dent leading to loss-of-face in the market. It is inevitable but true! How does a company manage a crisis? What are the ramifications? How does it limp back to normalcy? Chapter 10, *Restoring Confidence and Reengineering Stakeholder Frames in 'The Eye of the Storm': Crisis Management*, provides cues for understanding the telltale signs of an impending crisis, suggests ways to devise a crisis communication strategy, emphasises leadership role and communication in such situations while establishing a link between crisis and reputation.

The chapter in Section IV, Strategising Corporate Reputation underscores the importance of strategic planning. While companies and leaders have often been charged with not 'walking the talk' or lauded for possessing capabilities to 'walk the talk', are they also able to 'talk the walk'? The last chapter of the book, *'Walk the Talk' and 'Talk the Walk': Strategising Corporate Reputation*, discusses the need and ability to develop a vision, narrate stories, craft a communication plan and strategise the process of understanding, building and managing corporate reputation for corporate excellence.

Acknowledgements

Now that we reflect on it, it will be difficult for us to assign a date when the writing of the book commenced and closed. As we moved in and out of classes, conceptualising chapters and recollecting examples, we had a team of two Academic Associates, IIMA working with us—Ms Chitralekha Chakrabarty and Dr Nameeta Chandra—who took the burden off our shoulders by making good and concrete suggestions, searching articles and examples, and editing. We are of the view that giving credit to Chitra and Nameeta at the head of this section is truly justified. Acknowledgements are also due to Sudhir Kr. Pandey, Academic Associate, IIMA and Ms Uzma Aamir, Manager, School of Liberal Studies, Pandit Deendayal Petroleum University for helping with the literature review in the initial part of the book writing.

Mr Shoebmohmed Chobdar, IIMA, with a smile, has helped punch in content, work on the references, etc. Thanks, Shoeb. We would like to extend our gratitude to Mr Vinod Parmar for providing timely help in recreating more appealing diagrams in CorelDraw.

We would also like to acknowledge the suggestions of Dr Vidhi Chaudhuri, Assistant Professor at Erasmus University, Rotterdam, who is equally passionate about corporate reputation. After she read the first chapter on Corporate Social Responsibility, her response was prompt and critical: 'Do you want the book to be an authoritative treatise on the subject? Be more comprehensive!' Thanks, Vidhi! We also managed to rope her in for doing a chapter on Corporate Governance.

Over the last four years, as we taught the course, Communicating Corporate Reputation, the feedback of IIMA students was of immense value. We would like to acknowledge the support of each and every student who took the elective, showed interest in the reputation-building exercise of organisations and made noteworthy suggestions and contributions.

As we stop today and reflect on the process, we know that it would have been difficult for us to complete the book without the support and cooperation of our families. Moments when we refused to go out or party, burnt the midnight oil, could not attend to issues at home were overlooked. We think it appropriate to close this note with profound thanks to Mrs Vimla Kaul and Late Shri G. N. Kaul, Dr K. K. Kaul, Shri R. G. Desai and Mrs Uma Desai, Shri Sharad Desai and Mrs Vasanti Desai, for being pillars of support. Harsh, Anand, Rupa, Rohini, Akash and Vishwesh, would we be where we are today if you would not have been around?

Asha Kaul
Avani Desai

1

An Overview of Corporate Reputation: A Hammer or a Tool?

Reputation is an idle and most false imposition: oft got without merit, and lost without deserving.

—WILLIAM SHAKESPEARE[1]

Objectives:

- Provide a definition of reputation
- Understand the difference between image, identity and reputation
- Study techniques of managing reputation
- Identify the role of reputation in securing competitive advantage
- Craft a framework for communicating reputation
- Assess the importance of corporate reputation

INTRODUCTION

Our reputation is more important than the last hundred million dollars.

—RUPERT MURDOCH[2]

Why and how have companies across the globe begun to speak the same language—the language of reputation management? Why have words as frauds, debacles, stellar

---

Key Words

- Behaviour
- Communication
- Competitive advantage
- Customers
- Framework
- Identity
- Image
- Mission
- Multidimensionality

- People
- Performance
- Planet
- Profits
- Reputation
- Stakeholders
- Transparency
- Triple bottom line
- Unidimensionality

---

performances, profitability, corporate stewardship, regulations, investor relationships, stakeholder perceptions and media relations begun to crowd corporate reputation scholarship? The answer is simple. The rules of the game have changed. For instance, no longer is the success of a company measured only by its financial performance. Causative factors as internationalisation and globalisation have led companies to focus on communicating what they have done, what they are doing and what they plan to do to enhance the triple bottom line that is, people, planet and profits.

The shift in focus from profits to people and planet is not inadvertent but stems from the logic that if stakeholders are nurtured and environment is preserved, profits will accrue. Companies have begun to realise that it is critical to build a character that commits to integrity and transparency through well-enunciated vision and mission statements. Being

---

Vedanta Resources: Reputation for Sustainability under the Scanner

Vedanta Resources plc, headquartered in London, is a 15 billion US$[3] natural resources conglomerate with interests in copper, zinc, silver, aluminium, oil and gas, iron ore and power segments.

The company's stated belief is: 'to meet our strategic objectives and to create and preserve value for all of our stakeholders, it is essential that at all levels we conduct our business in a sustainable manner.'[4] It also emphasises its commitment to 'minimising our environmental footprint from the start of operations to closure and beyond.'[5]

One look at the awards and accolades received by the group's various companies in the area of sustainable development for 2013 alone—The CII Sustainability Award (BALCO), The International Green Apple Award from The Green Organization, London (BALCO), The Good Green Governance Award from Srishti Publications Pvt. Ltd., New Delhi (BALCO), the OISD Safety Award 2012 from Oil Industry Safety Directorate (Cairn India Ltd.) and the Golden Peacock CSR Award 2012 (Cairn India Ltd.)[6]—would convince one about its rigorous focus on sustainability issues and its robust reputation for the same.

However, the company's plans to drill for bauxite in Odisha's Niyamgiri hills in 2009 led to a wave of protests beginning with the tribal residents of the region and finding support all the way to London. For the last four years, demonstrations have been held inside and outside its annual general meetings in London.[7] Amid allegations of environmental devastation, anti-union action, corruption and even deaths of protesting tribals, some organisations as Foil Vedanta are trying to get Vedanta de-listed from the London Stock Exchange.[8]

Will this issue escalate and impact the company's reputation? In the present scenario, is the reputation of Vedanta Resources a hammer or a tool?

on a constant vigil, thwarting negative influences and developing competencies to manage internal stakeholders and build external allies require consistent time, effort and persistence, which rarely, if ever, go unrewarded. We would not be far from the truth if we were to state that reputational capital can be generated by creating an exemplary company character that is governed by cognitive (performance) and affective (sympathetic) dimensions.

The advantages of a good reputation are multiple. It:

- Helps in making financial decisions that are accepted by stakeholders
- Aids in selling a product at a premium price
- Is an indicator of legitimacy
- Helps in building trust
- Heralds success

Small wonder then, that reputation has been the 'poster term' for multiple disciplines including sociology, accounting, strategy and others, as reflected in Table 1.1.

Table 1.1   Concept, Characteristics and Requirements of Reputation under Various Parameters

S. No.	Disciplines/ Theories	Concept of Reputation	Characteristics of Reputation	Requirements for Building Reputation
1	Sociology[9]	A social identity; the main determinant of status	Can be inherited through family or caste characteristics. Entities must be active in shaping environment, rather than being passive influencers	Organisation must increase overlap between projected image and actual attributes
2	Accounting[10]	Maximising value for all stakeholders	Profit is a short-term goal; value maximisation is more important	Using tools as Balanced Scorecard to determine extent of impact of financial and non-financial measures on various stakeholders
2.1	Transaction Cost[11]	Reputation (positive) reduces transaction costs	Implies visibility and trust, causing the entity to be monitored and evaluated more easily	Requires building on visibility to ensure that searching costs for the entity are lowered
3	Strategy[12]	The idiosyncratic capital of an entity	Affects sustainable competitive advantage	Requires non-transferable idiosyncratic investments as reputation is built for specific stakeholders
4	Organisation Theory[13]	An asset specific to a certain entity	Reputation can be correlated if more entities co-organise communication	Requires assessing the degree to which reputation can be redeployed by alternative uses/users without sacrificing its value

(Table 1.1 Continued)

(Table 1.1 Continued)

S. No.	Disciplines/ Theories	Concept of Reputation	Characteristics of Reputation	Requirements for Building Reputation
4.1	Network[14]	Reputation is heavily conditioned by actions of institutional investors and media accounts	An organisation can acquire the reputation of another entity by networking with it	Requires developing long-term networks whose membership is based on certain aspects of reputation which together make up the network's reputation
4.2	Cultural[15]	Reputation affects mental programs leading to persons exhibiting more or less the same behaviour in similar situations at individual, collective and universal levels	Affects organisational culture	Requires an understanding of the stable components of culture that lead members of an organisation to exhibit certain behaviours
5	Economics[16]	The perception of a company held by external observers	Has an informational content; is functional as it generates perceptions	Requires allocating resources to activities that can create a perception of reliability and predictability to outside observers
5.1	Legitimation[17]	Social legitimation in the context of economic exchange	Leads to legitimacy if reputation is at a certain acceptable minimum level	Requires achieving legitimacy by conforming to societal ideologies about the mode of functioning of organisations

Table 1.1 exemplifies the interdisciplinary and vast nature of 'reputation' and spells out a need to converge and synthesise ideas across disciplines that add value to the corporate world.

Reputation and its management have gained mammoth proportions in the current changing economic scenario. Reasons are multiple:

- Increasing globalisation has shrunk boundaries, removed entry barriers and increased global presence and enhanced emphasis on governance be it with respect to employees or carbon footprints.
- Entry of private sector players into domains that were hitherto controlled by the public sector.
- Diverse, educated and sophisticated group of stakeholders who are pressurising companies to consider informed decisions based on the ease and speed at which information is disseminated.

- Increased focus of stakeholders and activists on humanitarian and environmental issues.
- Filtering purchase decisions based on company behaviour and conduct along aforementioned dimensions.
- Rankings and ratings assigned to companies by agencies that publicly compare and evaluate performance.[18]

Hence, our focus on reputation is not unjustified! Beginning with a modest introduction to the subject, we discuss in this chapter what is a reputation, present the company perspective in managing and developing reputation, differentiate between identity, image and reputation, study the role of reputation in securing competitive advantage, posit a framework for crafting and communicating reputation and present its importance.

WHAT IS A REPUTATION?

Corporate reputation should be considered as much more than simply a brand emblem in the marketplace. Rather, it is a window to the fundamental character of a company and its leaders and as such is relevant to all stakeholders…

—STEPHEN GREYSER[19]

Over the years, scholars and researchers have posited various definitions and interpretations of corporate reputation. The discussion has primarily focussed on stakeholder impressions and dimensionality of reputation. Stakeholder impressions suggest that all stakeholders have a similar view about the company and variances if any, are not significant enough to be addressed. The concept of dimensionality proposes an understanding of corporate reputation as a combination of admiration, respect, trust and confidence in a company or a 'collective assessment of the company's ability to provide valued outcomes to a representative group of stakeholders'.[20] It scores multidimensionality over unidimensionality and posits that 'the customer's overall evaluation of a firm [is] based on his or her reactions to the firm's goods, services, communication activities, interactions with the firm and/or its representatives or constituencies (as employees, management or other customers) and/or known corporate activities.'[21] This implies that customer perceptions are shaped by company willingness to satisfy their needs, how management treats its employees and pays heed to their interests and the level of competency in the employees. Multidimensionality also refers to internal and external business stakeholders and their perceptions of company activities in the society.

This construct of multidimensionality can be measured on three reputational dimensions: financial, managerial and product (refer Fig. 1.1). All three are independent and represent different aspects of corporate reputation. The financial refers to the profitability of the company where customer expectations and desire to invest resources are shaped by perceptions of managerial prowess. The social and environmental factors capture the stakeholder belief in management generating societal goodwill by positive contributions

Figure 1.1   Multidimensionality of Corporate Reputation

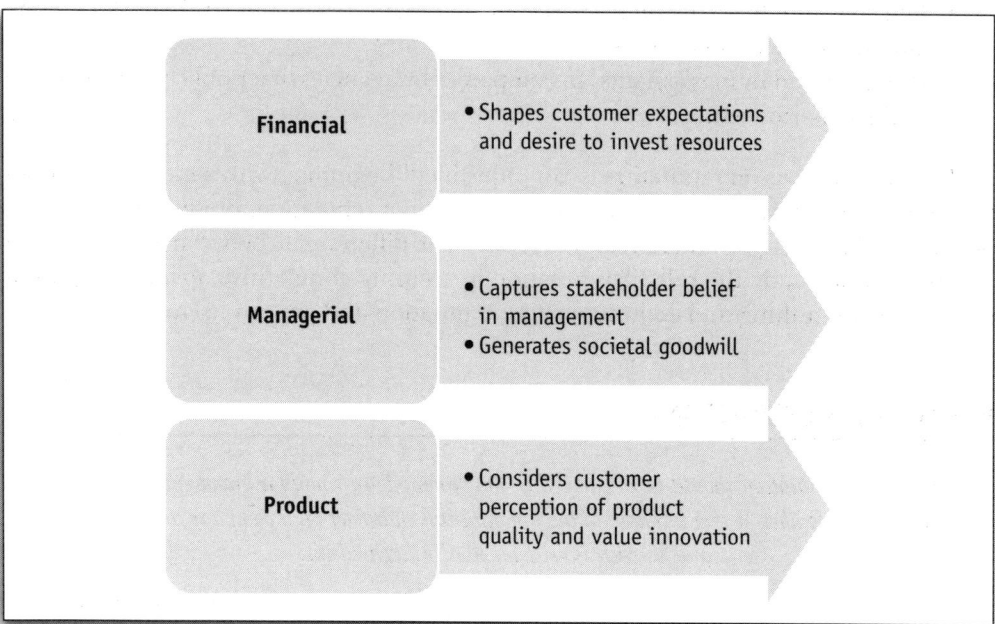

to the society and environment. The dimension of product and quality service takes into account customer perceptions of the product, its inherent quality and value innovation.

Based on the above propositions, it can be stated that a good reputation signals stakeholder loyalty. Are stakeholders willing to provide positive recommendations or word-of-mouth referrals? A simple yes is reflective of the trust, transparency and appreciation of company operations over the years.

Reputation through Referrals: Tata Consultancy Services Ltd.

Mr Kedar Shirali,[22] Head Global Investor Relations, Tata Consultancy Services Ltd. (TCS) believes that positive recommendations from other stakeholders as investors are equally important contributors to the reputation of the company. He shares an instance of Mr Jeff Chowdhry, Head of Emerging Market Equities at F&C Asset Management plc stating that TCS is head and shoulders above other companies in its sector due to good communication of its consistent and well-implemented strategy to shareholders. Even in a difficult external environment, with possibly low orders, companies as TCS score high because of their strategic choices and decisions.[23]

Reputation evolves over time and is earned and bestowed by stakeholders. It is a consequence of direct and indirect experiences that may differ across groups or segments.

For instance, an environmental stewardship may be viewed positively by a select group of elitist shareholders yet may be perceived suspiciously by activists. Hence, we would not be far from the truth in stating that reputation is the perception of stakeholders based on the sum of their expectations and company dialogue and behaviour (honest and transparent). The rising or plummeting reputational quotient can satisfactorily be addressed through appropriate communication with stakeholders. It is not only what the company does and says but also what it does not do or does not state that impacts reputational quotient. In short, the reputation and value associated develops through interaction between and among stakeholders. It is a combined assessment that creates an image, strengthened by the role and accountability of the leader/leadership team.

It has been found that the most reputable organisations have CEOs who have proved their worth in terms of respect, credibility and integrity. For example, in its January–February 2013 issue *Harvard Business Review*[24] lists Mr Y. C. Deveshwar (ITC Ltd.) at seventh position among the world's best performing CEOs. His credibility and personal reputation have undoubtedly influenced the reputation of ITC, which has also been ranked among the top three at the *Fortune India*'s Most Admired Companies 2013.[25]

HOW DO COMPANIES MANAGE AND DEVELOP REPUTATION?

There is no advertisement as powerful as a positive reputation traveling fast.

—Brian Koslow[26]

Corporate reputation management can be understood as a composite of constituent relationships, reputation building practices and organisational issues. Some key actions relate to associating with constituents (internal and external), designing practices, building strategies and systems, organising and assigning responsibilities for various actions. Reputation thus can be referred to be a sum of performance, behaviour and communication (refer Fig. 1.2).

As an integrated process, reputation management involves doing, communicating, listening and seeing. Companies with a good reputation follow a consistent policy of informing stakeholders about products, services, operations, history and identity, using multiple channels to communicate their message.

Figure 1.2 Constituents of Corporate Reputation[27]

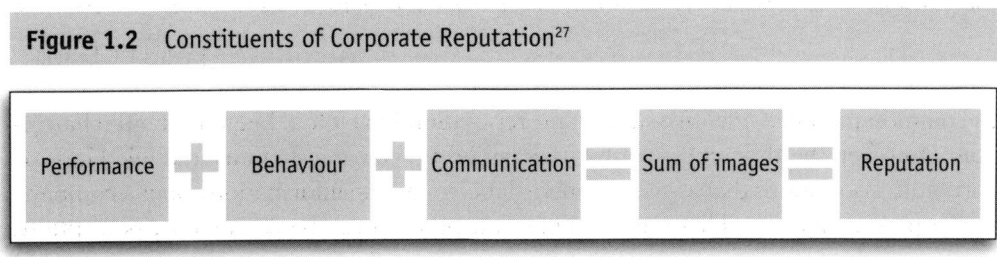

Performance + Behaviour + Communication = Sum of images = Reputation

One Message, Many Media: ITC Ltd.

ITC Ltd. is a prime example of a company that effectively uses multiple channels to provide relevant information to stakeholders. Information about its huge product portfolio of 50 brands is shared through its website, various print and television advertisements, and even forms 10 colourful pages of its annual report. The CEO, Mr Y. C. Deveshwar, uses a wide range of platforms, ranging from management discussion and analysis section of the annual report, the sustainability report, speeches at the company's AGMs as well as interviews in the media to reiterate the identity of the company as one 'creating world-class brands that put India first'.[28]

Reputation-building communication requires that an attempt be made to understand constituents' perspective and concerns which could act as content for developing corporate messages. Communication centring on 'being' and 'doing' is what lends credence and reputational capital to organisations. Companies with a higher reputation ranking have been found to be more effective and superior in terms of doing and communicating than companies with a comparatively lower reputation ranking. For acquiring this status, companies need to intensely and aggressively 'walk the talk' and 'talk the walk' to communicate their presence and identity.

Walking the Talk: Mr Azim Premji

Mr Azim Premji, Chairman, Wipro Ltd. transferred 295.5 million equity shares, representing 12 per cent of the shares of Wipro Ltd., to an irrevocable trust (the Azim Premji Trust). This is the largest philanthropic transfer by any individual in the country and is a part of the Giving Pledge, a promise by the world's richest persons to commit a large portion of his wealth to philanthropy. Mr Premji publicly stated: 'I strongly believe that those of us who are privileged to have wealth should contribute significantly to try and create a better world for the millions who are far less privileged.'[29]

DOES REPUTATION LIE IN THE EYE OF THE BEHOLDER?

For good or for ill, the reputation of an organization is made through the words and deeds of its members.

—James O'Toole[30]

In common parlance, identity, image and reputation have often been used interchangeably. However, the difference can be understood by viewing them as multiple kinds of corporate associations that assign a 'generic label for all the information about a company that a person holds'.[31] These associations can be of three types: identity, perceptions of internal stakeholders; intended image or mental associations created by leaders for intended stakeholders; construed image or mental associations of external stakeholders.

A fine line demarcates the three concepts of identity, image and reputation. 'Identity' is the manner in which key constituencies conceptualise the company and is 'the construed external image of the firm. What a member believes outsiders think about the organization'.[32] 'Image' is the 'view of the organization developed by its stakeholders; the outside world's overall impression of the company'.[33] 'Reputation' is the manner in which key stakeholders develop perceptions about the company and is 'a collective presentation of all participants' image, built over time and based on programmes of company identity, its performance and perceptions of its behaviour'.[34] A favourable impression of the company or positive reputation is transmitted through corporate communication that removes uncertainty, helps shareholders appreciate operational issues and builds an intangible asset for the company, which cannot be openly traded in the market but adds value to the organisation.

Company reputation is composed of a set of beliefs about the company and the industry in which it operates. In other words, a combination of corporate image and corporate identity is what finally shapes corporate reputation. The corporate image denotes stakeholder belief and identity attributes used to describe an organisation. In other words, 'what do people think about you?' and 'who are you?' The beliefs of an organisation are based on relationship with stakeholders, knowledge of company character, capability, products, services and behaviour. Further, a reputational quotient is generated based on the company's past behaviour, with use of descriptive terms to define the company, and authentication of beliefs that match with stakeholder values. An organisation with a good reputation can thus be classified as one in which its identity and image match the stakeholder values and beliefs.

In summary, based on the company's performance (in terms of its quality of products/services and financial performance), its behaviour (including quality of engagement with stakeholders) and its corporate communication, key stakeholders develop an image which comprises their beliefs, feelings and perceptions about the company. The company's identity is its own projection of attributes created through symbols, verbal and visual communication and behaviour, which influences its key stakeholders. Both, identity and image, together shape corporate reputation (refer Fig. 1.3).

To elaborate further, reputation is based on the five facets of identity:[35] professed—what the company professes; projected—the identity projected to different stakeholders in varying hues; experienced—what the stakeholders experience about the company or its product/service; manifested—what the company has manifested through its behaviour over the years and attributed—what stakeholders attribute to a company based on their experiences.

Based on the identity, situation and relationship, individual stakeholders form opinions about a company that may or may not overlap with the collective impression. However, in scholarly discussions, 'reputation' is viewed as a collective phenomenon attributed to a group of people rather than a single individual. This in no way implies that individual

Figure 1.3   Identity, Image and Reputation

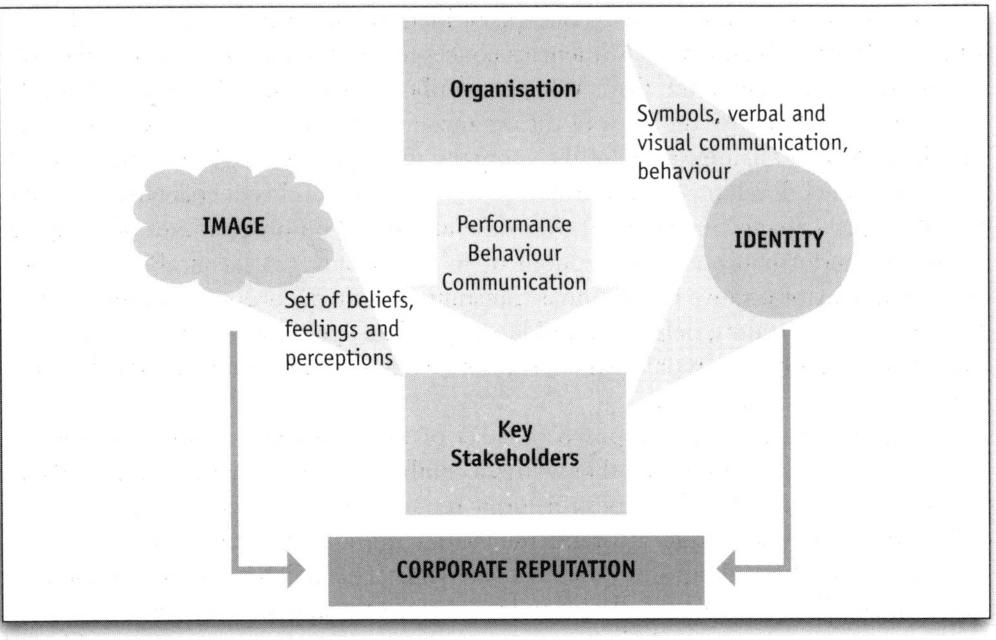

Facets of Identity: Larsen & Toubro Ltd.

Larsen & Toubro Ltd.'s (L&T) vision professes it to be 'committed to total customer satisfaction and enhancing value; ... constantly creating value and attaining global benchmarks ... meeting expectations of employees, stakeholders and society'.[36] It projects this identity through its advertisements where it shows how its activities help in 'building India'.[37] These professed and projected identities are experienced by its stakeholders in the form of L&T's products and services, and an increased CAGR in sales and recurring profits.[38] The identity is then manifested and attributed by way of various awards received by the company: for example, L&T is the only company in the engineering and construction sector to be ranked among the top 10 'Best Indian Brands' in an Interbrand and Economic Times Survey,[39] to have been the recipient of the NDTV Profit Business Leadership Award and Golden Peacock National Quality Award 2013.[40]

Its professed identity of meeting expectations of stakeholders is also manifested in its various stakeholder-oriented and sustainability awards: second in India in the All Asia Investor Relations Perception Study conducted by *Institutional Investor* magazine,[41] among the Top five overall and first in Engineering and Automotive sector in *Business Today—People Strong* 'Best Companies to Work For',[42] ICC Corporate Governance and Sustainability Vision Award, 'Caring Company Award' by World CSR Congress and CII Sustainability Award.[43] Collectively, these identities enable it to build a robust reputation; evident in its being figured among Top five in *Businessworld* 'India's Most Respected Companies 2013'[44] and among Top 10 in *Fortune* 'India's most Admired Companies 2013'.[45]

views are insignificant. The challenge before companies is to convert individual perceptions to collective impressions. An accurate comprehension of reputation and its management begins with an assessment of individual impressions followed by continuous social pooling of sensibilities to minimise variations across time and zone.

DOES REPUTATION HELP SECURE COMPETITIVE ADVANTAGE?

I repeat: Today we're in an all-out war for reputation. Our companies are battling—
to an unprecedented extent—for our most vital assets: our own identities.

—MILES D. WHITE[46]

Can reputation be used for gaining competitive advantage? Let us begin examining this question by listing the drivers (subsequent chapters in the book attempt an in-depth understanding of reputation drivers) of corporate reputation: size—larger companies enjoy greater fame; prior performance—an aggregate of financial performance over the last three to five years; media exposure—what the media says and does; dividend policy and strategy as reflected in the investment decisions, investments in charitable causes and environmental stewardship.

As a good strategy, companies should compete on existing reputation or use reputation as a tool taking into cognisance all stakeholders. Identifying with the local stakeholders and investing in local communities without flaunting commercial success is the best strategy for securing competitive advantage. For this to happen, the company should be perceived as credible with required expertise; authoritative with desired power and influence and likeable, suggesting similar beliefs as those of the stakeholders.

How do companies assess which stakeholder group is the most important? This can be done by revisiting the statement of intent and measures of control. Some companies have more than one internal statement to describe their image that may be reflected in their credo, while others may use a more formal strategic plan comprising vision and mission statements and/or a code of business ethics and governance practices. A process of periodically measuring and validating market position ascertains the success of the strategy adopted. Companies can begin by asking the question, is our reputation merely useful or strategic? If the answer is 'useful' then attempts should be made to weave it in the corporate strategy. If the response is 'strategic', then it should be communicated at large to all stakeholders.

Research points to tangible and intangible assets as measures for providing competitive advantage. Undoubtedly, a good corporate reputation reduces transactional costs and improves financial and non-financial results. For companies to employ reputation as a tool for securing competitive advantage, they need to initiate programmes that give shape to their identity and create a positive image. By crafting a corporate reputation framework companies may decide to foster a reputation that either matches the expectations of a large group or restricts it to those who matter.

CAN A FRAMEWORK OF CORPORATE REPUTATION BE CRAFTED?

A corporate reputation is an overall evaluation that reflects the extent to which people see the firm as substantially 'good' or 'bad'.

—GRAHAME R. DOWLING[47]

Companies can develop a framework for building and maintaining corporate reputation (refer Fig. 1.4). The first step in the process is assessing current reputation by auditing internal responses from employees. A critical review brings to the table the strengths and weaknesses of the company, the set of values and principles it espouses and the strategic direction it has chalked for itself. Following the review is the process of prioritisation and alignment of stakeholder or influencer (financial community, media, government, activists and advocacy) groups. The prioritisation is based on the relative importance of stakeholders in achieving company objectives and meeting goals. For example, Tata Steel Ltd., ranked as 'India's Most Admired Company' in 2013 by *Fortune*, uses a stakeholder-mapping approach to identify its most important stakeholders, gauges the degree of inter-relationship between groups and formulates the correct strategy of engaging with each.

Once this process is over, the company is able to decipher the attributes that stakeholders consider important in assessing company reputation. Subsequently, companies decide to add any unique or industry-specific attribute that give it the winning edge. The advantage of this step is that it allows the company latitude in focussing or refocussing its strategies, reallocating or investing resources based on attribute selection.

The second phase is developing a reputation strategy in which specific objectives are laid down, perceptions of business captured and a business strategy defined. Companies may decide to begin with the five pillars of building reputation: people, pacesetters, products, performance and purpose which represent employees and workplace environment,

Figure 1.4   Developing a Framework for Corporate Reputation

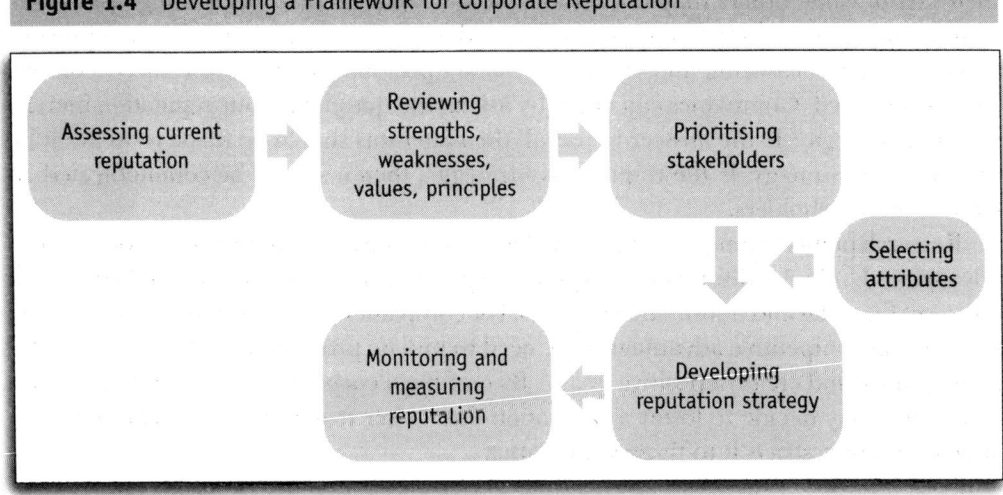

leadership, vision and governance, value related to products, company performance at the financial and operational level and the company approach and commitment to humanitarian and environmental issues.[48] The time-phase for implementing the strategy that addresses gaps and strengthens the company forte is also documented.

The third phase is of monitoring and measuring activities as process identification; performance measurement linked to change, implementation and output; definition of metrics that help track changes in stakeholder perceptions, if any. Successful implementation is reflected in:

- Leadership support
- Employee engagement
- Defined corporate values
- Ongoing commitment and investment

However, these success measures need to be communicated.

A Strategy for Building Reputation: Tata Motors Ltd.

The stellar reputation of Tata Motors Ltd. can be attributed to a conscious strategy for building and managing reputation. Periodic employee satisfaction surveys and employee feedback-based performance review plans denote strong employee engagement. The company's vision of being 'most admired by our customers, employees, business partners and shareholders for the experience and value they enjoy from being with us'[49] indicates leadership support. Its defined core values of inclusion, integrity, accountability, customer, innovation, concern for the environment, passion for excellence and agility[50] imply its focus on maintaining the company 'character'. Regular feedback from every stakeholder group including customers, shareholders, suppliers, dealers, investors and government bodies demonstrates an ongoing commitment to stakeholder engagement. The success of these measures has finally contributed to its current reputation as Tata Motors Ltd. has been ranked first in *AC Nielsen's* 'Corporate Image Monitor 2011–12', eighth in *Businessworld's* 'India's Most Respected Companies'[51] (2011) and 6th in *Fortune* 'India's Most Admired Companies' (2012).[52]

HOW IS CORPORATE REPUTATION COMMUNICATED?

Being good may not be good enough if it is not communicated.

—MACE DOLLINGER, PEGGY GOLDEN AND TODD SAXTON[53]

Corporate reputation management derives legitimacy through its triple bottom line. While profits are most important, social and environmental concerns are of equal significance. Can constancy and legitimacy be achieved in advocating reputation? A periodic validation of corporate reputation helps a company achieve constancy in reputation management. Based on an understanding of the economic assets, stakeholders as investors and analysts find it easy to validate reputation by collecting tangible information about the range, price, quality and performance. However, the same does not hold true for other stakeholders. There is a natural tendency for many to accept or dismiss evidence that does not match with their current beliefs. In recent years, there has been an increasing focus on building relationships, as mutual trust and co-operation provide companies a competitive advantage. The commitment and complementarity in relationships help in engaging, bonding and revealing excellence in operations. Engagement through constant communication is the first step in generating a desired emotional appeal. This creates a favourable inclination towards the company, its products and programmes.

Transparency in communication of company policies is yet another important reputation-building strategy, through which misappropriations are avoided and moral high-ground maintained. Transparency is affected by the ownership and governance structure and reflected in the composition of the board of directors. It can be communicated to multiple stakeholders through mission statements that create a framework, demonstrate distinctiveness, establish an emotional connect and provide a 'sense of mission'.[54] The formulation of the mission statement and documentation serves as a constant reminder to concerned stakeholders of what the company stands for and its ethical code of conduct. It helps express a distinctive identity and enables stakeholders to develop images of the company, which can have positive reputational impact and also accord competitive advantage.

The objective of writing mission statements is to challenge and inspire organisational direction; and, please critical constituencies with a language that spells out the variance in attentiveness across societies, shareholders and employees. The language used in the mission statement is a rhetorical tool for addressing concerns of stakeholders. It is symbolic and expresses intent to accomplish. This sense-giving and symbolic function unifies stakeholders with companies and creates long-term value. As response patterns of individuals are aligned with expressive and symbolic rather than substantive action, mission statements may also be used as a tool for building reputation and impression management. The ability to respond to stakeholder values, needs and concerns yields rewards that may be difficult to replicate in the short term. Table 1.2 illustrates mission statements of some Indian companies featuring in the top 10 positions in reputation rankings in 2012.

CONCLUSION

We know what we are, but not what we may be.

—William Shakespeare[55]

Why is a good reputation important? The benefits clearly underscore the importance of a good reputation. Companies high on the reputational quotient secure

Table 1.2   Sample Mission Statements

Tata Consultancy Services Ltd.	'To help customers achieve their business objectives by providing innovative, best-in-class consulting, IT solutions and services. To make it a joy for all stakeholders to work with us.'[56]
ITC Ltd.	'To enhance the wealth generating capability of the enterprise in a globalising environment, delivering superior and sustainable stakeholder value.'[57]
Tata Steel Ltd.	'Consistent with the vision and values of the founder Jamsetji Tata, Tata Steel strives to strengthen India's industrial base through the effective utilization of staff and materials. The means envisaged to achieve this are high technology and productivity, consistent with modern management practices.'[58]
Aditya Birla Group	'To deliver superior value to our customers, shareholders, employees and society at large.'[59]
Tata Motors Ltd.	'To be passionate in anticipating and providing the best vehicles and experiences that excite our customers globally.'[60]
Life Insurance Corporation of India	'Explore and enhance the quality of life of people through financial security by providing products and services of aspired attributes with competitive returns, and by rendering resources for economic development.'[61]

shareholder confidence, advantages at the operational front, improved profitability, market-to-book value, total sales and a premium price for their products. It has been found that a good reputation coupled with a good image impacts 35 per cent of investment decisions.[62] While a good reputation can be a tool and yield multiple benefits to a company, a poor or bad reputation can act as a hammer and mar the company's progress. Hence, companies need to be cautious in devising strategies for reputation management.

Building a stellar reputation requires a cohesive strategy that addresses concerns of the internal and external stakeholders who eventually exercise control over business operations. This bonding provides companies the required competitive advantage for trading in crowded market arenas. Reputations are not created overnight. They need to be built, supported and managed through an honest reflection of business philosophy, performance and behaviour.

For building a good corporate reputation companies should:

- Build trust through commitment and integrity
- Be transparent
- Create frameworks for managing triple bottom line
- Nurture relationships
- Communicate through mission statements
- 'Walk the Talk' and 'Talk the Walk'

Key Points

- Internationalisation and globalisation have led companies to focus on communicating what they have done, what they are doing and what they plan to do to enhance the triple bottom line, that is, people, planet and profits.
- A good reputation helps in making financial decisions that are accepted by stakeholders; aids in selling a product at a premium price; is an indicator of legitimacy; helps in building trust and heralds success.
- Reputation construct is based on the concept of multidimensionality that can be measured on three reputational dimensions: financial, managerial and product.
- Reputation is the perception of stakeholders based on the sum of their expectations and company dialogue and behaviour (honest and transparent).
- Companies with a higher reputation have been found to be superior to companies with a comparatively lower reputation in terms of being, doing and communicating.
- Companies 'walk the talk' and 'talk the walk' to intensely and aggressively communicate their presence and identity.
- A fine line differentiates the concepts of identity, image and reputation.
- Identity is the manner in which key constituencies conceptualise the company and is the construed external image of the firm.
- Image is the organisational perception in the mind of stakeholders, the overall company impression.
- Reputation is the manner in which key stakeholders develop perceptions about the company and is a collective view based on image, identity, company performance and perceptions.
- An organisation with a good reputation is one in which its identity and image match the stakeholder values and beliefs.
- Reputation is based on the five facets of identity: professed, projected, experienced, manifested and attributed.
- A good corporate reputation reduces transactional costs and improves financial and non-financial results.
- Reputations can be developed and managed by building relationships based on mutual trust and co-operation.
- Engagement through constant communication and transparency help generate a desired emotional appeal.
- Transparency is communicated through the mission statement that creates a framework, demonstrates distinctiveness, establishes an emotional bond and provides a 'sense of mission'.

END NOTES

1. Brainy quote, website http://www.brainyquote.com/quotes/quotes/w/williamsha386690.html (accessed 24 August 2013).
2. 'Funny and inspirational quotations from leaders and experts about reputation', website http://retail-industry.about.com/od/retailleaderquotes/a/Funny-Inspirational-Quotations-Reputation-Quotes-Business-Leaders-Experts-Famous.htm (accessed 24 August 2013).

3. Vedanta resources, 'Financial highlights', website http://www.vedantaresources.com/news-media/media-kit.aspx (accessed 24 August 2013).

4. Vedanta resources, 'Responsible stewardship', website http://sustainability.vedantaresources.com/responsible_stewardship (accessed 24 August 2013).

5. Vedanta resources, 'Committed to minimising our footprint', website http://sustainability.vedantaresources.com/responsible_stewardship/enviroment_our_approach (accessed 24 August 2013).

6. Vedanta resources, 'Latest awards', website http://sustainability.vedantaresources.com/reporting/awards?cat_select=true (accessed 24 August 2013).

7. Richard (2009, July 27), 'Worldwide protests against Vedanta', *London Mining Network*, website http://londonminingnetwork.org/2009/07/worldwide-protests-against-vedanta/ (accessed 24 August 2013).

8. K. Sinha, 'Activists plan protest at Vedanta's London meet tomorrow', *The Times of India* (2013, 1 August), website http://timesofindia.indiatimes.com/world/uk/Activists-plan-protest-at-Vedantas-London-meet-tomorrow/articleshow/21520942.cms (accessed 24 August 2013).

9. G. Vlasic and J. Langer, 'Concept of reputation: Different perspectives and robust empirical understandings', *Trziste* (2012), 24(2), 219–244.

10. Ibid.

11. M. J. Dollinger, P. A. Golden and T. Saxton, 'The effect of reputation on the decision to joint venture', *Strategic Management Journal* (1997), 18(2), 127–140.

12. Ibid.

13. Ibid.

14. Ibid.

15. G. Hofstede, *Culture's Consequences: International Differences in Work Related Values*. SAGE: Beverly Hill, CA (1980).

16. P. T. DiMaggio and W. W. Powell, 'The iron cage revisited: Institutional isomorphism and collective rationality in organizational fields', *American Sociological Review* (1983), 48(2), 147–160.

17. C. J. Fombrun, 'The reputational landscape', *Corporate Reputation Review* (1997), 1(1), 5–13.

18. A. Pearce, 'The reputation challenge', *Prophet*, website http://www.prophet.com/thinking/view/290-the-reputation-challenge (accessed 24 August 2013).

19. Reputation quotes, website http://www.reputationrx.com/Default.aspx/CEOREPUTATION/CEOQUOTES (accessed 25 August 2013).

20. C. J. Fombrun, N. A. Gardberg and J. M. Sever, 'The Reputation Quotient: A multi-stakeholder measure of corporate reputation', *Journal of Brand Management* (2000), 7(4), 241–255, p. 243.

21. G. Walsh and S. E. Beatty, 'Customer-based corporate reputation of a service firm: Scale development and validation', *Journal of the Academy of Marketing Science* (2007), 35(1), 127–143, p. 129.

22. K. Shirali, Global Head, Investor Relations, Tata Consultancy Services Ltd., personal communication, 5 February 2013.

23. J. Choudhry, interviewed by Vivek Law, Bloomberg UTV's Market Guru (July 2012), website http://www.youtube.com/watch?v=pylxqik5ue4 (accessed 24 August 2013).

24. M. T. Hansen, H. Ibarra and U. Peyer, 'The best performing CEOs in the world', *Harvard Business Review* (January–February 2013), website http://hbr.org/2013/01/the-best-performing-ceos-in-the-world (accessed 24 August 2013).

25. 'Hay Group-Fortune release annual study of India's Most Admired Companies, TCS tops the charts', Hay Group (2013, 15 July), website http://www.haygroup.com/in/press/details.aspx?id=37630 (accessed 24 August 2013).

26. 'Funny and inspirational quotations from leaders and experts about reputation', website http://retail-industry.about.com/od/retailleaderquotes/a/Funny-Inspirational-Quotations-Reputation-Quotes-Business-Leaders-Experts-Famous.htm (accessed 24 August 2013).

27. C. J. Fombrun and V. Rindova, 'Reputation management in global 1000 firms: A benchmarking study', *Corporate Reputation Review* (1998), 1(3), 205–212.

28. Y. C. Deveshwar, ITC Ltd. Report and accounts (2013), ITC Ltd., website http://www.itcportal.com/about-itc/shareholder-value/annual-reports/itc-annual-report-2013/content.aspx (accessed 24 August 2013), p. 1.
29. 'Azim Premji has his heart in the right place', website http://www.rediff.com/money/report/azim-premji-has-his-heart-in-the-right-place/20130223.htm (accessed 24 August 2013).
30. CEO quotes, website http://www.reputationrx.com/Default.aspx/CEOREPUTATION/CEOQUOTES (accessed 25 August 2013).
31. T. J. Brown and P. A. Dacin, 'The company and the product: Corporate associations and consumer product responses', *Journal of Marketing* (1997), 61(1), 68–84, p. 69.
32. J. E. Dutton, J. M. Dukerich and C. V. Harquail, 'Organizational images and member identification', *Administrative Science Quarterly* (1994), 39(2), 239–263, p. 239.
33. M. J. Hatch and M. Schultz, 'Bringing the corporation into corporate branding', *European Journal of Marketing* (2003), 37(7/8), 1041–1064, p. 1048.
34. P. A. Argenti and B. Druckenmiller, 'Reputation and the corporate brand', *Corporate Reputation Review* (2004), 6(4), 368–374, p. 368.
35. G. Soenen and B. Moingeon, 'The five facets of collective identities. Integrating corporate and organizational identity', in B. Moingeon and G. Soenen (eds), *Corporate and Organizational Identities: Integrating Strategy, Marketing, Communication, and Organizational Perspectives* (pp. 13–34). London: Routledge (2002).
36. L&T Ltd., 'Vision', website http://www.larsentoubro.com/lntcorporate/common/ui_templates/HtmlContainer.aspx?res=P_CORP_AABT_ACOM_CVIS (accessed 24 August 2013).
37. L&T Ltd., 'Corporate ads', website http://www.larsentoubro.com/lntcorporate/common/ui_templates/HtmlContainer.aspx?res=P_CORP_EMID_DCOR (accessed 24 August 2013).
38. L&T Ltd., 'Investor presentation' (July 2013), website http://www.larsentoubro.com/lntcorporate/Uploads/L&T%20Investor%20Presentation-%20July%2013.pdf (accessed 24 August 2013).
39. L&T Ltd., 'L&T in Top Ten Indian Brands', website http://www.larsentoubro.com/lntcorporate/LnT_NWS/PDF/InterbrandETBestBrandSurvey.pdf (accessed 24 August 2013).
40. L&T Ltd., 'Awards and recognitions', website http://www.larsentoubro.com/lntcorporate/common/ui_templates/HtmlContainer.aspx?res=P_SIA_REC&tabid=SIA_6 (accessed 24 August 2013).
41. Ibid.
42. L&T Ltd., 'L&T in Top Five "Best Companies to Work For"', website http://www.larsentoubro.com/lntcorporate/LnT_NWS/PDF/BusinessToday18072013.pdf (accessed 24 August 2013).
43. L&T Ltd., 'Awards and recognitions', website http://www.larsentoubro.com/lntcorporate/common/ui_templates/HtmlContainer.aspx?res=P_SIA_REC&tabid=SIA_6 (accessed 24 August 2013).
44. L&T Ltd., 'L&T Among India's Top 5 Most Respected Companies', website http://www.larsentoubro.com/lntcorporate/LnT_NWS/PDF/MostRespectedCoBW22082013.pdf (accessed 24 August 2013).
45. Hay Group, 'Hay Group-Fortune release annual study of India's Most Admired Companies, TCS tops the charts', website http://www.haygroup.com/in/press/details.aspx?id=37630 (accessed 24 August 2013).
46. CEO quotes, website http://www.reputationrx.com/Default.aspx/CEOREPUTATION/CEOQUOTES (accessed 24 August 2013).
47. G. Dowling, 'Corporate reputations: Should you compete on yours?', *California Management Review* (2004), 46(3), 19–36, p. 20.
48. A. Pearce, 'The reputation challenge', *Prophet*, website http://www.prophet.com/downloads/whitepapers/reputation-challenge.pdf (accessed 5 September 2013).
49. Tata Motors Ltd., 'Corporate Sustainability Report' (2012–13), website http://www.tatamotors.com/sustainability/pdf/annualSustainabilityReport2012-13.pdf (accessed 25 August 2013).
50. Ibid.
51. A. Biswal, 'Most Respected Companies of India 2011—Businessworld Survey', website http://amitbiswal.blogspot.in/2011/08/most-respected-companies-of-india-2011.html (accessed 13 July 2013).

52. 'TCS replaces Tata Steel as India's most admired', *The Business Standard*, website http://www.business-standard.com/article/companies/tcs-replaces-tata-steel-as-india-s-most-admired-113070900674_1.html (accessed 13 July 2013).

53. M. J. Dollinger, P. A. Golden and T. Saxton, 'The effect of reputation on the decision to joint venture', *Strategic Management Journal* (1997), 18(2), 127–140, p. 138.

54. A. Campbell and S. Yeung, 'Creating a sense of mission', *Long Range Planning* (1991), 24(4), 10–20, p. 10.

55. William Shakespeare quotes, website http://www.brainyquote.com/quotes/quotes/w/william-sha164317.html (accessed 24 August 2013).

56. Tata Consultancy Services Ltd., 'Heritage and values', website http://www.tcs.com/about/heritage_values/Pages/default.aspx (accessed 25 August 2013).

57. ITC Ltd., 'The ITC mission', website http://www.itcportal.com/about-itc/values/vision-mission.aspx (accessed 25 August 2013).

58. Tata Steel Ltd., 'Vision and mission', website http://www.tatasteelindia.com/corporate/vision-and-strategy.asp (accessed 25 August 2013).

59. Aditya Birla Group, 'Vision and values', website http://adityabirla.com/About-Us/vision-and-values (accessed 25 August 2013).

60. Tata Motors Ltd., 'Mission', website http://www.tatamotors.com/know-us/pdf/mission.pdf (accessed 25 August 2013).

61. LIC India, 'Mission vision', website http://www.licindia.in/mission_vision.htm (accessed 25 August 2013).

62. J. Pfeffer, *Managing with Power: Politics and Influence in Organizations.* Boston, MA: Harvard Business School Press (1992).

Understanding
Corporate Reputation

2

Waltzing with Stakeholders to Score on Corporate Reputation

You can't control what you can't measure.

—TOM DEMARCO[1]

Objectives:

- Learn techniques of measuring and managing corporate reputation
- Identify and analyse stakeholders
- Align and leverage stakeholder support
- Comprehend methods of influencing stakeholders
- Assess measures of building and managing stakeholder relationships

INTRODUCTION

A business's reputation is valuable on two counts: first, its intrinsic current value as an intangible asset; and secondly, its ability to create—or destroy—future value.

—JEAN-PAUL LOUISOT AND JENNY RAYNER[2]

Growing trends in the business environment as market interpenetration, media framing, vocal stakeholders and commoditisation of industries and products[3] have forced corporates to revisit the concept of reputation, its development and management. In the midst of this

23

Key Words

- Alignment
- Attitude centrality
- Bridging
- Change curve
- Cognitive economy
- DEAR process
- Emotional appeal
- Foresight model
- Functional appeal
- GOREL model
- Kelly Repertory Grid
- Laddering
- Measurement
- Natural grouping
- Perceptual ranking

- Photosort
- Psychological contract
- Q-sort
- Rankings
- Ratings
- Reputation audit
- Stakeholder performance appraisal
- Stakeholder relationship audit
- Stakeholder theories
- Value change scoreboard
- Value creation

changing environment, how does a company develop a reputation?—By creating ground for experience, constantly reiterating product-related information, entertaining dialogue and paying heed to stakeholder needs. This creates both a functional and emotional appeal that generates positive perceptions in the minds of the stakeholders.

The functional addresses a set of tangible, measurable traits as a review of the balance sheet in the annual report. The emotional relates to the perceptions developed on the basis of individual experiences about the company or its products as association with a FMCG product. Companies target the intellect, belief, perceptions and expectations of stakeholders in the hope that it will influence their purchase decisions. Building on the value chain through innovative mechanisms, the functional and emotional choices of stakeholders are influenced. This provides companies with competitive advantage, enhanced performance and, thereby, consumer/stakeholder trust and confidence.

How is the success of the aforementioned strategy measured? There is a perceptible growth in reputational assets, which though difficult to measure, assign a favourable

One Concept—Different Facets: Measuring Corporate Reputation in India

India can proudly proclaim its own rankings for corporate reputation since the last decade or so. The country now has three different indices that rank leading companies specifically on their reputation quotient—*Businessworld* magazine's 'India's Most Respected Companies' initiated in 1983, *AC Nielsen's* 'Corporate Image Monitor' that started in 2002 and *Fortune* magazine's 'India's Most Admired Companies' that was initially announced in 2012.

Out of these, *Businessworld* and *AC Nielsen* have a slightly different take on the concept of reputation. According to *Businessworld* editor Mr Prosenjit Datta, 'Respect is not something that can be earned by super normal revenues or profits alone. To gain respect, a company not only has to perform well in financial terms, but also develop a way of working that makes its peers look upon it with respect.'[4]

For Mr Dinesh Kapoor, Executive Director, *AC Nielsen* India, 'The Corporate Reputation Index is a testament to a brand's reputation, by people that matter most to it. For stakeholders, this implies they feel the brand is reliable and sustainable in difficult times.'[5]

These rankings are different approaches to measuring corporate reputation. Are there any other ways in which corporate reputation can be measured? While rankings as these may rely on surveys of peer companies, how does an organisation gauge its own reputation?

industry position to the company. This rank may be specific to a company attribute or may be an overall score. For instance, it may relate to a product/service or may be an aggregate of overall performance on multiple parameters. This ranking of companies is normally done by outside agencies, the validity of which has been debated in various academic circles and among practitioners. Though there is a lack of consensus among researchers and practitioners on measurement techniques, they are unanimous in their agreement on the need for a scale to evaluate corporate reputation.

In this chapter, we discuss the techniques of measuring corporate reputation, strategies for building reputation with stakeholders and connecting with them, choice of communication strategies and related benefits.

CAN CORPORATE REPUTATION BE MEASURED?

Don't measure yourself by what you have accomplished, but what you should have accomplished with your ability.

—John Wooden[6]

Over the last two decades, evaluation of corporate reputation has begun to receive increased attention. Various measures and attributes have been proposed by scholars and academics who view reputation as a reflection of financial performance, quality of management, product or service quality, innovativeness, long-term investment value, ability to attract, develop and keep talented people, responsibility to the community and the environment and wise use of corporate assets.[7] In other words, company reputation implies a set of financial and non-financial variables perceived, attributed and assimilated by the public. Companies provide informational cues as market, accounting, institutional, strategy[8] and legitimation[9] to stakeholders that aid in reputation assessment.

However, the mechanism of human information processing emphasises that there is a limit to the ability of assimilating information over a period of time. The mind works through a process of categorisation, through which stakeholders form impressions about products and processes. Based on the principle of 'cognitive economy'[10] a halo effect is created and positive or negative relationships developed. A positive halo enables companies to secure for themselves a 'forgive and forget' position from the perspective of stakeholders in case of misconduct or crisis. However, the same does not hold true for companies with a negative halo.

Given that the quantum of benefits in the organisation–stakeholder relation is huge, the measurement of reputation is an imperative. There are three ways of measuring the same:

- Company behaviour, processes, strategy, governance, employees, culture
- Board composition and governance practices that are convincing and persuasive
- Value proposition created and ability to address varied concerns

These three measures provide sufficient data for comparison of company attributes with those of competitors. Interestingly, the assessment by all stakeholders is never the same. In more situations than not, responses are varied and based on differences in interaction patterns, complexity in relationships and importance assigned to the company. Can developing a corporate reputation index be a solution to ironing out such differences?

Corporate Reputation Index

Reputational assets yield high returns and place the company at a vantage position. Companies can now command higher price for their products and stock offerings, attract more applicants to the jobs with increased loyalty and productivity, pay lower prices and draw suppliers to their fold and lower the risk of crisis. The value creation finally flows to the financial statement of the company and translates into good market positioning. There are various value creation indices that have been proposed and implemented for measurement of corporate reputation. Some of these utilise historical and expected rates of returns that are different for tangible and intangible assets.[11]

A Corporate Reputation Index (CRI) addresses the corporate and academic concern of reputation measurement. As discussed above, it includes financial statements as well as corporate strategy, visibility, organisational culture, ethics and integrity, governance processes and leadership, product services, strategic alliances and business partnering and innovation.[12]

The Value Change Scoreboard[13] is another measure that quantifies non-economic assets as indicators of performance. This acts both as a tool for decision making and a means for disclosure. Most of the proposed indices attempt to address specific attributes that impact corporate reputation or measure intangible assets or liabilities. We provide an elaboration of the same in the following text.

Managing product or service reputation is the primary method of value creation and developing brand image. The product is the basic interface with the consumer/customer and a leading driver of corporate reputation. Companies may find it difficult to enhance their reputation if the customer is not able to associate value or has a negative value association with the product.

Employees are the next most important in the measurement index. The actions of the leadership team, senior and middle management create an organisational image. The loyalty of employees helps companies win the trust of all other stakeholders. The length of time that an employee remains with the company is an indicator of employee satisfaction that is often shared by word of mouth and reflected in the number of applicants for a position within the company. Undoubtedly, this is another indicator of goodwill created by the company.

Company culture has been found to affect employee motivation and trust. The onus of managing cultural change rests with the leadership team in general and CEO in particular. Through their actions, their 'walk the talk' and 'talk the walk', they affirm their stand and implicitly influence employees to be part of a committed, credible and honest corporate climate. Creating an ethical climate and embedding it in the cultural fabric of the organisation is another strategy used by companies for building reputation. Violations of any sort in the nurtured climate can begin a negative chain reaction among the public and severely dent the reputation. Hence, measurement indices also address the issue of governance practices and ethical policies. Some questions which become critical to assessment and evaluation are: have channels been provided to employees for reporting ethical violations, is the senior leadership team aware of ethical concerns of employees, is the ethical policy being reinforced sufficiently, has priority been assigned to ethical issues?

Financial reporting has been suggested to be an important tool for reputation management as it helps release company information in the public domain, most of which is favourable. Shareholders trust this information as it provides them accurate information concerning company performance and helps them in taking financial decisions. An example of the same would be a disclosure of any kind that creates a favourable impact.

Additionally, the external relationships with suppliers, partners, investors, competitors and vendors also merit consideration. The extent of investor confidence is a measure of ascertaining faith and trust. Well-respected companies are able to secure a much faster response from investors and external stakeholders than those who have neglected their reputation.

Innovation and value creation help enhance the corporate portfolio by focussing on customers and their need for innovative products and services. It has been found that customer satisfaction relates more to innovation than market value and is an important driver[14] in assigning merit to a company. Metrics which can be used to assess the relationship between customer satisfaction and innovation are per cent sales of new product over the last three years, per cent of projected growth of company over the next three years and per cent of sales in the last three years through each channel of marketing.[15]

Finally, intangible liabilities created by corporate actions may be implicit or explicit. Some of these liabilities may be unrecognised future claims, past actions that impact the future growth, etc. Some of the internal and external liabilities relate to processes, information, configuration and human issues.[16]

Attempts have been made to assign a weight to the various components of corporate reputation. The most important of these is the product/service that is assigned a maximum weight, followed by employees, external relationships, innovation and value creation. However, this may vary based on the sector in which the company operates and the requirements thereof. For reliability in assessment, companies hire an external consultant to audit corporate reputation, as this helps in arriving at an authentic overall value score revealing stakeholder perception of the company as neutral, good or bad.

There has been considerable debate in the academic circle concerning measures used for assessing corporate reputation and its validity across cultures. To date there has been no consensus on how to measure corporate reputation, and what actually needs to be measured. There have been various definitions and measures proposed by researchers, practitioners and magazine surveys. An attempt is being made by academics, based on the available data set, to develop a scale which will hold good across cultures.

Stakeholder impressions can be created by informational cues as market, accounting, institutional, strategy and legitimation. Company attributes as product/service reputation, employee loyalty, external relationships, innovation and value creation, and financial reporting. In addition, company actions related to its processes, information sharing, configuration and human issues further give shape to stakeholder impressions. The sum of these impressions, when assessed, can provide a measure of the organisation's corporate reputation (refer Fig. 2.1).

Rankings and Ratings

Prevailing uncertain conditions and high transaction risk together with proliferation of the Internet have altered business dynamics. To play it safe customers have begun to engage only with well-established companies. They have begun to rely on rankings and ratings, which are viewed as objective measures for assessment, reflection, engagement and action.

The process of assigning ranks to companies began as early as 1982 with the publication of *Fortune* magazine's survey of America's 'Most Admired Companies'. Though it

Figure 2.1   Measuring Corporate Reputation

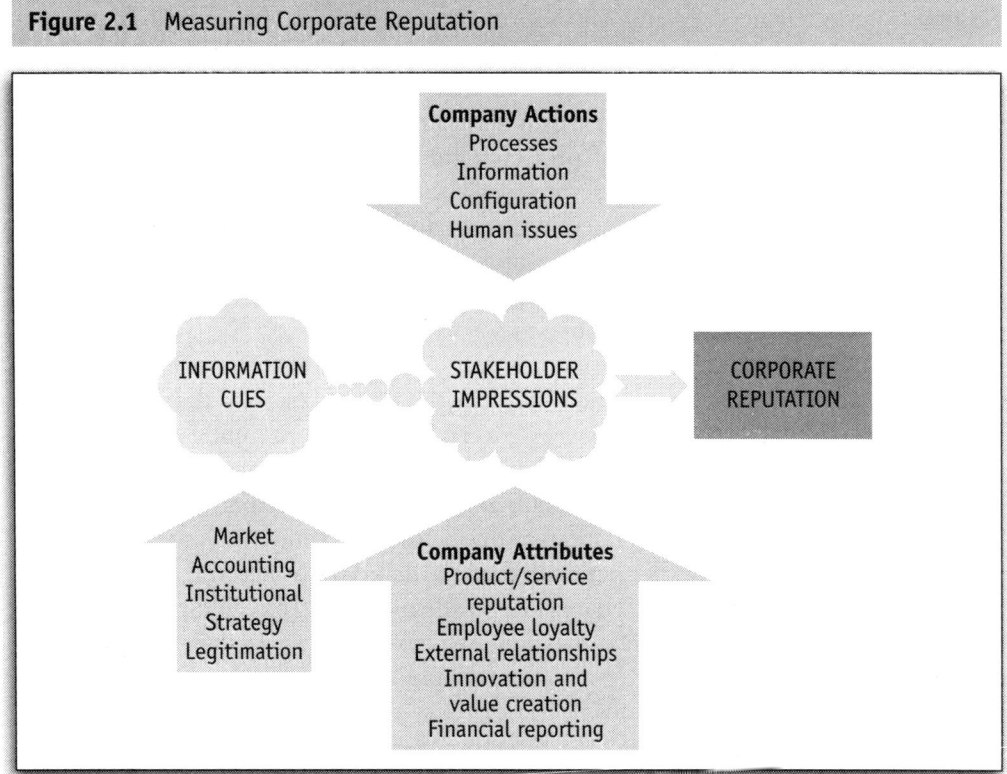

gained immediate fame, there was much criticism levied against the report. According to companies, the survey was biased as it evaluated only large, mostly US-based companies and focussed only on financial indicators. Still, the popularity of the survey had many other publications in Europe and Asia replicate the methodology.

A similar methodology has continued over the years with *Fortune* inviting almost 10,000 senior executives to assign a rank to 10 largest companies in their own industry on eight 'excellent' criteria (according to *Fortune*): quality of management, quality of products and services, innovativeness, long-term investment value, financial soundness, ability to attract, develop and retain employees, responsibility to the community and the environment and wise use of corporate assets.[17] Some of the well-known magazines that follow a similar process are: *Asian Business* ('Asia's Most Admired Companies'), *Far Eastern Economic Review* ('Review 200'), *Management Today* ('Britain's Most Admired Companies') and *Financial Times* ('Europe's Most Respected Companies'). For all these media surveys, some of the ranking criteria are similar and some different.

There are also specialised publication houses that rate and rank companies. For example, we have the *Business Ethics* ('America's 100 Best Corporate Citizens') and *Working Mother's Magazine* ('The 100 Best Companies for Working Mothers'). Books have also been published in the West, which assess companies on different parameters as 'The 100 Best Companies to Work for in America', 'The Best Companies for Minorities', 'The Best Companies for Women' and 'The 100 Best Companies for Gay Men and Lesbians'. There are various social monitors that have conducted studies to assess intent-to-purchase decisions, reward social stewardship and penalise those companies that have scored low on socially desirable parameters. Companies are awarded for responsible leadership. However, none of these rankings or ratings can be referred to as being totally unbiased. With growth in reputation scholarship and emphasis on corporate reputation, the indices need to be strengthened and be able to capture cross-cultural dimensions. India, unfortunately, is lagging behind the West in devising scales for measurement. At present there are four sets of ratings that attempt to assign a rank to companies on specific attributes as well as on overall reputation (refer Table 2.1).

Measurement techniques for analysis of corporate reputation fall under the category of primary and secondary. At the primary level we have workplace environment, products and services. The focus of the secondary level is on environmental responsibility, emotional appeal, vision, financial performance and leadership. In this list, the last variable has been documented as the most important. Corporate reputation scholarship emphasises that 48 per cent of the image of the leader or CEO impacts company reputation.[18] Focus on industry and country of origin have also been considered as important parameters for measurement. Other general principles of measuring reputation are generic and take into account multiple stakeholder concerns as organisational information, audit data, investment analysis, insights from journalists, rumour and brand activities.[19]

Analysis of corporate reputation emphasises the strategic and stakeholder approach. The antecedents of the strategic approach are profitability, firm size, charity, quality of

Table 2.1   Reputation Rankings in India

Name of the Survey	Companies under Review	Parameters	Methodology
Fortune 'India's Most Admired Companies'[20]	Companies from 15 countries were shortlisted on the parameters of size, contribution to national GDP, growth rate, maturity of industry, competition within the industry, the minimum number of players in the industry and their national presence	Quality of management, quality of products/ services offered, innovativeness, value as a long-term investment, soundness of financial position, ability to attract, develop and keep talented people, responsibility to the community and/ or the environment, wise use of corporate assets, effectiveness in conducting its business globally	507 executives across 291 companies were surveyed between October 2011 and January 2012. Peer rating method was used. Senior executives were asked to rate companies from their industry (other than their own company), to arrive at an overall cross-industry implied ranking
Businessworld 'India's Most Respected Companies'[21]	249 companies across 20 sectors selected in terms of revenues or profits (for listed companies) and significant presence (for unlisted companies)	Innovativeness, depth and quality of top management, financial performance and returns, ethics and transparency, quality of products and services, people practices and talent management and global competitiveness	Peer survey within 20 sectors for sector-wise rankings, followed by across-sector survey for overall rankings
AC Nielsen 'Corporate Image Monitor'[22]	40 leading companies in India across sectors	Product and service quality, vision and leadership, workplace management, financial performance, operating style and social responsibility	Survey of over 1,700 respondents, consisting of policy makers, influence groups, the financial community, investors, corporate peers and elite and the general consumer

inputs, media intensity, product characteristics and its consequences, access to capital, customer loyalty, ability to attract and retain customers and community support.[23] There are several studies which also examine the stakeholder approach and analyse approaches for measuring behavioural intentions and outcomes. The experiences and observations of stakeholders create a belief that leads to an intention to purchase. However, this view is restrictive as it considers only the antecedents and consequences of one group of stakeholders, namely customers/consumers.

What is critical is that companies should develop reputation by aligning all stakeholders.

HOW DOES A COMPANY BUILD REPUTATION WITH STAKEHOLDERS?

Every stakeholder group within the industry has strong thoughts and ideas about what's in the best interest of their group, as one would expect them to.

—DANNY DAVIS[24]

The definition of 'who are the stakeholders' has changed over time. The earlier definition of 'those groups [stakeholder] without whose support the organisation would cease to exist'[25] was later modified to 'all of those groups and individuals that can affect, or are affected by, the accomplishment of organisational purpose'.[26] An understanding of the stakeholders is followed by analysis of this target segment. To build reputation with them, it is critical to comprehend their expectations from the company, which can create sustained economic, social and environmental value, transparency and good governance. Creating a holistic model that comprises all three and merges with the business philosophy is often the key to the problem. Analysis of stakeholders begins with questions as: who are the stakeholders? What are their needs? What is the control they exercise over the company? How do they help in building reputation? What communication strategies should be adopted for signing the psychological and emotional contract? An answer to these questions helps in building a relationship that is one of mutual reciprocity and forms the base for making the business successful in the long term. Beginning with an understanding of stakeholders, we discuss these questions in the subsequent sections.

Understanding Stakeholders

Three theories have been proposed by researchers to help organisations understand stakeholder behavioural patterns (refer Table 2.2).

Out of these theories, normative is the most relevant as it extends organisational responsibility beyond economic and legal expectations to include societal expectations of good corporate behaviour and governance.

The theories discussed above are based on the premise[27] that the organisation and its multiple stakeholders are intricately linked to one another and each is affected by the other; this relationship is based on the processes and outcomes of the two involved entities and there

Table 2.2   Stakeholder Theories

Theory	Concept
Instrumental[28]	Focusses only on powerful stakeholders who can affect value
Descriptive[29]	Identifies and categorises stakeholders without considering their legitimacy/power
Normative[30]	Considers rights and duties of all actors and defines strategies for managers in assessing issues related to moral code of conduct

is an intrinsic value associated with legitimate stakeholder interests with focus on managerial decision making. How then should a company proceed? By categorising stakeholders on their attributes as latent, dormant, discretionary, demanding, expectant—dominant, dependent and dangerous and definitive.[31] Strategies for understanding and wooing customers are devised based on the power, legitimacy and urgency exercised by different groups.

Stakeholder Analysis

A business comprises a mix of internal and external stakeholders. There are five key stakeholders who perform a major role in the growth of business (refer Fig. 2.2). Employees form the talent pool and help in business functioning and operations; customers aid in patronage and revenue; suppliers provide the material and resources; community gives the sanction to operate and, investors provide financial support.[32] All five groups are indispensable to the functioning of the business.

Figure 2.2   Key Stakeholders

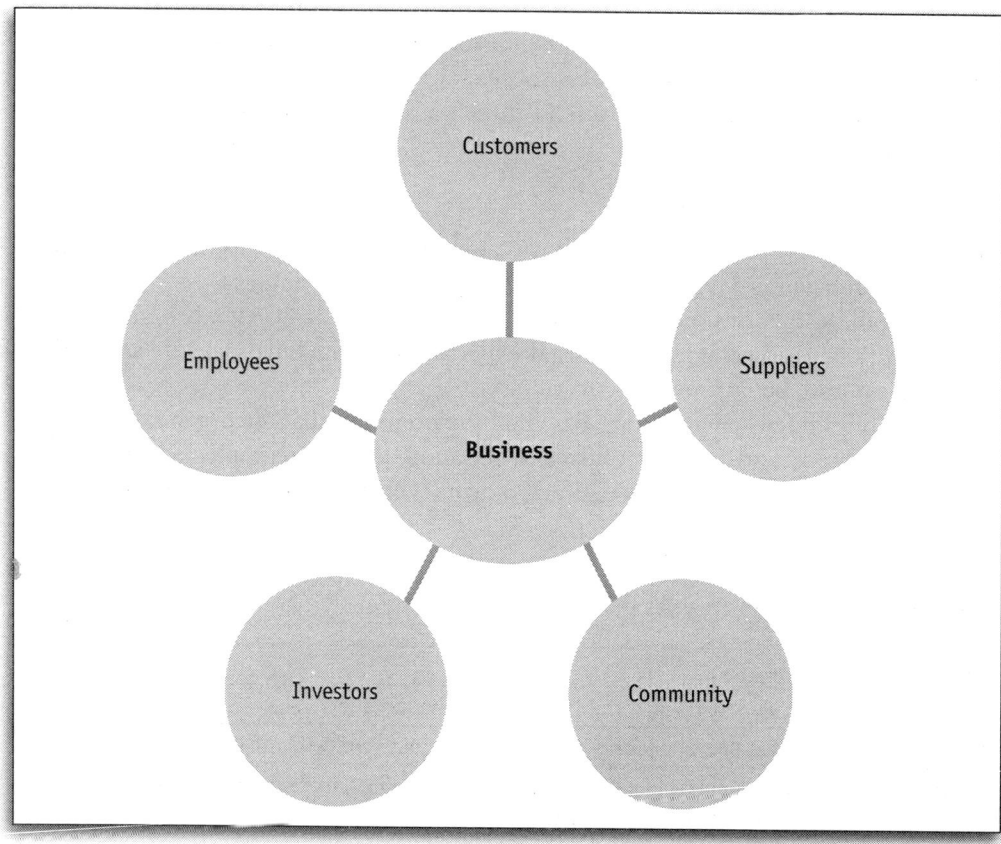

Companies should ideally form coalitions with stakeholders; comprehend ways in which they can contribute to organisational growth; identify criteria to keep them appeased and, enrich performance matrix for winning them over. As resource providers, stakeholders possess the power of cutting off the resource flow in case their interests are left unattended.[33] Hence, it is critical to identify and define stakeholders; understand their interests in the organisational processes; comprehend interests and conflict of interests, if any.

Companies use the results of stakeholder identification as a tool to understand the environment and the resulting threats and opportunities.[34] Within companies there is a constant struggle to woo the wide variety of stakeholders who are considered important for the management. Beginning with an examination of the internal statement of intent and measures of control, companies craft a vision and mission statement, spell out their code of business ethics, define their corporate brand value proposition or formal strategic plan that describes the desired image and intent. Control mechanisms, internal and external, are also presented. The standard accounting and control system are two such internal mechanisms to manage any kind of reputational risk. External mechanisms include balanced scorecard, triple bottom line reporting (economic, social and environmental), corporate governance and building on organisational social responsibility. Apart from these internal and external measures, personal controls are also advocated and reflected in the Key Performance Indicators. The final responsibility of setting the agenda and establishing standards of corporate behaviour rests with the board and the top management.

Establishing standards of behaviour, also labelled as the DEAR process—decisions evaluated against reputation,[35] acts as a guiding post for stakeholders to view the company favourably and make judgements or evaluations. This, hypothetically, indicates that profits are directly related to the reputation of a company. Additionally, goodwill created in the market by presenting of identity attributes or publicly trading on good name is another method of shaping stakeholder perceptions. In summary, this understanding and analysis helps companies persuade stakeholders to match their beliefs with those of the company through a process of sharing identity, disclosing attributes and generating emotional connect. Only credible, attractive and powerful companies are able to connect with stakeholders.

HOW DO COMPANIES CONNECT WITH STAKEHOLDERS?

If with your inferior, speak no coarser than usual; if with your superiors, no finer. Be what you say; and, within the rules of prudence, say what you are.

—ALFORD[36]

A resource-based strategy helps a company build connects and project a positive image to the stakeholders. For operationalising this concept, companies make reputation enhancement a part of strategy formulation. Reputation has been found to send a credible signal in the market about past company performance that can be used to predict future action. It can be used to signal broad-based 'goodness'. Periodic demonstrations of 'goodness' and clarifications set the expectations of stakeholders and help the public self-select the companies they wish to associate with or avoid.

The process of building connects with stakeholders can be better understood with the 'Governance of Relationships' (GOREL) model.[37] The nine-step GOREL model details the following steps: envisioning, identifying and listening, defining specific objectives, involving potential stakeholders, relating with issue influencers, convincing opinion leaders, rolling out content, evaluating and resetting. The GOREL model proceeds on the assumption that stakeholders are aware of organisational goals and are keen to associate with them.

Focussing on key stakeholder relationships is important from the perspective of the organisation and its stakeholders. What is the reason for maintaining these relationships? Some reasons are performance-linked and others are at the core of business existence. These relationships are based on the concept of mutual interdependence where one cannot survive without the other. There exists a 'system of primary stakeholder groups, a complex set of relationships between and among interest groups with different rights, objectives, expectations and responsibilities'.[38] Companies hope to win the loyalty and satisfaction of stakeholders through these relationships, while the focus of stakeholders is on quality and services. There may also be some negative repercussions, situational and inherent risk variables associated with commitment to this relationship. Stakeholders may decide to continue with their loyalty and forego better alternatives. Undoubtedly, there are situational variables as type of product, level of service and contact frequency between the two entities and inherent risks as financial and performance risks and costs associated with termination.[39] The most important, from the stakeholder perspective, are quality of product and service, trust and availability of alternatives. Managing trust and satisfaction through good quality products and services and remaining competitive are essential for maintaining customer base.

Strategies Adopted for Internal and External Stakeholder Connect

While there are many metrics to measure the success of a company, the ultimate test is the market share that has a positive effect on existing and potential employees, shareholders and emerging reputation. For building reputation, leaders provide an empowering environment for the employees by training them to develop skill sets, educating them in values, vision and mission and supporting their needs. Rewards and incentives for superior performance are also provided which motivate employees to give their best to the company.

Apart from employees, the concerns of shareholders, too, need to be addressed. Keeping them informed of the present scenario and future prospects are two tactics that provide a strategic focus to shareholder management. As shareholders form an important segment of the stakeholder group, companies attempt consistency in messages and speed in sharing information. There is always a lurking fear that competitors may create a frame, a reference point that is more appealing to the shareholders.

Empowering Employees: Google India

'It's really the people that make Google the company it is', states the Google website,[40] and its employee practices tend to make one believe that the company does follow this dictum. The company that was ranked first by *The Economic Times* 'India's Best Companies to Work for—2013', has trained its employees to avoid being mediocre, look for success beyond hierarchies, never be complacent and work in teams, all part of its basic culture which it attempts to retain even after 15 years of its being a start-up.

Google India ensures that its employees pass the 'airport test'[41]—the ability to strike up an interesting conversation on a non-work topic with a stranger at an airport, one of the ways in which it teaches employees the importance of having multiple skills, and fulfilling their need for work–life balance by cultivating external hobbies and interests.

Employee empowerment is further strengthened through knowledge sharing programmes as 'Googler 2 Googler', which allows employees to share with peers on subjects ranging from tightrope walking to advanced Python programming. Special budgets for engagement activities, called 'play dough', are created for entertaining group activities outside the workplace. 'We have an incredibly empowering environment and let people figure out how they get to their goals',[42] states Rajan Anandan, MD, Google India.

Clearly, Google India has mastered the art of creating a positive reputation among employees, which undoubtedly helps it to attain a strong overall reputation.

Media is often used as a channel for communicating messages to external stakeholders. This zeroes in on the question of the quality and quantum of information to be shared with the media. Though the choice is deliberate, there is still hesitation on how it will be scripted and received. Only those bits are shared which, when presented by the media, generate emotional appeal. However, there is an inherent danger in interacting with stakeholders through the media. In case of partial or incomplete information, the media may acquire and process information from other sources which may be negative and create an undesired effect.

Interacting with the government, civil societies and communities has its positive and not-so-positive effects. Stringent rules that are pithy and require time to implement, clamouring demands of civil societies and addressing local needs at the site of operations

Positive Effects of Community Interaction: Tata Steel Ltd.

Tata Steel Ltd. has been actively involved in the development of Jamshedpur city since its renaming in 1919. In October 1923, Mr JRD Tata told shareholders, 'We are constantly accused by people of wasting money in the town of Jamshedpur. We are asked why it should be necessary to spend so much on housing, sanitation, roads and hospitals and on welfare.... Gentlemen, people who ask these questions are sadly lacking in imagination. We are not putting a row of workmen's huts in Jamshedpur—we are building a city.'[43] Even today, the company's commitment to the city and its administration remains strong.

Various initiatives including the public–private partnership project providing safe drinking water to every resident, and the CEO Water Mandate, in association with UNGC, which aims at better utilisation of natural resources, have greatly enhanced the quality of life of Jamshedpur residents. Tata Steel Rural Development Society and Tribal Culture Centre work towards developing the rural economy around Jamshedpur, in association with the government, district administration and international organisations. The company's endeavour for a clean, green city began with Jamsetji Tata's vision of the massive Jubilee Park in the heart of the city, and is still continued through regular tree plantation drives. Additionally, the Sir Dorabji Tata Park and the Tata Zoo add to the ecological richness of the town. The famous JRD Tata Sports Complex, with its capacity of 40,000 and Tata Football Academy, Tata Athletics Academy and Tata Steel Adventure Foundation give Jamshedpur its reputation as the sports capital of Jharkhand. The Tata Main Hospital, Tata Memorial Cancer Centre and the Meherbai Tata Memorial Hospital together contribute to the excellent healthcare infrastructure in the city. The R. D. Tata Technical Education Centre and the Tata Auditorium are the company's gifts to education and culture in the city.[44]

Community satisfaction is evident; citizens rated Jamshedpur as India's second-best city to live in, during an ORG MARG Nielsen study in 2008.[45]

are all challenges which require attention. Companies assessing the benefits of engaging local communities and civil societies have begun focussing on sustained value creation. A balanced approach enables companies to address competing interests of all stakeholders without risking exclusion of any one.

As mentioned earlier, companies need to be able to address the demands of civil societies and address local requirements at their respective sites of operations. Failure to do so can result in a severe backlash.

It Can Backfire Too: Nirma Ltd.'s Run-in with Local Community at Mahuva

Nirma Ltd., the Gujarat-based detergent giant, is experiencing the negative effects of community inter-relationships in the form of a public and legal conflict with local communities over its upcoming cement plant in Mahuva, Bhavnagar, Gujarat. Farmers in Mahuva, led by their MLA have opposed the state government's allotment of 268 hectares of land to the company, on the grounds that it consists of wetland and a government-constructed water reservoir meant to counter salinity in the area. They claim that this environmental disruption will affect 5,000 families in more than 15 villages.[46]

The protesting farmers from 12 villages have so far taken out rallies, arranged padayatras (journeys on foot) to the state capital, submitted a memorandum to Chief Minister of Gujarat, Shri Narendra Modi and filed a public interest litigation in the High Court of Gujarat under the Shree Mahuva Bandhara Khetiwadi Pariyavaran Ran Bachav Samiti,[47] all amidst heavy media coverage.

After an initial stay order in March 2010, the High Court of Gujarat allowed the company to resume construction work after returning 46 hectares of the allotted land, in addition to the 54 hectares already relinquished.[48] In March 2011, the Ministry of Environment and Forests (MoEF), issued a show-cause notice to Nirma and asked it to stop construction, which the company strongly opposed.[49] Later, in December 2011, the MoEF revoked permission for the plant, against which the Supreme Court of India permitted the company to approach the National Green Tribunal. In a surprising verdict, the National Green Tribunal fined the Mahuva farmers and the MoEF.[50]

Throughout this controversy, Nirma Ltd., with a vision statement that visualises the company as '... widely admired ethical corporate citizen'[51] believing in 'fulfillment of ... role as a responsible part of the society and environment in which one operates',[52] has been silent and has not made any definite efforts to reach out to the community in any manner to reduce the reputational damage caused.

Situations of the type presented above create an organisational image in the mind of the stakeholders that perpetuates perceptions and generates a positive or negative halo for the company. Hence, it becomes imperative to measure corporate image for understanding stakeholder impressions of company intent and acts of commission and omission.

Methods of Measuring Corporate Image

There are six dimensions on which image can be measured. Out of these six, only two follow a closed method (refer Table 2.3).

The number of respondents for each of these techniques can vary from 10 to 100 with low to high degree of involvement. For all these measurement techniques, costs involved and ease of conducting analysis range from low to high.[53]

Which of the methods to select: open or closed? It is a choice based on the desired end result. A close-ended questionnaire provides converging results. However,

Table 2.3   Dimensions for Measuring Corporate Image

Type	Measure	Description
Closed	Questionnaire/attitude scale	Measures respondent beliefs
	Q-sort	Oral interview in which participants are asked to sort cards according to normal distribution
Open (oral interviews)	Photosort	Respondents are asked to validate a photo deck that matches with the company
	Laddering	Respondents are repeatedly asked the 'why' question with the objective of discovering a cause–effect relationship
	Kelly Repertory Grid	Objects are provided and respondents are asked to pick two out of three that match the 'best' and 'worst' of the company and spell out the reason
	Natural grouping	Objects on cards are split into homogeneous groups

an open-ended analysis elicits more details that may at a later date help a company brainstorm and use as input for further close-ended analysis. When comparisons are to be made or trends to be measured, a close-ended questionnaire is the best. However, when attributes lack clarity or greater information is required to understand stakeholder perspective, an open-ended methodology is the most appropriate.

Soliciting Feedback from Stakeholders: Tata Motors Ltd.

Tata Motors Ltd. has certainly created a strong industry-wide and overall reputation for itself. In terms of external assessments of reputation, it was at first position in *AC Nielsen*'s Corporate Image Monitor 2011–12, eighth in *Businessworld*'s 'India's Most Respected Companies' and 12th in *Fortune* 'India's Most Admired Companies'. The company also won the 'Best in Class' for product and service quality and vision and leadership distinction in the Nielsen survey.[54]

In terms of internal assessment, the company has invested substantial time and effort and used different data collection tools to gauge stakeholder satisfaction.

For shareholder feedback, Tata Motors Ltd. conducts shareholders' satisfaction surveys. During 2011–12, almost 2,287 shareholders participated in this survey and 70 per cent gave the company perfect scores on all parameters. The company assesses customer satisfaction using different customer satisfaction surveys—the globally renowned J. D. Power survey for passenger car business and TNS survey (by TNS Global) for commercial vehicles business. For 2011–12, Tata Motors Ltd. scored 785 on 1,000 points in J. D. Power Customer Satisfaction Index Score and was ranked seventh; while it pulled in 83 and 86 points, respectively (on a 200-point scale) for its Medium & Heavy Commercial Vehicles Truck and Medium Commercial Vehicle Bus segments. Periodic employee satisfaction surveys have thrown up insights that have been used for developing future policies and addressing learning needs. In 2011–12, the company launched Performance Assessment and Coaching Tool, which was a newer version of its performance management and rewards system, and was based on employee feedback.

For measuring the impact of its community initiatives, Tata Motors Ltd. has conducted review assessments using the 'Tata CS Protocol'. Annual dealer and vendor satisfaction surveys have enabled the company to understand satisfaction levels of these groups. Similarly, for stakeholder groups as investors, government and regulatory bodies, Tata Motors Ltd. has used action plans and minutes of meetings held with these groups as sources of data to assess satisfaction levels.[55]

This across-the-board strategy of obtaining stakeholder reactions gives the company an edge in tailoring its offerings to meet stakeholder expectations, which go a long way in generating reputational capital.

Is there a Return On Investment (ROI) on building relationship with stakeholders? The ROI is reflected in the triple bottom line philosophy of the company. To assess the ROI, various measurement techniques have been developed as Stakeholder Relationship Audit, Attitudinal Management Planning Model, Stakeholder Performance Appraisal, which are advanced and variant forms of the Foresight Model.[56]

The most important component in all these models is attitude centrality, which suggests that 'important or involving attitudes are more extensively linked to other components of cognitive structure as other attitudes, values and self-concept. Unimportant or uninvolving attitudes are structurally isolated'.[57] This network of attitudes among consumers or buyers can often create resistance to change. Consumers will continue to live with their own perceptions and stereotypes in the absence of compelling evidence concerning product or company. Often buyers have lack of direct experience about the product and find it difficult to build a product attitude. Building on extrinsic cues provided by the company, they form or transfer their product judgements.

WHAT COMMUNICATION STRATEGIES TO SELECT?

When people talk, listen completely. Most people never listen.

—ERNEST HEMINGWAY[58]

Organisational communication scholarship emphatically asserts the need for companies to assess measures for influencing and aligning with stakeholders in their quest for building reputation (refer Fig. 2.3). In this process, alignment with employees through internal communication is the first step. As brand ambassadors, employees play a critical

Figure 2.3   Aligning with Stakeholders

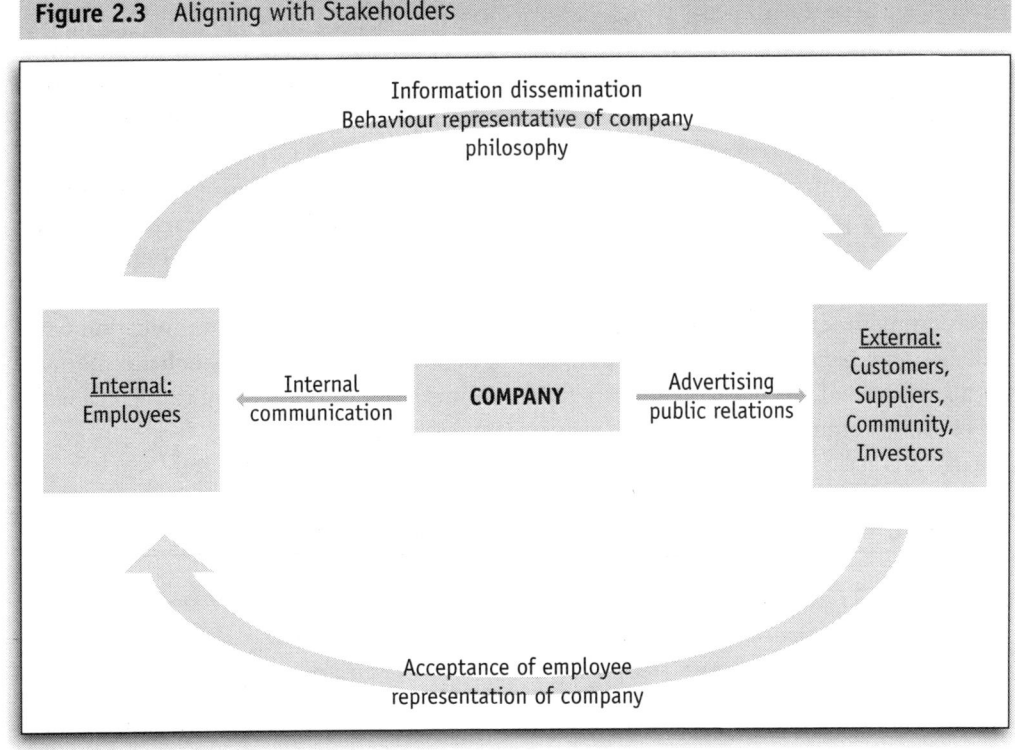

role in information dissemination. Chances of success are high if employees internalise and communicate values, and demonstrate the same through behaviour that is truly representative of company philosophy. The loop does not close at this point. Customer acceptance of employee representation of the company, based on perception and experience, should also be high.

The second step is getting external stakeholders on board through advertising, public relations, etc. and is critical from the perspective of attributing goodwill to the company and making important decisions that directly affect business operations. However, from the point of building reputation, employees are far more significant than external stakeholders. Companies that value their employees more than shareholders stand to gain higher and better returns than otherwise. Good communication helps change employee attitudes, behaviour, style of working and relationships.

With organisational change, there is also a shift in internal communication, which caters to expectations of employees. The classic 'change curve'[59] suggests measures companies adopt which border on emotions as satisfaction, complacency, denial, rejection, resistance and anger. For this change to be communicated the senior management articulates the vision and shows commitment to it; and, middle management facilitates and reinforces through actions with the aim of securing commitment and enthusiasm of employees at all levels and stages. The process of implementing change begins with extensive research that provides insights into processes and functions highlighting attitudes and behaviour.

For such scenarios, various measures have been proposed. For instance, communicating 'psychological performance'[60] which relates directly to the present experiences of stakeholders or expression of self-concept. Adherence to 'social expectations' from company and behaviour in the market place is the second communication method. Company conduct and performance is communicated through corporate personality defined as 'those characteristics of the person or of people generally that account for consistent patterns of behaviour'.[61] Stemming from the aforementioned discussion is the concept of trust that is 'the subjective probability that one assigns to benevolent action by another agent or group of agents'.[62] Communicating trust, thus, is a process of predicting social behaviour in which are embedded concepts of reliability, benevolence and honesty.[63] Reliability is the ability to maintain the promise made by the company through its communication with stakeholders; benevolence is the willingness to behave in a mutually beneficial manner for all concerned parties and, honesty fulfils promises and reflects corporate credibility. All of these communicate expertise, trustworthiness and sincerity.

WHAT ARE THE BENEFITS OF STAKEHOLDER ENGAGEMENT?

Imagine an organization full of people who come to work enthusiastically, knowing that they will grow and flourish, and intent on fulfilling the visions and goals of the larger organization. There's ease, grace, and effortlessness about the way they get things done.

—Peter Senge[64]

There are various advantages associated with enhancing relationships with stakeholders. Good organisation–stakeholder relationships provide companies leeway to charge a premium price for their product, simplify the new product launch process and provide a reputational shield to be used in moments of crisis. Other associated advantages are strategic positioning, successful market penetration, availability of different resources, cost reduction, increased motivation and productivity, easier recruitment of employees and higher profits.[65]

Multiple Benefits of Stakeholder Engagement: Hindustan Unilever Ltd.

Hindustan Unilever Ltd.'s (HUL) corporate purpose proclaims that 'to succeed requires the highest standards of corporate behaviour towards everyone we work with, the communities we touch and the environment on which we have an impact'.[66] This focus on maintaining integrity and an ongoing commitment to sustainable operations, and taking all stakeholders along is also reflected in its unique 'purpose and principles' statement.

With a huge product portfolio of over 35 brands spanning 20 categories, HUL has always been able to command premium prices, since its first entry into the Indian market in 1888. In spite of stiff competition, HUL brands as Annapurna, Brooke Bond, Bru, Closeup, Dove, Fair & Lovely, Kissan, Knorr, Kwality Walls, Lakme, Lifebuoy, Lux, Liril, Pears, Pepsodent, Ponds, Rin, Surf and Vim have been foremost in sales, even in categories where they are pricier than competing products.

Every new product launched under each of these brand umbrellas—be it multi-grain Annapurna Atta, specialty Bru coffees, Dove hair oils, Lux and Pears bathing products, Ponds and Lakme cosmetics or newer versions of washing products under the Rin, Surf or Vim brands—have received favourable responses from the market.

The company's robust reputation, as evidenced by its No. 2 position in *Fortune* 'India's Most Admired Companies' 2012 and 2013, also enables it to ward off the negative effects of crises. In spite of an ongoing skirmish regarding alleged mercury waste dumping in the South Indian tourist town Kodaikanal, the company's reputation does not seem to have suffered.

Associating with stakeholders and inviting them to participate in the decision making process increases both, financial performance and commitment.[67] With increased focus on accountability and freedom of expression, the company involvement through stakeholder engagement has today become a necessity and is no longer an option.

The interdependence between stakeholders and the organisation increases when corporates adopt systems and practices that get reflected in increased allegiance and commitment. A good example of the same is the CSR policy adopted by companies in the interest of the local communities, be it education, women empowerment, etc. This clearly demonstrates organisational capability of working in coalition with stakeholders by the process of consultation, monitoring and reporting. Researchers record that these strategic partnerships, also termed as 'bridging', lead to engagement and grant stakeholders the power to influence organisational activities.[68]

Another functionality of building relationships is one of mutual benefit in which there are positive business returns and ethical advantages. The moral engagement or commitment is marked through communication. For a company to achieve 'real success' its strategic intent should be deeply embedded in the company culture and shaped by ethical and moral considerations in performance and management. Stakeholder interests and concerns should not be treated as 'add-ons' but be managed coherently and integrated in the overall strategic planning.[69]

Profit as a 'Lag' Measure: Tata Group

Mr R. Gopalakrishnan, Executive Director, Tata Sons, and a member of the Group Executive Board, Tata Group, believes that the reason why the Tata Group continues to flourish even after 140 years of existence is its core philosophy of giving back to society.

According to him, the Tata Group of Companies has always emphasised collaborative growth and this embedded intent is one of the reasons behind its stellar reputation in India and globally.

He provides several examples to illustrate how stakeholder interests are built into the Group's core philosophy and strategic planning. Tata Steel Ltd., founded in 1882, considered self-reliance of the country and its people as its primary concern; profits were secondary. It was a pioneer in introducing good labour practices including 8-hour work days, leave with pay and employee provident fund. Its efforts at community development were initially mocked. Still, the company continued to act upon its beliefs. Over a period of time, its focus on employee and community welfare made Tata Steel Ltd. figure as one of the most reputed companies in India.

Another example he shares is about how community development is ingrained in every Tata company, without any formal instructions to the effect. Performance review presentations made by every group company invariably include their contribution to the surrounding community; trusteeship is ingrained in the very fabric of the company.

The shareholding pattern of the Tata Group, with the parent company Tata Sons Ltd. being a private unlisted company and the emanating companies being listed ones, allows it to stay faithful to its perspective. A large portion of Tata Sons Ltd. is owned by a group of charitable trusts, and this reminds all the employees that from their efforts of earning extra profits, two-thirds will go to charity. This is a convincing example of a business putting social responsibility at the core of its activities, which results in other 'lag' measures like profits to automatically follow.[70]

In summary, organisations need to adopt a systematic approach and move away from an issues-based intervention policy to a more comprehensive and collaborative structuring. With increased and enhanced stakeholder relationships they stand to benefit in terms of commitment, building of exchange and communal relationships, increased interaction, empowered relationships and enhanced two-way communication. Further, these relationships make the organisations socially responsible and accountable along with better quality of management.

Balancing Stakeholder Interests and Measuring Engagement

The recent spate of corporate scandals has brought to the fore the importance of assigning attention to stakeholder management. Balancing stakeholder interests and needs is a long drawn-out process that requires identification, assessment and action in the interests of those who have a stake and genuine interest in the functioning of the organisation. It helps organisations manage divergent and different requirements.[71]

For example, Kudremukh Iron Ore Mining Company Ltd., a profitable export-oriented government undertaking in Karnataka had to discontinue its 29-year-old mining operations in December 2005 following a Supreme Court of India ruling that its mines were part of the Kudremukh National Park. The company now uses outsourced haematite iron ore for manufacturing iron oxide pellets at its nearby Mangalore plant. Though this withdrawal had a negative financial effect, the company has been able to satisfy stakeholder requirements and ensure conservation of the ecological system in the area.[72]

Stakeholder engagement can be measured in the following ways:

- Frequency of complaints in a given period of time
- Number of employees assigned to address complaints
- Number of targets achieved as against number assigned
- Efficiency in operations and process management
- Higher investments
- Higher revenues and profits
- Acceptance in local communities
- Governmental approvals

CONCLUSION

To disregard what the world thinks of us is not only arrogant, but utterly shameless.

—Marcus T. Cicero[73]

Reputation scholarship primarily focusses on the role, conditions and sources of company reputation that can create expectations about offerings from potential buyers. The issue becomes critical when there is little or no knowledge about the offering. Reputation enhancement can happen by providing high-quality offerings, maintaining all channels of information transmission and engaging stakeholders.

Can stakeholder engagement be institutionalised? Yes! By following a four-step process of plan, act, observe and reflect in an iterative cycle. The first step in this process is integration of core group of external with other important stakeholders, followed by measurement of success. Observation and consultation between and among stakeholders improves relationship between key constituencies and promotes engagement.

Universally acceptable and applicable measurement techniques of corporate reputation and stakeholder engagement are yet to be documented. Though the process has begun, there is still much ground to be covered.

There are some steps companies adopt to garner stakeholder trust and confidence:

- Generate a positive company image
- Create a functional and emotional appeal
- Measure reputational quotient on a regular basis and work towards a per cent increase
- Build relationships with stakeholders by understanding, listening to and assessing their needs
- Communicate psychological performance, company conduct and performance, and adhere to social expectations

Key Points

- Companies create reputation by creating ground for experience, reiterating product-related information, entertaining dialogue and paying heed to stakeholder needs.
- Positive perceptions of the company are shaped by the functional and emotional appeal of the company.
- Companies provide five informational cues to the stakeholders: market, accounting, institutional, strategy and legitimation.
- Stakeholders create impressions through the principle of cognitive economy and assign a positive or negative halo to a company.
- The quantum of benefits in the organisation–stakeholder relationship is huge which makes measurement of reputation an imperative.
- Reputational assets yield high returns and place the company at a vantage position.
- A corporate reputation index and the value-change scoreboard help in reputation measurement.
- Components of corporate reputation are product/service, employees, external relationships, company culture and ethics, innovation and value creation.
- Ranking and ratings provided by external agencies accord a reputational quotient to a company that helps in business excellence.
- Understanding and analysing stakeholders, their preferences and needs is the most critical in the chain of reputation enhancement.
- Building connects with the stakeholders can commence by a proper application of the GOREL model.
- Communicating using concepts of psychological performance, corporate personality, social expectations and trust help in bonding with stakeholders.
- The interdependence between stakeholders and the organisation increases when corporates adopt systems and practices that get reflected in allegiance and commitment.

END NOTES

1. Tom DeMarco quotes, website http://thinkexist.com/quotation/you-can-t-control-what-you-can-t/347396.html (accessed 4 July 2013).

2. J. Louisot and J. Rayner, 'Managing risks to reputation: From theory to practice', website http://www.risk2reputation.com/files/Managing_Risks_to_Reputation_From_Theory_to_Practice.pdf (accessed 4 July 2013).

3. N. A. Gardberg and C. J. Fombrun, 'The global reputation quotient project: First steps towards a cross-nationally valid measure of corporate reputation', *Corporate Reputation Review* (2002), 4(4), 303–307.

4. 'Giving due respect', website http://businessworld.in/en/storypage/-/bw/giving-due-respect/r388735.0/page/0 (accessed 13 July 2013).

5. Nielsen, 'Tata Motors tops Nielsen's Corporate Image Monitor study', website http://www.nielsen.com/in/en/nielsen-pressroom/2012/tata-motors-tops-nielsen-s-corporate-image-monitor-study.html (accessed 13 July 2013).

6. John Wooden quotes, website http://thinkexist.com/quotation/don-t_measure_yourself_by_what_you_have/148159.html (accessed 4 July 2013).

7. A. Caruana, 'Corporate reputation: Concept and measurement', *Journal of Product & Brand Management* (1997), 6(2), 109–118.

8. C. J. Fombrun and M. Shanley, 'What's in a name? Reputation building and corporate strategy', *Academy of Management Journal* (1990), 33(2), 233–258.

9. H. Rao, 'The social construction of reputation: Certification contests, legitimation and the survival of organizations in the American automobile industry: 1895–1912', *Strategic Management Journal* (1994), 15(Special issue), 29–44.

10. A. Caruana, 'Corporate reputation: Concept and measurement', *Journal of Product & Brand Management* (1997), 6(2), 109–118, p. 114.

11. B. Lev, *Intangibles: Management, Measurement and Reporting*. Washington, DC: Brookings Institution Press (2001).

12. K. Cravens, E. G. Oliver and S. Ramamoorti, 'The reputation index: Measuring and managing corporate reputation', *European Management Journal* (2003), 21(2), 201–212.

13. Ibid.

14. G. Baum, C. Ittner, D. Larcker, J. Low, T. Siesfeld and M. Malone, 'Introducing the new value creation index', *Forbes ASAP* (3 April 2000), 140–143.

15. R. F. Lusch, 'Creating long-term marketing health', *Marketing Management* (2000), 9(1), 17–22.

16. M. G. Harvey and R. F. Lusch, 'Balancing the intellectual capital books: Intangible liabilities', *European Management Journal* (1999), 17(1), 85–92.

17. C. J. Fombrun, 'Indices of corporate reputation: An analysis of media rankings and social monitors' ratings', *Corporate Reputation Review* (1998), 1(4), 327–340.

18. R. W. Grupp and L. Gaines-Ross, 'Reputation management in the biotechnology industry', *Journal of Commercial Biotechnology* (2002), 9(1), 17–26.

19. C. J. Fombrun, *Reputation: Realizing Value from the Corporate Image*. Boston, MA: Harvard Business School Press (1996).

20. Hay Group, 'Hay Group releases India's 50 Most Admired Companies' rankings', website http://www.haygroup.com/in/press/details.aspx?id=33153 (accessed 7 July 2013).

21. P. Datta, 'Beyond mere numbers', *Businessworld*, website http://www.businessworld.in/en/storypage/-/bw/beyond-mere-numbers/r383635.30752/page/0 (accessed 7 July 2013).

22. Nielsen, 'Aditya Birla Group leads Nielsen's Corporate Image Monitor 2012–13', website http://www.nielsen.com/in/en/nielsen-pressroom/2013/aditya-birla-group-leads-nielsens-corporate-image-monitor-2012-1.html (accessed 11 July 2013).

23. H. M. Shamma, 'Towards a comprehensive understanding of corporate reputation: Concept, measurement and implications', *International Journal of Business and Management* (2012), 7(16), 151–169.

24. Danny Davis quotes, website http://www.quotesea.com/quotes/by/danny-davis (accessed 4 July 2013).

25. R. E. Freeman, *Strategic Management: A Stakeholder Approach*. Boston, MA: Pitman (1984), p. 31.

26. Ibid., p. 46.

27. E. W. Mainardes, H. Alves and M. Raposo, 'Stakeholder theory: Issues to resolve', *Management Decision* (2011), 49(2), 226–252.

28. H. Spitzeck and E. G. Hansen, 'Stakeholder governance: How stakeholders influence corporate decision making', *Corporate Governance* (2010), 10(4), 378–391.

29. Ibid.

30. A. L. Friedman and S. Miles, *Stakeholders: Theory and Practice*. Oxford: Oxford University Press (2006).

31. R. K. Mitchell, B. R. Agle and D. J. Wood, 'Toward a theory of stakeholder identification and salience: Defining the principle of who and what really counts', *The Academy of Management Review* (1997), 22(4), 853–886.

32. B. Murphy, K. Stevens and R. McLeod, 'A stakeholderism framework for measuring relationship marketing', *Journal of Marketing Theory and Practice* (1997), 5(Spring), 43–57.

33. R. C. Gomes and L. de O. M. Gomes, 'Performance measurement and stakeholder perceptions: Assessing performance through the dimensions of stakeholder', website http://web.ebscohost.com/ehost/detail?vid=3&hid=104&sid=9a454f5f-6aaa-41b6- b895-740e7323670f%40sessionmgr115&bdata=JnNpdGU9ZWhvc3QtbGl2ZQ%3d%3d#db=bth&AN=6001434 (accessed 6 July 2013).

34. R. E. Freeman, *Strategic Management: A Stakeholder Approach*. Cambridge: Cambridge University Press (2010).

35. J. M. T. Balmer, 'Corporate identity and the advent of corporate marketing,' *Journal of Marketing Management* (1998), 14 (8), 963–996.

36. Communication quotes, website http://www.aphids.com/cgi-bin/quotes.pl?act=ShowListingsForSub&Subject=S54 (accessed 4 July 2013).

37. T. Muzi-Falconi, *Global Stakeholder Relationship Governance*. Miami: Institute for Public Relations (2010), website http://www.instituteforpr.org/wp-content/uploads/Global_Stakeholder_Relationship_Governance.pdf (accessed 4 July 2013).

38. M. B. E. Clarkson, 'A stakeholder framework for analyzing and evaluating corporate social performance', *The Academy of Management Review* (1995), 20(1), 92–117, p. 107.

39. C. S. Alexander, P. Miesing and A. L. Parsons, 'How important are stakeholder relationships?', *Academy of Strategic Management Journal*, (2005), 4, 1–7.

40. Google India, 'Our culture', website http://www.google.co.in/about/company/facts/culture/ (accessed 11 July 2013).

41. D. Sengupta, 'Best companies to work for 2013: Google's care quotient for employees helps it stay on top', *The Economic Times* website http://articles.economictimes.indiatimes.com/2013-06-24/news/40166697_1_google-india-rajan-anandan-meetings (accessed 11 July 2013).

42. ET Bureau, 'Google best workplace in India, followed by Intel and American Express', *The Times of India*, website http://timesofindia.indiatimes.com/business/india-business/Google-best-workplace-in-India-followed-by-Intel-and-American-Express/articleshow/20738436.cms (accessed 11 July 2013).

43. R. Gopalakrishan, 'Beyond consumer capitalism: Towards sustainability and fair trade', Speech at Caux Conference on Trust and Integrity in the Global Economy (13 August 2010), website http://www.caux.iofc.org/en/node/50133 (accessed 13 July 2013).

44. Tata Steel Ltd., 'The Jamshedpur story', website http://www.tatasteelindia.com/corporate-citizen/corporate-sustainability/jamshedpur-story.asp (accessed 12 July 2013).

45. 'Discover Jamshedpur', website http://www.jamshedpurlive.net/discover-jamshedpur/factfile/inthe-limelight.aspx (accessed 12 July 2013).

46. 'It's poor farmers vs. Modi and Nirma in Gujarat', website http://www.rediff.com/money/slide-show/slide-show-1-farmers-versus-gujarat-government-and-nirma/20110104.htm#2 (accessed 12 July 2013).

47. 'Rally against Nirma cement plant', *The Hindu*, website http://www.thehindu.com/business/companies/rally-against-nirma-cement-plant/article1543213.ece (accessed 12 July 2013).

48. 'Gujarat HC gives green signal to Nirma's Mahuva cement plant', website http://deshgujarat.com/2010/04/26/gujarat-hc-gives-green-signal-to-nirmas-mahuva-cement-plant/ (accessed 12 July 2013).

49. 'Mahuva project: Nirma refuses to follow Centre's directive', *The Times of India* website http://articles.timesofindia.indiatimes.com/2011-03-15/ahmedabad/28690973_1_cement-plant-mahuva-moef (accessed 12 July 2013).

50. 'Mahuva farmers fined for opposing proposed Nirma cement plant', *The Indian Express*, website http://m.indianexpress.com/news/mahuva-farmers-fined-for-opposing-proposed-nirma-cement-plant/1132994/ (accessed 12 July 2013).

51. Nirma Ltd., 'Vision, mission and philosophy', website http://www.nirma.co.in/vision_mission.htm (accessed 13 July 2013).

52. Ibid.

53. C. B. M. van Riel, N. E. Stroeker and O. J. M. Maathuis, 'Measuring corporate images', *Corporate Reputation Review* (1998), 1(4), 313–326.

54. 'Aditya Birla, Tata Motors, LIC top reputation index: Nielsen', *The Economic Times*, website http://articles.economictimes.indiatimes.com/2013-03-25/news/38010478_1_nielsen-s-corporate-image-monitor-aditya-birla-group-executive-director-dinesh-kapoor (accessed 13 July 2012).

55. Tata Motors Ltd., 'Corporate Sustainability Report 2011–12', website http://www.tatamotors.com/sustainability/pdf/annualSustainabilityReport2011-12.pdf (accessed 13 July 2013).

56. R. Slaughter, *The Foresight Principle: Cultural Recovery in the 21st Century*, London: Adamantine (1995).

57. A. H. Eagly and S. Chaiken, *The Psychology of Attitudes*. Fort Worth, TX: Harcourt Brace Jovanovich College Publishers (1993), p. 149.

58. Communication quotes, website http://www.aphids.com/cgi-bin/quotes.pl?act=ShowListingsForSub&Subject=S54 (accessed 4 July 2013).

59. J. Harkness, 'Living and breathing the brand: The role of internal communication', *Journal of Communication Management* (1999), 4(1), 87–94, p. 89.

60. J. E. Swan and L. J. Combs, 'Product performance and consumer satisfaction: A new concept', *Journal of Marketing* (1976), 40(2), 25–33, p. 26.

61. L. A. Pervin, *Personality, Theory and Research*. New York: John Wiley (1989), p. 4.

62. B. Nooteboom, H. Berger and N. G. Noorderhaven, 'Effects of trust and governance on relational risk', *The Academy of Management Journal* (1997), 40(2), 308–338, p. 311.

63. S. Ganesan, 'Determinants of long-term orientation in buyer-seller relationships', *Journal of Marketing* (1994), 58(2), 1–19.

64. Quote—Employee stakeholder engagement, website http://deonbinneman.com/2011/07/13/quoteemployee-stakeholder-engagement/ (accessed 4 July 2013).

65. C. Ljubojevic and G. Ljubojevic, 'Building corporate reputation through corporate governance', *Management* (2008), 3(3), 221–233.

66. HUL, 'Purpose and principles', website http://www.hul.co.in/aboutus/purposeandprinciples/ (accessed 13 July 2013).

67. J. Simmons, 'Balancing performance, accountability and equity in stakeholder relationships: Towards more socially responsible HR practice', *Corporate Social Responsibility and Environmental Management* (2003), 10(3), 129–140.

68. M. L. Sinclair, 'Developing a model for effective stakeholder engagement management', *Asia Pacific Public Relations Journal* 12(1), 1–20.

69. M. Hitt, R. Freeman and J. Harrison, *The Blackwell Handbook of Strategic Management*. Hoboken, NJ: Wiley-Blackwell Publishers Ltd. (2001).

70. R. Gopalakrishan, 'Beyond consumer capitalism: Towards sustainability and fair trade', Speech at Caux Conference on Trust and Integrity in the Global Economy (13 August 2010), website http://www.caux.iofc.org/en/node/50133 (accessed 13 July 2013).

71. S. J. Reynolds, F. C. Schultz and D. R. Hekman, 'Stakeholder theory and managerial decision-making: Constraints and implications of balancing stakeholder interests', *Journal of Business Ethics* (2006), 64(3), 285–301.

72. KIOCL, 'The story of KIOCL', website http://kioclltd.in/history.shtml (accessed 16 July 2013).

73. Quotes about reputation, website http://quotationsbook.com/quotes/tag/reputation/#sthash.a4zC-DO7D.dpbs (accessed 4 July 2013).

Building
Corporate Reputation

3

Redeeming Corporate Trust and Reputation: A Systemic Look at Corporate Governance and Ethics*

In its broadest sense, corporate governance is concerned with holding the balance between economic and social goals and between individual and communal goals.... The aim is to align as nearly as possible the interests of individuals, of corporations and of society.

—Sir Adrian Cadbury[1]

Objectives:

- Examine the relevance of Corporate Governance (CG) in the contemporary environment
- Provide an overview of CG legislation in India
- Illustrate the implications of CG and business ethics for corporate reputation and trust
- Understand the symbiotic relationship between (corporate) fraud and (political) corruption
- Advance a systemic perspective for understanding and implementing CG
- Argue the centrality of leadership and values in good governance

INTRODUCTION

The time is always right to do right.

—Martin Luther King, Jr[2]

* This chapter is contributed by Vidhi Chaudhri, Assistant Professor, Erasmus University Rotterdam, The Netherlands.

Key Words

- Accountability
- Bad apples
- Compliance
- Corporate governance
- Corporate reputation
- Corruption
- Culture
- Ethics
- Fraud
- Globalisation
- Leadership
- Legal
- Management
- Profits
- Shareholders
- Stakeholders
- Systemic perspective
- Transparency
- Trust
- Values

A quick glance at the pervasiveness of management fraud in Table 3.1 is likely to generate first reactions ranging from the incredulous to the dismissive with a sprinkling of variations in between. What is new, one might ask? A valid question, indeed, for numbers, by themselves, are unremarkable. There is no dearth of academic articles, books, surveys and industry reports on the state of Corporate Governance (CG) and ethics in the contemporary business environment. Yet scholarship has not kept pace with the growing frequency

Table 3.1 Management Fraud in India, 1997–2012[3]

- *Size of Fraud:* The average size of management frauds has increased from ₹282 crores before 2009 to ₹502 crores in the period 2009–2012. 2009 was a turning point with the value of fraud topping ₹138 crores.

- *Firm Type:* While fraud has occurred in companies of all sizes, about 60 per cent of fraud has taken place in small companies with revenues of up to ₹200 crore. However, there has been a 7.5 per cent rise in the average revenue of companies involved in frauds after 2009 (from ₹200 crore to ₹1,500 crore).

- *Motive(s):* Personal gain through siphoning off funds by promoters/top management (36 per cent) at the cost of stakeholders appears to be the primary motivation to commit fraud. Other key motives include defrauding lenders (17 per cent), defrauding the Government (13 per cent), defrauding investors (13 per cent) and evading taxes (12 per cent). These motives have remained unchanged in the last 15 years.

- *Predictability:* Although 24 per cent of the companies covered in the report were audited by the Big Four* consulting firms, there appears to be no correlation between the type of auditors and fraud propensity and/or detection as none of the frauds were detected by auditors.

- *Prevention:* The report notes that codified CG norms (e.g. Clause 49) have not been instrumental in preventing fraud. Among the sample of defaulting publicly listed companies, most companies had 50–75 per cent Independent Directors (IDs) on its Board; financial statements of all companies had been certified and approved by the Chief Financial Officer (CFO) and the Chief Executive Officer (CEO); and in 70 per cent of the companies, the audit committees had more than three independent members but were still not able to detect these frauds.

- *Punishment:* The report finds that monetary penalties and criminal prosecution were hardly deterrents as the fines imposed for fraud are often miniscule and most legal cases against the promoters/management were pending at various stages. Further, public information regarding the final punishment meted out to perpetuators of fraud was not readily available.

- *Result:* Post fraud detection, majority (43 per cent) of the companies ceased to exist or was being liquidated while 30 per cent continued business at reduced levels. A small percentage (5 per cent) continued operations following a change in management and/or merger with another entity.

Note: *PricewaterhouseCoopers (PwC), Ernst & Young (E&Y), KPMG and Deloitte are referred as the Big Four.

and regularity of governance scandals and ethical transgressions. This chapter makes no claims to summarise an extensive and vibrant area of research; instead, it argues that stakeholder trust and corporate reputation are central to organisational sustainability, performance and long-term value creation.

Perhaps it is an understatement that businesses do not exist in a vacuum or separate from the larger socio-political contexts in which they operate. Certainly, the conduct of business is guided and constrained by the institutional, regulatory and legal environment, and macroeconomic policies. However, the legitimacy of business as a key actor goes beyond compliance with laws and regulations to a keen awareness of its economic, ethical and social responsibility towards stakeholders and communities. The interdependencies among business, society and government and the need to recognise the 'total' impact of corporate conduct necessitate a holistic look at issues of CG.

This chapter reviews the state of CG in India especially noting the symbiotic relationship between governance at the macro and micro levels, the imperative of good governance for trust and reputation and the centrality of responsible leadership in fostering an ethical culture.

WHAT IS CORPORATE GOVERNANCE?

How a company is managed, in terms of the institutional systems and protocols meant to ensure accountability and sound ethics. The concept encompasses [...] disclosure of information to shareholders and board members, remuneration of senior executives, potential conflicts of interest among managers and directors, supervisory structures, etc.

—FINANCIAL TIMES[4]

CG is a broad concept that is variously defined. The Organisation for Economic Co-operation and Development (OECD) defines CG as:

> ... Procedures and processes according to which an organisation is directed and controlled. The corporate governance structure specifies the distribution of rights and responsibilities among the different participants in the organisation—as the board, managers, shareholders and other stakeholders—and lays down the rules and procedures for decision-making.[5]

In a nutshell, CG refers to the processes and practices that are necessary for the accountable and ethical conduct of business. Global guidelines issued by the OECD[6] conceptualise good governance in terms of six principles: (a) the need for an effective CG framework; (b) protecting the rights of shareholders; (c) the equitable treatment of shareholders including minority and foreign shareholders; (d) recognising the role and rights of stakeholders; (e) transparency and timely and accurate disclosure and (f) the responsibilities of the board to provide strategic guidance and monitor company management.

Although there is no single or universal model for CG because of variations in ownership structures and cultures, most CG principles are built around common elements

---

Figure 3.1 Stakeholders in the CG Framework

Figure 3.1 Stakeholders in the CG Framework

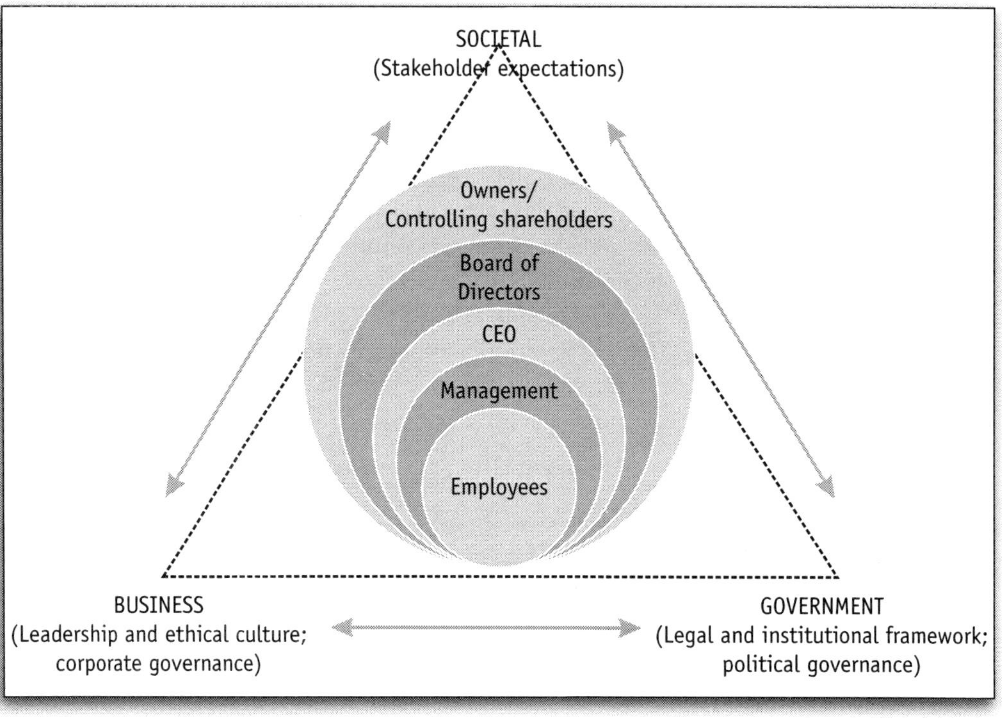

as those outlined by the OECD. An independent Board, transparency in dealing with stakeholders, measures to improve accountability and the ability of the management and the Board of Directors to work together in the best interests of the stakeholders provide the foundation for effective governance (refer Fig. 3.1). These stakeholders exist in a mutually reinforcing and interdependent relationship and a consideration of their interests and participation is integral to good governance. Indeed, how businesses operate and in whose interests are questions that lie at the crux of CG.

Enablers of CG

There are several mechanisms that organisations can and do have in place to govern, control and guide the conduct of business. Documented in the CG policies of the organisation, these internal systems and structures are designed to align with (and in some cases, go beyond) regulatory norms in the particular context.

Clause 49 of the Listing Agreement issued by the Securities and Exchange Board of India (SEBI) lays out a set of mandatory and non-mandatory provisions with which Indian listed companies must comply. Non-compliance with Clause 49 (which officially came into effect on 1 January 2006) is subject to de-listing and stiff financial penalties (refer Table 3.2).

Clause 49 is a part of the comprehensive framework of CG norms in India that have evolved over the years (see CG in India: A Primer). The effectiveness of this robust

Table 3.2 Clause 49[7]

Mandatory Provisions in Clause 49	Highlights
Board of Directors	• Combination of executive and non-executive directors with 50 per cent non-executive directors
	• Definition and eligibility criteria for IDs
	• Restriction on membership of board committees
	• All Board members and senior management to comply with a code of conduct
Audit committee	• Minimum three directors as members; two-thirds to be IDs
	• All members to demonstrate financial literacy and at least one member to have expertise on financial management or accounting
	• Chairman to be an ID
	• Defined role and powers of the audit committee
Subsidiary companies	• At least one ID of holding company must be on the board of material non-listed Indian subsidiary
	• Financial statements, especially pertaining to investments of subsidiary companies, to be reviewed by the Audit committee of holding company
Disclosures	• Related-party transactions; Differences, if any, between accounting treatment and prescribed standards; Risk assessment and minimisation procedures; director compensation; conflict of interest
	• Shareholders to be kept informed of director movement/new appointments
	• Setting up a Shareholders/Investors Grievance Committee
	• Quarterly results and presentations to be posted on company website
CEO/CFO certification	• Review and sign-off on the company's annual financial statements
Report on CG	• Separate section on CG in the Company Annual Report.
	• Quarterly compliance report to be submitted to stock exchanges
Compliance with Clause 49	• To be certified by Auditors or practicing company secretaries
Non-mandatory provisions	• Whistle-blowing policy: establish and communicate to the organisation a whistle-blowing mechanism to encourage employees to report on fraud, ethical and company violations. If necessary, whistle-blowers to have direct access to the firm's audit committee Chair.

framework, though, is questionable as is the extent of compliance. A 15-year study of management fraud in India (refer Table 3.1) attests to the limited effectiveness of Clause 49—findings confirmed in other studies as well. CG disclosures in Annual Reports, for instance, vary significantly according to company size such that the quality and quantity of disclosure is generally higher among large companies, and only a small percentage of companies fully conform to the mandatory provisions of the clause.[8]

CG in India: A Primer[9]

- The Companies Act, 1956 provides the basic framework for the responsibilities of companies and was the first piece of legislation on CG in India. Propelled by liberalisation reforms in the 1990s, a number of important initiatives were undertaken to codify governance norms.
- 1996: The Confederation of Indian Industry (CII) set up a task force to develop a code for CG and issued its report, *Desirable Corporate Governance: A Code*, in 1998.
- 1999: The Kumar Mangalam Birla Committee on CG set up by SEBI. The committee outlined the roles and responsibilities of shareholders, board of directors and the management with a goal to ensuring accountability, transparency and equal treatment of all stakeholders.
- 2002: The Naresh Chandra Committee, established by the Ministry of Finance and Corporate Affairs, was a response to the US corporate scandals of 2001–02. Committee recommended strengthening corporate audits, disciplinary mechanisms for auditors and CEO/CFO certifications about internal control and financial reporting, similar to provisions in the US Sarbanes-Oxley Act of 2002.
- 2003: The Narayana Murthy Committee, established by SEBI, made recommendations on a variety of issues that were later incorporated into the modified Clause 49 of the Listing Agreement (see Table 3.2).
- 2009: In the aftermath of Satyam, CII set up a task force under the chairmanship of Naresh Chandra that recommended separating the offices of the Chairman and CEO (in keeping with international norms) and introducing measures to ensure independence of auditors.
- In December 2009, the Ministry of Corporate Affairs issued the Corporate Governance Voluntary Guidelines.[10] Key recommendations related to appointments to the board, certification and tenure of IDs (six years), remuneration policy and the encouragement of whistle-blowing.
- The Companies Bill 2012[11] is the most recent piece of legislation. It was passed by the Lok Sabha in December 2012 and is expected to replace the Companies Act, 1956. Key recommendations include: (a) provision for class action suits; (b) mandatory rotation of auditors every five years, and auditing firm every 10 years; (c) firms to appoint at least one woman director in an effort to increase diversity (with less than 7 per cent of women directors in Indian firms, India ranks 28th in a 2012 study, significantly lagging behind Norway (37.23 per cent), Sweden (27 per cent), Finland (24 per cent), South Africa (17.31 per cent) and the US (16.67 per cent);[12] and (d) The Companies Bill also stipulates that companies with high net worth (₹500 crore), turnover (₹1,000 crore) or net profit (₹5 crore or more) in any financial year, must set up a Corporate Social Responsibility (CSR) committee and spend at least 2 per cent of their net profits for CSR.

KEY REGULATORY ACTORS IN INDIA

Multiple actors are responsible for regulatory oversight of the policies and legislation listed above, often leading to overlapping responsibilities and adding multiple layers of bureaucracy.

- The Reserve Bank of India: Responsible for banking sector regulation
- SEBI: Regulates capital markets

- Ministry of Corporate Affairs
- Auditors
- Industry associations [e.g. CII, Confederation of Indian Industries (CII), The National Association of Software and Services Companies (NASSCOM)]
- Professionals associations as the Institute of Chartered Accountants of India; Institute of Company Secretaries of India.

DOES CG MATTER?

It takes many good deeds to build a good reputation and only one bad one to lose it.

—BENJAMIN FRANKLIN[13]

CG is not a new business concept, yet, driven by the speed and scale of globalisation, it has assumed greater importance and scrutiny since the beginning of the 21st century. Contemporary arguments in favour of CG point to its enabling role in improving economic efficiency, securing (foreign) investment, reducing the cost of capital, managing risk and enhancing investor confidence in domestic and foreign markets—factors that can help organisations deliver value in an increasingly competitive business environment. By instituting internal structures and systems of control that allow organisations to achieve their goals in an ethical and accountable manner, with due regard to the interests of shareholders and stakeholders, CG ultimately contributes to long-term profitability and growth.

But does it pay to be good and does CG matter to investors? The response to this ubiquitous question is a resounding yes. In a survey of investors conducted by the International Finance Corporation, 100 per cent of the respondents cited CG as 'a critical factor' influencing investment decisions in emerging economies. Asserting that transparency and disclosure was the decisive criterion in making investment decisions, investors indicated willingness to pay a 10–20 per cent premium for well-governed organisations in emerging markets.[14]

These findings are echoed in the perceptions of domestic and foreign institutional investors regarding CG in India.[15] Quality of financial reporting (followed by reputation of the promoter/owner, company management and board of directors, respectively) is cited as the most important parameter for evaluating potential investments. While investors (95 per cent) equate CG with high shareholder returns, they equally highlight the perils of poor governance especially in the form of exit from investee companies. The survey concludes that while good CG is a necessary precondition for high returns, investors also consider factors as management capability and competitive positioning of the company in selecting investment targets.

Here is a caveat, though. The preponderance of the legal and economic narrative is at best, only a partial perspective and, at worst, a problematic one—problematic because it highlights the role of formal rules and privileges financial gains from CG above all else.

Sure, a legal system may establish certain minimum standards for compliance; however, sole reliance on a legal framework is more likely to function as a security blanket. In other words, the existence of legislation is not a sufficient solution in and of itself.

What prevents companies from abiding with these principles in form as opposed to substance? By no means a novel argument but certainly one that merits repetition is that we need to go beyond a legal-compliance approach to embracing issues of ethics, trust and reputation in the context of CG. Put another way, if business is a part of the larger socio-economic, institutional context in which it exists, it must take into account issues of ethics and demonstrate consideration of (shifting) societal interests and expectations. Doing so is critical for gaining societal 'license to operate' and for sustained value creation. Legislation can provide the "'form' to ensure standards" but the 'substance is inexorably linked to the mindset and ethical standards of management'.[16]

Likewise, the business case that seeks to identify the link between CG and firm performance has, until recently, privileged shareholders over stakeholders and financial gain over larger socio-environmental concerns. Global discourses of sustainability and corporate CSR manifest a collective shift in thinking about the role of business in society. Likewise, CG needs to be situated within the context of stakeholder expectations, and as integral to corporate reputation and trust.

WHY CARE? WHY NOW?

It is trust, trust of the management, its policies, of the employees and what they do, that is the essential bedrock of economic success.

—NIALL FITZGERALD[17]

Global events as the financial meltdown have heightened the interest in the indispensability of good governance and the consequences of governance problems. Indeed, no discussion of CG, CSR and business ethics is complete without the mention of Enron. Once lauded for being an exemplary corporate citizen, Enron's corporate fraud in 2001 signalled 'the dark side of shareholder value'[18] and the consequences of a one-sided pursuit of profit. Investigations pointed to a failure in CG practices, specifically conflicts of interest at the board and management levels, a lack of oversight and monitoring of executive compensation and circumventing rules to set up special purpose entities to distribute risk and maximise returns.

Only the first of massive corporate failures, Enron was quickly followed by others as WorldCom, Tyco, Qwest Communications, Parmalat, Adelphia, Global Crossing, Duke Energy and Merck to name a few. In the wake of Enron came a flurry of corporate and accounting reforms (the Sarbanes-Oxley Act of 2002), corporate codes of conduct and stricter penalties. Despite stiff regulation, white collar crime has purportedly grown and losses from corporate fraud in the US were estimated at $638 billion in 2005 (up from $600 billion in 2002 and $400 billion in 1996).[19] Even as the world was reeling from the residual effects of large-scale corporate crises across the globe, the financial recession of 2008 dramatically changed the business landscape. The fall of Lehman Brothers, the $58 billion Ponzi scheme crafted by Bernie Madoff, the US$1.5 billion accounting scandal at Satyam in 2009 and the systemic mismanagement at Ranbaxy Laboratories Ltd., more recently, serve as constant reminders for the need for stronger CG.

Recurring corporate scandals have prompted a downward spiral of confidence in business and questioned the integrity of corporate leaders. At Davos 2013, Klaus Schwab, Executive Chairman of the World Economic Forum, noted that the trust deficit caused by the global recession, rampant unemployment and anti-business discontent manifest in global social movements (e.g. Occupy) required stronger leadership and a departure from the old ways of 'business-as-usual'.[20] Schwab posited that 'leadership based on vision and values will go a long way to regaining trust and beating the burnout',[21] but warned that leaders would need to 'prove through concrete actions that social responsibility and moral obligations are not just empty words'.[22]

Trust and reputation are not easily earned, and if lost, are difficult to repair. Once considered a fuzzy concept, reputation is today the most important intangible asset for any organisation. A 'collective representation of a firm's past actions and results',[23] reputation is deemed among the most important indicators of an organisation's ability to deliver long-term stakeholder value. Arguably, we live in a reputation economy in which stakeholders make decisions about purchase, employment and investment based primarily on perceptions of 'trust, admiration and appreciation for the companies and institutions that stand behind them'.[24] Said another way, reputation is ultimately a matter of trust.

So how do stakeholders respond to the loss of trust in organisations? According to The Chartered Institute of Management Accountants, stakeholders reactions (disappointment to outrage) and the extent of trust damaged (questioned to completely lost) depends on the severity and type/intent of organisational action (inconsistency of actions to fraud and embezzlement). Whereas cases of inconsistency in behaviour or poor judgement may elicit disappointment and surprise respectively, the loss of trust from managerial incompetence, questionable decision making and illegal activity is likely to be severe and permanent.[25]

Good governance is a key driver of the relationship between an organisation and its stakeholders. Although the argument about reputational gain from CG is implicit in most scholarship, it is difficult, if not futile, to isolate the effect of CG on corporate reputation. A composite measure of governance, products/services, innovation, workplace, citizenship, leadership and financial performance, reputation is recognised as the basis of stakeholder commitment and loyalty, the ability to attract and retain talent and as a key differentiator. Consider this: People's willingness to recommend their organisation as a place for investment (90 per cent) and work (80 per cent) depends less on their perception of products and services and more on corporate reputation.[26]

Companies today are also cognizant of the reputational risks accruing from weak CG. Three-fourths of the respondents in a 2012 Ernst & Young study[27] confirmed that loss of reputation was the most serious (perceived) damage accruing from corporate fraud.

Unfortunately, the threat of a bad reputation might also act as a deterrent to reporting fraud for fear that such information in the public domain may result in revenue loss, lower market capitalisation and downgraded ratings. As such, reputation can be a double-edged sword, facilitating ethical behaviour while encouraging complicity for fear of repercussions.

The Case for CG in India

India is no stranger to corporate fraud. The Companies Bill 2012 defines fraud as a deliberate act that involves misuse of authority for advancing narrow interests or:

> … Any act, omission, concealment of any fact or abuse of position committed by any person or any other person with the connivance in any manner, with intent to deceive, to gain undue advantage from, or to injure the interests of, the company or its shareholders or its creditors or any other person, whether or not there is any wrongful gain or wrongful loss.[28]

Satyam (meaning 'truth' in Sanskrit; see inset) has the unenviable top spot among CG failures in India for being the biggest, if not the first, case of corporate fraud.[29]

Riding the Tiger: Scandal at Satyam Computer Services Ltd.

Incorporated in 1987, Satyam Computer Services Limited was, in 2008, India's fourth-largest technology services and consulting firm (after Infosys, Tata Consultancy Services and Wipro) employing 53,000 people across 66 countries to service its 185 Fortune 500 clients. Recognitions for the organisation included, among others, the entrepreneur of the year (awarded by Ernst & Young, 2007), top three employers (Mercer and Hewitt, 2007) and the Golden Peacock for global excellence in CG (2008) that was later revoked by the World Council for Corporate Governance on account of 'non-disclosure of material facts'.[30]

On 7 January 2009, B. Ramalingu Raju, then Chairman and CEO of Satyam, confessed to a US$1.5 billion accounting fraud notoriously dubbed 'India's Enron'. Raju confessed that he had falsified and inflated financial statements to outperform competitors and demonstrate high financial returns. US$1.04 billion in cash and bank loans which the company stated as assets were non-existent. Raju's letter dated January 8, 2009 claimed innocence of the Board and the company management, and admitted full personal responsibility:

> What started as a marginal gap between actual operating profit and the one reflected in the books of accounts continued to grow over the years.... Every attempt made to eliminate the gap failed.... It was like riding a tiger, not knowing how to get off without being eaten.[31]

Upon revelation of the fraud where, unlike Enron, the CEO blew the whistle on himself, Indian authorities moved swiftly to manage the situation: investigations were launched, arrests were made, the Satyam board was superseded and a new board instituted. At stake was rebuilding the trust and confidence among the organisation's national and international partners and customers, the future of 53,000 employees and bolstering India's reputation as the 'IT capital'. Satyam's share price plummeted from ₹179 (on 6 January) to ₹23.85 (on 9 January), and Satyam was removed from the Sensex and Nifty.[32]

To ensure transparency in the recovery process, the government-appointed Satyam board held an open auction to select a new owner for the beleaguered organisation. On 21 June 2009, Satyam was rebranded as Mahindra Satyam. Four years later, in May 2013, Mahindra Satyam announced its first dividend (30 per cent) since the takeover in 2009.[33]

Although the scandal was dismissed by some as an isolated incident that was unlikely to 'taint' the entire Indian IT industry, the fraud raised questions about regulatory oversight in India and the fate of the company's auditors, Lovelock & Lewes, a member of the PricewaterhouseCoopers (PwC) network. As Satyam's auditors for close to a decade, PwC's failure to note irregularities suggested incompetence or, worse, collusion with the company in perpetuating the fraud. For its failure to comply 'with some of the most elementary auditing standards and procedures',[34] PwC's appeals to innocence were dismissed and the organisation continues to grapple with the reputational damage both in India and internationally.

Acknowledging the need for reform, the CII introduced a set of voluntary guidelines in December 2009 that proposed separating the office of the CEO and Chairman (Raju wore both hats at the time of the scandal), and actions to ensure the independence of auditors.

The prevalence of fraud and deceit raises questions about motivation, regulatory oversight and the fallout of governance problems. Three points merit attention in this regard. First, while management fraud is often the most visible manifestation of improper governance, it is only symptomatic and embedded in a larger context of corruption and weak political governance. Consider this: The 2012/2013 Kroll Global Fraud Survey[35] finds that outside of Africa, India reports the highest levels of fraud globally (68 per cent). Eight out of the 10 types of frauds investigated in the report were more widespread in India than anywhere else in the world, and more importantly, the average financial loss accruing from the prevalence of fraud in India averaged 1.2 per cent of revenues, significantly higher than the global average of 0.9 per cent.

Second, the cost(s) associated with poor governance and ethics extend far beyond economics. While there are financial and 'tangible' implications of poor governance, that is only half the picture. What is at stake is organisational legitimacy, even survival.

Finally, although India has a framework of CG laws and policies in place (refer the CG primer) that, at first blush, might seem to provide reasonable safeguard against governance problems, legislation is no guarantee for proper governance. What is missing? The effective implementation, monitoring and enforcement of policies to prevent, detect and punish corporate fraud. The ability of perpetrators—whether individual or corporate—to circumvent these legislations is a sad commentary on the state of CG in India.

WHY DO WE NEED A SYSTEMIC PERSPECTIVE?

Good governance is perhaps the single most important factor in eradicating poverty and promoting development.

—KOFI ANNAN[36]

As stated before, most explanations of CG focus on the legal and economic issues as separate from politics. CG is ultimately about power and responsibility, and '… like other decisions about authority, corporate governance structures are fundamentally the result of political decisions. Corporate governance systems reflect policy choices.'[37] The political economy guides, enables and constrains corporate behaviour such that (corporate) fraud and (political) corruption exist in a symbiotic relationship, feeding off each other and perpetuating an (un)ethical culture.

The World Bank notes that corruption may take various forms (e.g. bribery; theft; political and bureaucratic; isolated and systemic and private sector corruption) with far-reaching negative consequences on macroeconomic stability, business efficiencies, inflow of foreign investment, entrepreneurship, socio-economic equality and overall national development.[38] The 2011–12 anti-corruption movement led by Anna Hazare, India's largest social movement since the 1977 emergency that mobilised 60,000 supporters at its peak was, arguably, an expression of simmering discontent against a corrupt environment. Although the movement waxed and waned and was plagued by its own political troubles, the fundamental cause clearly resonated with people affected by systemic corruption.

Evidence documenting the national and international ramifications of corruption is readily available. India's rankings in the annual Corruption Perception Index consistently finds the country in the bottom half (among countries and corruption scores; see Table 3.3). A 2012 CLSA study of CG[39] places India seventh among 11 Asia-Pacific countries (Singapore is first and Indonesia is last) and notes that although regulatory enforcement is improving in India, political challenges continue to impede improved CG performance.

A public opinion study by Transparency International indeed found that not only did 74 per cent of Indian respondents report an increase in levels of corruption in 2010–11, most believed that the police and political establishment (political parties and the Parliament) were the biggest perpetrators and beneficiaries of corruption. Moreover, these groups were perceived to be the least effective in alleviating the situation. It is estimated that politicians and government officials in developing economies receive anywhere between US$20 billion and US$40 billion in bribes every year.[40]

Additionally, corruption has an adverse impact on the global competitiveness of a nation. One cannot ignore the commentary of India's losing battle against China in light of sluggish inflows of foreign direct investment and the ease of doing business. In 2012, India attracted only $27 billion in foreign direct investment (down from $32 billion in 2011) as compared to China's $111.62 billion,[41] attributable in part to the difficulty of starting and running a business in India (India ranks 132 out of 185 countries on 'Ease of Doing Business'; China ranks 91).[42]

Table 3.3 Corruption Perception Index (CPI):[43] India's 10-year Performance

Year/Ranking	India's Ranking (viz. Total Number of Countries)	CPI Score (0 = Highly Corrupt)
2002	71 out of 102	2.7
2003	83 out of 133	2.8
2004	90 out of 145	2.8
2005	88 out of 158	2.9
2006	70 out of 163	3.3
2007	72 out of 179	3.5
2008	85 out of 180	3.4
2009	84 out of 180	3.4
2010	87 out of 178	3.3
2011	95 out of 183	3.1
2012	94 out of 174	3.6

Paying a High Price: 60 Years of Corruption (1948–2008)[44]

- Since independence, India has lost a total of $213 billion in illicit financial flows (or illegal capital flight) primarily due to tax evasion, corruption, bribery and kickbacks, and criminal activities.
  - Adjusted estimates put this figure at $462 billion, more than twice the external debt of $230 billion.
- Between 2004 and 2008, India lost assets at an average rate of $19 billion per year.
- Total financial flows outside India represented about 16.6 per cent of India's GDP for year 2008.
- Private companies, high net-worth individuals, as well as India's underground economy were key drivers for illicit financial flows.

How does this matter? As stated before, a macro environment of corruption creates a climate that provides all three pre-requisites for fraud: motive, opportunity and rationalisation. Corruption affects the cost of doing business, reduces efficiency, increases inequality, results in value erosion and necessitates reforms both internally and externally. What makes corruption a systemic problem in India (and elsewhere) is the widespread political–business nexus, as illustrated in the 2G spectrum scam in India. The political–business nexus is in no way unique to India. In fact, in an interview with *The New York Times*, Bernie Madoff alleged that banks and hedge funds 'had to know' about his Ponzi scheme (that lasted 16 years) but chose to turn a blind eye and failed to scrutinise the discrepancies in his filings. Their attitude, Madoff opined, was one of 'if you're doing something wrong, we don't want to know'.[45]

Deep Complicity: The 2G Spectrum Scam[46]

A notorious example of the business–political nexus spearheaded by then Telecom Minister, A. Raja, the 2G scam involved issuing telecom licenses to private players at throwaway prices without due process. In 2008, licenses were issued at prices equivalent to the rates in 2001 and were issued to companies that did not meet the eligibility criterion and/or lacked previous experience. Against the advice of the Telecom Regulatory Authority of India, Raja followed a preferential 'first-come-first-served' approach. Telecom Regulatory Authority of India had recommended inviting bids and auctioning the spectrum at market rates.

In return for meting out favours, Raja reportedly received paybacks worth several crores from the beneficiaries who in turn made huge profits. Swan Telecom Pvt. Ltd., for example, got licenses worth ₹1,537 crore and sold off a 45 per cent stake for ₹4,200 crore to UAE's Etisalat.[47]

According to the Comptroller and Auditor General of India, the spectrum scam was worth ₹1.76 lakh crores. Raja has been charged with conspiracy, cheating, criminal misconduct and abusing an official position for personal gain, and was arrested in 2011. In February 2012, all 122 licenses allocated to nine beneficiary companies were revoked by the government.

More recently, such complicity has been challenged. In 2012, Coal India Ltd. experienced an incident of shareholder activism when UK-based The Children's Investment (TCI) fund accused the company of manipulating the price of coal. TCI—Coal India's second largest shareholder after the government—noted that the prices were discounted to the tune of 70 per cent to international market prices, and undertaken at the behest of the government.[48] For not protecting the interests of minority shareholders and for bad management, TCI demanded the resignation of the company's Chairman, and filed a lawsuit in Indian court. Amidst the ongoing legal battle, TCI has, since April 2013, sold 19 per cent of its shareholding in company.[49]

These scams have fully exposed the deep business–government nexus that has long existed but only recently become apparent to the common person. They highlight the deeper problems of governance and ethics that cannot entirely be resolved with political reform. Without a systemic change effort across individual, organisational and institutional levels towards sustainable business practices, India's deep-rooted governance problems will not disappear soon.

Digging Deeper: An Indian Approach?

In Indian culture, interpersonal relations at work are modelled on family and kin relations. You pay respect to your superiors, seek their blessings, propitiate them with gifts and humble yourself before them [...] As soon as you can, you make your superior your 'uncle', his wife becomes your mausi [aunt]. You are expected to invest resources in maintaining your status in your workplace.[50]

Economist and professor emeritus at London School of Economics, Lord Meghnad Desai[51] has proposed that ingrained family values and blurred boundaries between interpersonal relations and professional behaviour are responsible for widespread corruption in India. Advancing a behavioural perspective on a systemic problem, he argues that in the absence of a clear distinction between formal rules of behaviour and family relations, people become participants in perpetuating a societal culture in which favours (no matter how questionable) for the sake of the kinship become a way of life.

There is no denying the supremacy of family and associated values in Indian society. These informal values and patterns of behaviour especially become dominant in an organisational set-up when formal rules, their enforcement and oversight are weak. Dinesh Thakur, the whistle-blower in the Ranbaxy case (discussed later in the chapter), confirms the hierarchical culture in Indian organisations—'your manager knows what is right and you essentially follow that line of thinking'[52]—contrasting that with the merit-based culture in US counterparts ('it is more about what you know than who you are').[53] In an editorial,[54] Thakur reflects on how the unquestioned obedience to authority, the need for creative solutions within constraints (loosely translated to *jugaad*) and an attitude of *chalta hai*[55] collectively result in maintaining the status quo. Together, these cultural beliefs have inhibited resistance to questionable and immoral practice and induced a culture of compromise and acquiescence that is detrimental to quality. Given their embeddedness in everyday behaviour, Thakur cautions that 'it is not the big ethical line that we need to worry about. Rather, we need to worry about all the thousands of little situations we are presented with in our daily lives…'[56]

One would be remiss to suggest that individual ethics and personal values do not have a role in managerial or political decision making; rather, the argument being made is that it is extremely important to attend to the contexts in which these actions take place. Generally, the tendency has been to treat corporate failures as the case of 'a few bad apples'. By this logic, corporate misdeeds have been explained in terms of the failure of individual moral codes and as the actions of a handful of aberrant individuals (or organisations) without adequate attention to the systemic problems of governance, ideologies, practices and policies that combine to encourage ethically questionable behaviour.[57]

Looking at issues of governance and ethics in an integrated manner, then, requires a change in thinking about corporate decisions and behaviour and a departure from the traditional paradigm of business-as-usual. Doing so mandates a fundamental shift in perspective from a focus on the financial bottom-line to examining the total impact of business conduct.

A Holistic Approach to Implementing CG

The preceding discussion has pragmatic implications for how organisations may think of CG practices. Systemic problems require systemic solutions, and the starting point is usually the establishment of and compliance with standardised mechanisms, processes and codes of conduct. Simultaneously, for sustainable trust and reputation, organisations need to ensure congruency and alignment among interrelated factors as business strategy, systems, structures, organisational culture, leadership and management practices[58] (refer Fig. 3.2).

Figure 3.2   Factors Impacting Corporate Governance

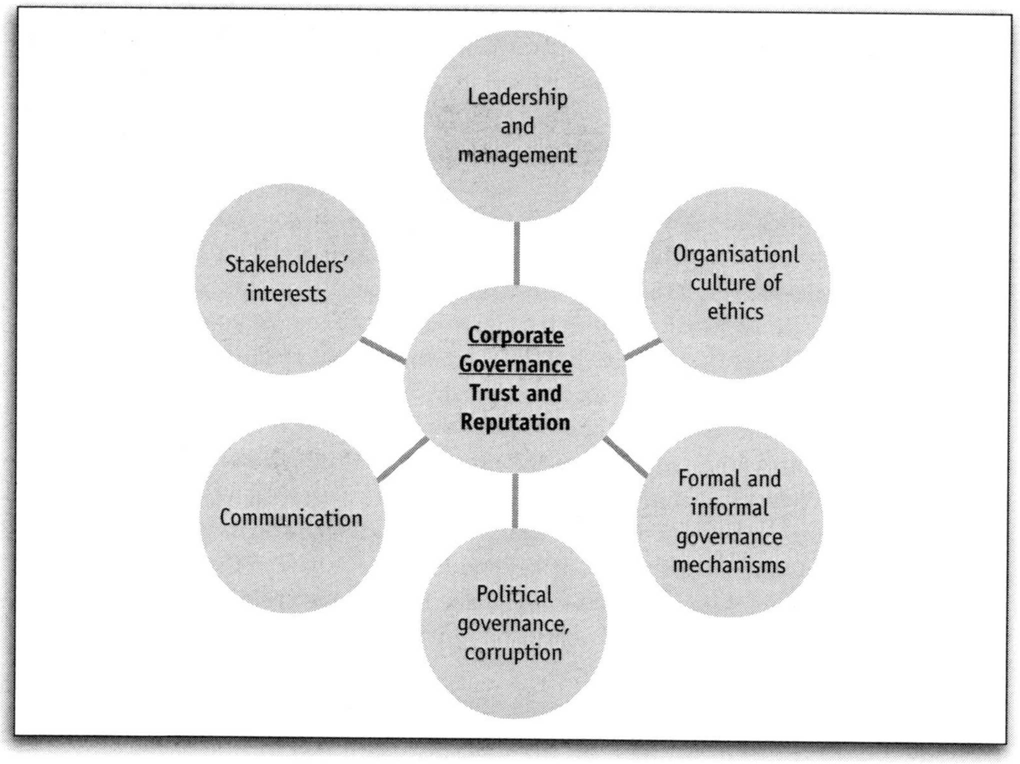

Globally, corporations today confront a crisis of trust amidst an environment that has, thus far, rewarded only financial results often overlooking the means employed to achieve those. The spate of global failures has illuminated a paradox of competing and contradicting values where financial performance is the sole standard for success by which corporate leaders are measured and lauded as heroes on the one hand, and degraded as villains on the other.[59] In the case of Enron, for example, in-depth investigations have attributed the fall of the firm along with the erstwhile Arthur Andersen LLP to a corporate culture of 'winner takes all' and pressure to maximise shareholder returns. In an interesting analogy, Enron's corporate culture, with its emphasis on winning, has been compared to a tournament, where 'Enron's managers, with a belief system biased towards winning, lost touch with both hard economic constraints and the rules of the game.'[60]

Closer home is the case of Reebok India and fraud by its two top executives. In a recent interview, Ravi Venkatesan, former Chairman of Microsoft India, shared his observation about the Reebok case describing it as, 'a failure of leadership choice and a failure of culture. Reebok bet on the wrong guy, and the whole industry knew it. And then, they chose to ignore it, as long as the results were good.'[61]

Winning at All Costs: Reebok India

Reebok India's managing director Subhinder Singh Prem and chief operating officer Vishnu Bhagat were accused of a ₹870 crore accounting fraud in 2012. German parent Adidas AG filed an FIR and fired the two executives for perpetrating the fraud by diverting merchandise to secret warehouses which were used to stock material that was billed but not delivered to the customers or franchisees. Both executives denied the charges of 'criminal conspiracy' and 'fraudulent' practices brought against them by the parent company.[62]

Directed by the Ministry of Corporate Affairs, and led by the Serious Fraud Investigation Office, the Economic Offences Wing of the Gurgaon police, and the IT department, fraud investigation found evidence of systemic mismanagement in business operations and corporate conduct. Specifically, the report noted a manipulation of accounts, tax evasion, maintenance of secret warehouses and an overall non-compliance with guidelines of the Companies Act. Investigations revealed that the secret warehouses were in existence since 2009 and Reebok India reportedly paid rent to elusive owners of these warehouses amounting to a total of ₹1.4 crore. Drawing monthly salaries of ₹20 lakh (Prem) and ₹10 lakh (Bhagat) respectively, the two accused reportedly owned several premium residential and commercial properties across India.[63] Both executives were arrested on 21 September 2012.

The case of Phaneesh Murthy, the disgraced CEO of IT outsourcing firm iGate, is also instructive. Once considered a shining star of the IT industry, Phaneesh was ousted from Infosys in 2002 in the wake of a sexual harassment lawsuit filed by a US employee that the company settled out-of-court for $3 million. After leaving Infosys (where he was credited with growing the firm's revenues from $2 million to $700 million),[64] Murthy joined iGate where he was CEO from 2008 to May 2013. Once again, though, Murthy was found guilty of pursuing a relationship with a subordinate (again in the United States) that violated company policy and the employment contract and although he dismissed the allegations as blackmail, he was fired from the top job on 20 May 2013. Reports suggest that in the aftermath of his dismissal, the company had lost a $200 million technology outsourcing contract and risked losing another. iGate stock was down 10 per cent on the Nasdaq, and at $14.82, company shares closed at the lowest level in over a year. Ironically, Phaneesh Murthy's leadership (likely evaluated in terms of financial returns) was a key criterion for the company's biggest investor to invest in iGate.[65]

The case is noteworthy for at least two reasons. First, it is remarkable that all cases of sexual misconduct brought against Murthy came from his American colleagues. The fact that he did not face any charges or accusations of sexual misconduct in his entire career in India alludes to a culture of tolerance and leniency towards such behaviour.[66] The second reason is that iGate chose to hire Murthy despite his earlier transgressions, focussing primarily on his track record of economic performance. Turning a blind eye to his behaviours and actions probably signalled to Murthy that the company valued financial gains above all else and would probably overlook his unethical behaviour.

WHERE DO WE GO FROM HERE? LEADERSHIP AND ETHICAL CULTURE

To change cultures, we must change the 'unwritten rules' that guide people, which they learn from the stories they are told and the people they admire.

—ARUN MAIRA[67]

A culture based on sound ethical principles and values is the cornerstone of effective governance. More than any other factor, the tone and example set by senior management is decisive in fostering an ethical culture and climate. What differentiates one organisation from another is certainly a factor of leadership, of leaders 'walking the talk'. The CII Task Force Report on CG explicitly notes that the dedication to run business in a legal, ethical and transparent manner is a commitment that must emanate from 'the very top and permeate throughout the organisation'.[68]

While most prescriptions emphasise the establishment of a codified ethics policy, building an ethical organisational culture is a combination of formal (e.g. code of ethics, ethics training, compliance officer, rewards and punishments) and informal (the everyday enactment of the principles laid out in the code of ethics, leading by example and empowering people to make difficult ethical decisions) systems. How values and principles laid out in the ethics codes translate to everyday practices and actions of organisational members is critical. So while the role of leadership in exemplifying ethical behaviour is important, it assumes critical mass when the importance of ethics is communicated, imbibed and practiced across all levels of the organisational hierarchy.

Whistle-blowing is an apt example in this context. In the absence of a mandatory provision for whistle-blowing and adequate mechanisms of protection, employees will be reluctant to expose questionable organisational practices. Even if, for the sake of compliance, organisations made provisions for whistle-blowing, it would not be effective unless employees knew they were safe doing so, their identities were kept confidential and their grievances were acted upon. Here, human resources have a decisive role, along with company leaders, in creating an enabling environment for debate, expression of dissent and empowering as well as rewarding employees for making ethical decisions. An ethical workplace climate has been associated with greater job satisfaction, commitment, motivation, trustworthy relationships and security in reporting wrongdoing and expressing dissent.

The case of Ranbaxy (see inset on page 69) reveals the dark side of leadership and a culture of deceit. Since accusations of selling spurious drugs and life-saving medication and the $500 million settlement with US authorities, Ranbaxy's management has attempted to dismiss or minimise the (potential) threat to human life resulting from the company's actions.

While Daiichi is considering legal action against Ranbaxy and the company shares fell as a fall-out of the fraud, the more important narrative(s) relate a culture of mismanagement within the organisation that thwarted dissent, the state of CG in India, and how the Indian government and regulator (the Drug Controller General of India) have failed to pursue action against the company. Thakur's decision about approaching

---

Playing with Lives: Fraud at Ranbaxy Laboratories Ltd.[69]

On 13 May 2013, Ranbaxy Laboratories Ltd. admitted to serious charges brought against it by US regulators under the Federal Food, Drug and Cosmetic Act. The felony charges, to which Ranbaxy pleaded guilty on 13 May 2013, include selling adulterated drugs with the intent to defraud, not reporting that its drugs failed to meet specifications and making intentionally false statements to the government. Ranbaxy agreed to pay a total fine of US$500 million ($150 million for criminal charges, and $350 million to settle civil claims), making this the largest drug safety settlement with a generic drug manufacturer.

Established in 1961 with global headquarters in Gurgaon, India, Ranbaxy's mission is to develop, manufacture and market 'high quality, affordable medicines'.[70] With operations in 43 countries and customers across 150 countries, the company's product portfolio spans medical specialties (e.g. cardiovascular, neurology, dermatology), medication type (e.g. generic, branded generic) and dosage forms (e.g. tablets, vaccines). In 2008, the promoters of Ranbaxy (Malvinder and Shivinder Singh) sold their holding in the company to Japan's Daiichi Sankyo. The acquisition was reportedly guided by Daiichi's strategy to grow its presence in the generic medication space and in developing markets.

The key player in the unravelling of the fraud was Dinesh Thakur, former Director and Global Head, Research Information and Portfolio Management, at Ranbaxy. During his tenure at Ranbaxy (2002–05), Thakur discovered systematic falsification of drug data and violation of manufacturing and laboratory practices at two of Ranbaxy's plants in India. Thakur's testimony to the US Food and Drug Administration reveals that Ranbaxy scientists were directed to 'substitute cheaper, lower-quality ingredients in place of better ingredients, to manipulate test parameters to accommodate higher impurities and even to substitute brand-name drugs in lieu of their own generics in bio-equivalence tests to produce better results'.[71] A few months earlier, in November 2012, Ranbaxy was forced to recall its anti-cholesterol drug from the US market after glass contaminants were found in some batches.

Thakur's efforts to apprise the management of questionable practices were dismissed or thwarted. So deep-rooted was the fraud, Thakur noted, that it took 'eight years to help government authorities unravel a complicated trail of falsified records and dangerous manufacturing practices that threatened to compromise the quality and safety of Ranbaxy drugs'.[72] For blowing the whistle on Ranbaxy, Thakur is set to receive a compensation of $48.6 million from the US government's federal government's share.

---

the US regulator over the Indian regulator suggests a lack of trust in Indian systems and processes. Even a public interest litigation to probe the manufacturing and distribution of substandard drugs by Ranbaxy was dismissed by the Supreme Court of India citing the lack of India-specific evidence, 'show us material that things are happening in India and it adversely affects right to life of people here'.[73]

The Ranbaxy case has also raised questions about Board oversight and its role as the organisation's conscience and/or as a trustee of the shareholders. Ranbaxy had an illustrious board comprising eight IDs; however, successive resignations of senior executives in 2004–05 (including then CEO R&D head and her successor Rajinder Kumar, and Thakur) failed to draw the Board's attention to the events in the company. Prior to his mysterious resignation, Kumar had reportedly apprised the Board of manufacturing lapses and data mismanagement in the organisation without any follow-up action from the Board. The jury is still out on this issue (the opposing view holds that the fraud was so well-concealed that the directors themselves were likely victims[74]) and the impact of the case on Board due diligence, supervision and oversight of fraud risk management remains to be seen.

Fortunately, some oft-cited positive examples provide a glimmer of hope as organisations navigate the complex terrain of CG. At the Tata Group, a comprehensive Code of Conduct provides the ethical guidelines for its members while ensuring that these principles are integrated with the company's purpose and core values (integrity, understanding, excellence, unity and responsibility). Reaffirming the centrality of ethics and good governance in everyday practices, R. Gopalakrishnan, director, Tata Sons, stated in an interview, 'we do business the way we do, not because we have clear evidence [that] it has a better chance of success. We do it because we know no other way.'[75] Perhaps a lasting legacy of the group's former Chairman, Ratan Tata, comes from having legally and ethically grown the group's revenues manifold to over $100 billion in 2012. Narayana Murthy, Chairman emeritus and co-founder of Infosys, has credited Ratan Tata's leadership, 'the highest level of integrity and with courtesy, grace and humility'[76] as an exemplar for the business world.

Narayana Murthy himself defines the purpose of leadership as creating wealth through legal and ethical means. As someone who is known to 'walk the talk', Murthy has fostered a culture of CG that is embedded in the organisation's culture, policies, company values and relationship with stakeholders.[77] A testimony to his leadership and reputation is the response to the recent announcement that Murthy would return as Executive chairman of the Board and Additional Director to his firm that has been losing market share to competitors. The announcement of his return on 1 June 2013 witnessed a spike in investor confidence as Infosys share prices rose 7 per cent on the Bombay Stock Exchange.[78]

CONCLUSION

The tipping point is that magic moment when an idea, trend, or social behaviour crosses a threshold, tips, and spreads like wildfire.

—Malcolm Gladwell[79]

In summary, CG is a system of processes and practices that guide how an organisation is managed. The CG challenges confronting India are manifold. Globally, businesses are prompted (even forced) to re-examine their roles and relationships with stakeholders and society at large. The purpose of business is clearly being introspected and in some cases, redefined, in this 'age of transcendence'.[80] The primacy of profit maximisation and shareholder value (the most widely taught management mantra) that has, thus far, marginalised issues of ethics is being vociferously questioned.

CG assumes ever more importance in a time of widespread distrust and uncertainty. Even though CG issues generally surface and escalate in times of crisis, they are central to the ongoing conduct of business, and best understood in the context of the interlinkages among business, society and government. The argument advanced in the chapter is that CG problems, corruption and fraud exist in a symbiotic relationship and require systemic solutions both within organisations and in the regulatory environment.

The need of the hour is to institute robust internal and regulatory measures for good governance and ethical corporate behaviour. From a macro perspective, the introductions of the Right to Information Act as well as public interest litigations are important steps in facilitating transparent and accountable business practices. As is normally the case with any new legislation, its true potential takes time to manifest. The Right to Information Act empowers citizens to query the governments on anything as long as it is not related to national security. Initial attempts to utilise its provisions have had a mixed response from authorities but as the citizens understand the power of this tool, it is likely to uncover more facets of corruption.

Alongside changes in the macro environment, business may work on creating internal mechanisms to ensure good governance. Some recommendations to this effect include:

- Conduct regular and frequent audits to assess the risk/propensity of CG problems. Borrowing from a fire analogy, firms may select a strategy of remediation (fire extinguisher to control damage), early detection (smoke detector to assess risk) and deterrence (removal of causal factors). Addressing the underlying causes (i.e. a strategy of deterrence) through organisational change is likely to reduce opportunities for committing fraud.[81]
- Formulate a code of conduct that guides the behaviour of employees, facilitates decision making in ethical conflict situations and encourages ethical practices in everyday actions. Businesses have to develop unique codes aligned to their respective core values.
- As stated before, simply writing a code is not enough. Corporate codes of conduct need to be understood, learned, taught, assessed and revised on a regular basis.
- Set a strong, exemplary tone at the top. Strong leadership and an ethical culture guided by core values are decisive in building competitive and trustworthy organisations. Parallely, empower members at all levels in the organisation to take ownership of building an ethical culture.
- Review the corporate message about what is valued in the organisation. If the message is one of financial performance, above all else (i.e. the end justifies the means), organisational members will be encouraged, induced or even pressured to achieve results at all costs. On the contrary, an ethical organisation will not only attract like-minded employees but will also weed out those with a propensity for fraud.
- Institute fraud detection mechanisms. Only a few companies have a whistle-blowing mechanism and protection for whistle-blowers. Doing so is critical for facilitating detection and reporting.

- Create a safe and secure environment for fraud reporting. Encourage reporting in the company's code of ethics. Reward fraud reporting.
- Regularly communicate with stakeholders about the measures taken to ensure ethical conduct, invite feedback and share best practice.

The state of CG in India undoubtedly presents a grim picture. However, it also presents an opportunity for businesses to become the change agents, to withstand the pressures of rationalising corruption as a way of doing business, to encourage accountability and to make ethical choices in favour of sustainable business practices. Long-term survival, competitiveness and value creation cannot be achieved with a short-term perspective.

How long before India hits its tipping point?

Acknowledgements

The author thanks the editors for the opportunity to contribute a chapter.

The author also thanks Sameer Kapoor, ex-Director, PricewaterhouseCoopers (PwC) and co-author of the TARI study ('Understanding the Demand and Supply Equations of Corruption and Fraud'), for providing valuable insight and feedback on previous drafts of this chapter.

Key Points

- Corporate governance refers to the processes and practices that are necessary for the accountable and ethical conduct of business.
- An independent Board, transparency, accountability and the ability of the management and the Board of Directors to work together in the interest of stakeholders provide the foundation for effective governance.
- Good governance is linked with long-term profitability and growth, economic efficiency, securing investment, reducing the cost of capital, managing risk and higher investor confidence in domestic and foreign markets.
- Good governance is a key ingredient in the relationship between an organisation and its stakeholders, and one of the drivers for corporate reputation.
- Trust and reputation are not easily earned, and if lost, are difficult to regain.
- Global corporate scandals have prompted scrutiny of governance problems and questioned the integrity of corporations and their leaders.
- The tendency to treat corporate failures as the case of 'a few bad apples' is flawed and overlooks the systemic nature of governance problems.
- Corporate governance is best understood in the context of the interlinkages among business, society and government.
- Corporate governance is not limited to compliance with the law. Businesses have to take into account their economic, ethical and social responsibility towards stakeholders and communities.

- Legislation can provide the 'form' to ensure standards but the 'substance' comes from an organisation's ethical culture and leadership.
- Corporate governance requires systemic solutions both within organisations and in the regulatory environment. An integrated approach is important for gaining societal 'license to operate' and for sustained value creation.
- The tone and example set by senior management is decisive in fostering an ethical culture and climate.
- Communication is decisive to creating an ethical culture, encouraging ethical decision making across all levels of the organisation, empowering people to report questionable practices and sharing best practices.

END NOTES

1. Global corporate governance forum (2003), website http://www.gcgf.org/wps/wcm/connect/429797 0048a7e4ef9f87df6060ad5911/GCGF_Annual_Review.pdf?MOD=AJPERES&CACHEID=429797 0048a7e4ef9f87df6060ad5911 (accessed 8 July 2013).
2. Brainy quote, website http://www.brainyquote.com/quotes/quotes/m/martinluth106169.html (accessed 1 July 2013).
3. K. Dutta and S. Kapoor, 'Understanding the demand and supply equations of corruption and fraud', thought Arbitrage Research Institute, website http://www.tari.co.in/public/report/1372144861Understanding%20the%20demand%20&%20supply%20equations%20of%20 corruption%20&%20fraud%20-%20final.pdf (accessed 20 June 2013).
4. 'Lexicon', *Finance Times*. website http://www.lexicon.ft.com/Term?term=corporate-governance (accessed 17 January 2014).
5. Glossary of statistical terms: Corporate governance, website http://stats.oecd.org/glossary/detail. asp?ID=6778 (accessed 20 May 2013).
6. 'OECD principles of corporate governance', 2004, website http://www.oecd.org/corporate/ca/ corporategovernanceprinciples/31557724.pdf (accessed 10 May 2013).
7. Clause 49, National stock exchange of India Ltd., website http://www.nseindia.com/getting_listed/ content/clause_49.pdf (accessed 20 June 2013).
8. A. Sen, 'Corporate governance in India: Clause 49 of the listing agreement', *JM International Journal of Management Research* (2011), 1(2), 162–171.
9. 'Consultative paper on review of corporate governance norms in India', Securities and Exchange Board of India, website http://www.sebi.gov.in/cms/sebi_data/attachdocs/1357290354602.pdf (accessed 20 June 2013).
10. Ministry of Corporate Affairs 'Corporate governance voluntary guidelines 2009', website http://www. mca.gov.in/Ministry/latestnews/CG_Voluntary_Guidelines_2009_24dec2009.pdf (accessed 21 June 2013).
11. Ministry of Corporate Affairs, 'Companies Bill 2012', website http://www.mca.gov.in/Ministry/pdf/ The_Companies_Bill_2012.pdf (accessed 21 June 2013).
12. 'India ranks 28th in women representation on company boards: Survey,' *NDTV Profit*, website http:// profit.ndtv.com/news/corporates/article-india-ranks-28th-in-women-representation-on-company-boards-survey-318882 (accessed 18 November 2013).
13. Brainy quote website http://www.brainyquote.com/quotes/quotes/b/benjaminfr385547.html (accessed 4 July 2013).

14. 'The emerging markets investor survey 2012', International Finance Corporation, website http://www.ifc.org/wps/wcm/connect/dbfd8b004afe7d69bcb6bdb94e6f4d75/IFC_EMI_Survey_web.pdf?MOD=AJPERES (accessed 7 July 2013).
15. 'Institutional investors: Driving force for good governance' Survey conducted by the CII and IIAS, website http://www.moneycontrol.com/news_html_files/news_attachment/2012/CII%20IIAS%20Survey%20Sept%202012.pdf (accessed 1 July 2013).
16. 'Report of the SEBI Committee on corporate governance, 2003', website http://www.sebi.gov.in/cms/sebi_data/attachdocs/1293094958536.pdf (accessed 21 June 2013).
17. Unilever, 'Unilever Chairman Niall FitzGerald addresses shareholders,' (2003), website http://www.unilever.com/mediacentre/pressreleases/2003/20030507_chairmans_address.aspx(accessed 2 July 2013).
18. W. W. Bratton, 'Enron and the dark side of shareholder value', *Tulane Law Review* (2002), 76, 1275–1361.
19. J. W. Shoen, 'Corporate fraud alive and well in U.S.', *NBC News*, website http://www.nbcnews.com/id/12762573/ns/business-corporate_scandals/t/corporate-fraud-alive-well-us/ (accessed 22 May 2013).
20. K. Shwab, 'Davos 2012: Beating the burnout with actions, not words', *The Times*, January 2012, website http://www.thetimes.co.uk/tto/public/davos/article3296735.ece (accessed 4 July 2013).
21. Ibid.
22. Ibid.
23. N. A. Gardberg and C. J. Fombrun, 'The global reputation quotient project: First steps towards a cross nationally valid measure of corporate reputation', *Corporate Reputation Review* (2002), 4, 303–308.
24. Reputation Institute UK, 'Corporate reputation: The main driver of business value', May 2012, website http://www.reputationinstitute.com/frames/press/CRO%20White%20Paper_%20RI%20UK.pdf (accessed 21 May 2013).
25. 'Corporate reputation: Perspectives of measuring and managing a principal risk', 2007, CIMA, website http://www.cimaglobal.com/Documents/Thought_leadership_docs/Corporate%20reputation%20perspectives%20of%20measuring%20and%20managing%20a%20principal%20risk.pdf (accessed 28 June 2013).
26. 'Navigating the reputation economy: A global survey of corporate reputation officers', June 2012, Reputation Institute, website http://reputationmatters.me/wp-content/uploads/2012/12/2012_CRO_Global_Whitepaper.pdf (accessed 28 June 2013).
27. 'India fraud survey 2012', Ernst & Young, website http://www.ey.com/Publication/vwLUAssets/Fraud_and_corporate_governance_changing_paradigm_in_India/$FILE/Fraud_and_corporate_governance_changing_paradigm_in_India.pdf (accessed 15 May 2003).
28. 'Companies Bill 2012', Ministry of Corporate Affairs, website http://www.mca.gov.in/Ministry/pdf/The_Companies_Bill_2012.pdf (accessed 21 June 2013).
29. 'Top ten scams in India', September 2011, MSN News, website http://news.in.msn.com/specials/news_photos.aspx?cp-documentid=5389341 (accessed 29 June 2013).
30. B. Behan, 'Governance lessons from India's Satyam', 16 January 2009, Businessweek.com, website http://www.businessweek.com/stories/2009-01-16/governance-lessons-from-indias-satyambusinessweek-business-news-stock-market-and-financial-advice (accessed 17 May 2013).
31. 'Satyam: Full text of Raju's letter to the Board', 8 January 2009, *The Economic Times*, website http://articles.economictimes.indiatimes.com/2009-01-08/news/27640204_1_maytas-balance-sheet-account-of-inflated-profits (accessed 17 May 2013).
32. 'Chronology/Satyam computer: History of events, share price movement', 23 November 2011, NDTV, website http://profit.ndtv.com/news/market/article-chronology-satyam-computer-history-of-events-share-price-movement-43806 (accessed 17 May 2013).
33. 'Time for reflection, quiet appreciation on Mahindra Satyam: Mahindra', 17 May 2013, *Business Standard*, website http://www.business-standard.com/article/companies/time-for-reflection-quiet-appreciation-on-mahindra-satyam-mahindra-113051700591_1.html (accessed 17 May 2013).

34. 'Satyam scam: US finds PwC 'India' guilty', 18 October 2012, *The Indian Express*, website http://www.indianexpress.com/news/satyam-scam-us-finds-pwc-india-guilty/772584/ (accessed 17 May 2013).

35. 'Global fraud report 2012/13', Kroll advisory solutions, website http://www.krolladvisory.com/library/KRL_FraudReport2012-13.pdf (accessed 3 July 2013).

36. 'What does "good governance" mean?' 9 February 2012, United Nations University, website http://unu.edu/publications/articles/what-does-good-governance-mean.html (accessed 1 July 2013).

37. P. A. Gourevitch and J. Shinn, *Political Power and Corporate Control*. Princeton, NJ: Princeton University Press (2007), p. 3.

38. 'Corruption and economic development', The World Bank, website http://www1.worldbank.org/publicsector/anticorrupt/corruptn/cor02.htm (accessed 24 June 2013).

39. 'CG watch 2012: Market rankings', September 2012, ACGA, website http://www.acga-asia.org/public/files/CG_Watch_2012_ACGA_Market_Rankings.pdf (accessed 25 May 2013).

40. 'Global corruption barometer 2013', Transparency International, website http://gcb.transparency.org/gcb201011/results/ (accessed 24 May 2013).

41. K. Merchant, 'Foreign direct investment to India slows', 31 March 2013, Livemint, website http://www.livemint.com/Money/RjQHyvDbIgVA2SwIp2wUGO/Foreign-direct-investment-to-India-slows.html (accessed 25 May 2013).

42. 'Doing business', Economy rankings for 2013, website http://www.doingbusiness.org/rankings (accessed 25 May 2013).

43. Compiled with data from Transparency International, website http://www.transparency.org/research/cpi/overview (accessed 24 May 2013).

44. 'The drivers and dynamics of illicit financial flows from India: 1948–2008', November 2010, Global financial integrity, website http://india.gfintegrity.org/ (accessed 4 July 2013).

45. D. B. Henriques, 'From prison, Madoff says banks "had to know" of fraud', 15 February 2011, *The New York Times*, website http://www.nytimes.com/2011/02/16/business/madoff-prison-interview.html?ref=bernardlmadoff (accessed 1 July 2013).

46. 'What is the 2G spectrum scam?' 19 October 2012, *India Today*, website http://indiatoday.intoday.in/story/what-is-the-2g-scam-all-about/1/188832.html (accessed 23 May 2013).

47. 'What is 2G spectrum scam?' 5 May 2011, *NDTV*, website http://www.ndtv.com/article/india/what-is-2g-spectrum-scam-66418 (accessed 23 May 2013).

48. N. Malpani, 'Coal India faces a surprising case of shareholder activism in India', 2012, website http://www.policymic.com/articles/6356/coal-india-faces-a-surprising-case-of-shareholder-activism-in-india (accessed 9 July 2013).

49. 'TCI sold nearly 19% of its Coal India stake', 25 June 2013, *Business Standard*, website http://www.business-standard.com/article/companies/tci-sold-nearly-19-of-its-coal-india-stake-113062500310_1.html (accessed 9 July 2013).

50. M. Desai, 'Why is India corrupt?' July 15, 2012, *The Indian Express*, website http://www.indianexpress.com/news/why-is-india-corrupt-/974515/1 (accessed 29 June 2013).

51. Ibid.

52. C. Kalbag and E. K. Sharma, 'FDA has learnt from the Ranbaxy case: Dinesh S. Thakur', 23 June 2013, *Business Today*, website http://businesstoday.intoday.in/story/whistleblower-dinesh-s.-thakur-ranbaxy-us-drug-setllement/1/195490.html (accessed 4 July 2013).

53. Ibid.

54. D. Thakur, 'The Indian way? No way.' 13 June 2013, *The Hindu* (Op-ed), website http://www.thehindu.com/opinion/op-ed/the-indian-way-no-way/article4804513.ece (accessed 4 July 2013).

55. Although the term defies easy explanation, it roughly translates to an attitude of "it will go" or "it goes" and usually implies a lack of caring or botheration (who cares?) with contentious practices (e.g. corruption).

56. D. Thakur, 'The Indian way? No way.' 13 June 2013, *The Hindu* (Op-ed), website http://www.thehindu.com/opinion/op-ed/the-indian-way-no-way/article4804513.ece (accessed 4 July 2013).

57. C. Conrad, 'Setting the stage: Introduction to the special issue on "Corporate Meltdown"', *Management Communication Quarterly* (2003), 17(5), 5–19.

58. R. F. Hurley, N. Gillespie, D. L. Ferrin and G. Dietz, 'Designing trustworthy organizations', *MIT Sloan Management Review* (2013), 54(4), 75–82.

59. J. C. Lammers, 'An institutional perspective on communicating corporate responsibility', *Management Communication Quarterly* (2003), 16(4), 618–624.

60. W. W. Bratton, 'Enron and the dark side of shareholder value', *Tulane Law Review* (2002), 76, 1275–1361, 1330.

61. H. Timmons, 'A conversation with:' 12 April 2013, *The New York Times*, website http://india.blogs.nytimes.com/2013/04/12/a-conversation-with-ravi-venkatesan-former-chairman-of-microsoft-india/?_r=0 (accessed 18 April 2013).

62. 'Corporate fraud probe body to question Reebok officials in ₹870-crore fraud case', 10 June 2012, Profit.NDTV, website http://profit.ndtv.com/news/corporates/article-corporate-fraud-probe-body-to-question-reebok-officials-in-rs-870-crore-fraud-case-305914 (accessed 20 June 2013).

63. S. K. Ahuja, 'Reebok fraud accused invested crores in realty', 31 October 2012, *The Hindustan Times*, website http://www.hindustantimes.com/India-news/Haryana/Reebok-fraud-accused-invested-crores-in-realty/Article1-952486.aspx (accessed 20 June 2013).

64. 'Rise and fall of Phaneesh Murthy', 21 May 2013, *The Hindustan Times*, website http://www.hindustan-times.com/business-news/CorporateNews/Rise-and-fall-of-Phaneesh-Murthy/Article1-1063310.aspx (accessed 28 June 2013).

65. J. Mendonca and I. Nandakumar, 'Rough road ahead for iGate post Phaneesh Murthy's sexual harassment scandal', 23 May 2013, *The Economic Times*, website http://articles.economictimes.indiatimes.com/2013-05-23/news/39475702_1_igate-shares-murthy-ceo-phaneesh (accessed 28 June 2013).

66. S. Rai, 'The real Phaneesh Murthy scandal', 3 June 2013, *The Indian Express*, website http://www.indianexpress.com/news/the-real-phaneesh-murthy-scandal/1124142/0 (accessed 28 June 2013).

67. A. Maira, 'The values we choose to live by', 12 May 2005, *The Economic Times*, website http://articles.economictimes.indiatimes.com/2005-05-12/news/27472632_1_corporate-governance-indian-banking-business-destination (accessed 5 July 2013).

68. 'Introduction' in CII task force report on corporate governance, 2009, http://www.mca.gov.in/Ministry/latestnews/Draft_Report_NareshChandra_CII.pdf (accessed 21 June 2013).

69. K. Eban, 'Dirty medicine', 14 May 2013, *Fortune*, website http://features.blogs.fortune.cnn.com/2013/05/15/ranbaxy-fraud-lipitor/ (accessed 27 June 2013).

70. 'Mission and values', Ranbaxy, website http://www.ranbaxy.com/about-us/mission-values/ (accessed 27 June 2013).

71. K. Eban, 'Dirty medicine', 14 May 2013, *Fortune*, website http://features.blogs.fortune.cnn.com/2013/05/15/ranbaxy-fraud-lipitor/ (accessed 27 June 2013).

72. P. T. Jyothi Dutta, 'Ranbaxy issue, a wake-up call for India', 14 May 2013, *The Hindu* Business Line, website http://www.thehindubusinessline.com/companies/ranbaxy-issue-a-wakeup-call-for-india/article4715034.ece (accessed 27 June 2013).

73. 'Supreme Court dismisses pleas against Ranbaxy', 26 June 2013, *The Economic Times*, website http://articles.economictimes.indiatimes.com/2013-06-26/news/40206971_1_ranbaxy-labs-arun-sawhney-mohali (accessed 27 June 2013).

74. A. K. Bhattacharya, 'Corporate governance failure at Ranbaxy?' 9 June 2013, *Business Standard*, website http://www.business-standard.com/article/opinion/corporate-governance-failure-at-ranbaxy-113060900607_1.html (accessed 5 July 2013).

75. A. Graham, 2010, 'Too good to fail', Strategy+Business, 58, http://www.strategy-business.com/media/file/sb58_10106.pdf (accessed 2 July 2013).

76. 'Ratan Tata's legacy has many lessons for business leaders: Narayana Murthy,' *The Economic Times*, website http://articles.economictimes.indiatimes.com/2012-12-28/news/36036388_1_ratan-tata-cyrus-mistry-tata-group (accessed 2 July 2013).

77. 'Corporate governance', n.d., Infosys, website http://www.infosys.com/investors/corporate-governance/pages/index.aspx (accessed 2 July 2013).

78. A. Sen, 'Infosys shares rise as Narayana Murthy returns', 3 June 2013, Livemint, website http://www.livemint.com/Money/DYWtf1kkQH6J2hbeRklRCJ/As-Narayana-Murthy-returns-Infosys-shares-climb-9.html (accessed 3 July 2013).

79. M. Gladwell, *The Tipping Point: How Little Things Can Make a Big Difference.* Boston: Little Brown (2002) (2nd ed.).

80. R. Sasodia, D. B. Wolfe and J. Sheth, *Firms of Endearment: How World-Class Companies Profit from Passion and Purpose.* New Jersey: Wharton School Publishing (2007), p. xxii.

81. J. P. Martin, 'The impact of fraud on organizations', 1 July 2012, SmartBusiness, website http://www.sbnonline.com/2012/07/the-impact-of-fraud-on-organizations/ (accessed 29 June 2013).

4

Orchestrating the Song and Dance of Reputation: The Role of Leaders

Leadership is all about moving ahead with two basic instruments: the compass and the clock. One which confirms the direction you are moving in and the other which tells you how fast you will get there.

—DEEPAK PAREKH[1]

Objectives:

- Understand leader reputation and how it is crafted
- Examine the leadership style most suited to building reputation
- Assess the relationship between leader and organisational reputation
- Recognise consequences of leader reputation
- Identify strategies for leader communication

INTRODUCTION

When people can see which direction the leaders are going in, it becomes easier to motivate them.

—LAKSHMI MITTAL[2]

All of us have heard of executives in senior leadership positions who have made it big or failed miserably in the art of taking people and company along. Historically, leadership has been understood as a trait essential for corporate tsars to surge ahead with their teams. Their success or failure has been attributed to building and maintaining organisational reputation in the eyes of the stakeholders. Stemming from this hypothesis, multiple questions have been debated in the academic circle, as: How does a leader create an image for self and the organisation? Is image synonymous with reputation? To what extent does the reputation of the leader impact the organisation and vice versa?

The focus on image and reputation is well-justified in the current scenario.

Key Words

- Accountability
- AC²ID Test
- Communicate
- Communication strategies
- Conversational sensibility
- Goal centricity
- Identity
- Image
- Integrity
- Leadership
- Leadership style
- Reputational capital
- Reputational quotient
- Social capital
- Stakeholders
- Trust
- Vision

Changes in the environment as economic, organisational, global, generational and technological have forced leaders to focus on corporate image building in the current business arena for future organisational demands. The standards espoused in the past are, in today's context, no longer appropriate in addressing organisational, societal and stakeholder expectations and needs. In this current scenario of complexity and diversity, leaders have to interact with specialists and generalists as business, country and functional heads in a manner which orchestrates and builds their own reputation and that of the organisation, improves organisational ranking and perception, reflects character and matches changing expectations of the environment.

In the midst of this diversity, uncertainty and unpredictability, there are opportunities galore, which can be tapped by competencies and skill sets (Table 4.1).

A 'Gem' of a Reputation: Ratan Tata

Mr Ratan Tata, the recently retired Chairman of the Tata Group, has left very large shoes for his successor to fill. During a tenure spanning 21 years, he led the Tata Group from strength to strength, to become one of the most trusted global conglomerates. Many believe that if Indian business has a reputation abroad, it is solely due to Mr Ratan Tata. Initially faced with criticism and scepticism and thought to have nothing more to his credit than his surname, Mr Ratan Tata forged a reputation for leadership that is unparalleled, and that only added to the corporate reputation of the Tata Group, both domestically and internationally. Ranked higher in reputation than Queen Elizabeth, Barack Obama and even the Pope,[3] Mr Ratan Tata showed how the 'Most Powerful CEO'[4] can also be the most ethical one, 'guarding the group's reputation for high ethical standards in a country rife with corruption'.[5] The close connection between his personal reputation and that of the Group is not incidental. As Ms Zia Mody, Managing Partner, AZB & Partners, legal advisors to the Tata Group, once pointed out, 'The reputation of the group and its guiding principles are uppermost in his [Ratan Tata] mind while taking decisions.'[6]

Table 4.1   Required Competencies for Leaders

Competencies	Characteristics
Behavioural	Curiosity, self-awareness
Mental	Empathetic, motivational, cognitive skills
Functional	Ability to participate, challenge, interpret, decide, align and learn

We have heard stories and narrations of leaders who meet these competencies, possess the skill set and are able to lead their organisations to pinnacles of success with unmatched inspiration, vision and energy. Interestingly, there is more to these stories than is evident to the naked eye. The vision and the mission, developed over the years by leader/s, earns for the company an intangible asset, 'reputational capital' which translates into positive relationship with internal and external publics through which they exchange knowledge, skills, experience and information. Small wonder then, that for leadership positions, organisations hire people who command respect and have a clout in the market so that the company can 'look good' and earn the recognition of being highly reputed.

Emphasis on the organisational reputation does not, in any way, undermine the role of the leader who is pivotal in developing harmonious relationships with stakeholders through indicators as trust, control mutuality, commitment and satisfaction.[7] Integrity, dependability and competence are critical in establishing trust; control mutuality emphasises the unspoken agreement between two parties where one is entrusted with the power to influence the other; commitment can be procedural or emotional; and, providing satisfaction to stakeholders is a process of reinforcing existing relationships with them. The stakeholders interpret leader communication through the symbols shared and actions undertaken. This demonstration of responsible leadership generates 'value' through social capital accrual, yielding tangible results for the organisation.

Arguably, the role of the leader and his/her reputation are important for organisational success. In this chapter, we discuss concepts related to creation of leader reputation and its importance and what are some of the critical considerations; which leadership style is most suited for building a reputation; what are the consequences of leader reputation; how do leaders communicate, the role of the leader as a storyteller; and, the juggling act performed by leaders in trying to maintain a balance between tangible and intangible assets, internal and external stakeholders.

WHAT IS LEADER REPUTATION AND HOW IS IT CREATED?

The way to gain a good reputation is to endeavour to be what you desire to appear.

—SOCRATES[8]

Leader reputation has been defined as, '... a perceptual identity reflective of the complex combination of salient personal characteristics and accomplishments, demonstrated behaviour, and intended images presented over some period of time as observed directly and/or as reported from secondary sources.'[9] The identity of the leader is constructed in consonance with the organisation reflecting leader reputation and vice versa.

When we talk of identity creation, we emphasise stakeholder perception which can be measured by an AC^{2}ID Test (refer Table 4.2).

An amalgam of these five identities creates positive reputational capital. In an ideal situation, organisations should be able to manage all identities. A misalignment between two or more identities creates a reputational risk by sullying the image of both, the leader and the organisation.

It is crucial to elaborate on the intimate relationship between leader and corporate reputation, as a dent on one can seriously impact the other. For instance, the generally held view is that the personal traits of the leader give the organisation the required fillip. For instance, in a start-up, a charismatic leader can give a boost to stakeholders' perception of the company. The flip side of it also holds true. For example, if a previously successful company faces financial and reputational loss, the leader, on most occasions, is the scapegoat and blamed for inefficiencies, suboptimal results and irresponsible leadership. In such cases, the reputations of both, the leader and the company, suffer a major set-back.

We would not be far from the truth if we stated that leaders are the cynosure of all eyes. Research has emphasised and 'romanticized'[10] leader effectiveness and importance. There is a small body of research which considers the contribution of specific leaders to organisational performance minimal. What is agreed upon is that leader behaviour is continuously evaluated by external and internal stakeholders in every situation, be it one of high trust and low accountability, or low trust and high accountability. Based on past actions, leaders may develop a positive or negative market reputation. A positive reputation engenders trust, creates confidence and faith leading to a situation where leader credibility is viewed as a consequence of reputational capital rather than actual show of positivity. Interestingly, in such situations, even if the leader demonstrates negative behaviour, stakeholder perception of leader attribution to crisis is mild and negativity is

Table 4.2   AC^{2}ID Test[11]

A	Actual identity	What an organisation is in the real sense
C	Conceived identity	What are the perceptions created for identity
C	Communicated identity	Identity communicated in a controlled fashion by the organisation
I	Ideal identity	The positioning of the organisation in an optimum manner
D	Desired identity	What the organisation desires the external stakeholders to be cognisant about

attributed to factors inherent in the situation. Additionally, if leader reputation is above average and performance is average or contrary to expectations, there is tolerance or forgiveness. The above discussion on attributing or not attributing outcome to the leader stems from the perspective of according respect, based on past experience and knowledge, to motives that govern behavioural display.

In other words, the perspective of the leader and those evaluating his/her actions is extremely important in building an image of responsible leadership. The responsibility of the leader can be defined as a legal, moral and/or mental accountability. The question worth probing is responsibility to whom and for what.

How Does a Leader Create an Image?

A leader creates an image in the mind of the stakeholders by defining reality. This is done by a process in which a vision is crafted for the company and its employees, and systems of meaning are created to which all members within the organisation are able to relate.[12] The image the leader creates, often acts as a role model for employees and a symbol for external stakeholders. The images thus created, hold the company in good stead, as confidence in the leader is translated into belief and trust in company operations.

How accurate is the leader in defining the reality? In this case it may be difficult to assign a value. However, based on hindsight, experiences, interest, values and vision, the leader defines reality, a guiding factor for all strategic decisions where company strategy and leadership intertwine, creates a vision and a value framework. The congruence between values expressed in words and actions, and consistency between the two develops integrity in company actions and enhances reputational capital. For leaders it is crucial to build on this intangible asset, for a loss in the same requires time and effort to repair.

Articulating Vision: Infosys Ltd.

According to Mr Narayana Murthy, Founder and Executive Chairman, Infosys Ltd., the company's vision is to be a globally respected corporation. He admits that their vision, in spite of being a good one, would have failed unless the leadership brought 'exhilaration, joy, enthusiasm, and energy to the minds of our people to translate this vision to reality'.[13]

Infosys leaders use quotes to communicate their values to employees easily and directly. Their value system is aptly summed up by the adage, 'The softest pillow is a clear conscience' and their commitment to transparency is reflected in the often-quoted, 'When in doubt, disclose.'[14]

Organisations too, create an ethical climate to which all members, including leaders, subscribe. These ethical standards are introduced either through formal or informal channels or organisational structures. The leader develops a climate of trust, to which all employees willingly and happily contribute. A culture is developed within the organisation in which all attempt to imitate leader traits. Thus, leaders 'walk the ethics talk'[15] to secure compliance and commitment from internal stakeholders and buy-in from external stakeholders which more often than not is reflected in market confidence.

Building Trust to Build Reputation: Housing Development Finance Corporation (HDFC) Ltd.

Mr Deepak Parekh, Chairman, HDFC, describes how trust is the 'cement of meaningful relationships and an open and creative management style'.[16] HDFC leadership has strived to build trust among its employees and empower them to develop a participatory management style. This has enabled them to build a learning and adaptable organisation, a characteristic which greatly contributes to the reputation it enjoys today.

Why Is Leader Reputation Important?

Leader capital is the most important resource a company possesses. The success of some important organisational decisions as investments, alliances and mergers, hiring of employees and building employee confidence are based on the reputational capital generated by the leader. Studies prove that performance metrics as revenue, net income and share price are always superior in leadership-branded companies.[17] The role, position and action of the leader get magnified in moments of adversity. How well was the situation addressed? What was the stand of the leader? What was said and done to counter the situation? Appropriately addressing these questions aids in improving performance and maintaining trust of all stakeholders.

Transparency as a Leadership Tenet: Mr Raghav Bahl

Transparency is a leadership tenet for Mr Raghav Bahl, MD, Network 18 Media and Investments Ltd. He believes that 'anything left hidden becomes fodder for speculation'.[18] When Reliance Anil Dhirubhai Ambani Group's Anil Ambani invested in Network 18, it stoked much corporate gossip, even leading to speculation that ownership would soon change hands; but Mr Bahl's conviction in making documentation public to secure the support of shareholders, regulators and employees paid off and stakeholder trust was maintained.

Corporate leaders are beacons of light in providing guidance, direction and inspiration which they effectively manage through direct and indirect communication channels with all concerned stakeholders.

What Are Some of the Important Considerations for Building Leader Reputation?

There has arisen a need for innovative ways to process and share information in flatter structures and hierarchies, which have a greater geographical reach and higher diversity. Additionally, with an increase in digital networks and powerful social media platforms, communication patterns have undergone a radical change. In these changing times, communicating vision through leadership has emerged as an important determinant (the others being competitive effectiveness, marketing leadership, customer focus, familiarity/ favourability and corporate culture)[19] of corporate reputation.

Leadership Is about Vision

In the words of Mr Kumar Mangalam Birla, Chairman, Aditya Birla Group:

Leadership is all about plugging into the minds and hearts of people. It is about rallying them around to a compelling and exciting vision of the future. It is about upping the quality of imagination of the organisation. It is about encouraging a spirit of intellectual ferment and constructive dissent so that people are not bound by the status quo, and mavericks are given space and free play.[20]

In such a scenario, leaders should be risk takers, learn to disagree, focus on giving and receiving feedback, avoid use of destructive language at work and avoid concerns related to being liked or respected.[21] Some practices which leaders follow to build reputational capital are: create reputational oversight and coordinate responsibilities for executives, provide global leadership education and training at all levels within global units, conduct an annual global reputational audit and compete for selected leadership awards and reputational rankings.[22]

Challenges for leaders in projecting credence are multiple as they focus on both internal and external stakeholders. The issue of stakeholders can be addressed if the leader is sure of the team, the people, the processes and the culture within the organisation. With internal stakeholders the demands are relatively lower. Creation of an enabling environment with positive attributes creates a good image in the minds of employees. For external stakeholders as investors and analysts, it is the quality of interaction with senior leadership team which is important, and which directly contributes to the stock market performance. Challenges in building connects with stakeholders can be addressed by acceptance of financial and social demands at the same time; differentiation or recognition of the uniqueness of differing demands and integration of the conflict between financial and social goals which are so closely interwoven that the difference between them is blurred.[23]

> ### Building Reputation among Multiple Stakeholders: ICICI Bank Ltd.
>
> Ms Chanda Kochhar, MD & CEO, ICICI Bank Ltd., maintains that clear communication about the organisation's position and strategy with its multiple stakeholders as customers, investors, regulators and employees is imperative. Throughout the financial crisis of 2009 and 2010, ICICI Bank leadership followed a conscious strategy of regular communication, responding to queries and convincing employees about the consolidation undertaken by the bank. The efforts were fruitful, and ICICI Bank Ltd. was able to build confidence among its multiple stakeholders even in the midst of a volatile operating environment.[24]

WHICH LEADERSHIP STYLE IS MOST SUITED FOR BUILDING REPUTATION?

Leaders, who can stay optimistic and upbeat, even under intense pressure, radiate the positive feelings that create resonance. By staying in control of their feelings and impulses, they craft an environment of trust, comfort and fairness. And that self-management has a trickle-down effect from the leader.

—Daniel Goleman[25]

Study of leadership styles has been a favourite topic of discussion and analysis among researchers for decades. However, focus on reputation and accountability has been a recent phenomenon which has drawn attention to individuals entrusted with the capability to mobilise outcomes. When companies hire an executive for a leadership position, it is the leadership capabilities in working towards pre-defined goals, which is the most important, followed by an ability to contribute to the team achievements and the ability to act as a catalyst possessing a good mix of personal humility and intense professional will. The last has been referred to as Level 5 leadership[26] (an elaboration of Level 5 leadership is provided in Table 4.3). This type of leadership focusses on a compelling modesty followed by an unwavering resolve that takes into account developing core values and communicating them to the stakeholders.

Analysis of leadership styles points to a bouquet of traits an individual possesses which are a reflection of personality, mental ability and skills. While it may be difficult to arrive at a consensus concerning required personality traits, there is an overall agreement that personality is best represented by agreeableness, conscientiousness, emotional stability, extraversion and openness to experience.[27] While the personality of the leader is important, his/her intelligence—social, emotional, practical and self-monitoring—helps in interpersonal effectiveness. Together with these traits, we also need to consider the strategies to be adopted by the leader. He/she should be able to project situationally appropriate behaviour, should conform and adapt to social norms and be in control of emotions and expression. Undoubtedly, this would be referred to as

Table 4.3   Hierarchy of Leadership Levels

Level	Type	Interpretation
5	Executive	A leader who combines personal humility with intense professional resolve
4	Effective leader	A leader who acts as a catalyst in achieving high organisational performance by promoting commitment towards and focussed pursuit of a clear vision
3	Competent manager	A manager who efficiently organises human and other resources for achieving organisational objectives
2	Contributing team member	A person who contributes significantly in group achievements and works harmoniously in a team environment
1	Highly capable individual	An individual whose talent, knowledge, skills and work ethic lead to valuable contributions to the organisation

a political skill, which packages all aforementioned behaviours and inculcates a strong sense of adaptability in performance.

For a leader to develop an appropriate style, Plato's question: would you like to be '... an unethical person with a good reputation or an ethical person with a reputation for injustice?'[28] reverberates in the corporate scenario, as he/she juggles between what is right and wrong; what is ethical and unethical and what can and cannot be done. This style, also referred to as 'ethical leadership', was discussed almost 70 years ago by Chester Bernard, who entrusted the leader with the responsibility of creating and conforming to a 'complex code of morals'.[29] Compliance with this code requires adherence to and behavioural display of traits as integrity, honesty and trustworthiness, and projection of value-based decision-making abilities, which are objective and ethical.

In summary, doing the right thing the first time with a keen eye on the long-term vision and benefits is what differentiates a leader from an executive. Factors enabling reputation management are grit and determination coupled with an ability to challenge established systems, and an intention to innovate and create, without losing focus on people.

Defining Leadership Style for a Global India: Mr Mukesh Ambani

Mr Mukesh Ambani, CMD, Reliance Industries Ltd., maintains that 'an enlightened, bold and purposeful leadership is critical to successfully pursue the three pathways of economic, technological and social leadership to attain true global leadership.'[30] According to him, global pressures lead business leaders to adopt measures and take actions which extend way beyond quarterly profits and deal with issues as global poverty and unequal distribution of wealth.

A leadership style in which a leader gives due consideration to the anxieties of the team and workforce, as well as to the problems and aspirations of society as a whole, is critical. Humility and a strong-minded focus are crucial to success and leader reputation.

Mr Ambani defines the most important features of a leader as: 'the ability to formulate a shared vision of the world over the next 50 years, the ability to be rooted in the present but with an eye firmly fixed on the future, the capacity to handle ambiguity and uncertainty, the flexibility to adapt, change and constantly think on their feet, and the wisdom to lead without any cultural bias and prejudice.'[31]

WHAT ARE THE CONSEQUENCES OF LEADER REPUTATION?

Unfortunately, your reputation often rests not on your ability to do what you say,
but rather on your ability to do what people expect.

—Bryant H. McGill[32]

The most important of the consequences of leader reputation is generation of trust which involves a feeling, an expectancy that leader behaviour will be predictable and will not focus on the self or harm the other. Two factors emerge through this understanding of trust: competency (ability, skill set, etc.) and value orientation (motives, integrity, ethics, etc.). The first refers to confidence in the capabilities of the leader: the ability to steer safely in adverse situations, the belief that under his/her able stewardship nothing can go wrong and the conviction that the leader has high ethical standards. The second factor is a consequence of accountability or expectation of individual performance in a specific manner. The advantage of this consequence is that leaders are viewed to be responsible for their actions. Accountability can be of various types: formal or informal, external or internal, process or outcome oriented.

The relationship between trust and accountability has been found to be inversely proportional. If the leader has been able to generate trust through reputation, key stakeholders will place lesser emphasis on monitoring or accountability. Conversely, when the focus on accountability or monitoring is high, the element of trust takes a backseat. Building high levels of trust and reputation help organisations in cutting monitoring costs without experiencing an accompanying reduction in employee performance.

How do leaders develop trust in the minds of the stakeholders? Stakeholder trust is built on a leader's reputation. The factor of accountability for leaders is more cosmetic than real because of their high status in society. In some cases, the combination of high trust and low accountability can be fatal to organisational reputation, as was revealed in the case of Satyam Computers and the 2G scam.

Building Stakeholder Trust: Aditya Birla Group

The Aditya Birla Group is one of the finest examples of fast, inorganic growth through a series of international mergers and acquisitions that have transformed it from a $2 billion group in 1995 to a $40 billion behemoth in 2012.

Mr Kumar Mangalam Birla, Chairman, attributes a large portion of this stream of successful growth to a key element: stakeholder trust. For him, it is important to build trust among internal and external stakeholders. He categorises employees of acquired companies as internal customers. The external ones range from customers to regulators and several other groups of people who may sometimes not appear connected to the company.

During his numerous acquisitions, Mr Birla employed this basic tenet of creating trust among his stakeholders, leading to success in acquisition and long-term reputation gain for the entire group. Each example is interesting: soon after acquiring Novelis Inc., Mr Birla made key appointments at the acquired company and then trusted them to choose their own executive teams.

When one of the group companies, Hindalco Industries Ltd., acquired a mining asset in Australia, the local employees who had only heard stories of operations of Indian firms, were apprehensive to the extent that a rumour emerged about the new management planning to compel all of them to turn vegetarian. In this and similar situations, the top management of the Aditya Birla Group ensured that fears were allayed and an environment of trust created by familiarising the new management with their own working style.

After completing an acquisition deal in North America, the entire senior management of the acquired company was invited to visit India to enable them to better understand Indians. Naturally, the Americans found it difficult to accept the differences in culture. To make things easier for the visitors, the head of Group Human Resource Engagement Activities, invited the German CEO of Siemens Ltd. to talk about what he had learned of the country and its culture. Additionally, he asked Ms Nina Woodward, an American HR trainer with many years of Indian experience, to talk to workers and managers in America and allay their fears.[33]

This series of incidents from one organisation alone points to the fact that building trust among stakeholders is crucial and efforts should be made in that direction.

To be able to successfully build self and organisation reputation, a leader is required to have skills as anticipating, challenging, interpreting, deciding, aligning and learning, along with behavioural, mental and functional traits. Combining these with personal leadership style, a strong vision and mission, personal integrity, compelling modesty, charisma and capabilities, the leader acts as a catalyst to mould perceptions of internal and external stakeholders. Stakeholder perceptions are further shaped by the environment of trust, credibility, fairness and adherence to ethics created by the leader in the organisation. In this process of engaging stakeholders, strategies of acceptance, differentiation and integration are also used. These leader attributes and behavioural traits create leader reputation, which ultimately builds corporate reputation through the twin consequences of trust and accountability (refer Fig. 4.1).

Figure 4.1 How Leaders Build Corporate Reputation

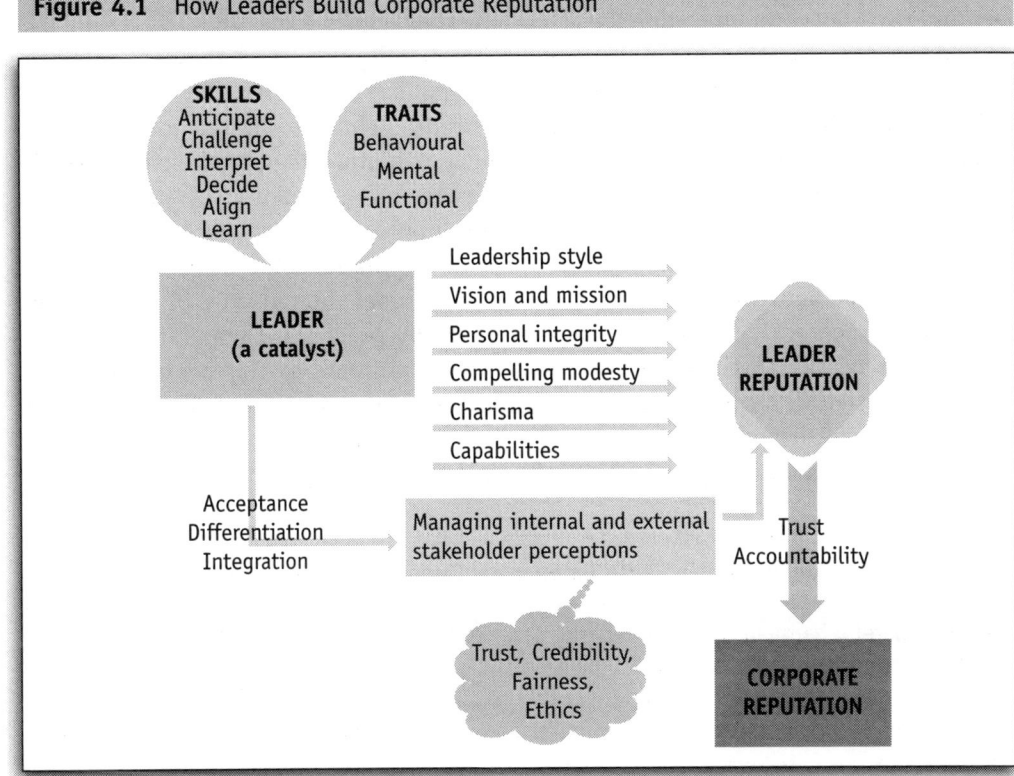

HOW DO LEADERS COMMUNICATE?

Great communication depends on two simple skills—context, which attunes a leader to the same frequency as his or her audience, and delivery, which allows a leader to phrase messages in a language the audience can understand.

—John Maxwell[34]

Almost 70–90 per cent of the time leaders are communicating to internal and external stakeholders through texts, cell phones, telephones, video conferencing, intra and Internet, newsletters, etc. Hence, acquiring skills for communication is desirous for executives aspiring to move to leadership positions. The higher the position, the greater is the requirement for effective and efficient communication.

The question which excites debate is why this focus on communication? Organisations function on systematic sharing of knowledge which is also part of the cultural heritage. Understanding cultural assumptions and building trust in existing systems require communication, comprehension and commitment. The end goal is belief in a single core philosophy which shapes the values of the organisation and assigns a reputational quotient.

Executives in leadership positions open avenues for developing channels which promote easy and two-way communication for achievement of higher goals.

Leaders and companies are improvising techniques through which they can enhance the quality of communication with internal stakeholders so that they are able to build better teams, solve problems and bring about strategic change. The authoritarian approach or one of command and control has shifted to a more democratic style in which the emphasis is more on creating value through constant interactions with stakeholders. In such situations, managing the flow of communication and creating stakeholder-friendly communication patterns are important for building reputational quotient.

Conversation between leaders and followers is personal and reflective of one-on-one personal interaction that generates employee-friendly practices, co-operative cultural norms and a 'conversational sensibility'[35] within the organisation. The task of the leader is to create a friendly environment in which interactions with employees are face-to-face and where the leader talks 'with' instead of 'to' them, enabling 'operational flexibility, high levels of employee engagement, [and] tight strategic alignment'.[36]

Communicating with Employees: Godrej Industries Ltd.

Mr Adi Godrej, Chairman, Godrej Industries Ltd., stresses on the importance of interaction and communication with employees. He admits that unlike a few years ago, when he did not always pay attention to what others had to say, he has made a conscious change in his manner of communication. He now makes an effort to listen carefully to his employees' suggestions.

He also feels that tough decisions can be respected if they are communicated more effectively. Leaders should ideally take the time to explain their decisions instead of making one-line announcements.[37]

In this process of cultivating 'conversational sensibility' the leader develops an intimacy with the stakeholders, more specifically, the employees. Understanding the differences between self and employees helps in bridging gaps, if any. However, the process is long and tedious where the leader has to speak with conviction and listen with empathy. Promoting interactivity by talking with employees about personal concerns through unscripted texts is a good way of earning trust. Mere statement of values is often dismissed as contrived leadership talk. A good way to begin is through the storytelling process where detailed description of how values affect or have affected the leader can be presented to secure the buy-in of the team. The stand thus taken is empathetically perceived by the followers.

By creating an inclusive culture, employees become part of developing the company story and are 'front-line content providers'.[38] This expansion of the role shifts emphasis from the leader to the team where different employees may perforce take upon themselves the role of brand ambassadors, thought leaders and storytellers. This new strategic dialogue framework requires a paradigmatic shift from removing hierarchies to promoting a flat structure in which all listen and are listened to.

> ### Building Teams for Building Reputation: Wipro Ltd.
>
> Mr Azim Premji, Chairman and MD, Wipro Ltd., insists that developing a culture of teaming is critical for creating excellence which builds reputational capital. As he puts it, 'while great individuals are important, one cannot have pockets of excellence.'[39] Creating cross-functional teams can cut through bureaucracy, eliminate the tendency of personal empire building and lead to unimaginable savings—all attributes that enhance the reputation of the organisation. In the long term, the teaming culture spreads to the rest of the organisation and soon becomes a way of life.

As a conscious decision, leaders should create an agenda and pursue it relentlessly for communication to be focussed, directional and meaningful. As a meaning-maker the agenda of the leader is governed by how to build trust, how and what to share and communicate and how to make the climate more inclusive. Leaders demonstrate strategies as showing trust in employees, and encouraging constructive confrontation. This brings forth alternative perspectives for examination and discussion which, if found suitable, are adopted in the decision-making process. The advantage of this process is that the same strategies are employed by the employees in reciprocity, creating a culture where everyone is on the same page. It is important for leaders to realise that they 'not only need to have visions and plans for achieving them, but also must be able to articulate their visions and strategies for action in effective ways so as to influence their followers'.[40]

Effective leaders listen to their teams, and involve them in decision making. Creative ideas are discussed and not challenged by the leaders. Words as 'and', 'however' are used to provide the link to progression of idea. To as great an extent as possible, the use of 'but', a delinking word, is avoided. For example, 'If I understand you correctly, [paraphrase the concept]. However what are your suggestions?'

> ### Being Accessible to Employees: Mr Raghav Bahl
>
> Mr Raghav Bahl, MD, Network 18 Media and Investments Ltd., maintains that being accessible to employees is a cornerstone of leadership. He considers himself one of the most accessible persons to his employees. He reports that in the initial phases of his leadership position, employees could walk into his room almost anytime. However, now with tighter schedules there is a slight change in the pattern. He still continues with easy accessibility through quick email responses.[41]

As a key communicator of messages, trustworthiness, commitment and credibility, the leader/CEO defines the corporate image to the internal and external audiences. Using influence and power, an attempt is made to impact employee perceptions, attitudes and performance. This is critical as employee perceptions are closely linked to their 'engagement' levels. Higher the degree of company perception, greater is the involvement/

engagement of the employees. However, this in itself is not sufficient. To secure the buy-in of the teams, leaders follow strategies of selective demonstration of weakness/es; capitalisation on strengths or unique features; reliance on intuition to process decisions and employee management with 'tough empathy'.[42]

This leadership communication is based on strategic interaction and engagement which is purposive, goal-centric and falls in the category of 'intentional–automatic continuum'[43] where both 'intentional' and 'automatic' are interwoven. Any attempt to separate the two leads to artificiality in the process. For instance, the leader's carefully designed communication with the media about accomplishments and strategies creates a positive image. However, not all information can be provided or documented. The onus is on the leader to selectively frame messages which communicate and yet do not present all information. The leader should be cautious that no negative image is created by the media which may erode the already well-established impression in the minds of the stakeholders. Leaders often maintain their reputation through ambiguity in messages, which generates speculation in the minds of the stakeholders and forces them to search for situational interpretations.

The leader, as a brand ambassador of a company, earns the same respect from the stakeholders as is enjoyed by the company. What should a leader do? How engaged is the leader in conducting business? Is there social commitment? Does he/she have a vision? The last of these questions is the most important. In ideal situations the leader should have a vision which is compelling enough to secure stakeholder engagement. In addition to a vision, the leader should also possess the capability of encapsulating and articulating it in a manner which has emotional and rational appeal. Once the vision is well developed, answers to all questions (posited in the earlier part of the paragraph), begin to fall in place.

How is a vision crafted? What is the basis for vision development? Does a vision capture the salient points of the business, appeal to all and orchestrate resources to achieve higher standing in the market? Crafting a vision, sharing it with other stakeholders and building conviction, appreciation and appeal is what gives the leader the razor edge. The vision should possess the capability of energising stakeholders, their interest and activity levels.

The recipe for successfully building reputation entails that the leader should:

- Be high on agenda and demands
- Have credibility in the eyes of the investors
- Be clear on critical success factors
- Be able to manage expectations
- Be able to manage reputational risk

Leader as a Storyteller

Leaders are intermediaries between internal and external stakeholders and the environment. What they say and how they say it, impacts stakeholder perception and helps build or

> ### Success in Building Excellence Leads to Superior Reputation: Mr Azim Premji
>
> Mr Azim Premji, Chairman and MD, Wipro Ltd., shares his recipe for building organisational reputation. His simple mantra is, 'an obsession for excellence'.[44]
>
> Stressing the need for a leader to be high on agenda and demands, he explains how he believes in creating an obsession for excellence, encouraging people to look at global standards of excellence in quality, cost and delivery and not rest till they are surpassed.
>
> Clarity on critical success factors is deeply ingrained in the employees. Mr Premji has made it clear that at Wipro, excellence is about doing the best, and speed lies in doing it quickly. These two critical success factors, which are important elements of quality and excellence, are hence, part of the Wipro culture.
>
> Mr Premji also stresses upon managing expectations of internal and external stakeholders. According to him, people in any organisation must realise that they cannot be the best in everything they do; hence, it is important to define what they are likely to be/would like to be best at and what someone else can do better. Defining one's own core competencies and outsourcing other processes to experts in their own fields is one of the ways of ensuring excellence that contributes to reputation.

reduce reputational capital. What strategy should they adopt to make this communication effective? Storytelling is one technique through which leaders sell their ideas to employees, interact with them and develop newer stories for higher acceptance of content. The two stories often narrated address the financial and the human angle within the organisation. While the first is relatively simple and number-centric, important to sustenance in the market, the second is comparatively tougher and culture- and value-centric, important to building and maintaining reputation in the market. Both types of stories are important to create and communicate 'sense' within the organisation by projecting values and culture, and sharing performance-related data. Employees connect, identify with these stories, reinforce their belief and build trust in existing values and culture. These stories become guiding posts for future course of action.

Stories can be built around mission, vision, values and strategic intent of the organisation. They possess the capacity to unite all members within the organisation by a common thread. All employees should be able to relate to and see logic in the story. There should be transference of knowledge and development of capabilities which will help in negotiating with the external environment, more specifically, in moments of economic crisis. Influencing customers, clients and shareholders through stories of success, mission and social stewardship has been commonly practised by leaders. The impact of this influence is almost always reflected in development of positive perceptions of the products, services, decisions to invest and willingness to consider the company as a potential recruiter.

Stories of reputed and successful organisations emanate from leaders and employees in collaborative environments. Leaders narrate to create an impact, influence their team and align them to the larger goals. Employees, who are in tune with the strategic vision of the leader take on the baton and transmit the same stories to multiple stakeholders as per their understanding. This group/community shares its perceptions of the stories at various structured/unstructured venues and formal/informal gatherings. The information shared by the circle of employees is used by leaders to understand employee interpretation of values and culture and use it as feedback to amend existing stories and reshape future strategies (refer Fig. 4.2).

Figure 4.2 Storytelling Loop

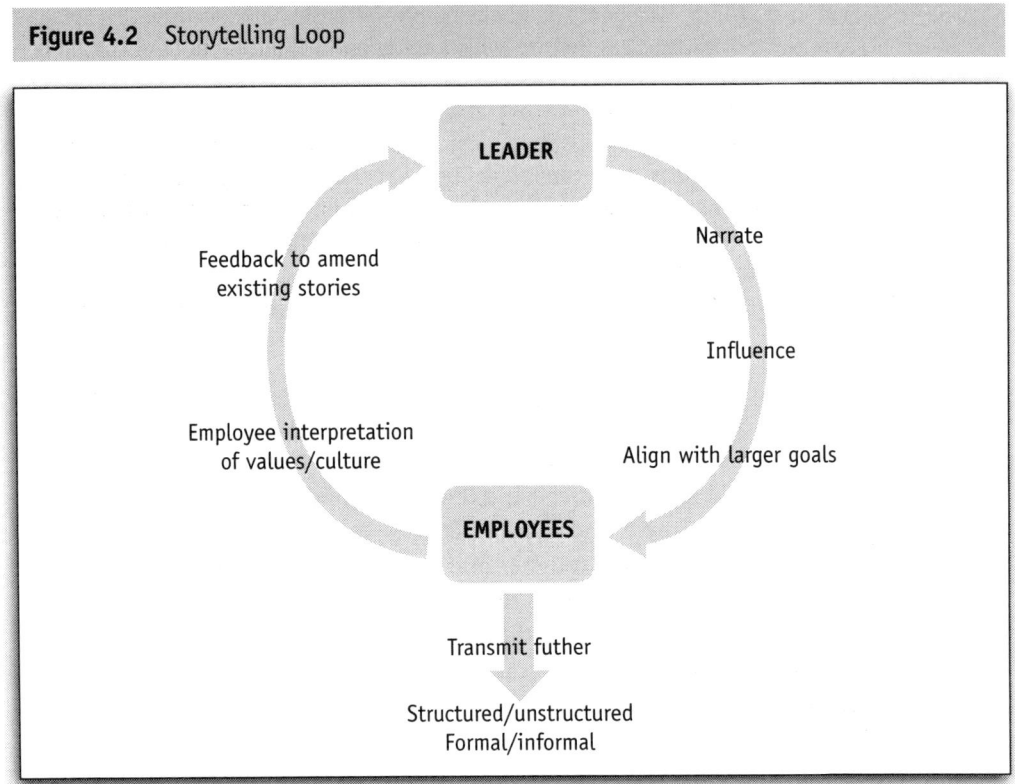

Storytelling at Infosys Ltd.

Mr Narayana Murthy, Founder and Executive Chairman, Infosys Ltd., is known as a great storyteller who effectively uses personal stories to communicate key organisational messages around vision, mission and values. He is adept at using the three key elements that make a good story: colour, repetition and structure,[45] which ensure that key ideas are spread throughout the organisation with fidelity. For example, everyone at Infosys Ltd. has heard and used the story of how the founders started the company with an initial investment of just ₹10,000 in a make-shift office in Mr Murthy's home.[46]

IS LEADERSHIP A JUGGLING ACT?

The challenge of leadership is to be strong, but not rude; be kind, but not weak; be bold, but not bully; be thoughtful, but not lazy; be humble, but not timid; be proud, but not arrogant; have humour, but without folly.

—JIM ROHN[47]

Managing reputation with multiple stakeholders through communication is not simple for the leader. While the focus of the investors is on the tangibles, employee concentration is on the intangibles. Bringing about a balance in communication and behaviour is a challenge for the leader. The raising and fulfilling of differing expectations is important.

Maintaining a balance between the two types of stakeholders is important. As leaders, there should be emphasis on both the tangibles and the intangibles. For instance, if there is excessive emphasis on financials or numbers, it will keep the team focussed on the target, but not draw them into the fold as part of the regeneration process. In such situations, leadership may be viewed as 'number-centric' making furtive attempts to secure investor and analyst buy-in without creating and nurturing an environment in which all are equal partners. Bonding is slow or does not happen at all, with power entrusted in the hands of a few who are hierarchically in leadership positions.

The level of difficulty in the act of juggling and balancing the tangibles and intangibles is compounded by the individual and combined influence of employees, clients and the media, which can also affect company performance and purpose. The list can be expanded to include financial target groups, government/politics and the labour market.

Finally, NGOs as target groups also need to be addressed. The challenge is to create equity while projecting an image of care and nurturance.

Some tips for channelising communication are:

- Communicate with passion
- Be clear and specific
- Address the smallest details without leaving room for speculation
- Ensure organisational fit[48]

IS THERE A LINK BETWEEN LEADERSHIP AND COMMUNICATION?

Good leaders make people feel that they're at the very heart of things, not at the periphery. Everyone feels that he or she makes a difference to the success of the organisation. When that happens people feel centred and that gives their work meaning.

—WARREN G. BENNIS[49]

What kind of a leader does a company want? Autocratic, charismatic, democratic? Definitely, one who will be able to show consistent good performance. However, building reputation is much more than focussing on the tangibles. The question which needs to be deliberated upon is: can the leader create meaning for stakeholders? As meaning- and sense-makers, leaders often confuse authenticity with rational thinking. The point needs to be understood with caution. Weber defines this modern focus on thinking as 'technical rationality',[50] also referred to as 'instrumental reason'[51] where the rationality of the act is assessed by the relationship between means and ends. In this, the rational act is stripped of morality. Any act can be defined on the basis of rationality. The question is: can all acts then be justified and help build reputation?

Focus on the ethical stand is imperative for leaders, for they need to use a yardstick by which they can influence, impact and align with stakeholders. Rationality will help enhance performance but adherence to the same, plus a higher objective will help leaders influence and align needs, build relationships, understand behaviours and co-ordinate using the value umbrella.

CONCLUSION

Leadership is about building the highest levels of empathy, without compromising on fairness and without running a popularity contest.

—Kumar Mangalam Birla[52]

Company reputations can be built and managed only by leaders. Creating, shaping and reshaping perceptions of internal and external stakeholders is slow and requires concerted effort. Beginning with the employees, the leader can initiate this process through appropriate communication of the vision, mission and intent to act. The 'what' and 'how' of this communication strategy creates an empathetic image generating a positive or negative response. Once employees are energised by the vision and compelled to action, they become company advocates transmitting and managing both values and performance.

Some of the steps leaders can follow are:

- Develop a vision
- Select a leadership style suited to their personality
- Craft a story
- Develop a communication strategy
- Share the values, vision and mission with all stakeholders
- Build, shape and reshape perceptions
- Secure employee confidence
- Win customer support
- Revisit strategies—change or reinforce
- Communicate the same!

Key Points

- Leader reputation is important in the light of current environmental changes as economic, organisational, global, generational and technological.
- The required global competencies for leaders focus on basic traits which are behavioural, mental and functional.
- Leaders earn for their companies, an intangible asset 'reputational capital' which translates into positive relationships with internal and external public.
- Relationships are developed with stakeholders through indicators as trust, control mutuality, commitment and satisfaction.
- Leader reputation is a perceptual identity which reflects personal characteristics and accomplishments, demonstrated behaviour and intended images.
- Reputation of the leader and the company are intertwined and adverse publicity of one can impact the other.
- The effectiveness and importance of leaders is often emphasised and 'romanticised'.
- The leader develops a climate of trust and employs the strategy of 'walk the ethics talk' to secure compliance and commitment.
- Credibility of the leader is translated into higher recognition of the company, its products and services.
- To earn reputation, leaders should be risk takers; learn to disagree; focus on giving and receiving feedback; avoid use of destructive language at work; avoid concerns related to 'being liked' or 'respected'.
- Leaders should possess traits which are a reflection of general personality, mental ability and skills.
- Leader reputation is built by demonstration of grit and determination, together with an ability to challenge established systems, an intention to innovate and create, without losing focus on people and publics.
- Consequence of leader reputation is generation of trust which emphasises trust and value orientation.
- Leaders initiate a 'conversational sensibility'.
- As a 'meaning maker' the agenda of the leader is governed by how to build trust, how and what to share and communicate and how to make the climate more inclusive.
- Leaders create a vision which possesses the capability of energising the interest and activity levels of people who have a direct stake in it.
- Leaders don the role of storytellers and narrate stories which address the financial and the human angle within the organisation.
- Leader stories are built around mission, vision, values and strategic intent of the organisation.
- Leader stories possess the capacity to unite all members within the organisation by a common thread and by creating a 'sense making' model.
- Leaders build reputation by communicating with passion, being clear and specific, addressing all details and ensuring organisational fit.

END NOTES

1. D. Parekh, 'Imprints of the past and what it will take to succeed in the future', in AIMA (ed.), *Leaders on Leadership: Insights from Corporate India* (pp. 58–68). New Delhi: SAGE Publications (2013), p. 60.
2. Motivational quotes, website http://www.selfhelpcollective.com/motivation-quotes.html (accessed 20 April 2013).
3. Reputation Institute, 'Global leader Rep track', website http://www.reputationinstitute.com/events/14_Sept_11_PR_New%20_York_Leader_RepTrak_Results.pdf (accessed 22 March 2013).
4. 'India Inc's most powerful CEOs', *The Economic Times*, website http://economictimes.indiatimes.com/features/corporate-dossier/mostpowerfullceo.cms (accessed 20 March 2013).
5. 'Ratan Tata retires, gives reins of Tata Group to Cyrus Mistry', website http://www.biztechreport.com/story/2366-ratan-tata-retires-gives-reins-tata-group-cyrus-mistry (accessed 24 March 2013).
6. 'The amazing story of how Ratan Tata built an empire', website http://www.rediff.com/money/slide-show/slide-show-1-tata-special-amazing-story-of-how-ratan-tata-built-an-empire/20121228.htm#7 (accessed 24 March 2013).
7. The Institute for Public Relations Report (1999) cited in P. S. Brønn, 'Relationship outcomes as determinants of reputation', *Corporate Communications: An International Journal* (2007), 12(4), 376–393.
8. BIM, website http://95tatman24715.blogspot.in/2012/05/way-to-gain-good-reputation-is-to.html (accessed 20 April 2013).
9. G. R. Ferris, F. R. Blass, C. Douglas, R. W. Kolodinsky and D. C. Treadway, 'Personal reputation in organizations', in J. Greenberg (ed.), *Organizational Behaviour: The State of the Science* (2nd ed.). pp. 211–246. Mahwah, NJ: Lawrence Erlbaum (2003), p. 215.
10. J. R. Meindl, S. B. Ehrlich and J. M. Dukerich, 'The romance of leadership', *Administrative Science Quarterly* (1985), 30(1), 78–102, p. 96.
11. J. M. T. Balmer and S. A. Geyser, 'Managing the multiple identities of the corporation', *California Management Review* (2002), 44(3), 72–86.
12. L. Smircich and G. Morgan, 'Leadership: The management of meaning', *Journal of Applied Behavioural Science* (1982), 18(3), 257–273.
13. N. R. N. Murthy, 'Lessons from the Infosys journey', in AIMA (ed.), *Leaders on Leadership: Insights from Corporate India* (pp. 1–12) New Delhi: SAGE Publications (2013), p. 6.
14. Ibid.
15. L. K. Trevino, L. P. Hartman and M. Brown, 'Moral person and moral manager: How executives develop a reputation for ethical leadership', *California Management Review* (2000), 42(4), 128–142, p. 138.
16. D. Parekh, 'Imprints of the past and what it will take to succeed in the future', in AIMA (ed.), *Leaders on Leadership: Insights from Corporate India.* (pp. 58–68) New Delhi: SAGE Publications (2013), p. 64
17. V. McLaughlin and C. Mott, *Leadership Brand Equity.* London: Oliver Wyman (2009).
18. R. Bahl, 'The audacity of ambition', in AIMA (ed.), *Leaders on Leadership: Insights from Corporate India.* (pp. 69–81). New Delhi: SAGE Publications (2013), p. 74.
19. S. A. Greyser, 'Advancing and enhancing corporate reputation', *Corporate Communications: An International Journal* (1999), 4(4), 177–181.
20. K. M. Birla, 'The turning points in our journey of transformation', in AIMA (ed.), *Leaders on Leadership: Insights from Corporate India.* (pp. 42–57) New Delhi: SAGE Publications (2013), p. 57.
21. B. Bence, 'How leaders earn brand-loyalty for life: The top 5 behaviours that can damage your leadership personal band', *Supervision* (2009), 70(9), 9–10 p. 9.
22. J. A. Petrick, R. F. Scherer, J. D. Brodzinski, J. F. Quinn and M. F. Ainina, 'Global leadership skills and reputational capital: Intangible resources for sustainable competitive advantage', *Academy of Management Executive* (1999), 13(1), 58–69.
23. W. K. Smith, M. L. Besharov, A. Wessels and M. Chertok, 'A paradoxical leadership model for social entrepreneurs: Challenges, leadership skills, and pedagogical tools for managing social and commercial demands', *Academy of Management Learning & Education* (2012), 11(3), 463–478.
24. C. Kochhar, 'Practicing leadership in contemporary India: A personal experience', in AIMA (ed.), *Leaders on Leadership: Insights from Corporate India* (pp. 95–108). New Delhi: SAGE Publications (2013).

25. 'Leading thoughts: Building a community of leaders', website http://www.leadershipnow.com/disciplinequotes.html (accessed 20 April 2013).
26. J. Collins, 'Level 5 leadership: The triumph of humility and fierce resolve', *Harvard Business Review* (2001), 79(1), 67–76.
27. L. R. Goldberg, 'The structure of phenotypic personality traits', *American Psychologist* (1993), 48(1), 26–34.
28. Cited in L. K. Trevino, L. P. Hartman and M. Brown, 'Moral person and moral manager: How executives develop a reputation for ethical leadership', *California Management Review* (2000), 42(4), 128–142.
29. C. I. Barnard, *The Functions of the Executive*. Cambridge, MA: Harvard University Press (1968), p. 279.
30. 'A leader for a global India Inc.—Mukesh Ambani', *Business Today*, website http://businesstoday.intoday.in/story/a-leader-for-a-global-india-inc—mukesh-ambani/1/1190.html (accessed 13 January 2008).
31. Ibid.
32. Brainy quote, website http://www.brainyquote.com/quotes/quotes/b/bryanthmc168283.html (accessed 20 April 2013).
33. C. Paul, 'Kumar Mangalam Birla: A man for all seasons', *Forbes India*, website http://forbesindia.com/article/leaderhip-award-2012/kumar-mangalam-birla-a-man-for-all-seasons/33839/0 (accessed 22 March 2013).
34. J. C. Maxwell, '94 leadership quotes for you and your church', website http://www.sermoncentral.com/articleb.asp?article=john-maxwell-94-leadership-quotes (accessed 20 April 2013).
35. B. Groysberg and M. Slind, 'Leadership is a conversation', *Harvard Business Review* (2012), 90(6), 76–84 p. 78.
36. Ibid.
37. S. Dave and T. Behl, 'I am much less autocratic now', *The Hindustan Times*, website http://www.hindustantimes.com/business-news/InterviewsBusiness/I-am-much-less-autocratic-now/Article1-822344.aspx (accessed 14 January 2013).
38. Ibid.
39. 'Azim Premji's leadership style', website http://www.azimpremji.org.in/azim-premji-leadership-style.htm (accessed 20 March 2013).
40. J. A. Conger and R. N. Kanungo, *Charismatic Leadership in Organizations*. Thousand Oaks, CA: SAGE Publications (1998), p. 54.
41. R. Bahl, 'The audacity of ambition', in AIMA (ed.), *Leaders on Leadership: Insights from Corporate India* (pp. 69–81). New Delhi: SAGE Publications (2013).
42. R. Goffee and G. Jones, 'Why should anyone be led by you?', *Harvard Business Review* (2000), 78(5), 63–70 p. 64.
43. J. H. Fleming, 'Multiple audience problems, tactical communication and social interaction: A relational-regulation perspective', *Advances in Experimental Social Psychology* (1994), 26, 215–292 p. 272.
44. 'Azim Premji's leadership style', website http://www.azimpremji.org.in/azim-premji-leadership-style.htm (accessed 20 March 2013).
45. R. F. Dennehy, 'The executive as storyteller', *Management Review* (1999), 88(3), 40–43.
46. P. 'K. Nair, 'Make story telling a part of your communication tool kit', *Infosys Ltd.*, website http://www.infosysblogs.com/leadership/2011/12/make_story_telling_a_part_of_y.html (accessed 20 March 2013).
47. Jim Rohn quotes, website http://thinkexist.com/quotation/the_challenge_of_leadership_is_to_be_strong-but/261556.html (accessed 20 April 2013).
48. R. Van der Jagt, 'Senior business executives see communication and reputation as a crucial part of their leadership role', *Corporate Reputation Review* (2005), 8(3), 179–186.
49. S. M. Heathfield, 'Inspirational quotes for business and work: Leadership', website http://humanresources.about.com/od/workrelationships/a/quotes_leaders.htm (accessed 20 April 2013).
50. R. Goffee and G. Jones, 'Why should anyone be led by you?', *Harvard Business Review* (2000), 78(5), 63–70, p. 64.
51. Ibid.
52. K. M. Birla, 'The turning points in our journey of transformation', in AIMA (ed.), *Leaders on Leadership: Insights from Corporate India* (pp. 42–57). New Delhi: SAGE Publications (2013), p. 57.

5

Increasing Crescendo:
Wooing Investors for Market
Valuation and Visibility

IR is booming in India. Rapid growth in the corporate sector is leading to an increasing appreciation of a discipline which ensures management and investors are as informed as possible.

—DAVID SWEET[1]

Objectives:

- Describe the evolution and concept of Investor Relations (IR)
- Explain the benefits, structure and mechanics of IR in the organisational context
- Summarise the IR communication process and outline IR message, media and audiences
- Understand the challenges of IR
- Demonstrate the link between corporate reputation and IRs

INTRODUCTION

…structured reporting is what the company has to do to meet its legal requirements. In theory, this is all anyone would need to know about a company. But theory is very different from practice, and potential investors usually want to know considerably more about a company than just what's happened in the past.

—DONALD ALLEN[2]

With increasing complexities in the world's capital markets and growing competition for funds, investors require more sophisticated information to make investment decisions. Companies have begun to realise the importance of communicating relevant information to their financial stakeholders as investors, analysts, regulatory bodies and the government. They have also begun to understand that this communication is not only limited to informing them about past performance, but also providing assurance about the soundness of future prospects. At the same time, there is a need for ensuring that the company is seen and appreciated as a 'transparent' organisation, as well as creating and maintaining lasting relationships with providers of capital.

Key Words

- Analysts
- Communication
- Cost of capital
- Disclosure
- Financial community
- Financial reporting
- Forecasts
- Information asymmetry
- Internet
- Investment thesis
- Investor
- Investor relations
- Liquidity
- Media
- Metrics
- Performance
- Reputation
- Stakeholders
- Strategic value proposition
- Trading volume
- Transaction costs
- Valuation
- Visibility

Inaugural IR Awards in India

Indian companies are gradually realising the importance of IR, and this has come to light with the announcement of the inaugural Extel India Investor Relations Awards 2012. At an IR event jointly organised by Deutsche Bank and Thomson Reuters in association with the IR Society, India and Bombay Stock Exchange, awards were declared for the best Indian IR company, CEO, CFO and IR professional.

The awards are the culmination of the Extel India IR Survey, which represents the views of more than 200 investment professionals and analysts. According to Mr Steve Kelly, MD, Extel Global, 'The level of response in itself indicates the growing role, influence and importance of the profession.'[3]

IR is the means to achieve the aforementioned ends. It addresses the information needs of the companies' financial stakeholders, and, as the word 'relations' suggests, also takes concrete steps towards creating and maintaining close relationships with them.

IR has been described as the connect between a company and the financial community,[4] the financial side of the communication function[5] and the continuing interactive relationship between a company and its investors.[6] It has been defined as:

a strategic management responsibility that integrates finance, communication, marketing and securities law compliance to enable the most effective two-way communication between a company, the financial community and other constituencies, which ultimately contributes to a company's securities achieving fair valuation.[7]

In this chapter, we discuss how IR can contribute to the reputation of a company. We analyse the concept of IR; its evolution, role and benefits to the organisation; how it is structured; the audiences, messages and media most relevant to IR communication the challenges faced by the IR function and the link between IR and corporate reputation.

HOW DID THE CONCEPT OF IR EVOLVE?

The 'parents' of investor relations are public relations and finance.

—WILLIAM F. MAHONEY[8]

Researchers believe that the roots of IR lie in the separation of management and ownership of companies. IR was initially recognised as a management function in the USA. Ralph Cordiner, Chairman of General Electric Corporation, created the first IR department in 1953 to look after all shareholder communications. Till 1985, only 16 per cent of the Fortune 500 companies had an IR department, which sharply escalated to 56 per cent in 1989.[9] This sudden appearance of IR departments was attributed to pressure from social activists and financial analysts, compelling organisations to espouse rights of shareholders and indicate their commitment to the same through the creation of boundary-spanning structures.[10]

Compared to the global scenario, IR in India is in the evolving stage. A recent study revealed that around 67 per cent of the top 150 listed Indian companies have an IR department (under the finance director or the company secretary or as a separate department) or officer, of which around 60 per cent have been in existence for more than five years.[11]

WHAT IS IR?

IR is a story about how you position your company in the market.

—VIVEK SADHALE[12]

It may be difficult to point to a single theory which explains all aspects of IR. However, we can make an attempt by studying voluntary disclosure and organisation visibility.

Voluntary Disclosure

The minimum level of corporate disclosure (generally provided through financial reports and other regulatory filings) is determined by regulatory authorities. Organisations communicate voluntarily using press releases, investor/analyst presentations, conference calls, management forecasts and other corporate reports, collectively termed as voluntary disclosure. The company's decision regarding the need for and extent of voluntary disclosure about accounting and other relevant information depends on various factors arising from agency and cost–benefit theory.

Agency Theory

An agency relationship is 'a contract under which one or more persons (the principal/s) engage another person (the agent) to perform some service on their behalf which involves delegating some decision-making authority to the agent'.[13] In the framework of the company, the manager is an agent acting on behalf of the principal, the shareholder. The manager may have an information advantage, leading to information asymmetry. Such asymmetry may also occur when some investors have access to private information affecting the value of the organisation, while others only possess public information.

Any form of information asymmetry hampers the efficient allocation of resources and introduces adverse selection into buyer–seller transactions,[14] which can have several undesirable outcomes as higher transaction costs, lower liquidity and, ultimately, mispricing of the organisation's shares.[15] One way to mitigate the undesirable effects of adverse selection and to reduce information risk is to disseminate information to less informed parties through voluntary disclosure. In the process, companies also build a reputation for transparency.

Cost–Benefit Theory

The question before us is: when do companies engage in voluntary disclosure? They do so only in situations where they realise that the perceived benefits are greater than the perceived costs. These costs are both direct, as data collection, processing, production and auditing, and indirect (also called proprietary), that arise when useful information is provided to external, and potentially, oppositional parties as suppliers, employees, unions and competitors.[16] Such proprietary costs may motivate companies to avoid disclosure of additional information; and it is only after a consideration of all such costs involved, that a company determines its strategy for voluntary disclosure, which ultimately forms the base of its IR programme.

Organisation Visibility

The benefits of voluntary disclosure can be realised only in a scenario where a company is visible in the market. Visibility attracts the investment community, reduces uncertainty about the organisation's prospects,[17] eliminates information asymmetries and brings greater efficiency in trading the stock.[18]

Many companies are overlooked by investors due to their low visibility. Researchers refer to a low visibility organisation as one getting lesser attention from financial analysts, institutional investors and the media. Securities with low market visibility may have to compensate for deficiency of information through higher premiums, leading to greater capital costs.[19]

In an attempt to build visibility and attract investors, companies endeavour to use intermediaries as analysts and the media, with the intention of building coverage by both. Analyst and media coverage have an impact on institutional investor following, as well as on each other. These three factors together also influence, and are themselves influenced by organisation visibility.[20]

Thus, the foundation for IR is laid by disclosure and visibility, highlighting the potential importance of a set of activities that can contribute to both.

Increased Visibility, Thanks to IR: Persistent Systems Ltd.

Persistent Systems Ltd. has seen a huge rise in its visibility after the initiation of IR activities. According to Mr Vivek Sadhale, Company Secretary and Head, Legal & IR, the difference in the number of people who knew about Persistent earlier, and those who do so now, is very large. In spite of being a relatively young mid-cap (just short of three years as a listed company), Persistent has about 40 analysts following it. For example, one of its conference calls in 2012–13 saw participation from an overwhelming 190 analysts/investors; an achievement which the company attributes entirely to its IR activities.

WHAT IS THE ROLE OF IR?

The primary role of IR is to bridge the gap in understanding and thinking between the company and the investor community.

—AVISHEK LATH[21]

The IR role encompasses providing present and prospective investors with a precise depiction of a company's present performance and future prospects,[22] creating common long-term interaction between a company and its investors[23] and ensuring an organisation's fair relative market value.[24]

It is believed[25] that the role of IR has progressed through three phases:

- Simply communicating the company's actions
- Increased emphasis on finance as a function, and financial results
- Development of trend towards active marketing

The final stage of evolution encouraged investors to buy or hold the company's shares while ensuring fair valuation.

With time, as IR assumes more and more elements of a communication role, the concentration is shifting from mere figures to the manner in which they are communicated to various stakeholders. Its scope has expanded from simply publishing mandatory annual/interim reports to providing regular, in-depth and pre-emptive two-way communication.

One of the most important functions of IR is the task of building and maintaining strong relationships with financial stakeholders. It helps increase trust, co-operation and commitment by managing crucial stakeholder relations with financial market participants,[26] and is able to create a base of loyal shareholders who support the company during periods of crises. The IR function satisfies an image-building or sense-giving role too, as it feeds the financial community with necessary inputs for their understanding of the company and its prospects. It is sometimes considered similar to public relations, as both these roles are directed at creating a positive reputation.

IR has also been described as a strategic marketing activity[27] as it aims to increase the visibility of the company in capital markets and win approval of financial stakeholders by impacting their perceptions and opinions.

Increasingly, it is felt that IR is not just a megaphone for outbound messaging, but also a microphone for incoming messaging[28] that brings issues and inputs from investors to the top management and board of directors; it is a means by which top management receives feelers from the market. This feedback can include investor perceptions of financial performance, management credibility, company strategy and any other issues that influence investors' decision to buy, hold or sell the stock, enabling top management to truly understand market sentiment.[29]

Bringing the 'Outside' In

The IR head of one of the leading Indian IT companies emphasises the role of IR in facilitating top management in market analysis. He believes in showing them the impact of their actions from a market perspective and making them plan strategies for addressing reactions from the financial community. It has to include an 'outside in' mechanism rather than being an 'inside out' function alone.

In the aftermath of corporate disasters as Enron and Satyam, the significance of IR is emphasised as it can help rebuild investor trust.[30]

On a practical note, the various roles of the IR function can be broken into:

- Financial reporting and disclosures
- Marketing the company's investment thesis
- Communicating corporate governance
- Creating a public presence for the company[31]

A Host of Functions: IR at Infosys Ltd.

Infosys Ltd. uses its IR function to communicate its plans, objectives, strategies and business updates to the investment community as well as solicit investor feedback so that suggestions can be provided to management for appropriate changes in corporate functioning and strategies.

The broad activities covered by the IR team at Infosys are: timely reporting with a deadline of announcing quarterly results within two weeks of quarter-end, posting a calendar of investor events on the IR website and the annual report in advance. It is also responsible for the company's Insider Trading Policy prescribing the level of restraint to be exercised by employees.

> In aiming for world-class transparency and disclosure levels, the IR team follows clear and concise analysis of business conditions and operating results, striving to be ahead of legislation in financial reporting and disclosures. Its fair disclosure practices include: non-discrimination, adherence to Generally Accepted Accounting Practices of India and USA and compliance with Regulation FD of the Securities & Exchange Commission, USA.

WHAT ARE THE BENEFITS OF IR?

The biggest benefit of IR is that it enables a company to build trust among the analyst community and the market.

—Vivek Sadhale[32]

IR creates disclosure of new information, as well as media visibility through press releases and coverage, leading to revision in estimates of organisation value by market participants, which is finally reflected in trading volumes and better prices.[33] By increasing the precision of private and public information, IR also leads to higher accuracy of analyst forecasts and greater consensus among them.[34] It not only stimulates higher level of analyst following, but also contributes to raising the market demand for their reports by increasing the size of the public information set available for interpretation.

IR strategies are targeted at institutional investors in order to increase market following and expand the shareholder base. Proactive IR strategies attract institutional investors by lowering the initial set-up costs required to initiate coverage of an organisation and lead to increases in the number as well as percentage of institutional ownership.[35]

An organisation's market valuation is also found to be influenced by IR. Companies hiring IR consulting firms or those with good IR practices are found to experience improvement in market valuations and earn positive higher returns over the year.[36]

What They Repaid ...

Two of Infosys Ltd.'s often-quoted dictums—'When in doubt, disclose' and 'The softest pillow is a clear conscience' also apply to its IR function. Following this, the company believes that timely disclosure and business updates in a proactive manner will help investors take informed decisions and ensure consistency, accessibility and transparency across regions. As Mr Avishek Lath, IR Associate, states, 'The value of business is less to do with physical and financial assets and more to do with intangible items like reputation. Good IR helps build reputation and good reputation pays for itself. Investors do not mind paying premium for a well-governed company.'[37]

In the words of Tata Consultancy Services (TCS) Global IR head, Mr Kedar Shirali, 'We believe that a strong IR programme has ensured a fair valuation of our stock, thus protecting shareholder value from any erosion due to market misperceptions. Today, TCS stock valuation fully reflects the company's consistent performance and investor expectations of future growth. TCS does not need to raise any funds; else, the lowered cost of capital would have been the most tangible benefit.'[38]

Mr Vivek Kumar, Manager, IR, at Maruti Suzuki India Ltd. considers a high degree of visibility, good quality interaction with analysts/investors and larger number of reports generated on Maruti Suzuki India Ltd. as the benefits of its IR programme. 'We consider ourselves to be one of the most highly covered companies. Apple Inc. has 40 analysts following it; we have 60.'[39]

'We have gained the reputation of being a well-governed company that provides information without playing hide and seek, and gives access to its people when demanded. For a young company, in its third year of listing, this is the most critical element',[40] says Mr Vivek Sadhale of Persistent Systems Ltd.

HOW DO COMPANIES STRUCTURE AND MANAGE IR?

A committed senior management team that devotes time to IR is a pre-requisite for success. The focus should be on value creation day in and day out.

—Avishek Lath[41]

The degree, to which an organisation formalises the IR function, reflects its acceptance of the importance of IR. It may be organised as a separate department or as part of another department as Legal, Secretarial or Finance. About one-fourth of large Indian listed companies are found managing IR through a separate IR department; the rest carry out IR activities as part of the finance or company secretary's department.

Typically, the operational IR head reports to the Chief Financial Officer (CFO)/Treasury Head, and is also given close access to the CEO, Corporate Planning Cell and the Company Secretary to ensure that the top management has an 'IR fit'. The number of persons working with the operational IR head depends upon the company size and the extent of activity undertaken by the IR team. In most large organisations, the IR team focusses only on institutional investors, whereas the retail investors are taken care of by the Company Secretary's department. As and when the situation demands, a management team comprising the CEO, CFO, IR head and on occasions, business unit or geographical unit heads may be formed to address the investors.

It All Comes from the Top ...

From the award-winning IR head of one of India's leading IT companies:

'IR is merely the communication arm for the largely organisational perception of governance. It could be structured as a stand-alone function, but if the underlying approach of the management to minority shareholders or corporate governance is not right, IR has no role to play. The fundamental strengths of the company are due to its governance standards, not due to its IR team. If the CEO is seen as a strong figure who believes in practicing good governance, it contributes to the share price; and not the activities of the IR officer alone.'

'These come from the top management, and hence it is imperative that IR should have an organisational mandate. It must be involved in top management discussions for all major decisions in the first place. Because our organisation involves IR in every major decision, be it an important acquisition or a demerger, we are able to decide the type and quantum of information to be shared, preempt the questions likely to arise and gauge reactions of the investment community.'

'We are like spokespersons—we toe the party line. It is difficult to build the credibility of IR if there is no credibility of the top management.'

IR officers attach a great deal of importance to involvement of top management in the IR process, as well as to their own inclusion in strategic discussions for the success of the IR function. Some of the ways in which top management executives, especially the CEO and CFO can be involved in the IR function are:

- Attending analyst meetings, presentations and conference calls
- Creating a culture of IR and investing in IR teams as well as getting into a regular planning cycle on investor engagement models
- Becoming the face of the company by being accessible to institutional investors and media
- Ensuring that the IR team is a part of strategic discussions at an early phase of important company events or milestones

Top Management Support to IR: Tata Consultancy Services Ltd. (TCS)

Mr Kedar Shirali, TCS, feels that it is very important for top management to be the face of IR for the organisation. Between the two, the CFO is better suited to own the IR function, especially because time commitments from the CEO may not do justice to the function.

At TCS, I've been fortunate to have a very proactive and supportive CFO, Mr S Mahalingam, who not only understood the importance of IR but wholeheartedly participated in this activity. As against the norm of 75–80 hours a year spent on IR by CFOs in North America, Maha routinely spent thrice as much. That has ensured a very robust, well-structured investor outreach programme that draws much appreciation from investors. Moreover, his clarity of thought and communication helped communicate our strategy to the markets very effectively.[42]

As with any other corporate function, IR too, needs to be clear about its annual goals and create strategic and operational plans on a yearly basis. Increasing credibility, relevance and timeliness of disclosure; reputation and relation building; maintaining and increasing visibility of the company and increasing analyst attention and research coverage are recognised as objectives of any company's IR team.

For a recently listed company, Mr Vivek Sadhale, Persistent Systems, believes that the most urgent goals of the IR programme would be to ensure that analyst coverage does not drop, by engaging meaningfully with them, providing them access to top management, addressing their information needs and meeting their clients to enhance confidence.

Another IR head of a leading IT company divides annual IR goals into two parts: regular work and new initiatives. Regular IR functions would include compiling statistics, analysing the positives and negatives of the previous period and assessing the extent to which the company's core message is being captured and presented. New initiatives are activities that the IR team would like to add to its portfolio, as additional use of technology, posting videos of analyst meets, modes of improving quality of interaction with sell-side (brokers and investment bankers) and buy-side (mutual funds, banks, insurance companies) analysts, to name a few.

Mr Vivek Kumar, Maruti Suzuki India Ltd., feels that being associated with a Japanese company has led them to look for continuous improvement (Kaizen). Every year, their IR team takes a look at the activities undertaken and identifies scope for improvement. The number of interactions between top management and the investor community are planned, and the extent of disclosure in terms of quantity and quality are discussed in consultation with the corporate planning department.

Whether IR goals have been achieved and its benefits realised or not, can only be assessed through performance evaluation of the IR function. About half of large Indian listed companies are found to evaluate the performance of their IR teams.[43] Various forms of evaluation include: securing direct feedback from analysts/investors; measuring the quality and level of analyst/media coverage; tracking changes in the composition of investor base; undertaking financial market perception studies; measuring shareholder returns and tracking price to fundamentals ratios.

TCS follows the practice of tracking their valuations vis-à-vis peers on a regular basis, monitoring movements in institutional holdings, preparing target lists and drawing up and executing investor outreach plans every quarter. In addition to measuring the level of IR activity on a monthly basis, it relies on subjective feedback from investors/analysts and the stock valuation (not the price). Feedback from the investment community is obtained through the company's own surveys as well as from polls by organisations like Asiamoney, Institutional Investor and Thomson-Reuters Extel.

Customised Evaluation Techniques: Maruti Suzuki India Ltd. (MSIL)

In addition to the available options, MSIL is exploring customised evaluation techniques. For example, in addition to the detailed stock price data available, the IR team at MSIL conducts its own research by tracking specific events (as Yen appreciation) in the life of the company and assessing the impact of such events on the share price, pre and post the event.

The MSIL IR team's tracking of the Japanese Yen when it began appreciating in November 2012 helped the company to accurately assess its impact on their component imports from Japan.

Such customised tracking tools enable the IR team to inform the top management about the effect of specific events on the company's share price and provide valuable feedback.

HOW DO COMPANIES COMMUNICATE IR?

Be prepared to tell [investors] why they should invest in your company. If they're already shareholders, explain why they should continue to hold the company's stock or perhaps buy more. And provide analysts, money managers, brokers and specialized financial media with information so that they can recommend the stock to their customers and back up the recommendation with solid information.

DONALD ALLEN[44]

The IR communication process targets both internal and external audiences on a regular basis (refer Fig. 5.1). Taking inputs from the finance, legal/secretarial and corporate communication departments, regulatory mandated communication is initiated, which targets existing individual (retail) and institutional investors and regulatory authorities. This is usually done through annual/interim reports, the IR website and press releases. Based on the company's own assessment, and the information needs of the financial stakeholders, voluntary information sharing is done with the earlier mentioned audiences as well as with buy-side and sell-side analysts, financial intermediaries and the

Figure 5.1   The IR Communication Process

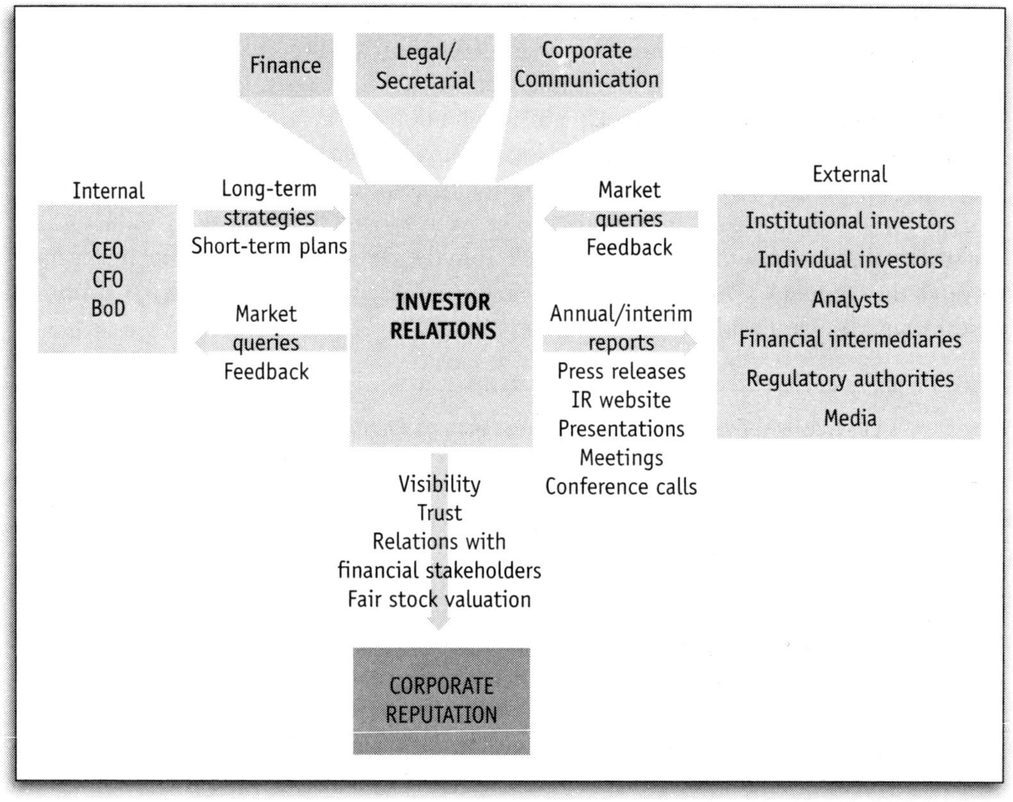

media, using communication channels as meetings, presentations, conference calls and even the IR website. During its regular interactions with financial stakeholders, the IR department receives queries about the company's performance/prospects and feedback about its image. It passes these on to the top management, thus bringing an 'outside in' perspective. Due to its close contact with the CEO and CFO, the IR department is able to address queries and share information about the company's long-term strategies and its short-term plans. These IR activities together ensure better relations with and create trust among financial stakeholders, enhance the visibility of the company and have an impact on the valuation of its shares, which finally helps build corporate reputation.

Why Should I Invest in This Company?

Investors face information risk. They are unsure whether they possess precise information to make intelligent investment decisions. The information overload created by regulatory filings, media reports, website data and even investor blogs makes it difficult for investors to sift through and identify if they have sufficient and relevant data to help them make sound investment decisions.

Analysts are crucial intermediaries influencing investment decisions of both individual (sell-side) and institutional investors (buy-side). While both 'buy side' and 'sell side' analysts have different perspectives, they use the same information to evaluate the company. Their focus is on calculating the value of the company's share to determine whether it is under-valued or over-valued. Analysts' interpretation of the company's future prospects can have a large bearing on the valuation of the company and therefore it is critical to help them arrive at a correct estimation.

To achieve the above mentioned objective, how does a company ensure clarity in the message? Most IR practitioners agree that the company's 'story' should be well-defined and clearly communicated. It should be developed in consultation with the top management. The storyline could be revenue growth, cost reduction or industry leadership.[45] What is required is a right combination of 'narrative and numbers'.[46] This pre-planning helps the target audience make a correct assessment of the company prospects.

In order to stay invested in a company long-term, its financial stakeholders are interested in knowing about the 'strategic value proposition' or 'investment thesis', which is a statement of the satisfaction that investors will obtain in exchange for their committed funds.[47] It is the answer to 'Why should I invest in this company?' Companies usually discuss their strategies in detail in annual reports or investor presentations, but often shareholders and analysts are unclear about the actual business of the company, its future growth directions, the metrics to look out for, the time frame in which milestones will be achieved and the return expected for shareholders, along with the risks. A clear 'strategic value proposition' gives less reason for shareholder activism, even when the company has been underperforming.[48] A thorough understanding of these key points enables analysts to rate the company favourably, and encourages investors to stay invested for a longer period. Getting this message across is one of the biggest challenges and achievements of the IR function.

Communicating the Investment Case: Maruti Suzuki India Ltd. (MSIL)

Mr Vivek Kumar, MSIL, elaborates the choice of IR message for his company, which is the largest Indian automobile maker and of general interest to investors.

MSIL interacts regularly with analysts and investors at global investor conferences, at least six times every year, unless there is a specific requirement for more information to be shared. 'In our investor presentations, we do not limit ourselves to financial numbers. There are a lot of auto analysts doing number crunching who provide numbers to investors. We try to talk about something new.' The company tries to come up with a theme for every investor conference and introduces a new dimension or area of benchmarking. It may talk about its new concept of 'cost of ownership' for its cars, by considering factors as initial purchase price, fuel efficiency, cost of spares and servicing and the residual value; or its fuel strategy, or even about its operations for the last five years.

Our business model is quite simple—introduce new models and expand dealership/service network, which is not difficult to replicate. In fact, all automobile companies in India are doing the same. Hence, we feel that we need to provide new information that will emphasise our investment case, especially to an audience that comprises portfolio managers more interested in knowing about the investment potential of any company.

Most of our competitors in India are subsidiaries of foreign companies, who do not disclose much information. Being publicly listed, we are bound by mandatory disclosure norms. However, we believe in going one step ahead and sharing more than what is required.[49]

MSIL's policy of providing additional information not only makes the task of investors easier, it also promotes a reputation of transparency.

The investment thesis can be communicated by:

- Explaining the factors and forces behind results, instead of simply talking about recent financial metrics
- Sharing with investors multiple metrics that best show the value of the company, which will increase understanding of performance and decrease stock volatility
- Being consistent in providing access and information flow even in bad times
- Tracking movements of investors regularly to thoroughly understand stock movements and find out about the effectiveness of the IR programme itself.[50]

Telling the Story Well

An award-winning IR head of one of India's foremost IT companies feels that articulating the company's story well is the key task of IR.

According to him, providing more quantity and better quality of information including substantial data on operational metrics can help investors understand the company's business better. It may invite a lot more questions from investors, but at the same time it leads to a much higher degree of transparency.

Sharing good and bad news with the same degree of regularity and forthrightness enables the company to build its reputation for transparency. For example, revenue productivity may move upwards and downwards for any IT company. When the company provides data during both upward and downward trends, it sends out a message that it values transparency.

In the long run, investors look for this quality among companies rather than core financials. They should be made to feel that the company is not a 'black hole', from which no information emerges. If sufficient information, in the form of multiple metrics, is provided proactively, and coupled with regular management access, it leads to lesser scrutiny and more confidence from investors.

Understanding and Targeting the Audience

The target audience for IR comprises individual (retail) and institutional investors, both current and prospective. Carefully analysing databases of sell-side and buy-side can help sort and identify investment styles of investors with company characteristics.

Institutional investors can be classified into: momentum investors (who are interested only in upward price movement and not in the company's message); growth investors (who primarily look at growing industry sectors, and companies within) and value investors (who seek out undiscovered or recovering companies with growth potential). Retail investors could be smaller investors as students, pensioners or housewives, or larger, High Networth Individuals.

Which Media to Select?

The IR function has a host of private and public communication channels at its disposal in order to reach out to its target audience. Private communication channels (as one-to-one meetings) are perceived to be an important means of influencing analysts and institutions. On the other hand, public channels of communication as the annual report and the investor website are essential to reach out to a diverse, geographically dispersed target audience. IR needs to create a balance between public and private channels so that the company can reap benefits of providing information in the public domain (better quality information set, higher liquidity and lower cost of capital) without losing the benefits of exchange (preserving control of company, obtaining funds and shareholder support when required) of private disclosure.[51] Public disclosure about information as research and development may result in loss of competitive advantage. Hence, as a strategy, managers may choose to discuss such aspects in private channels with select members of the financial market. On the other hand, private meetings can create the perception of selective disclosure, causing a higher cost of capital.[52]

The annual report and the company's IR website are the two most important indirect channels of communicating with its various audiences. These modes are considered most important for IR communication by IR officers as well as by analysts and retail investors.

> **Focussing on the Basics: Annual Report at Persistent Systems Ltd.**
>
> Persistent Systems Ltd. believes that the annual report is a document which lives with you for a year, and hence requires to be taken seriously.
>   The IR team spends a lot of time, almost five months on its creation. Typically, the annual report preparation process starts every year in January itself.

Institutional investors need in-depth and specific information that helps them make better decisions about buying a company's shares. Face-to-face meetings are the most preferred mode of interaction for institutional investors, globally and in India. These interactions, in the form of conferences, meetings in investment manager offices, analyst days or even tours of company facilities, are important as they enable a personal assessment of senior management.[53] Both buy-side and sell-side analysts are usually keen to have on-site meetings and interactions with several members of senior management. Often companies make presentations at investor conferences hosted by brokerage houses, which may have huge numbers of retail and institutional investors in attendance. While such conferences enable reaching out to many investors in a couple of hours, it is also possible for the message to get lost in the crowd. The investment manager's office is also a popular venue for face-to-face meetings, where an IR or brokerage organisation accompanies company officers to meet with institutional investors. Analyst days, exclusive conferences at the company premises are also popular among sell-side analysts looking for additional information.

Institutional investors also prefer at least a quarterly conference call or investor presentation that gives them the opportunity to have their questions about company performance and future prospects answered.[54] Not filtering out small or first-time investors during the question–answer sessions can add credibility and reduce perceptions of 'scripting'. During earnings season, most companies hold conference calls or investor presentations on the same days and sometimes, even the same time. Providing the audio/video recordings of conference calls and investor presentations as well as the presentation slides on the IR website for at least one or two weeks after the event, is useful. Some companies maintain well-classified archives of all their conference calls, presentations and annual general meetings.

Individual (or retail) investors can be reached out through memberships in investment clubs (physical or online), advertorials in financial trade journals and public relations efforts in financial media as newspapers and news television shows. An impressive or charismatic Chairman or CEO, quoted frequently in the media is a huge credibility-booster with retail investors. With the all-pervasive effect of the Internet, social media is emerging as another strong tool for reaching out to retail investors.

Choosing the Right Communication Media: Tata Consultancy Services Ltd. (TCS)

According to Mr Kedar Shirali, TCS, there is no 'one-size-fits-all' answer to the correct communication media for investors. TCS has found personal interactions—at investor conferences, non-deal road shows or at one-on-one meetings at their own office—to be the most effective way of disseminating the investment thesis and the core messages. Financial and operational disclosures in the IT industry are very high, so investors are more interested in understanding the longer-term dynamics of demand, supply, etc. Such discussions are best had across the table.

Other tactical channels in descending order of importance include: investor presentations, analyst days, annual report, quarterly earnings calls, ad-hoc thematic conference calls, IR website and email broadcasts.

While Mr Shirali believes that social media offers a very effective platform for disseminating the investment thesis and establishing a two-way communication channel, it is better suited for markets where retail investors can make a material impact on a stock's valuation. For organisations where large institutional investors have a material impact on the valuation of stock, traditional channels and meetings are more effective. Belonging to the latter category, TCS uses social media as a secondary channel rather than the primary communication platform.

The positioning of the Internet as one of the key communication channels has brought increasingly new capabilities to the IR programmes of companies. A well-designed and content-rich IR website is usually the first port of call for every investor; retail or institutional. The substantial savings of time and money usually offsets the cost of creating the website, and also enhances the speed of information sharing. The company's two-way IR communication is also improved through email, Internet telephony services and videoconferencing, in a more cost-effective manner.[55]

The greatest advantage for Internet users is the simplicity of access and search. Investors can define the type and time frame of information they require. For instance, specific information not usually available in annual reports can be requested, and they can obtain more timely information, rather than waiting for annual or quarterly reports. Table 5.1 shows some of the most commonly found elements on Indian IR websites.

The combination of advances in information and communication technology and the prevalence of the Internet have transformed several forms of IR communication (Table 5.2). Investor meetings have now become increasingly 'virtual' and are being conducted through teleconferencing. Conference calls have emerged as a new genre of traditional face-to-face business meetings. Quarterly earnings announcements, earlier made during live meetings, are now usually communicated via earnings calls. Traditional written financial reporting, as annual reports and quarterly statements, is increasingly available in digital form on the company website. Companies are no longer content to put up their financial statements or annual reports as .pdf files on their IR websites; they invest heavily in creating digital reports that offer better readability, superior graphics and compatibility with new-age gadgets as iPads. New genres

Table 5.1 Common Elements on Indian IR Websites[56]

Corporate profile
Details of products/services
Interim statements of past years
Annual reports of past years
Annual report in pdf format
Share holding pattern
Code of conduct
Board of directors
Latest annual report
Asset or corporate officer images
Email to investor relations
Site map
Press/news releases
Search engine
Discrete annual reports section
Stock exchange listings
Security holders with more than 1 per cent shares
Environmental and social reports
Historical share price graph
Phone number to Investor Relations
Share registry details

of communicating with financial audiences have also emerged in the form of investor blogs, podcasts and investor chat-rooms.

WHAT ARE THE CHALLENGES FACED BY IR?

> *Sometimes, IR is neither proactive nor defensive. It's just plain old warfare and hard work, and making phone calls, talking to people, and battling misinformation.*
>
> —ALEXANDER L. CAPPELLO[57]

One of the foremost challenges of IR is the timing and amount of information disclosed to the market. 'Too much and you lose market credibility; too little and you lack visibility with your share price being undervalued by the market.'[58]

Table 5.2   Changes in Forms of IR Communication

Past IR Practices	Present IR Practices
Face-to-face investor meetings	Virtual meetings via teleconferencing, conference calls
Quarterly earnings announcement presentations	Earnings calls
Physical copies of financial reporting statements	Digital versions available on company's IR website
Traditional financial statements in printed form	E-statements in .pdf or flash formats with colourful images and sophisticated graphics
Telephone conversations	Investor blogs, podcasts, investor chat-rooms

Other challenges are both internal and external. For companies that have only recently realised the critical role of IR, the most frequent internal challenges are understaffed IR departments, the struggle for support of senior management and the process of showing the value that IR brings to the organisation.[59] The greatest strategic challenge faced by the companies when it comes to communicating with the market is the dichotomy between analysts' demand for short-term profit and the organisation's goal of building long-term value.

Freeing IR of the Stock Price Burden

One respondent from the country's leading IT company describes a unique outlook of his management, where the IR function is not made accountable for share price movements. The logic behind this is that if share price levels are used as an indicator of success/failure for the IR team, it would be overly focussed on prices and will communicate through stock price rather than other important metrics.

'My management does not pressurise the IR team for share prices. I am not stopped from saying something simply because it will have an effect on the share price. For example, if the next quarter is not expected to be very good, I don't defer communicating about it, but have the freedom to talk about it in a forthright manner.'

Such delinking of IR performance from the company's share price can be liberating for the IR team, encouraging long-term perspective and transparency, both of which are highly valued by investors.

The very nature of the IR role can also create challenges as its functions are unclear and undefined. IR job profiles and responsibilities vary across organisations and the function is performed differently based on whether it is part of the finance, communication or legal department.

Specific situations as share buy-backs, Initial Public Offerings (IPOs), private placement deals, mergers and acquisitions (M&A) and the odd crisis create further challenges for the IR function. It is essential for the company to have good IR practices during M&A transactions in view of the stringent SEBI regulations as well as in the interest of ensuring the success of the transaction. Most importantly, IR officers should be familiar with the rapidly evolving M&A regulations to ensure complete compliance.

Companies engaging in an IPO or even a secondary public offering will find that a thoroughly planned IR strategy is crucial. For any form of public offering, the IR team needs to clearly communicate its value proposition, key operating metrics and the company's position vis-à-vis its peer group, along with an evaluation of how long the differentiated position is likely to last. Companies usually go through a rigorous schedule of road-shows and presentations before a public offering. What will actually determine actual investment in the company is the content of such presentations and the ability to convince investors about the company's prospects. Stepping up on financial media relations efforts by aiming for coverage in regional/national news media can also have positive effects.[60]

Making the IPO a Success: Persistent Systems Ltd.

Mr Vivek Sadhale, Persistent Systems Ltd., feels that the key to managing a successful IPO from an IR perspective lies in starting early, communicating regularly and not discriminating among analysts.

> We began behaving like a public company in terms of regular financial disclosure and communication, even when we were not one. When asked about being market-ready and prepared to communicate, we could confidently reply in the affirmative.
>
> We took time to understand the entire process of IR, and also gathered intelligence by interacting with seniors in the IT sector. Realising the market's need for a differentiated 'story', we emphasised how our business model was different from that of IT services companies. This created interest among analysts and investors and led to frenzy at the time of the IPO to 'capture a differentiated story'.
>
> From the first year itself, we invited analysts to our facility and provided access to top and middle level management. This gave them an opportunity to see our team, what we were planning, whether we had the financial and human capacity for expansion and created a lot of goodwill.
>
> Our singular strategy of not discriminating between big-brand and non-brand investors/analysts has also paid off by generating massive interest among the financial community. Though it was overwhelming to meet a large number of analysts/investors and cater to their demands of time and information, the visibility generated has been worth the effort.[61]

Private placement deals bring an entirely different set of challenges in terms of IR practices. While IPOs demand intensive publicity, private placement requires seeking out a few large investors with utmost discretion. Here, the role of the IR team includes maintaining silence till the deal is announced, reviewing all corporate communications and ensuring that the deal is not revealed in any release or statement. The IR team's handling of the numerous meetings with the institutional investors and the information shared, makes or breaks the deal. Also, private placements may lead to a barrage of inquiries from existing shareholders, and it is up to the IR team to convince them about the rationality of the deal price and the appropriate use of funds raised—whether business expansion, or a new acquisition or reduction of debt.[62]

While regular IR is about maintaining relationships with the financial community and sharing information about the company's progress, crisis IR is about resolving problems, sometimes even before anyone outside the company is aware of them. There are multiple challenges, internal as well as external, faced by the IR team (refer Fig. 5.2) which if unattended can snowball into a crisis situation.

For the IR function, a crisis may be anything, from a rally in the company's shares to the cancellation of a new order. It may not be limited to negative news in the media or improper handling of a media person; but may include situations as diverse as proxy battles, earnings restatements, announcement of losses, unexpected management changes, product recalls and shareholder or other major lawsuits. A crisis IR strategy should be able to handle any situation that may have an impact on the market valuation of the company. The following are essential for tiding over an IR crisis:[63]

- Understanding the correct cause of the crisis and the concerns of the different audiences
- Communicating on time and proactively with all key audiences
- Preparing for other contingencies that may arise due to the current crisis
- Reacting appropriately (neither over, nor under) with a thorough risk-benefit analysis
- Ensuring consistency of message between various members of IR and top management

Figure 5.2   Challenges of IR

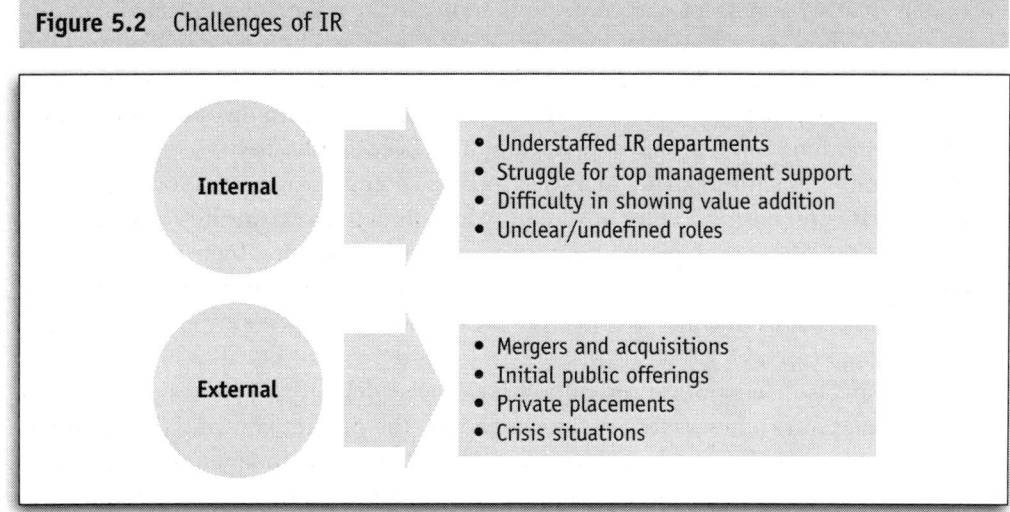

- Focussing on the solution along with the problem
- Being forthright about the facts and utilising the correct media for communication

IS THERE A LINK BETWEEN IR AND CORPORATE REPUTATION?

Investor relations officers must now play an integral role in managing and strengthening corporate reputation.

—HEATHER HARPER[64]

A large number of studies have found a link between financial performance and corporate reputation of an organisation. Researchers agree that financial and market performance history of an organisation is the variable that exerts the highest impact on its current reputation.[65] Even the *Fortune* 'Most Admired Companies' ratings are found to be greatly influenced by earlier financial performance.[66] Various measures of past financial performance as accounting returns, stock market returns, sales growth, size, operating leverage and so forth, have explained 42–53 per cent of the variance in overall rating of corporate reputation in the *Fortune* survey.[67]

This is evident with companies as Tata Steel Ltd., Hindustan Unilever Ltd. and Colgate Palmolive Ltd., whose consistently high profits, stock market returns and sales growth have led them to occupy the top three positions in *Fortune* 'India's Most Admired Companies 2012' list.[68] The impact of financial performance on corporate reputation is understandable, for interest levels of executives and industry analysts in financial performance are high and it is believed that while analysing corporate reputation, stakeholders are likely to put the highest emphasis on financial performance.[69]

Reputation is positively affected by a number of economic and non-economic factors, principal among which are profitability, risk and market value. Other factors found important in creating signals for corporate reputation are the company's reflected visibility in the media, the extent to which institutions hold their stock, their dividend yield to investors and their demonstrations of social concern.[70] All these indicators are communicated by the IR function through its activities of engaging with investors, and hence, its role in generating reputational capital cannot be over-emphasised.

The actions of institutional investors and media accounts heavily condition corporate reputations. By purchasing a company's equity in capital markets, institutional investors signal to other market participants about the merits of its activities. Increasing organisational visibility among media and institutional investors and, encouraging them to invest in the organisation are means by which the IR function further contributes to creating the reputational capital for the organisation.

Three aspects of corporate reputation have been defined: awareness, assessment and asset value. Awareness refers to the concept of the market knowing the organisation without any conclusion about its value. Assessment is the judgement made about it. Asset value indicates the dollar/rupee value of an organisation's reputation. IR impacts each of these aspects of corporate reputation. It contributes to awareness

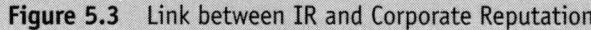

Figure 5.3   Link between IR and Corporate Reputation

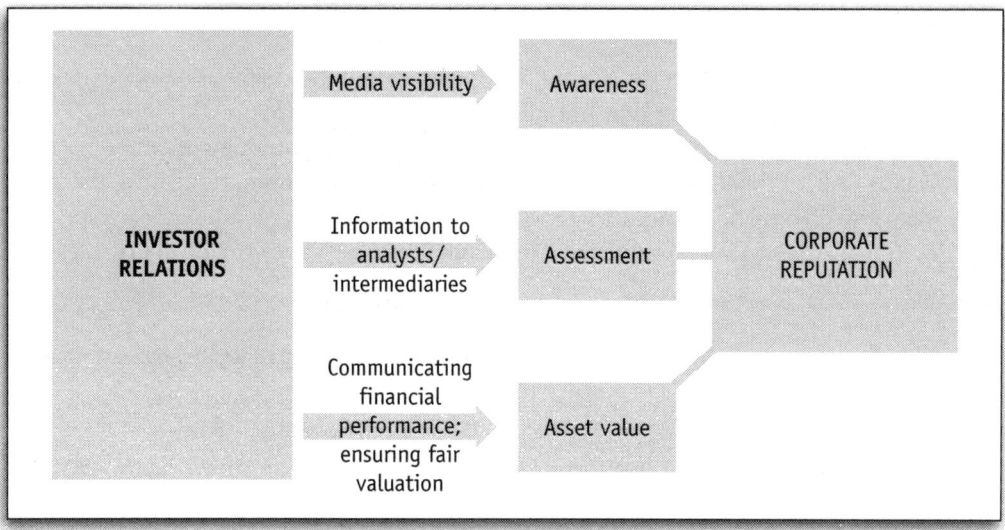

by creating media visibility. It adds to the assessment aspect by disseminating information to analysts and other intermediaries who then utilise it for their own judgements about the future earnings potential of the company. Finally, it impacts asset value by communicating the organisation's financial performance and ensuring fair valuation of its shares (refer Fig. 5.3).

Linking IR and Corporate Reputation: Tata Consultancy Services Ltd. (TCS)

Mr Kedar Shirali, TCS, emphasises that IR is an integral part of his company's reputation management, receiving a lot of top management attention.

By building a professional IR practice, we have been able to establish a reputation for promptness, openness, communicativeness, honest and consistent discourse which is much appreciated by institutional investors as well as sell-side analysts. The positive effect manifests itself not only in the valuation of the stock but also in the good things investors have to say about the company and its messaging.[71]

CONCLUSION

Investor Relations is a strategic lever for corporate development because of its influence on the cost of capital—share prices and credit ratings—and on reputation.

—ANNE GUIMARD[72]

Every company has a 'story' to narrate to the market, and its reputation depends on the degree to which stakeholders believe and trust that story. Reputation is also created if the company is able to 'talk to investors, analysts and financial media quickly, cogently and without an attitude'.[73]

Apart from information sharing, a good IR programme should focus on being flexible and adaptable; understanding that not all interactions can be planned in advance and closing the loop by providing 'inbound' communication to top management.

It is also critical for the IR function to cultivate the art of communicating the message—learn to go beyond mandatory reporting, consider the target audience perspective and develop answers to anticipated questions from their end. The crux of the IR message can be divided into:

- Communicating with clarity company values, business plan, strategy, risks, growth prospects, ability to deliver results and credibility.
- Differentiating the company's performance vis-à-vis competitors.
- Projecting the company as a leader in compliance, disclosures, transparency and corporate governance.
- Communicating the company's unique investment potential to the investing community.[74]

Key Points

- Investor relations (IR) is a strategic management responsibility that combines finance, communication, marketing and securities law compliance to enable effective two-way communication between a company and its financial stakeholders.
- The need for the IR function emerges from companies' requirements of providing adequate disclosure and creating visibility in capital markets.
- IR provides present and potential investors with a true picture of the company's performance and prospects, building and maintaining strong relationships with financial stakeholders and ensuring a fair market valuation for the company's shares.
- The benefits of IR include higher trading volumes and better market valuations for the company's shares; higher level of analyst following, more accurate analyst forecasts and more consensus among analysts and increase in the number of institutional investors and the percentage of institutional ownership.
- The target audiences for the mandatory and voluntary communication initiated by IR are: existing individual and institutional shareholders, regulatory authorities, buy-side and sell-side analysts, financial intermediaries and the media.
- The company should communicate its 'strategic value proposition' or 'investment thesis' clearly to its financial stakeholders.
- A balance should be sought between public and private channels of communication with financial stakeholders so that the public domain benefits are gained without compromising the exchange benefits of private disclosure.

- The greatest challenges of IR are: the timing and amount of information disclosed to the market, and the dichotomy between analysts' demand for short-term profit and the organisation's goal of building long-term value.
- Since prior financial performance is an important determinant in assessing corporate reputation, the quality of IR greatly influences corporate reputation.

END NOTES

1. M. S. Anand, *Investor Relations*. Hyderabad, India: ICFAI University Press (2007), p. 13.
2. D. Allen, 'Fundamentals of investor relations', in Benjamin Mark Cole (ed.), *The New Investor Relations* (pp. 3–22). New York: Bloomberg Press (2004), p. 10.
3. IR Society India, 'Thomson Reuters announces the winners of its inaugural Extel India Investor Relations Survey', website http://www.ir-india.com/transactions.asp (accessed 13 January 2013).
4. C. Marston, 'The organization of the investor relations function by large UK quoted companies', *Omega* (1996), 24(4), 477–488.
5. M. Regester, 'Why investor relations is growing in importance and requires special skills', *International Public Relations Review* (1990), 13(1), 4–7.
6. P. Tuominen, 'Investor relations: A Nordic school approach', *Corporate Communications: An International Journal* (1997), 2(1), 46–55.
7. National Investor Relations Institute, 'Definition of investor relations', website http://www.niri.org/FunctionalMenu/About.aspx (accessed 18 December 2007).
8. W. F. Mahoney, *Investor Relations: The Professional's Guide to Financial Marketing and Communications*. New York: New York Institute of Finance (1991), p. 3.
9. National Investor Relations Institute, USA, *Emerging Trends in Investor Relations* (2nd ed.). Washington, DC: NIRI (1989).
10. H. Rao and K. Sivakumar, 'Institutional sources of boundary-spanning structures: The establishment of investor relations departments in the Fortune 500 industrials', *Organization Science* (1999), 10(1), 27–42.
11. A. Desai, 'Investor relations of Indian companies', Unpublished Thesis, Dharmsinh Desai University, Nadiad, India (2011).
12. V. Sadhale, (formerly) Company Secretary and Head, Legal and Investor Relations, Persistent Systems Ltd., personal communication, 7 February 2013.
13. M. C. Jensen and W. H. Meckling, 'Theory of the firm: Managerial behaviour, agency costs and ownership structure', *Journal of Financial Economics* (1976), 3(4), 305–360 p. 309.
14. D. Easley and M. O'Hara, 'Information and the cost of capital', *the Journal of Finance* (2004), 59(4), 1553–1583.
15. K. G. Palepu and P. M. Healy, 'The effect of firms' financial disclosure strategies on stock prices', *Accounting Horizons* (1993), 7(1), 1–11.
16. S. J. Gray, L. H. Radebaugh and C. B. Roberts, 'International perceptions of cost constraints on voluntary information disclosures: A comparative study of UK and US multinationals', *Journal of International Business Studies* (1990), 21(4), 597–622.
17. C. B. Barry and S. J. Brown, 'Differential information and security market equilibrium', *Journal of Financial and Quantitative Analysis* (1985), 20(4), 407–422.
18. H. K. Baker, G. E. Powell and D. G. Weaver, 'Does NYSE listing affect organisation visibility?', *Financial Management* (1999), 28(2), 46–54.
19. A. Arbel, 'Generic stocks: An old product in a new package', *Journal of Portfolio Management* (1985), 11(4), 4–12.

20. M. Dahlquist and G. Robertsson, 'Direct foreign ownership, institutional investors and 'firm charac-teristics', *Journal of Financial Economics* (2001), 59(3), 413–440.

21. A. Lath, (formerly) IR Associate, Infosys Ltd., personal communication, 4 March 2013.

22. L. F. Brown, 'Getting a grip on investor relations', *Directors and Boards* (1994), 19(2), 44–46.

23. P. Tuominen, 'Investor relations: A Nordic school approach', *Corporate Communications: An International Journal* (1997), 2(1), 46–55.

24. R. H. Savage, 'Crucial role of investor relations', *Harvard Business Review* (1970), 48(6), 122–130.

25. B. W. Marcus and S. L. Wallace, *New Dimensions in Investor Relations: Competing for Capital in the 21st Century.* New York: John Wiley & Sons (1997).

26. A. O. I. Hoffmann, A. Tutic and S. Wies, 'The role of educational diversity in investor relations', *Corporate Communications: An International Journal* (2011), 16(4), 311–327.

27. H. Rao and K. Sivakumar, 'Institutional sources of boundary-spanning structures: The establishment of investor relations departments in the Fortune 500 industrials', *Organization Science* (1999), 10(1), 27–42.

28. J. MacGregor and I. Campbell, 'What every director should know about investor relations', *International Journal of Disclosure and Governance* (2006), 3(1), 59–69.

29. H. Harper, H. Rafkin-Sax and B. Goodwin, 'IR for blue-chip companies: The new look', in Benjamin Mark Cole (ed.), *The New Investor Relations* (pp. 23–40). New York: Bloomberg Press (2004).

30. M. Tonello, *Revisiting Stock Market Short-Termism.* New York: The Conference Board (2006).

31. H. Harper, H. Rafkin-Sax and B. Goodwin, 'IR for blue-chip companies: The new look', in Benjamin Mark Cole (ed.), *The New Investor Relations* (pp. 23–40). New York: Bloomberg Press (2004).

32. V. Sadhale, (formerly) Secretary and Head, Legal and Investor Relations, Persistent Systems Ltd., personal communication, 7 February 2013.

33. R.W. Holthausen and R.E. Verrecchia, 'The effect of informedness and consensus on price and volume behavior', *The Accounting Review* (1990), 65(1), 191–208.

34. O. E. Barron, O. Kim, S. C. Lim and D. E. Stevens, 'Using analysts' forecasts to measure properties of analysts' information environment', *The Accounting Review* (1998), 73(4), 421–433.

35. B. J. Bushee and G. S. Miller, 'Investor relations, firm visibility and investor following', *The Accounting Review*, 87(3), 867–897.

36. V. Agarwal, A. Liao, E. A. Nash and R. J. Taffler, 'The impact of effective investor relations on market value', Unpublished Manuscript, University of Edinburgh, Edinburgh, UK (2010).

37. A. Lath, (formerly) IR Associate, Infosys Ltd., personal communication, 4 March 2013.

38. K. Shirali, Global IR Head, Tata Consultancy Services, personal communication, 5 February 2013.

39. V. Kumar, Manager, IR, Maruti Suzuki India Ltd., personal communication, 1 March 2013.

40. V. Sadhale, (formerly) Secretary and Head, Legal and Investor Relations, Persistent Systems Ltd., personal communication, 7 February 2013.

41. A. Lath, (formerly) IR Associate, Infosys Ltd., personal communication, 4 March 2013.

42. K. Shirali, Global IR Head, Tata Consultancy Services, personal communication, 5 February 2013.

43. A. Desai, 'Investor relations of Indian companies', Unpublished Thesis, Dharmsinh Desai University, Nadiad, India (2011).

44. D. Allen, 'Fundamentals of investor relations', in Benjamin Mark Cole (ed.), *The New Investor Relations* (pp. 3-22). New York: Bloomberg Press (2004) p. 12.

45. Ungenwood, quoted in J. Hogg, 'The art of investor relations', *Charter* (2012), 26–28.

46. T. Murrell, 'Meeting the challenge of investor relations', *Keeping Good Companies* (2010), 337–342 p. 339.

47. J. MacGregor and I. Campbell, 'What every director should know about investor relations', *International Journal of Disclosure and Governance* (2006), 3(1), 59–69.

48. Ibid.

49. V. Kumar, Manager, IR, Maruti Suzuki India Ltd., personal communication, 1 March 2013.

50. H. Harper, H. Rafkin-Sax and B. Goodwin, 'IR for blue-chip companies: The new look', in Benjamin Mark Cole (ed.), *The New Investor Relations* (pp. 23–40). New York: Bloomberg Press (2004).

51. J. B. Holland, 'Private voluntary disclosure, financial intermediation and market efficiency', *Journal of Business Finance & Accounting* (1998), 25(1/2), 29–68.

52. D. Easley and M. O'Hara, 'Information and the cost of capital', *The Journal of Finance* (2004), 59(4), 1553–1583.
53. C. N. Orndorff, 'The information investment managers want from public companies', in Benjamin Mark Cole (ed.), *The New Investor Relations* (pp. 221–233). New York: Bloomberg Press (2004).
54. Ibid.
55. J. C. Kupermann, 'The impact of the Internet on the investor relations activities of firms', *Journal of Communication Management* (2000), 5(2), 147–159.
56. A. Desai, 'Investor relations of Indian companies', Unpublished Thesis, Dharmsinh Desai University, Nadiad, India (2011).
57. A. L. Cappello, 'Investor relations for private placements', in Benjamin Mark Cole (ed.), *The New Investor Relations* (pp. 105–117). New York: Bloomberg Press (2004), p. 109.
58. T. Murrell, 'Meeting the challenge of investor relations: A national study', *Keeping Good Companies* (2010), 337–342 p. 337.
59. A. Laskin, 'A descriptive account of the investor relations profession: A national study', *Journal of Business Communication* (2009), 46(2), 208–233.
60. D. M. Sherk, 'Investor relations for the IPO', in Benjamin Mark Cole (ed.), *The New Investor Relations* (pp. 119–137). New York: Bloomberg Press (2004).
61. V. Sadhale, (formerly) Secretary and Head, Legal and Investor Relations, Persistent Systems Ltd., personal communication, 7 February 2013.
62. A. L. Cappello, 'Investor relations for private placements', in Benjamin Mark Cole (ed.), *The New Investor Relations* (pp. 105–117). New York: Bloomberg Press (2004).
63. M. S. Sitrick, 'Crisis investor relations', in Benjamin Mark Cole (ed.), *The New Investor Relations* (pp. 139–147). New York: Bloomberg Press (2004).
64. H. Harper, H. Rafkin-Sax and B. Goodwin, 'IR for blue-chip companies: The new look', in Benjamin Mark Cole (ed.), *The New Investor Relations* (pp. 23–40). New York: Bloomberg Press (2004), p. 30.
65. C. Fombrun and M. Shanley, 'What's in a name? Reputation building and corporate strategy', *The Academy of Management Journal* (1990), 33(2), 233–258.
66. G. E. Fryxell and J. Wang, 'The Fortune corporate 'reputation' index: Reputation for what?', *Journal of Management* (1994), 20(1), 1–14.
67. J. Sabate and E. Puente, 'Empirical analysis of the relationship between corporate reputation and financial performance: A survey of the literature', *Corporate Reputation Review* (2003), 6(2), 161–177.
68. 'Tata Steel India's most admired company: Fortune', *The Business Standard*, website http://www.business-standard.com/article/companies/tata-steel-india-s-most-admired-company-fortune-112030600199_1.html (accessed 6 March 2012).
69. F. E. Webster Jr., 'The rediscovery of the marketing concept', *Business Horizons* (1988), 31(3), 29–39.
70. C. Fombrun and M. Shanley, 'What's in a name? Reputation building and corporate strategy', *The Academy of Management Journal* (1990), 33(2), 233–258.
71. K. Shirali, Global IR Head, Tata Consultancy Services, personal communication, 5 February 2013.
72. A. Guimard, *Investor Relations: Principles and International Best Practices of Financial Communications (Finance and Capital Markets)*, UK: Palgrave Macmillan (2008), p. xi.
73. D. Silver, 'The IR-PR nexus', in Benjamin Mark Cole (ed.), *The New Investor Relations* (pp. 59–74). New York: Bloomberg Press (2004), p. 62.
74. A. Lath, (formerly) IR Associate, Infosys Ltd., personal communication, 4 March 2013.

6

Seeking Relational Rent and Hedging Risk: Building Reputation with the Government

That government is best which governs least.

—Henry David Thoreau[1]

Objectives:

- Study business–government relationships and associated benefits
- Learn techniques of influencing the government
- Analyse importance of corporate political ties and activities
- Comprehend the PPP model and inherent advantages
- Assess value associated with regulation
- Learn techniques of establishing connects with regulators

INTRODUCTION

I believe government has no business to do business. Minimum government, maximum governance.

—Narendra Modi[2]

Competitive market structures and increasing competition, coupled with restrictive government regulations, have made growth in Indian markets difficult. The need of the hour is uniform governmental policies, rules and regulations, and structural changes which can help improve productivity. For companies to develop a growth strategy and create societal impact and build reputation, governmental support is required. Let us understand the relationships and dependencies among the three constituencies, viz. the company, the government and the society.

Companies play a legitimate role in public policy processes by advocating policies which are favourable with respect to market scenarios, business operations and competitive advantage.

Key Words

- Access strategy
- Astroturfing
- Bear hug
- Bridging
- Buffering
- Comparative advantage
- Co-optation
- Coregulation
- Corporate political activity
- Corporate political ties
- Delegation
- Direct lobbying
- Government
- Hidden lobbying
- Indirect lobbying
- Influencing
- Interest groups
- Lobbying
- Non-lobbying
- Partnerships
- Policies
- Policy makers
- Political capital
- Political rent
- Public–private partnerships
- Regulations
- Regulators
- Relational rent
- Return on political investment
- Rules
- Self-regulation
- Tripartite partnerships

Aiming to Improve Government–Business Relations

On 30 August 2013, the Planning Commission announced its intention to prepare a draft bill for an institutional mechanism that would hasten the process of resolving issues related to public contracts, by September 2013. It also proposed to prepare a separate note on the review of the government's experience with Public–Private Partnership (PPP) projects as well as to suggest measures for strengthening the system of financing and operating such projects.

Following a review meeting attended by the secretaries of economic affairs and road transport and highways, as well as representatives from the power, coal, civil aviation and urban development ministries, Planning Commission deputy chairman Montek Singh Ahluwalia said,

> This was a first review meeting about PPP projects. We have been asked by the Prime Minister … the finance ministry and Planning Commission together to come back with an assessment of how the [PPP] programme is going, what problems have arisen and how can we address them.[3]

These measures are part of an attempt to boost investor confidence and refresh the investment cycle. The government has planned for investments of $1 trillion in infrastructure projects in the five years ending March 2017, with about 50 per cent targeted from the private sector. The brief for this draft bill and note were given to the

Planning Commission by the Prime Minister of India, Dr Manmohan Singh amid concerns over delays in implementation and cost overruns in several PPP projects.[4]

PPPs are the most commonly found forms of government–business interactions. Serious consideration being given to ensure their success at the highest levels of the government indicates how crucial these relations are for achieving the goals of both, the government and the corporate sector.

They also need to adapt to public policies floated by the government through processes of legislation and regulation. Interestingly, these very same companies make strategic use of public policy[5] by supporting legislators and regulators who provide support against competition, substitute products, buyers and suppliers. Government focus on business rests on development and implementation of national economic strategies providing and enforcing subsidies, tariffs, price controls and entry barriers, which are often referred to as the private interest theory of regulation.[6] When public policies are developed by the government, companies act as interest groups and attempt to influence policy development. In such situations, companies use domain management strategies for addressing environmental uncertainties concerning government. Also referred to as 'politicisation of management',[7] this process evokes greater awareness in managers concerning government and politics and motivates them to influence government policies. While the relationship between the government and the company is one of interdependence, the link between the company and the society is one of dependency. Societies are dependent on the business sector for their macro-economic goals as employment and income.

Corporate houses use political influence to shape societal values which are also reflected in company behaviour and objectives. The company behaviour is driven by the goal of attaining competitive advantage, which brings into conflict public and private interest. However, a corporate political strategy would reference the societal need as a justification for supporting the private agenda of a company. Let us consider a public policy (protectionism with quotas and tariffs) trying to create societal and company impact. This policy will have a societal impact—full employment, protection of new or small industries; and will simultaneously affect the company by improving selling prices and increasing price-cost margin for domestic firms.

The question before us is: how do companies acquire political and financial capital which influences government and society and yields tangible and intangible returns? Acquiring this political capital together with financial is important as it helps them in securing a societal standing by building on reputation. Political capital is dependent on multiple factors subject to prioritisation by companies: company's public reputation and social legitimacy, development of capability to facilitate political strategies by leveraging on its size and financial resources, access to policy makers, knowledge of public policy arenas and expertise in design of strategies. The desire to develop a relationship with government and policy makers is based on trade-off between pressure of corporate-level control and respect for autonomous goals, knowledge and skills. Also referred to as 'firm filter model', this relationship represents the internal company characteristics, as structures, routines, resources and stakeholder dependencies. In the development of political involvement, the company response and adaptation to market and non-market signals mediates the relationship[8] and builds reputation.

Three distinct types of conflict emerge from the corporate-government relationship (Table 6.1).

An issue of dispute stemming from the above discussion is one which addresses concerns of companies on how to organise themselves to resolve the conflict of what is good and what needs to be followed for effective government and political engagement. The conflict resolution for the same can be centralised, shared or decentralised. In the centralised system there is one co-ordinating body which makes decisions and represents the company externally and alone possesses decision-making rights, power and authority to address intra-firm conflict. In the decentralised system each division independently determines distributive issues, advocacy position and representatives for advocating company interests. In between these two extremes lies a shared or co-ordinated system of the company which ensures that authority is placed in the hands of a co-ordinating group comprising representatives of each individual unit. Recommendations from each unit are shared with the central co-ordinating body which plans and determines a conflict resolution strategy. In such cases either a spokesperson from the corporate office or the individual business units may represent interest to political decision makers.

To further understand the complex web of relationships among companies, legislators, regulators and bureaucrats, we have divided the chapter into various sub-sections. We begin by an understanding of the comparative advantage which can be secured through government support; the associated benefits of Corporate Political Activities (CPAs) and ties; significance of PPPs and tripartite partnerships and the role of regulators and regulation in enhancing corporate performance.

Table 6.1 Types of Conflict[9]

Type	Description
Distributive	• Arises after a public policy/regulation has been implemented.
	• Companies/units conflict over dividing the yield or the returns or burdens of regulation.
Advocacy position	• Arises at the time of policy formulation.
	• Business units may have different views concerning preferred advocacy position for the company.
Representational	• Arises when benefits from existing policy and over a company's advocacy position reflect different interests within the company.

CAN COMPARATIVE ADVANTAGE BE SECURED WITH GOVERNMENT INTERVENTION?

> *Government help to business is just as disastrous as government persecution ... the only way a government can be of service to national prosperity is by keeping its hands off.*
>
> —Ayn Rand[10]

Almost all domestic and international business activities are shaped by government policies and strategies for profit optimisation by companies. Is there then, a need to regulate company operations? If yes, how? By making structural changes in policies that impact pricing, investment and entry decisions, environment and worker safety rules, etc. Based on the context, which may be the domestic or the international market, the policy decisions may vary from being 'company-friendly' to 'company-hostile'.

Whatever be the policy decision, governmental intervention (positive or negative), for sustenance of companies and building long-lasting comparative advantage is critical. Government influence in building comparative advantage for companies is a fulcrum for three distinct activities: market intervention that implements changes in the relative pricing schemes and tariffs in the domestic markets; export promotion with subsidised cost elements and, finally, funding investments in a foreign market. Comparative advantage is not always a result of natural endowments and need not necessarily be man-made but can change over time through influence, interventions and dialogue.

To elaborate further, we can begin studying the aforementioned activities of the government in three phases (refer Fig. 6.1).

In the first phase, the government assesses the desired long-term comparative advantage and the techniques for achieving success. For instance, if changes are required, they are implemented by altering relative prices through taxation, tariffs, restrictions on imports, etc. This phase is characterised by a bureaucratic decision making process. As the process matures, there is co-operation between government agencies and companies with emphasis on accumulated knowledge, skills and, enhanced direct and indirect

Figure 6.1   Phases of Government Influence

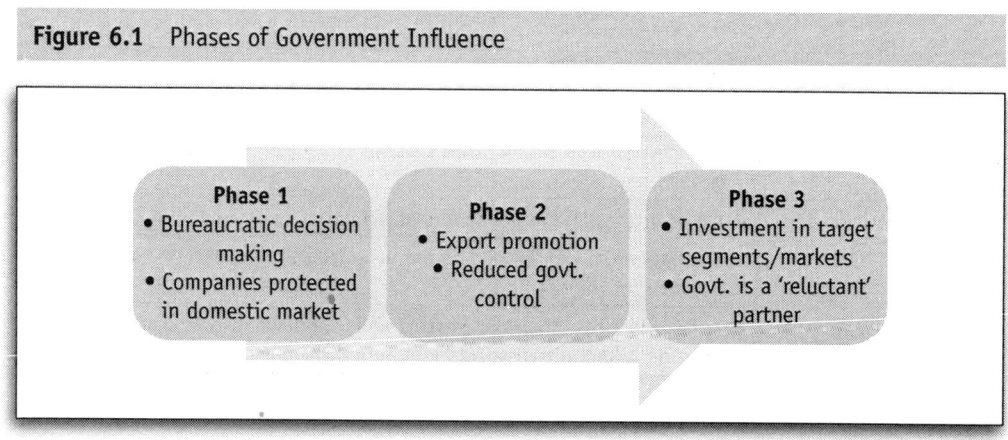

Phase 1
- Bureaucratic decision making
- Companies protected in domestic market

Phase 2
- Export promotion
- Reduced govt. control

Phase 3
- Investment in target segments/markets
- Govt. is a 'reluctant' partner

operational growth to achieve the desired target. Direct growth results in improved production, catering to the domestic and external markets. In indirect growth, companies begin to enhance production and export capacity with different product lines. In this situation, the companies are well-protected in the domestic market.

The second phase is export promotion where there is expansion of products and production levels increase. The development of this phase is based on the premise that there is small domestic consumption and companies exporting to large global markets can convert their status to price setters and takers. This is an important phase as it marks a period of transition in government-corporate relationship. Government takes on the role of a partner and with an increase in exports, its control over corporate houses decreases. This phase is marked by a steep incline in the corporate-level savings, which improve investment opportunities.

Following the success of the second stage, companies move to the next level of investing in target segments and markets. In this phase, the government still acts as a partner, albeit a reluctant one. The difference in interest between the government and the corporate houses begins to emerge. While the government, with focus on domestic markets, favours a process of internal consumption, the companies' motivation is to establish control over the export market, earn higher revenues and mitigate risks associated with trade policy changes in target markets. Companies plan direct investment in marketing and production areas with the objective of minimising risks and maximising profits. However, there can be situations of 'dependency risk'[11] when exports are targeted at only one or two foreign markets. To hedge risks, companies specifically make plans that in some sense help them gradually (phase-wise) steer away from government intervention. Viewing success in internationalisation of various corporate plans, the nature of government intervention also changes. For instance, policies may be designed, developed and implemented to meet basic consumer needs. There may also be initiation of processes like licensing and/or joint ventures with foreign firms.

In other words, we can state that government intervention, in the initial phase, is in the form of exercising control. However, with passage of time its role diminishes as companies move to the second and third phase. Strategies developed by the government aid companies to develop competencies and skills which help influence public decision making. Though competencies are developed, companies still cannot bypass or ignore political or bureaucratic activities as the same are essential to performance and survival of companies.

India is currently at the end of phase one and has begun moving into phase two.

WHAT IS THE RELATIONSHIP BETWEEN A COMPANY AND THE GOVERNMENT?

Few relationships are as critical to the business enterprise itself as the relationship to government. The manager has responsibility for this relationship as part of his responsibility to the enterprise itself. To a large extent the relationship to government results from what businesses do or fail to do.

—PETER DRUCKER[12]

The corporate-government relationship is embedded in global alliances, market and economic growth. Companies influence the government through their knowledge, expertise and relational skills. Government depends on companies for providing market information essential for making good policies and decisions. In short, there exists an interesting relationship that requires critical management between companies and public authorities. The relationship between the two entities is dynamic and keeps changing and developing over time as it is dependent on processes of strategy formation, dynamics of policy networks and changes in institutional organisations of market.

Companies strategise with the government through direct lobbying, grassroots activities and financial support to public office candidates for integrating their market and non-market activities. At the same time, policy makers too may sense a need to integrate their political activities with market actions.[13] However, the challenge stems from internationalisation of the market scenario which gives rise to multiple global issues as impact of employment on outsourcing to low-cost countries, child labour, media attention on environmental footprints, global warming, etc. making political activities of the companies more complex, varied and difficult to manage.

Influencing the Government

Complex engagement between government regulations and demand for favourable policies by companies has created an environment where influence and dialogue between the two has become an imperative. There are some company characteristics that play an important role in influencing decision making. For instance, large companies, with sufficient scale to enhance their effort, may provide government with decision-making infrastructure, or support by way of votes, income or post government service employment. Intense lobbying and ability to contribute to trade associations may also be used as techniques for influencing political decisions.

Company age is another important determinant in influencing governmental outcome. With passage of time and duration in the market space, older companies become more adept at understanding and influencing the government. Recognised by decision makers as high on survival, these companies are often successful in veering decisions in their favour through protracted and continuous interactions. A democratic government lends itself more to influence by companies in its executive and legislative branches. Similarly, a diversified government, with varied interests and affiliations, is also susceptible to the influence process.

Industry sector has been found to be another important driver in government influence. Multinational, exporting and government-owned companies are higher on the influence index than privatised or foreign-owned companies. Public sector companies that were later privatised have greater influence over government decision-making than companies which have always been privately owned. Competition in the market is another major influencer. Companies with no competition are higher on the influence indicator than companies with one to four competitors. Finally, decentralised governance systems can improve company effort in securing government support, and shaping political processes and policies.

Influencing Government Outcomes or Not? Monsanto India Ltd.

Monsanto India Ltd. has courted equal parts of success and controversy in India with allegations of its undue influence over governments. Beginning with the sales of herbicides in 1949, it has now grown into an organisation with a turnover of ₹1,000 crores.[14]

In addition to claims of its influence at the highest levels of the US government,[15] Monsanto is also alleged to have influenced the Indian government into getting its high-priced genetically modified seeds for cotton being used by farmers. Despite the high costs of its BT cotton seed, and its associated problems, strong advertising and government endorsement of its products initially helped persuade Indian farmers to take loans for buying the company's seeds.[16]

Recently, however, its relations with government in India seem to have taken a turn for the worse. In 2012, following public outcry over a genetically modified variety of brinjal, a native plant of India grown by millions of Indian farmers, the central government banned the Monsanto-created product, alleging violation of India's Biological Diversity Act.[17] In April 2012, the Gujarat government decided to discontinue distribution of Monsanto's maize seeds to tribals following criticism not only from within the state, but also at a national level from various agencies, including farmers' and tribal organisations, leaders and scientists.[18]

WHAT IS LOBBYING?

Lobbying is a constitutionally protected activity that plays an important role in the governmental process. It is precisely because of the importance of lobbying in the conduct of the public's business that it should be more open to the public's scrutiny.

—JIMMY CARTER[19]

Lobbying refers to the efforts made by companies to influence the government either directly or indirectly through actions across peer groups. As a direct or indirect process, lobbying is an informative sign to policy makers about the exact market and non-market situation. Direct lobbying is a way of influencing through 'voting, seeking interviews, attending government meetings, sending petitions, letter writing, email campaigns, phone-in efforts, campaign contributions and bribery'.[20] It can be divided into two categories. In the first category the models emphasise peer group influence and use of strategies through the election process. The second category focusses on pressure tactics exerted on politicians post elections. Indirect or grassroots lobbying is an influence attempt to shape the opinion of the general public, through 'public demonstrations (pickets, marches and meetings), media campaigns, sit-ins and occupation, or sometimes violence and sabotage'.[21]

Lobbying is extremely important in conveying information to policy makers and its impact is huge. Signals from the group lobbyists help regulators gather information, tailor policies and optimise the objective function of the same only when complete information is provided. Companies that undertake lobbying activities have preferences that are different from non-lobbying firms. In other words, the lobbying companies may bear government policy costs but not necessarily reap the benefits.

While studying lobbying and lobbyists, one needs to cognise the role of interest groups in legislative processes as they impact the rule-making process. Multiple organisations value participation in the rule-making process as critical to lobbying strategies. The same organisations are also of the view that their lobbying efforts are crucial in influencing policies and changes therein. Producer groups and their size contribute to the lobbying effort and help secure the 'political rent' by intervening in political activities. Small producer groups with focussed advantages are able to engage in lobbying more easily than others.

The importance of trade lobbyists cannot be undermined as they represent concerns of an individual company, which is instrumental in funding a lobbying effort. These trade associations create 'fronts' for a small group of companies. Though not a common norm, there may still be instances of information asymmetry or misrepresentation. Though registration requirements and disclosure laws reduce information asymmetry, they do not essentially provide the best means of control.

Lobbyists, though not completely harmless, can be controlled by governmental structuring of the environment and selection of strategies in anticipation of interactions. Formulation of stringent rules and regulations help prevent untoward activities by lobbyists.

Lobbying Strategies

Lobbying is used as a form of market exchange of political favours where the company exchanges market information, provides financial support and votes in favour of political benevolence. Various factors contribute to the lobbying efforts. The company size is an important determinant for it indicates both political and economic power. It is, in other words, also an indicator of the political engagement capability. Other critical factors are financial performance and assets. For instance, poor performing companies that require higher degree of lobbying also need larger capital assets to facilitate the lobbying process. Higher growth opportunities influence a company's decision to lobby. Companies consider the balance of power between shareholders and management when selecting measures for lobbying.

Companies adopt one of the following three lobbying strategies: bear hug, astroturfing and self-regulation. 'Bear hug'[22] is a strategy in which companies embrace opposition by providing financial support to interest groups with opposing views and subsidise the lobbying activities. Benefits associated with 'bear hug' imply that companies need to undertake socially responsible actions, which are also part of profit maximisation, e.g. strategic Corporate Social Responsibility (CSR). Prior to employing the 'bear hug' various issues as situation, insurance, etc. are deliberated upon. The strategy acts as an insurance against negative policy outcomes and can be ideally applied to situations where the company is unfamiliar with the environment.

Companies observe 'astroturfing'[23] when they are unaware of the actual state of the political world. The company subsidises the lobbying efforts of a group with similar views.

This tactic involves providing financial support to groups which hold almost identical opinions as the company. The astroturf strategy focusses on supporting an interest group with a negative bias. The policy outcome in such a situation is broad and lenient.

Finally, in self-regulation a company attempts to narrow the potential social harm from its activities. It involves substantive changes in company strategy and operations, which help mitigate the risk of social harm. This strategy is deployed by a company when it is unable to provide accurate lobbying information. Also a form of constant voluntary improvement, self-regulation helps in reducing the severity of a negative bias developing over a period of time. For instance, design measures for a new facility may minimise the risk of worst-case scenarios. Actions as these are accepted as credible commitments. Self-regulation can pre-empt a lobbying effort of interest groups by anticipating and minimising the returns (relative to costs incurred). It can improve the incentive of a positively biased interest group to share reports that are contradictory to the real state, leading to an informational loss. Though there are disadvantages associated with this form of lobbying, the government decision maker still benefits immensely from corporate self-regulation.

Impact of Lobbyists and Interest Groups

Lobbying, an influence attempt at political decision maker through a lobbyist who operates on behalf of the company or special interest group, can be extremely dangerous or beneficial. Lobbyists help formulate decisions, prevent some from being taken, and also shape the culture and context in a manner which ensures that certain decisions do not see the light of the day. The task of a lobbyist is to negotiate on behalf of interest groups and try to maximise benefits. Inability to achieve this target often sees them being replaced by other more effective and persistent lobbyists. Their importance can be gauged by the fact that they are often requisitioned by bureaucrats and politicians for providing balanced information on strong and weak interest groups. The problem begins when lobbying is hidden and done by groups that have strong incentives for action. However, these groups may be able to overcome issues related to collective actions more than other groups.

Does lobbying lead to corporate value creation? 'A company's return on lobbying and campaign contributions—let's call it return on political investment—is astronomically higher than any real investment it can make.'[24] Management is often forced to undertake lobbying investments so that they are able to create long term value for shareholders. It has been found that shareholder wealth is enhanced when a co-optation announcement with the government is made public. In such situations, political connections may be discussed and promotion of political ideologies may also be undertaken which may or may not yield any value returns. Agency theory argues that senior management, in pursuit of personal interests, may forgo such value creation. Positive and negative views have been posited concerning impact of lobbying on corporate values. The first view suggests that lobbying enhances value as well as promotes personal interests of management and the second view asserts that in lobbying, resources are misallocated.

Identifying New Areas for Growth: NASSCOM

National Association of Software and Services Companies (NASSCOM) announced its Analytics Special Interest Group in July 2013, comprising thought leaders from industry, academia and government. The primary objective of this group is to deliver thought leadership on shaping the growth policies for India to emerge as the global hub for analytics and help form all-inclusive strategies for developing talents and skills for these services, which are expected to grow at a CAGR of 19–20 per cent.

It has been predicted that the analytics and big data services, especially risk analytics, will burgeon to a $50 billion industry globally by 2020, of which there exists a $2.5 billion opportunity for Indian analytics services players.[25] The importance of risk analytics is becoming increasingly clear in complex and volatile environments as it helps companies in decision making.

This interest group will work towards increasing the visibility and relevance of analytics in India, providing consultations and capability-building services enabling firms to successfully execute analytics projects, address the talent gap for meeting the rocketing demand and resolve specific issues arising in the process of implementing analytics in the short and long term.

Is the value relevance of lobbying conditioned by the management? Companies with a strong management engage in greater lobbying activities than those with a weak one. Management may engage in lobbying for strengthening their corporate position, which would also determine their relative power with board of directors.

How does a lobbyist impact the target? By gaining access to decision makers or key decision points in the government. Access relates to 'facilitating intermediate objectives of political interest groups'.[26] While access is important for maintaining interest group influence through lobbyists, they rarely receive attention from political authorities. As assessment of influence level is difficult, their impact is suspect and often complicated. The problem is further compounded by the fact that it is equally difficult to estimate the level of engagement and integration of purpose or action of the lobbyists and government officials.

Substantially increasing number of lobbyists and their efforts have compelled legislators to make more demands for evidence of claims made by these groups. Legislators normally provide a structure of institutional norms for lobbyists to operate. For instance, they may be asked to register their affiliation and record their finances, which help in evaluation, data collation and communication with interest groups. Lobbyists are required to certify the measures advocated by them as being specifically approved by the organisation they represent.

Lobbyists that receive government money are under higher scrutiny and regulation than others. They are required to file extensive accounts of all the expenditures. They often act as a 'service bureau' providing on-demand information. However, their cost can be monitored by the legislators. The interaction between legislators and lobbyists is not only governed by the former but the latter also has a say and can indicate interest or lack of interest by choosing to attend or not to attend a public hearing.

WHAT ARE CORPORATE POLITICAL TIES?

Many businesses with unpopular products or inefficient production find it much easier to curry the favour of a few influential politicians or a government agency than to compete in the open market.

—CHARLES KOCH[27]

Corporate Political Ties (CPTs) are connects between companies and public authorities through organisational arrangement and are a part of corporate non-market strategies in both matured and emerging markets. Companies which are successful in developing this connect through corporate-government interactions, secure for themselves, invaluable political support and resources. However, CPT has been found to result in negative impact on company value and performance.

Extant research on CPT focusses primarily on profitability and outcomes. For instance, with a high ratio of CPT, companies provide political bodies with accurate and timely business-related information, financial and social political support. In exchange, the government helps these companies improve their power and legitimacy, and secure competitive advantage through multiple policy tools and resources.

Stemming from the economic perspective, there are three archetypes of CPT (Table 6.2).

Together with the economic, a social perspective too has been assigned to these relationships suggesting that companies require resources for ongoing social exchanges, which are well entrenched in organisational inter-dependencies. This implies that organisations

Table 6.2   Archetypes of CPT

Type	Manifestation	Benefit
Relationship between companies and political institutions	Affiliations and ownership arrangements	Help in alignment between strategic corporate goals and government incentives
Interpersonal relationships between corporate managers and authorities as politicians, bureaucrats	Reciprocity and long-term relationships	Strengthens company–government exchanges
Individual company connect with political authorities and between corporate managers and political institutions	Business–government interactions where companies 'purchase' information and support of policy makers by providing information, and, financial and political support	Develops trust; helps reduce the marginal transaction cost

Forging New Ties: Tata Motors Ltd.

The move of Tata Motors' Nano plant from Singur in West Bengal to Sanand in Gujarat is a classic case of a government facilitating the corporate sector through a strategic policy decision.

With the model unveiled, production in progress at Singur and commercial sales due by October 2008, Tata Group Chairman Mr Ratan Tata's promise of a ₹1 lakh car was on the verge of being fulfilled. The Singur plant, set up on 1,000 acres of land given by the West Bengal government, and employing around 4,000 employees, had begun trial production by August 2008. However, a major farmer's agitation under the leadership of West Bengal Chief Minister Ms Mamata Banerjee reached a crescendo on 28 August 2008 when the protestors created blockades outside the factory, threatened physical violence and even refused to let workers leave the plant. After talks with the agitating groups failed, the company announced its decision to move the plant out of the state on 3 October 2008.

The same day, Mr Ratan Tata got letters of invitation from four states and a SMS from Gujarat Chief Minister Narendra Modi, with the message, 'Welcome to Gujarat'.[28] By 7 October of the same year, a 1,100-acre plot in Sanand, near Gujarat's financial capital Ahmedabad, was allotted to Tata Motors Ltd. With astonishing speed, in three days, the Gujarat government acquired the land and made it available to Tata Motors Ltd. In the next 14 months, the company was able to construct its plant.

This speedily created alliance between Tata Motors Ltd. and the Gujarat government provided much needed support to the company and helped them to maintain their competitive advantage in being the first in the industry to come out with the ₹1 lakh car.

require resources from the environment which increases dependency on multiple resource providers. For this act they require political support so that hostile forces or elements, if any, in the environment and uncertainties, may be negated. In such situations, CPTs prove to be an important tool in achieving benefits of collaboration and co-optation. The flip side of the co-optation principle is that companies may face the risk of losing organisational autonomy, for political interests are often not in congruence with company agenda. However, the advantages of CPTs far outweigh the costs. The accumulated political capital, yields long lasting results, which can be enjoyed for years to come.

The value of CPTs is much higher in 'politically salient industries, as telecommunications and pharmaceuticals'[29] rather than in consumer electronics or goods. This suggests the importance of CPT in industries with specific characteristics.

Businesses can leverage these relationships by identifying the nature of political engagement. For instance, companies may decide to align corporate political and other non-market strategies as CSR. This would indicate that the two—CSR and CPAs can be jointly employed to strengthen CPT value. Another aspect companies need to cognise with is the presence of similar rival interest groups in societies. An unexpected change in the existing political environment may convert the original political asset into a liability. Additionally, in such situations social performance as CSR initiatives may face hostility from incoming political parties.

The value associated with politically connected companies can be impacted by the structure of political network and exchange mechanisms. Companies with high CPTs possess high bargaining power and relational content. This 'relational rent'[30] becomes the base for further bargaining and appropriation. An unjustified or unequal distribution of this rent may encourage companies to carve strategies through which they devote more time and resources to developing their bargaining powers. Non-state enterprises and smaller companies have a greater value for managerial and government ties than larger companies and state sector peers. Because of the nature and size of business, political ties hold greater value for them. In other words, organisational structure plays a key role in reducing CPT risks in emerging economies.

There are situations where CPTs can also become liabilities. There may be a potential conflict between company shareholders and corporate managers over political connections. Managers may voluntarily develop strong CPTs for personal benefits and incompetent managers may decide to use CPTs to make themselves indispensable. This can exacerbate the initial poor performance. Companies that rely heavily on CPTs become vulnerable to managerial connects and relationships with political actors and institutions, developed and strengthened over time. This indicates that senior managers are important actors in developing and managing CPTs in which relational ties are formed and governed by co-operative norms, mutual forbearance, trust and long-term commitment.

HOW AND WHY DO COMPANIES INDULGE IN CPA?

In political activity men sail a boundless and bottomless sea; there is neither harbor for shelter nor floor for anchorage, neither starting point nor appointed destination.

—MICHAEL OAKESHOTT[31]

CPA is a proactive measure adopted by a company to favourably impact politics and the public policy environment. Politics is an open arena where companies willing to pay the highest bid can secure a fee for their services and ascertain political favour and policy outcome. Democracy and competition between companies and within interest groups are important drivers of policy outcomes.

CPA can be studied at the macro or societal level and micro or company level. It is a well-known fact that public policy processes attempt a compromise, a choice between multiple interest groups and their competing goals. Public choice is a process that involves market-like exchange where both business actors and politicians seek favours or inducements from one another. This has also been referred to as 'rent-seeking'[32] and showcases company efforts in securing competitive advantage by influencing legislators and regulators. Micro or company level perspectives propose attempts by a company to use public policy processes for enhancing legitimacy. 'Corporate political strategies employ an organisation's resources to integrate objectives and to undertake coherent actions directed towards the political, social and legal environment in order to secure either permanent or temporary advantage and influence over other actors in the process.'[33]

Some of the outcomes of CPA relate to public policy while others to performance. There are five different tactics of CPA: 'PAC [Political Action Committees] contributions, advocacy advertising, professional lobbying, lobbying by senior executives and constituency building (organising grassroots feedback from employees, dealers, suppliers).'[34] Constituency building has been found to be the most effective technique of influencing.

Advocacy Advertising Converted to Constituency Building: Tata Global Beverages Ltd.

Tata Global Beverages (formerly Tata Tea) Ltd.'s 'Jaago Re' (wake up) advocacy advertisements were very popular since their launch in 2007 as they highlighted issues that the public was generally apathetic to. Taking this one step ahead, the company launched their website www.jaagore.com as a tool for Indians to bring about change through partnership with activists and organisations. The website has been conceptualised as a community platform where individuals can volunteer for the services of government approved Non-Governmental Organisations (NGOs). Visitors to the website can select from causes as women's empowerment, malnourishment of girl children, violence against women, corruption, education, etc. They can vote in online polls, participate in online discussions and even write articles.[35] Communities on Facebook and Twitter as well as a blog further support the campaign.

According to Mr Vikram Grover, Vice President & Head Marketing—South Asia, Tata Global Beverages Ltd.,

> Very often information and the tools of democracy are not understood well and therefore not utilised. While we at Tata Tea do realise the importance of awakening to issues that the nation is facing, we feel that it is equally important to have easy access to information in order to empower people to make a difference.[36]

The website and ongoing campaigns are a unique initiative by the company to organise grassroots feedback from customers and the community at large—a good example of constituency building.

What are some of the advantages associated with CPA? Companies, by entering into political transactions, are able to protect their economic transactions. It is equally important that politicians and bureaucrats also perceive benefits before they agree to be part of this exchange. Occasionally, CPA becomes a necessity for companies when they need to protect themselves against opportunism of other companies and poor legal systems that do not guarantee control or monitoring rights. Some of the important factors for securing favourable returns from government and society are company objectives, strategies, tactics and adherence to government rules and regulations. Mere statements do not suffice in the political arena; political attention too should be drawn towards them.

As a corporate-government engagement activity, CPA shapes policy in a way favourable to the company. It serves as a complement to governance practices, thus, hedging risk for company investments in the environment and engaging in political activity with the objective of improving company value. The engagement techniques are based on government dependence, company slack, diversification, ownership—foreign and domestic, age, formalised company structure, programme routine, political orientation. To elaborate further on each technique, dependence is contingent on the amount of sale to the government or the cost burden imposed from regulation; higher the slack, greater is the company activity in CPA; foreign vs. domestic ownership based on cultural attributes; the visibility of the company as its age, reputation, experience and credibility; formalised structures that facilitate and bring together professionals and other company resources. Programme routines help in interpreting and responding to environmental cues; and political orientation towards companies and sectors is based on their ability to perform and deliver.

In regulated industries there are direct costs associated with accessing decision makers, understanding their preferences and building trust. When investing time and resources with the policy makers, companies try and secure protection with a political promise concerning policy/policies to be implemented. The agreement focusses on an assurance that the policy will not be reversed or revoked at a time when the company is making an attempt to recover costs or secure a return on capital which is at least equivalent to the cost incurred in building CPA.

Not only companies but politicians also incur transaction costs: by committing to a policy, they are exposed to the electoral cycle and the probable illegitimacy of the political transaction makes them susceptible to risk of political attack. In this company–politician relationship, information provided by the companies should not be opportunistic or biased in favour of the company while giving the appearance of benefiting the competing politicians or bureaucrats. The result of competition among policy providers varies between politicians and bureaucrats. It has been found that a competitive environment among politicians leads to high benefits whereas the same among bureaucrats leads to low benefits.

Perceived success of CPA activities is based on the policy type expectations of the company and the degree of legitimacy. 'Legitimacy is a generalised perception or assumption that the actions of an entity are desirable, proper or appropriate within some socially constructed system of norms, values, beliefs and definitions.'[37] In addition to legitimacy, company reputation or credibility also account for success in CPA activities. Companies with a high reputational quotient are more trusted and information on financial incentives or number of votes promised is viewed as being more credible.

Over time, legislators develop policy reputations that are driven by the political agenda. Companies, central to helping develop these reputations, play an active role in political activities. The importance associated with a political issue helps a company take actions that are indicative of political affiliation. The ensuing strategies, with focus on political issues, accord companies a competitive advantage in the political and economic market.

Proactive versus Reactive CPA

CPA can be defined by two fundamental behaviours: 'buffering and bridging'.[38] Buffering is building on political affiliation by providing information to decision makers on the impact of legislation by contributing through lobbying, helping in political campaigns and other related activity. While buffering is proactive, bridging is reactive and includes activities as tracking regulations and norms to ensure that compliance is in place. Approaches to proactive and reactive CPA can be relational and long term, or transactional and ad-hoc with focus on issues. The end result of the two is the same: to secure political support through an overall 'access strategy',[39] based on providing financial incentives or commitments regarding information, money, votes in the political market. Implementing a CPA is critical as companies need to understand where and at what time they would need political and bureaucratic support.

There is a strong relationship between market strategy and CPA. Organising CPA, be it proactive or reactive, is a process of integrating political strategies with market position. Political strategies both complement and substitute market strategies and integration of the two can yield the best possible result. The market position of a company refers to external opportunities and threats and should be studied in relation to internal strengths and weaknesses of a company and its non-market position. Researchers have found that higher the diversification, greater is the chance of conflict and higher the cost of coordinating political activities.

WHAT ARE PARTNERSHIPS?

There is no peace among equals because equality doesn't exist in this universe. Either one prevails and the other follows, or both negotiate their differences and create a greater partnership.

—Harold J. Duarte-Bernhardt[40]

Beginning 1990s, companies have begun to engage in multiple partnerships with non-profit, non-governmental organisations referred to as social alliances. The concept of PPP where companies form alliances with government or international organisations has today, become the norm. There are both economic and non-economic objectives perceived in these partnerships. More recently, the trend has begun to include cross-sector partnerships with government agencies. This 'collaboration paradigm of the 21st century'[41] has helped solve complex problems as it exceeds the capabilities of any one sector and compliments those of the other. The effectiveness of these PPPs is highest when the strategic objectives of both the government and the company are suitably met and roles aligned to meet the target and address the scope of partnership.

Partnerships can be studied at the micro level (individual interests of companies and public) and are transactional or philanthropic; meso level (groups of actors) that are transactional and macro level (government), which are integrative. Micro partnerships focus on a specific activity and are primarily project-oriented; meso partnerships influence and impact sustainability in a certain sector and macro partnerships define wider issues and address multiple interests.

PPP is 'co-operation of some sort of durability between public and private actors in which they jointly develop products and services and share risks, costs and resources which are connected with these products'.[42] The definition suggests and emphasises co-operation and collaboration, risk sharing and jointly producing a product or service from which both parties benefit. Additionally, PPPs are institutional arrangements between public actors and private corporate houses. They also act as a governance tool, and are an expression of language which encompasses the established procedure in delivering public services. Often these partnerships are viewed synonymously with contracting.

PPPs have two dimensions: the financial and the organisational. Questions which stem from these two dimensions focus on the financial engagements of public and private actors and their organisational entrenchment. Concerning the financial dimension, partnerships help in alleviating global problems as environment and climate change resource. Examples of partnership patterns can be improvement of business environment promoting private participation in infrastructure, collaborating with CSR and base of pyramid business. This is possible only because 70–80 per cent of fund flow from developed to developing countries comes from the private sector.

There are four organisational structures associated with the PPP concept: co-operation for joint production and risk sharing; long term contracts with emphasis on outputs; public policy networks where loose stakeholder relationships are emphasised and, partnership symbolism in civil society and community development is adopted for cultural change and, urban renewal and economic development.

Building Roads through Partnership: PPP for Roads in India

The development of national highways in India is entrusted to the National Highways Authority of India, under a programme called the National Highways Development Project. While phases I and II largely used the engineering, procurement and construction mode, the later phases III–VII used the PPP route. Up to November 2011, 209 PPP projects were awarded.[43] PPP projects are awarded under the Build-Own-Transfer (BOT) model with a toll or annuity feature. Some projects are also awarded under the Operate-Maintain-Transfer (OMT) model. The method for award is through competitive bidding, and private sector participation is increasingly being seen through construction contracts, BOT for specific stretches based on either the lowest annuity or the lowest lump sum payment from the Government or BOT contracts permitting toll collection.[44]

Following a dip in investor interest in public works in the last fiscal year (less than 2,000 km of new road construction contracts against a target of 9,500 km), the government has been considering a shift in the method of financing such projects. It has gradually moved away from the PPP model, where developers fund the construction themselves in exchange for toll collection rights, to a form of contract where it funds part of the road building, taking on more of the associated project risk. The government's plan of investing $1 trillion into infrastructure over five years has come across roadblocks due to red tapism and over-cautious attitude of banks. To overcome this, plans have been formulated to fund 70 per cent of the 9,600 km of road projects aimed for the fiscal year 2013–14.[45] Policy changes have been envisioned to help investment in this sector by enabling developers to start construction without waiting for clearance from forest authorities.

These moves seem to have helped. For example, IL&FS Transportation Networks Ltd., has signed a $300 million (about ₹1,740 crores) contract in April 2013 to build a six-lane highway linking an eastern industrial zone to the nation's coal capital, Dhanbad.

The partnership between the business and the state is interesting for it shares a symbiotic relationship. Both need each other for their sustenance. The corporate sector is a powerhouse of investment, services and also a provider of jobs and incomes. Big business houses also add to the state status. Business houses need the state as a dominant client and partner for creating and maintaining proper work conditions. The moral sentiments required for a market economy are all embedded in the institutional setting over which the state has authority. Over the years, the relationship between the two entities has grown with almost equal distribution of power between the two. However, the relationship between the two is not always happy as is evident in the state-business interlock when corporate directors become advisory members in the state or hold management/ supervisory functions of institutions. Similar is the case when bureaucrats and political actors hold positions in a corporate house. In an ideal situation, the business–government interlocks should realise an exchange of knowledge, information and expertise.

PPPs are also used as a governance tool and provide a significant solution to governance problems. The governance model is determined by the private actors and their methods of conjoining activities. An important question in this structure is that of 'input legitimacy in terms of solving the democratic deficit, accountability and transparency problems of governance beyond the nation-state. Here, inclusion of non-state actors—both firms and non-for-profit sector—is said to increase the legitimacy of international negotiating systems'.[46] It is important to create networks which are all-inclusive rather than exclusive. The all-inclusive arrangement may result in lack of efficiency and reduce effectiveness. If the networks are exclusive there is lesser accountability and transparency. In short, a trade-off between legitimacy and effectiveness is required.

PPPs aid a company to increase its effectiveness in problem solving capacity and improve legitimacy by propelling democratic participation and accountability. Both hierarchical and non-hierarchical forms of steering can be employed. Steering can be accomplished through persuasion and/or by changing perceptual fields and providing a choice of alternatives. For this, learning, arguing and multiple forms of communication are required, which may help in changing the protagonist interest and identity. Hierarchical is reserved for states which possess the capacity to allocate values and enforce rules. Non-hierarchical can be further divided into the for-profit sector, i.e. companies and private interest groups and the not-for-profit sector and NGOs. Bargaining and governing by incentive are two forms of non-hierarchical steering, which also regulate protagonist behaviour by altering the cost–benefit calculation.

Types of PPPs

There are four distinct types of PPPs: co-optation, delegation, co-regulation and self-regulation in the shadow of hierarchy. The co-optation model is the weakest and least problematic form. The arrangement for this partnership is that non-state actors provide knowledge, expertise and legitimacy. In exchange they are able to secure better information and have greater access to resources. Under the second type of PPP, non-state actors are delegated functions as technical standardisation, contracting out of services, etc. This form of delegation covers PPPs in a wide array beginning from weak forms where private players are involved in outsourcing and contracting out to delegation under the ambit of hierarchy. The third type of PPP, co-regulation seems to have gained immense momentum in which non-state actors play an equal role in decision implementation. The main difference between co-optation, delegation and co-regulation model is that in the second and third, the non-state actors possess equal and legitimate powers, which is not the case in the first. The fourth type of PPP, self-regulation, is induced by many international organisations. Under the Indian government and political 'shadow of hierarchy', business actors are forced to accept more stringent privacy measures.

The frequency and significance of PPPs varies according to the types and associated purpose which may be a result of good governance, sustainable development and strengthening of civil society. PPPs are not very frequent in either rule-setting or implementation, as states are reluctant to delegate responsibility and authority to private players in the negotiation system. Concerning rule implementation, a managed compliance perspective serves as a facilitator for PPPs. The preference of private actors to regulate affairs and co-ordinate activities is relevant in situations of market or state failures.

Partnerships have been found to be instrumental in overcoming three kinds of 'failures' arising from unilateral actions taken by companies, government or civil societies: governance failure, limited ability of government to address developmental concerns; market failure, which limits the company ability to be ethical, i.e. awareness that CSR engagement cannot be effectively implemented without involvement of stakeholders and good intention failure, related to non-profit organisations with limited efficiency in idea implementation by co-financing organisations. Based on these dimensions, partnerships between state and corporates can address the policy rationale or the underinvestment problem in social capital, as the investment of neither the state nor the companies in isolation is sufficient.

Tripartite Partnerships

Tripartite partnerships with all three actors, i.e. state, companies and civil society aim at addressing problems resulting from 'institutional void'. Arising from retreating government or weak government structure, this void can be addressed by the tripartite partnerships. The advantage of this partnership is that there can be utilisation of complementary expertise with an opportunity to involve participation from all actors. One of the associated disadvantages is that these specific partnerships are supply-driven

---

PPP for Social Capital: National Skill Development Corporation (NSDC)

NSDC, a PPP, was announced by the Finance Minister in 2008–09. It was specifically set up to facilitate skill development programmes in the unorganised sector. Set up under Section 25 of the Companies Act (1956) with equity of ₹10 crores, the stakes of the government and private sector are 49 per cent and 51 per cent, respectively.[47] The objective of NSDC is to focus on developing skills through funding and incentivising, offering support services and providing momentum for larger scale participation by private players in the process of skill building. Twenty-one different industries as automobile/auto components, electronics hardware, textiles and garments, IT and software to tourism, real estate, banking, insurance and finance have been identified for the same.

NSDC works to bring together skill development initiatives by the Government as Khadi and Village Industries Commission, Ministry of Tribal Affairs, Ministry of Rural Development, Department of Rural Development, Ministry of Communications and Information Technology as well as industry associations as FICCI and CII.

---

and do not cognise local needs. Occasional free-rider behaviour in these partnerships may hinder progress.

These partnerships are integrated and strategic rather than philanthropic in nature implying that they share resources, knowledge and capabilities with objectives of joint and co-opt value creation. Such partnerships strategise operations with a 'we' rather than 'us vs. them' objective. In tripartite partnerships, there is immense clarity about the role division. Companies provide expertise, knowledge and funding; NGOs provide contacts, training, capacity building and local embeddedness and, the government facilitates the activities. In contrast to PPPs the inclusion of non-profit organisations almost always broadens the development focus. In these relationships, development activities are shaped by corporate core expertise. The governmental approach is to build the relationship, study corporate needs and manage operational problems.

Coming Together for an Environmental Cause: MoEF, ArcelorMittal SA and CEE

The Ministry of Environment and Forests (MoEF), ArcelorMittal SA, the global steel giant, and Centre for Environment Education (CEE), the Ahmedabad-headquartered research and development institute came together in a unique tripartite agreement to launch the Paryavaran Mitra (PM) project on 24 July 2010.

Conceptualised in two phases, the first phase involved school children electing an Environment Ambassador for India ('Kaun Banega Bharat Ka Paryavaran Ambassador'). The second phase envisioned creating 200,000 PMs across schools all over India through a process-oriented project which required action-based results. A PM was defined as a student who could demonstrate environmental citizenship and complete change in behaviour and action.

ArcelorMittal SA committed approximately $1.8 million (₹9 crores) over three years, while the Government allocated 10 times as much. The project had well-defined roles for all three participants: MoEF would facilitate contact with the environment and educational departments at the central and state levels and help in smooth functioning along with media exposure and event planning; ArcelorMittal would focus on resource material development and project review and monitoring in addition to financial assistance and, CEE would be the implementer, guiding schools and monitoring their progress.

There were gains for all three partners. For MoEF, the partnership was a practical mode of furthering its goal of preservation, conservation and protection of the environment. ArcelorMittal stood to increase its visibility with the pan-India scale of the project and its association with two major entities working towards environment protection. CEE, which was on the lookout for a viable and sustainable way to scale up its existing model, found a solution in this tripartite agreement.[48]

Level and Nature of Partnerships

Partnerships in terms of cogency and coherence between groups and activities cannot be completely conceptualised, planned and implemented. The general interest in partnership is mostly determined by the government as well as NGOs, who are representatives of stakeholders. It is this which makes the bonding more logical and structured.

What determines the nature of partnerships? Reputation and branding! It has been found that activity level of companies goes up once they see sectoral interest in partnerships, and the link between a company's core activities, individual strategies and engagement sought in the sector. There is a desire to address issues on a larger scale and willingness to take more risks, which is facilitated by the expertise and knowledge of other partners. Identifying potential in the project, the government often connects with the existing activities (mainly, development) of the companies and provides assistance in helping them to expand their scope to other regions and territories, and build links with other initiatives.

The nature of partnership varies with different partners, locations and objectives. Whatever be the nature of this partnership there are common dimensions to the process, which may be labelled as '(a) input; (b) throughput; (c) output; (d) outcome. In addition, partnerships can be evaluated on (e) efficiency and (f) effectiveness'.[49] Input refers to the means essential for carrying out a process, which may be tangible (money) or intangible (knowledge). Individual partners may have personal goals that are determined by societal affiliation or by their ethical code or values. It is important that at the beginning of the relationship partners become aware of types of failure, which may arise in the implementation stage. This sharing of possibility of failures enlarges the scope of partnership, secures the willingness to co-operate and improves the chances of success. Throughput defines the quantity and quality of participants, their roles, the degree at which internal dependencies and competencies are selected and their position as primary and secondary stakeholders. The output refers to the service activities undertaken by the partners. Other criteria for determining the output success are the level at which the project objectives are to be achieved, the sustainability and the exit possibility. The outcome of the partnership process is ascertained by goal fruition.

The success of the tripartite model is determined by the efficiency and the effectiveness of partnership. Efficiency, in this case, is assessed in terms of an added internal value and effectiveness by the impact of individual activities on different partners.

WHAT IS REGULATION AND WHY IS IT NEEDED?

The marvel of all history is the patience with which men and women submit to burdens unnecessarily laid upon them by their governments.

—WILLIAM H. BORAH[50]

Extant literature on government relationships has studied the impact of regulation on market structure and government influence in securing social objectives. It is widely acknowledged that company strategies are 'influenced by the environment/regime they operate in. The regime is broadly defined by a combination of variables capturing industrial structure, nature of technical knowledge and policy environment'.[51] Various frameworks for assessing regulation have been proposed, which impact a company's performance. Strategic, social and economic choices made by a company to improve its financial performance are affected by the extent of regulation in an industry. It is important for companies to deal with regulators and possibly arrive at negotiating outcomes. Companies less skilled in this competency are better off investing their resources in a domain which does not fall directly under regulators.

Regulators often have multiple obligations and face complex political issues. As they represent public interest of customers and shareholders, they must ensure that adequate services at reasonable rates are provided while helping companies maintain their financial stability. The positions adopted by regulators may vary from being extremely friendly to hostile towards the regulated company interests. Friendly actions are those that encourage regulations in favour of company interests, and hostile regulations are those that are far from company interests and may comprise actions as 'delays or refusals to issue operating permits, reductions in regulated rates or the imposition of costly new production standards'.[52] Managing these relationships, particularly in hostile environments, is difficult yet important, as good management is reflected in performance outcomes.

What are the reasons of hostility or constraints in regulators? Primary is the regulatory uncertainty arising from differing interests or relative power/preferences of interest groups. Additionally, political institutions that override negative externalities, market failures, globalisation, economic relationships and international regulations can create doubts in the minds of corporate bodies. Notwithstanding the regulatory uncertainty, companies have the right to seek direct support from regulators, e.g. by lobbying, or exerting influence by targeting legislators and bureaucrats who are responsible for framing regulatory policies. Large companies may decide to lobby individually when there is fear of sensitive information being leaked through trade lobbyists.

Issues related to regulation can be understood by scope, stringency, duration and degree of uncertainty.[53] Scope is the extent and stringency the degree of constraints; duration is the length of time the regulation has been in existence and degree of uncertainty is the change in the regulatory process. The duration often affects strategic choices to improve financial performance. The degree of regulatory uncertainty can be addressed by selecting the appropriate strategy and approach (refer Table 6.3).

While the table below focusses on strategies to be deployed in states of regulatory uncertainty, companies need to consider the key dimensions essential for developing political and governmental strategies in 'regulatory certainty': the choice of strategy—informational, financial, constituency building; level of participation—collective or individual and nature of relationship—relational or transactional. According to the life cycle model,[54] the timing for implementation of political strategies is important. To understand this concept, let us detour and understand the three-phased progression of a policy right from the stage of inception. Policy moves through three phases: public opinion formation, policy formulation, followed by implementation. Company intervention in policy processes is always aimed at securing maximum benefit. For this, it begins influence in the first phase and continues in the second.

Regulated companies operate in an environment that is typical to the industry and impacted by legal and economic constraints. Often regulated companies move out of

Table 6.3 Strategic Response to Regulatory Uncertainty[55]

Strategy	Approach
Avoid	Postponement
	Stabilisation
	Withdrawal
Reduce	Investigation
	Simplification
	Influencing
Adapt	Internal design
	Integration
	Co-operation
	Flexibility
	Imitation
Disregard	Substitution
	No-regret moves
	Business as usual

this environment and diversify so that they are able to earn greater return. In this game of regulation and diversification, organisational and political interests are integrated by corporate houses through environmental scanning, lobbying, political action committees, coalition building and adequacy advertising. Improved interaction with the government by the senior leadership team is often viewed as a defence against regulators. Additionally, it also provides the company a competitive advantage.

Regulations may be encouraged by companies to reduce industry demand and increase cost. Encouragement of such regulations by companies is interesting to consider as rivals can be threatened, market shares rearranged and size of total market reduced. Political power can be a complement and an alternative to market power in determining company performance. Weak companies solicit government protection because of their inability to compete on dimensions as efficiency, innovations and policy.

Company influence over regulators and regulatory agencies is marked by a lack of direct measure of influence and inability. This accounts for differences in the institutional environment with an almost singular focus on strengths of interest groups. Apart from traditional industry-level determinants, there are country and company level determinants which also impact a company's influence processes. Increase in number of competitors in the industry reduces the influence impact. This may be a result of enhanced divergence in regulatory influence-seeking activities. The common role of regulation can be equated to a 'fulcrum upon which contending interests seek to exercise leverage in their pursuit of wealth'.[56] This indicates the power of producer interests over the consumer. For transactions in the political market, political representatives are on the supply side and companies on the demand side.

Who should be the target of influence? Based on the roles and tasks, we can broadly state that for building reputation and deal making, the most important targets are the top echelons of the government; for operational management, influencing the lower levels of the government satisfies the objective; and, for multinationals, the ministry or department in charge of a specific industry should be nurtured and cultivated.

Attempting to Influence Regulation: Private Power Generators in India

In August 2013, the Association of Power Producers wrote to the Finance Minister with a demand to reconsider the proposed policy of purchasing domestically produced power equipment labelling such a policy 'retrograde' and 'anti-competitive'.[57]

This policy of mandatory domestic procurement of equipment, for ultra-mega power projects, has been proposed by the Ministry of Heavy Industries and Public Enterprises.[58] One reason cited for this policy is the largely underutilised new capacity by Indian power equipment makers as Larsen & Toubro Ltd., Thermax Ltd. and BGR Energy Systems Ltd., which may lead them to rake up losses of over ₹1,000 crores a year.[59]

According to Mr Ashok Khurana, director general of the Association of Power Producers, such a move, though profitable for equipment manufacturers, would raise the project cost for power generators and lead to higher electricity tariffs, directly affecting their sales.

CONCLUSION

The business of government is to keep the government out of business—that is, unless business needs government aid.

—Will Rogers[60]

In summary, businesses are interested in creating/maintaining interactions with three arms of the government: the policy makers (legislative), the executives (bureaucrats) and the regulatory bodies. Corporate interactions with policy makers with a view to influencing policies are termed lobbying. The affiliations with the executive and regulatory bodies may be in the form of CPA or CPTs. When the government and the corporate come together to achieve common aims, it is a partnership. Collectively or singly, these myriad relations with the government give a company a comparative advantage which ultimately helps build corporate reputation (refer Fig. 6.2).

Company influence 'on governmental decision making is measured by their reported influence on new national laws, rules, regulations or decrees that could have a substantial

Figure 6.2   Using Government Relations to Build Corporate Reputation

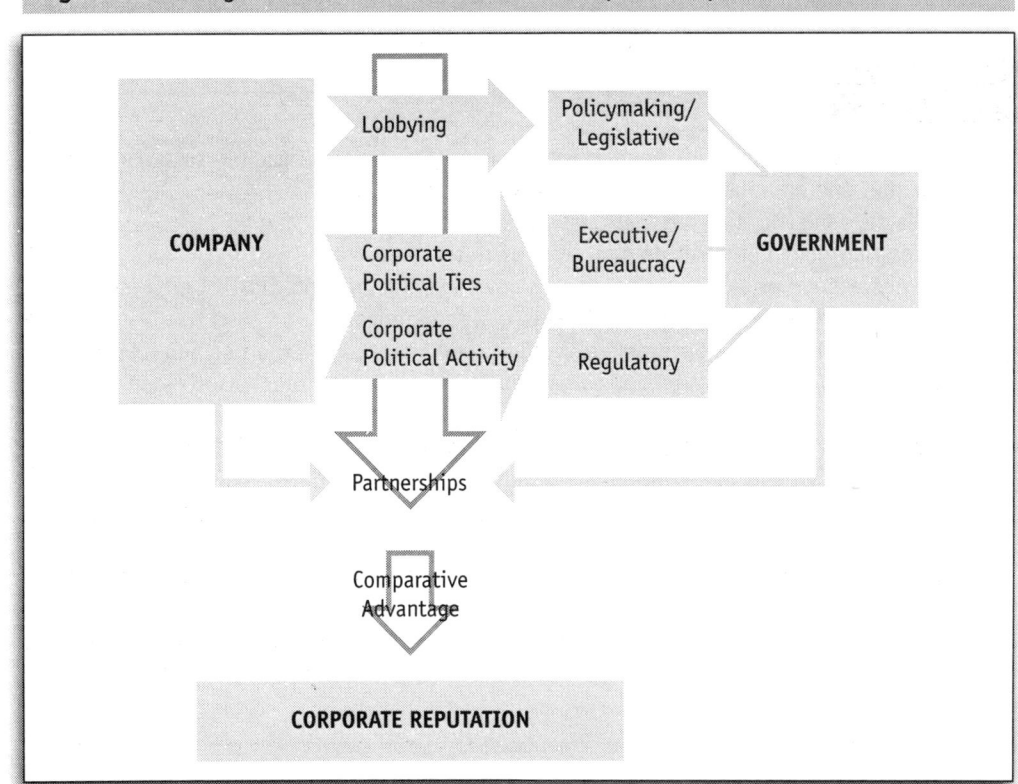

impact on their business across four distinct government entities: the executive, legislative and ministerial branches and regulatory agencies'.[61]

The question of why would a company try and influence the government, legislative and ministerial branches and regulatory bodies merits consideration. To reiterate, partnering with the government helps a company establish credibility in domestic and international markets. This indicates higher trust in their products and services, increases sales and overall impacts their bottom line. Being able to influence policy decisions in their favour enables companies to perform in conducive environments, which is again reflected in their growth and performance.

While what we have just stated is an ideal situation, there is much to be done at the company level to build reputation with the government. Some strategies which can be followed for a positive outcome are:

- Provide market information, financial support and votes
- Influence directly or indirectly through lobbying
- Build affiliations with public authorities and political institutions
- Enter into political transactions to protect economic transactions
- Invest time and resources with policy makers
- Develop products and services jointly with the government and share risks, costs and resources

Key Points

- Governmental intervention, be it positive or negative, is critical for sustenance of companies and building long lasting comparative advantage.
- Almost all domestic and international business activities are shaped by government policies and profit optimisation strategies of companies.
- Three distinct activities are associated with governmental influence: market intervention, export promotion and funding investments in a foreign market.
- Companies influence the government through their knowledge, expertise and relational skills. Government depends on companies for providing market information essential for making good policies and decisions.
- Companies, to integrate their market and non-market activities, use direct lobbying, grassroots activities and provide financial support to public office candidates.
- Lobbying refers to the efforts made by companies to influence the government either directly or indirectly.
- Lobbying is an informative sign to policy makers about the exact market and non-market situation.
- Lobbying is used as a form of market exchange of political favours where the company exchanges market information, provides financial support and votes in favour of political benevolence.

- Companies adopt one of the following three lobbying strategies: bear hug, astroturfing and self-regulation.
- Corporate Political Ties (CPT) are connects between companies and public authorities.
- Companies with high CPTs possess high bargaining power and relational content. This 'relational rent' becomes the base for further bargaining and appropriation.
- Corporate Political Activity (CPA) has been defined as proactive measures adopted by a company to favourably impact politics and the public policy environment.
- CPA can be studied at the macro or societal level and micro or company level perspective.
- Situations in which both business actors and politicians seek favours or inducements from one another is referred to as 'rent-seeking'.
- Public–Private Partnership (PPP) is a co-operation between public and private actors in which they jointly develop products and services and share risks, costs and resources which are connected with these products.
- The partnership between the business and the state shares a symbiotic relationship. Both need each other for their sustenance.
- There are four distinct types of PPPs: co-optation, delegation, co-regulation and self-regulation in the shadow of hierarchy.
- Tripartite partnerships with all three actors, i.e. state, companies and civil society aim at addressing problems resulting from 'institutional void'.
- Common dimensions to the partnership process are input, throughput, output and outcome.
- Four factors address issues related to regulation: scope, stringency, duration and degree of uncertainty.
- Strategic choices made by a company to improve its financial performance are affected by the extent of regulation in an industry.
- The positions adopted by regulators may vary from being extremely friendly to hostile towards the regulated company interests.
- Strategic responses to regulatory uncertainty are: avoid, reduce, adapt, disregard.
- Key dimensions essential for developing political and governmental strategies in 'regulatory certainty' are: the choice of strategy, level of participation and nature of relationship.
- Corporate influence of regulators should be based on task objectives and roles of regulators.

END NOTES

1. Government quotes, website http://www.searchquotes.com/search/Government_Relations34/ (accessed 30 August 2013).
2. Narendra Modi quotes, website http://blogs.reuters.com/india/2013/07/12/quote-unquote-narendra-modi/ (accessed 30 August 2013).
3. 'Plan panel to work on note for strengthening PPP regime', website http://www.livemint.com/Politics/Tq12JPEKLHFAMV2QU3drFM/Plan-panel-to-work-on-note-for-strengthening-PPP-regime.html (accessed 30 August 2013).

4. 'Plan panel to work on note for strengthening PPP regime', website http://www.livemint.com/Politics/ Tq12JPEKLHFAMV2QU3drFM/Plan-panel-to-work-on-note-for-strengthening-PPP-regime.html (accessed 30 August 2013).

5. D. J. Wood, *Strategic Uses of Public Policy: Business and Government in the Progressive Era.* Boston: Pitman Publishing Co. (1986).

6. M. D. Reagan, *Regulation: The Politics of Policy.* Boston: Little, Brown & Company (1987).

7. R. A. Harris, 'Politicized management: The changing face of business in American politics', in R. A. Harris and S. M. Milkis (eds), *Remaking American Politics* (pp. 261–285). San Francisco: West View Press (1989), p. 262.

8. D. Schuler and K. Rehbein, 'The filtering role of the firm in corporate political involvement', *Business & Society* (1997), 36(2), 116–139.

9. B. Shaffer and A. J. Hillman, 'The development of business-government strategies by diversified firms', *Strategic Management Journal* (2000), 21(2), 175–190.

10. Government relations quotes, website http://www.searchquotes.com/search/Government_Relations/4/ (accessed 30 August 2013).

11. A. O. Krueger, 'Import substitution versus export promotion', *Finance & Development* (1985), 20(2) 20–23, p. 20.

12. Lobbying quotes, website http://www.hillwatch.com/PPRC/Quotes/Lobbying.aspx (accessed 30 August 2013).

13. D. P. Baron, 'Integrated strategy: Market and nonmarket components', *California Management Review* (1995b), 37(2), 47–65.

14. S. Mukherjee, 'Monsanto in India: A success coexisting with controversies', *Business Standard* (12 August 2012), website http://www.business-standard.com/article/companies/monsanto-in-india-a-success-coexisting-with-controversies-112081200033_1.html (accessed 30 August 2013).

15. B. Adelman, 'WikiLeaks: More evidence of Monsanto's bullying and influence-buying', *The New American* (15 January 2012), website http://www.thenewamerican.com/usnews/politics/item/10049-wikileaks-more-evidence-of-monsantos-bullying-and-influence-buying (accessed 30 August 2013).

16. 'India: The suicide belt', website http://www.combat-monsanto.co.uk/spip.php?article549 (accessed 30 August 2013).

17. 'Indian government sues Monsanto over GM eggplant', website http://www.infowars.com/indian-government-sues-monsanto-over-gm-eggplant/ (accessed 30 August 2013).

18. 'Gujarat decides against distributing Monsanto maize seeds to farmers', *The Times of India*, website http:// articles.timesofindia.indiatimes.com/2012-04-27/vadodara/31421263_1_maize-seeds-monsanto-prabal (accessed 30 August 2013).

19. '19th and 20th Century quotes on lobbying & rent-seeking', website http://www.intellectualtakeout. org/content/19th-and-20th-century-quotes-lobbying-rent-seeking (accessed 30 August 2013).

20. B. L. Maux, 'Governmental behaviour in representative democracy: A synthesis of the theoretical literature', *Public Choice* (2009), 141(3/4), 447–465, p. 457.

21. Ibid.

22. T. P. Lyon and J. W. Maxwell, 'Astroturf: Interest group lobbying and corporate strategy', *Journal of Economics and Management Strategy* (2004), 13(4), 561–597, p. 561.

23. Ibid.

24. M. Miller, 'Make 150,000% today! Looking for a great return on investment? Hire a lobbyist', *Fortune* (February 2006), p. 153.

25. 'NASSCOM announces analytics special interest group to build India as the global hub for analytics', *Information Week*, website http://www.informationweek.in/services/13-06-27/nasscom_announces_analytics_special_interest_group_to_build_india_as_the_global_hub_for_analytics.aspx (accessed 30 August 2013).

26. D. B. Truman, *The Governmental Process.* New York: Alfred A. Knopf (1955), p. 264.

27. Government quotes, website http://www.woopidoo.com/business_quotes/government-quotes. htm#jSChsAs61xobrx71.99 (accessed 30 August 2013).

28. 'MoC: The Nano's journey from Singur to Sanand', website http://ibnlive.in.com/news/moc-the-nanos-journey-from-singur-to-sanand/167200-3.html (accessed 30 August 2013).

29. P. Sun, K. Mellahi and M. Wright, 'The contingent value of corporate political ties', *The Academy of Management Perspectives* (2012), 26(3), 68–82, p. 72.

30. Ibid., p. 77.

31. Political activity quotes, website http://www.searchquotes.com/search/political+activity/ (accessed 30 August 2013).

32. B. Shaffer, 'Firm-level responses to government regulation: Theoretical and research approaches', *Journal of Management* (1995), 21(3), 495–514, p. 500.

33. J. F. Mahon, 'Corporate political strategy', *Business in the Contemporary World* (1989), 2(1), 50–62, p. 51.

34. A. J. Hillman, G. D. Keim and D. Schuler, 'Corporate political activity: A review and research agenda', *Journal of Management* (2004), 30(6), 837–857, p. 849.

35. Shweta, 'Case study – Jaago Re Tata Tea', website http://www.webchutney.org/work/case-study-jaago-re-tata-tea/ (accessed 30 August 2013).

36. 'Tata Tea's Jaago Re site inspires people to make a difference', website http://www.mxmindia.com/2012/11/tata-teas-jaago-re-website-empowers-people-to-make-a-diff/ (accessed 30 August 2013).

37. M. C. Suchman, 'Managing legitimacy: Strategic and institutional approaches', *Academy of Management Review* (1995), 20(3), 571–610, p. 574.

38. A. J. Hillman, G. D. Keim and D. Schuler, 'Corporate political activity: A review and research agenda', *Journal of Management* (2004), 30(6), 837–857, p. 844.

39. Ibid., p. 845.

40. Public–private partnership quotes, website http://www.searchquotes.com/search/Public_Private_Partnership/1/ (accessed 30 August 2013).

41. J. E. Austin, 'Principles for partnership', *Leader to Leader* (2000), 18(Fall), 44–50, p. 44.

42. H. van Ham and J. Koppenjan, 'Building public-private partnerships: Assessing and managing risks in port development', *Public Management Review* (2001), 4(1), 593–616, p. 598.

43. 'The road ahead: Highways PPP in India', PWC report, website http://www.pwc.in/en_IN/in/assets/pdfs/publications-2012/the-road-ahead-highways-ppp.pdf (accessed 30 August 2013), p. 10–14.

44. Roads, website http://pppinindia.com/opportunities-roads.php (accessed 30 August 2013).

45. 'What it's taking to get new roads built in India', *NDTV*, website http://www.ndtv.com/article/india/what-it-s-taking-to-get-new-roads-built-in-india-380868 (accessed 30 August 2013).

46. T. A. Borzel and T. Risse, 'Public-private partnerships: Effective and legitimate tools of international governance?', in E. Grande and L. W. Pauly (eds), *Complex Sovereignty. Reconstituting Political Authority in the Twenty-First Century* (pp. 95–216). Toronto: University of Toronto Press (2005), p. 209.

47. 'All about NSDC', website http://www.nsdcindia.org/faq/about-nsdc.aspx#ac (accessed 30 August 2013).

48. A. Kaul and V. Chaudhri, 'ArcelorMittal in India: A partnership model for corporate responsibility', Unpublished Case, Indian Institute of Management, Ahmedabad.

49. A. Kolk, R. van Tulder and E. Kostwinder, 'Business and partnerships for development', *European Management Journal* (2008), 26(4), 262–273, p. 271.

50. Government quotes, website http://www.hillwatch.com/PPRC/Quotes/Government.aspx (accessed 30 August 2013).

51. R. Basant, 'Corporate response to economic reforms', *Economic and Political Weekly* (2000), 35(10), 813–822, p. 813.

52. G. L. F. Holburn and R. G. Vanden Bergh, 'Making friends in hostile environments: Political strategy in regulated industries', *The Academy of Management Review* (2008), 33(2), 521–540, p. 521.

53. K. Cook, S. M. Shortell, D. A. Conrad and M. A. Morrisey, 'A theory of organizational response to regulation: The case of hospitals', *The Academy of Management Review* (1983), 8(2), 193–205.

54. R. A. Buchholz, *The Essentials of Public Policy for Management* (2nd ed.). Englewood Cliffs, NJ: Prentice-Hall (1990).

55. C. Engau and V. H. Hoffmann, 'Corporate response strategies to regulatory uncertainty: Evidence from uncertainty about post-Kyoto regulation', *Policy Sciences* (2011), 44(1), 53–80.

56. S. Peltzman, 'Toward a more general theory of regulation', *The Journal of Law and Economics* (1976), 19(2), 211–240, p. 212.

57. R. Prasad, 'Power companies oppose government plans to make domestic gear sourcing mandatory', *The Economic Times*, website http://economictimes.indiatimes.com/news/news-by-industry/energy/power/power-companies-oppose-govt-plans-to-make-domestic-gear-sourcing-mandatory/articleshow/21925908.cms (accessed 30 August 2013).

58. 'Private power companies oppose mandatory domestic equipment sourcing', *The Economic Times*, website http://economictimes.indiatimes.com/news/news-by-industry/energy/power/private-power-companies-oppose-mandatory-domestic-equipment-sourcing/articleshow/21913371.cms (accessed 30 August 2013).

59. R. Prasad, 'Power companies oppose govt plans to make domestic gear sourcing mandatory', *The Economic Times*, website http://economictimes.indiatimes.com/news/news-by-industry/energy/power/power-companies-oppose-govt-plans-to-make-domestic-gear-sourcing-mandatory/articleshow/21925908.cms (accessed 30 August 2013).

60. Government quotes, website http://www.searchquotes.com/search/Government_Relations/34/ (accessed 30 August 2013).

61. J. T. Macher, J. W. Mayo and M. Schiffer, 'The influence of firms on government', *The B.E. Journal of Economic Analysis & Policy* (2011), 11(1), 1–25, p. 13.

Managing
Corporate Reputation

7

Unleashing the Potential of Social Responsibility for Reputational Gain: Managing Social Impact

In terms of power and influence you can forget about the church, forget politics. There is no more powerful institution in society than business.... The business of business should not be about money, it should be about responsibility. It should be about public good, not private greed.

—ANITA RODDICK[1]

Objectives:

- Understand the concept of Corporate Social Responsibility (CSR)
- Examine CSR as a strategic imperative for higher firm performance
- Analyse the relationship between societal investment and outcome
- Identify appropriate and effective communication strategies
- Assess the link between CSR and organisational reputation

INTRODUCTION

Corporate social responsibility is a hard-edged business decision. Not because it is a nice thing to do or because people are forcing us to do it ... because it is good for our business.

—NIALL FITZERALD[2]

Key Words

- Community
- Corporate social responsibility
- Discretionary
- Economic
- Environmental stewardship
- Ethical
- Leadership
- Legal
- People
- Planet

- Profits
- Reluctant volunteerism
- Reputational quotient
- Return On Investment (ROI)
- Shared value
- Societal investment
- Stakeholders
- Sustainability
- Triple bottom line

Companies, for years, have been spending a certain amount of their profits on charitable causes. While some refer to it as 'rejuvenating neighbourhoods', others consider it a strategic management tool to address and manage internal stakeholders and environment challenges. Multiple names have been assigned to this strategy as, 'Corporate Social Responsibility' (CSR), 'corporate social performance', 'corporate social responsiveness', 'sustainability measures/initiatives/development/entrepreneurship', 'triple bottom line', 'corporate citizenship' and 'environmental stewardship'.

Just as there is no one way of addressing CSR, there is no definite or specific formula for defining, conceptualising and implementing it. What is, however, definite is that India's

CSR in India

In India, debates on CSR, what is and what should constitute CSR and 'voluntary spend' have gained momentum and moved into the Parliament. The Companies Bill (2009), which was reintroduced in Parliament after the lapse of the 2008 Bill (with the dissolution of the 14th Lok Sabha), had a voluntary CSR clause. The Central Government reintroduced it in the Parliament in December 2011,[3] after which it was sent to the Parliamentary Standing Committee on Finance, chaired by former Finance Minister Mr Yashwant Sinha. In its June 2012 report, the Committee recommended that companies with net worth more than ₹500 crores or those with an annual turnover of more than ₹1,000 crores must set aside 2 per cent of their average net profits of three years for CSR. It also recommended creating a centralised fund where companies that have not utilised the ear-marked funds for CSR can deposit and utilise them for future schemes.

In its proposal to approve amendments to the Companies Bill (2011) in October 2012, the Cabinet accepted that the spending on CSR would be mandatory, preference would have to be given to local areas where the company operates for such spending, and an explanation would be required if the companies do not spend the required 2 per cent of their net profits on CSR.[4]

Playing its part in encouraging CSR disclosure, Securities and Exchange Board of India (SEBI), in early August 2012, mandated that Business Responsibility Reports be included in the annual reports of the top 100 listed entities [in terms of market capitalisation at the Bombay Stock Exchange (BSE) and National Stock Exchange (NSE)]. Voluntary disclosure for other listed companies was suggested, but not mandated. In response to the suggestion of mandatory disclosure by listed companies, the Ministry of Corporate Affairs categorically stated that, 'India will be the first country to include provisions on CSR in its Company Law'.[5]

'private giving' levels, at between 0.3 and 0.4 per cent of Gross Domestic Product (GDP), though not comparable to developed countries as the US and the UK,[6] are some of the highest among developing countries as China and Brazil.

Researchers, however, are quick to point out that donating money and other corporate resources to social causes is corporate philanthropy, not CSR. CSR encompasses legal compliance in letter and spirit; avoiding or alleviating any form of economic, social or environmental damage caused in the course of company operations and attempting to achieve sustainable development of natural resources.[7] Another viewpoint outlines three types of CSR: ethical, which is fulfilment of a company's economic, legal and ethical responsibilities; altruistic, which is satisfaction of philanthropic responsibilities for public welfare and strategic, which refers to community service initiatives that also help the company achieve strategic goals.[8] Seen from this perspective, while philanthropy is a step ahead of basic moral responsibilities of a company, it is much narrower in scope than CSR, which can be instrumental in achieving strategic goals.

In a report published in 2011, Bain and Company identified some of the challenges associated with CSR as:

- Lack of accountability and transparency
- Low awareness of channels for routing money
- Unfriendly tax laws for donations
- Influence of peers in donation amounts
- Requirements of capital for own business and focus on wealth creation[9]

In spite of challenges, corporate spend on CSR has increased partly due to governmental pressure and partly due to environment hazards which may cause damage to the company, or the stakeholders. If the company has a proven track record of community engagement and partnership, the public is willing to forgive and forget and provide an opportunity to the company to begin afresh.

Companies have devised ways of 'giving back to society' and community. Undoubtedly, the motives, principles, actions and outcomes become governing factors for CSR implementation. For instance, some companies have been driven by their leadership vision and initiatives, as seen in the case of Infosys Ltd. (Mr Narayana Murthy and Mrs Sudha Murthy), Wipro Ltd. (Mr Azim Premji), Aditya Birla Group (Mrs Rajashree Birla), etc. and have come to be recognised as socially responsible organisations. Some companies have demonstrated responsible leadership through building and enhancing stakeholder engagement by initiating company-driven programmes (e.g. IBM). Another category in which some of the large corporate houses (e.g. Tata Group and ITC Ltd.) fall, are driven by the philosophy of creating shared value. The guiding post is the desire to do something for the benefit of stakeholders in the value chain without losing sight of profits.

What are the benefits associated with CSR? How will it help a company? These are questions often asked by students and corporate executives alike. CSR helps companies enhance their reputational capital and build stakeholder and societal appreciation. With growth in economy and an increasingly competitive landscape, all companies are under threat of reputational loss. Increase in this asset, intangible though it is, proves to be a shield against unexpected calamities in years to come. CSR initiatives, when aligned with the corporate strategy and leadership vision, can boost and resurrect inadvertent loss of reputation. Small wonder then that one of the major objectives of large corporate houses is to protect themselves by pursuing activities that connects them to their immediate communities and provide them with the 'license to operate'.[10]

When and how did CSR become a signature statement has been debated across academic circles. The concept of CSR has been in existence since 1800s, though at times it was referred to as 'corporate philanthropy'. With passage of time, the word corporate was replaced by 'strategic' and it became a planned activity designed to achieve business objectives and realise corporate goals.[11] An interesting view was that stirrings in the global economy following industrial revolution, provided fertile ground for germination of CSR,[12] which evolved from the term 'philanthropy'. In due course of time, globalisation and 'governance gaps' in corporate management led to the emergence of our current understanding of CSR as a blend of performance, transparency and societal concerns, creating an organic link between business and society. This concept of CSR, though still nebulous, can be linked to an assessment of situational demands and stakeholder expectations.

In this chapter, we discuss the important question 'Why CSR?' and how it can help build the reputation of a company. To understand this, we analyse CSR as a concept, a notion; make a business case for CSR; study CSR influencers; appreciate CSR as a strategic imperative; develop skills for communicating CSR and identify tools for CSR communication.

WHY CSR?

We know that the profitable growth of our company depends on the economic, environmental, and social sustainability of our communities across the world. And we know it is in our best interests to contribute to the sustainability of those communities.

—Travis Engen[13]

Globally, there has been a steep incline in number of companies engaged in CSR activities. Participation of Indian companies in similar societal investments, according to researchers, is justifiably sound. Being the fourth largest economy in the world (on the basis of purchasing power parity exchange rates) and considered as one of the world's fastest-growing economies with a historical approach to social responsibility and a cultural ethos of nurturing and sharing,[14] the focus is well-timed. Additionally, increasing number of natural calamities, organisational lapses and economic blunders followed by societal misgivings create reputational risk. Companies attempt to anticipate such situations and plan strategically to abet face-loss. CSR is one such strategic tool, which can enhance reputation and provide both financial as well as non-financial benefits.

When we discuss the concept of CSR, there are some questions which immediately stem to the mind: 'Socially responsible to whom?', 'Socially responsive about what?', 'Social performance judged by whom and what standards?'[15] The same have also been raised by researchers and companies across the globe are still grappling to find answers to these questions. Failure to arrive at a satisfactory response to these questions has not deterred companies from rolling out CSR initiatives, either voluntarily or in response to calls by governmental, non-governmental organisations and market pressures ('reluctant' volunteerism), to contribute part of their 'wealth' to social and environmental causes. It may be difficult to differentiate between companies that practise CSR voluntarily and those that are 'reluctant' practitioners, as differences in intent are based on economic sustainability, market pressures on and social expectations from the company. However, the result in both cases is the same—a substantial growth in societal capital.

WHAT IS CSR?

CSR …means something, but not always the same thing, to everybody. To some, it conveys the idea of legal responsibility or liability; to others, it means socially responsible behaviour in an ethical sense; to still others, the meaning transmitted is that of 'responsible for', in a causal mode; many simply equate it with a charitable contribution; some take it to mean socially conscious…

—Dow Votaw[16]

Conceptualising and implementing CSR initiatives is based on stakeholder responses and influences. In recent years, companies have begun to expand their purview to societal responsibility, which provides them with the much needed licence to operate. Hence, many of the emergent questions in CSR scholarship focus on 'profit sharing' and 'engagement' with stakeholders and communities and inherent advantages and disadvantages. Should companies indulge in profit-sacrificing activities? Can these activities be continued on a sustainable basis? What are the expectations of stakeholders? To what extent should companies umbrella societal concerns and demands? Companies have been toying with these questions to achieve credence and acceptance in the market.

Extant literature on CSR has provided an answer to many of these questions and has sought to generate definitions which address issues as: What is social responsibility? What should be the dimensions projected by the company? For instance, '… social responsibility of business encompasses the economic, legal, ethical and discretionary expectations that society has of organisations at a given point of time'.[17] A somewhat narrower definition refers to CSR as 'societal expectations of corporate behaviour; a behaviour that is alleged by a stakeholder to be expected by society or morally required and is therefore justifiably demanded of business'.[18]

The approach to CSR can be understood better using the analogy of the heart and the soul. While social endeavours with an ethical credo and values for serving society (soul) are important, they must also be linked to and consistent with the objectives of earning profits (heart)[19] for 'the social responsibility of business is to increase its profits'.[20] Companies are waking up to the fact that while generating profits is essential for the sustenance of the company, a framework of 'shared values' can be created for earning profits and doing social good. 'There is one and only one social responsibility of business—to use its resources and engage in activities designed to increase its profits so long as it stays within the rules of the game …'[21]

The Purpose of Profit: Tata Group

The Tata Group, which has more than a century of experience in community initiatives, believes that the purpose of profit is community empowerment. According to Mr Anant G. Nadkarni, VP, Group corporate sustainability,

> Just referring to the number of wells dug up by a company as part of its community engagement programme does not mean much. But, when a company empowers a community by providing access to water resources, it tells an important story. That is the purpose of profit.[22]

Tata Group companies are encouraged to 'give a purchase order, not a charity cheque'.[23] With this philosophy in mind, Tata Teleservices (Maharashtra) Ltd. has launched its 'Amba' initiative, through which it directs office operations tasks to an NGO caring for mentally challenged children. In the same vein, Titan Industries Ltd. has set up 'Myrada', an NGO that trains differently-abled persons and assists them in obtaining employment.

While the focus on 'profits' is justified, other levels for CSR can be listed as 'compliance', 'caring', being 'synergistic' and 'holistic', as listed in Table 7.1.

Table 7.1 Levels of CSR[24]

Level	Interpretation	Motivation
Compliance-driven CSR	Welfare measures based on regulations stipulated by authorities	CSR is considered to be an obligation, and 'appropriate behaviour'
Profit-driven CSR	Social, ethical and environmental issues are integrated into business, as long as the activities contribute to profits	CSR is promoted if profitable
Caring CSR	Maintaining balance between economic, social and ecological issues by going further than mandatory or profit-motivated activities	Caring for people, society and environment is considered important
Synergistic CSR	Balanced solution for all concerned stakeholders	Sustainability in business and society
Holistic CSR	Integrated approach to CSR embedded in the core of organisational structure, culture, values and processes	Sustainability is imperative because of interdependence

Building on the concept of CSR, in 2007, Dr Manmohan Singh, Prime Minister of India, urged corporate India to work towards inclusive growth and a more humane society by presenting his 'Ten Point Social Charter'.[25] Beginning with the need to develop respect for workers and make efforts towards their welfare, he reinforced the need for defining CSR within the very philosophy of the company, and partnering with communities and regions in enhancing skills, developing environment-friendly technologies and promoting innovation.

Can we, then, consider investment in employee and worker welfare as the first step in the mandate for building a business case for CSR?

CAN A BUSINESS CASE BE MADE FOR CSR?

Business of business is business.

—MILTON FRIEDMAN[26]

Companies have been toying with the idea of making a business case for CSR which would mean benefits or returns on investments made. The company can thus 'do well by doing good'.[27] Alternately, the business case proposed should create value for the company in terms of enhanced performance, risk mitigation and societal consent.

Identifying specific risks and assessing their impact on the business and stakeholders, well in advance, is a prudent course of action, and is being adopted by companies to abet and mitigate risk[28] and to gain competitive advantage. Let us take the example of ITC Ltd., a company with a high dependence on agricultural inputs. ITC Ltd. faces a major risk from climate change and global warming which can disrupt agricultural patterns and yields. Such effects can impact the company as well as severely cripple farmers who are its suppliers. Additionally, the existence of two manufacturing plants in coastal areas exposes ITC Ltd. to the physical risks of climate change including destruction, and the less severe but equally draining, disruption in road and rail traffic. To mitigate these, ITC Ltd. has adopted a three-pronged strategy that:

- Identifies and evaluates climate-change risks for each business
- Reduces the impact of these risks on the company's processes, products and services
- Creates livelihood by promoting sustainable agricultural practices

It has also ensured protection of its assets in the coastal areas in anticipation of increased severity of storms and cyclones. This well-planned strategy has ensured that ITC Ltd. is prepared to meet contingencies and protect itself from threats to its reputational capital as well as become known as an organisation sensitive to the needs of communities and environment.

CSR helps in mitigating risk of damage in the long run. Issues as management of hazardous waste, emission control, effluent treatment and workplace safety can generate negativity or create an adverse image. In such situations, the stakeholders are of prime importance and viewed as part of the environment that requires control and good management. Ability to address stakeholder concerns, develop good CSR strategies and follow auditing practices lowers the risk and builds stakeholder confidence. Social investments, supported by core competencies have, over the years, helped companies generate sustainable performance and create 'shared value'. Another strategy of gaining an edge over competing market pressures is adapting to the external environment through appropriate allocation and direction of resources based on perceived demands of the stakeholders.

Creating Shared Value: Cairn India Ltd.

Cairn India Ltd., which is credited with about 20 per cent of India's oil production, has a large base of operations in the western Indian state of Rajasthan. It uses engagement processes to identify environmental, social and economic issues that are important to its local stakeholders, and bases its CSR initiatives on these.

For example, when farmers were worried about the effects of Cairn's pipelines on soil and farming, it developed the 'Cairn Farmer SMS Programme' in partnership with Reuters to reach out to 10,000 farmer families located along their 600-km long heated pipeline. This programme provided farmers with access to mobile phone technology, bringing huge savings in communications for them, as well as benefited the company in the form of timely information about issues as pipeline sabotage, leaks or maintenance problems. Additionally, farmers could also get information about prevalent market crop prices on their mobile phones, enabling them to make informed decisions while selling their produce.[29]

Sustainable opportunities for the company are created through a synergistic approach that aligns corporate philosophy with strategy for operations. An illustration is the Triple Bottom Line which focusses on people, planet and profits. Without losing sight of the reason for business, viz. performance/profits, focussing on stakeholders and environment creates a business case for CSR initiatives. A rethinking of the relationship between business objectives and societal concerns completes the conceptual loop, linking CSR (initiation and advocacy) to societal legitimacy.

Indian Maharatnas (Great Gems) Toeing the Triple Bottom Line

A September 2011 report by Deloitte and the Indian Chamber of Commerce revealed that Indian public sector companies are no longer strangers to the concept of triple bottom line. Indian Oil Corporation Ltd. (IOCL), Oil and Natural Gas Corporation (ONGC), Steel Authority of India Ltd. (SAIL) and National Thermal Power Corporation (NTPC) are some of the 'Maharatna' (great gem) companies that are pursuing the Triple Bottom Line.

For example, NTPC has taken major strides in education initiatives as part of its 'People' focus—ranging from its 48 schools benefiting 40,000 students, its 50 per cent subsidised coaching classes for students aiming for higher studies in engineering and medicine, its training programme for teachers and workshops for principals at Indian Institute of Management, Ahmedabad, and its introduction of the concept of inclusive education where children with special needs study alongside other children. In terms of its 'Planet' focus, NTPC has established the Centre for Power Efficiency & Environmental Protection (CenPEEP) in collaboration with United States Agency for International Development (USAID) to reduce greenhouse gas emissions, set up the Ash Utilisation Unit and has undertaken afforestation programmes in and around its projects in a concerted bid to counter the growing ecological threat. Its 'Profit' is right on track, by virtue of it being India's largest power producing company and Asia's second largest electricity generating company.[30]

Does CSR impact corporate financial performance and vice versa? Effects have been postulated, though not ascertained. Compelling evidence indicates that social responsibility has a positive relationship with an organisation's stock market performance. Social issues along with business factors lead to long-term benefits and better-quality relationships with significant stakeholders as banks, investors and government agencies.

A contrary view representing a negative correlation between CSR and company performance emphasises that companies high on CSR may have a disadvantage economically, when compared to less socially responsible organisations. Costs related to employee welfare programmes, charity, community development and establishing 'green' policies impact financial resources. Companies, hence, face a reduction in profits, firm value and shareholder returns.

While researchers have documented a negative correlation, studies in favour of positive and direct link between CSR and corporate performance are, by far, more and varied.

WHO ARE THE CSR INFLUENCERS?

> *Business social responsibility should not be coerced; it is a voluntary decision that the entrepreneurial leadership of every company must make on its own.*
>
> —JOHN MACKEY[31]

CSR scholarship discusses influencers and actors for implementing social investments at the institutional, organisational and individual levels.[32] The same can be studied at the level of initiatives and outcomes (business or societal benefits).

At the institutional level, stakeholders, society and regulative measures govern the nature of these investments. The stakeholders comprise shareholders, consumers, media, interest groups and local communities in which organisations operate. Their voice in critical organisational policy decisions, sometimes soft, cannot go unheard. For instance, if an organisation has identified a rural setting as the stage for operations, it has to work for the upliftment of the masses, be it in terms of education, environment or women empowerment. Societal consent for operations in such and other locations stems from multiple factors as community interest, desire or ability to relate to environmental stewardship and ethical behaviour of the organisation, in its day-to-day functioning. Together with consent, society also imposes implicit or explicit demands which act as a framework for company operations. Finally, governmental policies on what organisations should do for the communities in which they operate further gives shape to the procedural norms for design and implementation of CSR.

Community Interest Leads to Societal Consent: ITC Ltd.'s e-Choupal

The award-winning e-Choupal initiative of ITC Ltd. is a unique business model in response to stakeholder demands and provides societal consent to the organisation by delivering value to the community. The e-Choupal digital infrastructure connects farmers in rural India, and provides access to relevant knowledge, market prices, weather information and quality inputs for improving farm productivity and quality and obtaining better prices, and provides them an edge in national and global markets. Additionally, the 'Choupal Pradarshan Khet' programme provides customised agri-extension services and farmer training and familiarises farmers with the best practices in agriculture. Thus, by taking active interest in the communities it operates in, ITC Ltd. has created a digital–physical–human infrastructure that has greatly increased farmer income and productivity and 'transformed rural communities into vibrant markets'.[33]

At the organisational level, the primary concern of the leadership team is to secure stakeholder engagement (internal and external). Some questions which help them formulate plans are as follows: What are the objectives of the CSR initiative—societal or financial? What is the role of leadership team in making CSR a natural process to be observed and followed? How should values, philosophy, vision be embedded in the CSR processes of the organisation? How can CSR be part of the 'duty' structure which is implicitly woven in the HR policies? What responsibilities should be entrusted to employees and other stakeholders for smooth functioning of CSR activities? The nature of responses helps organisations chalk out or change the existing pattern of operations. For instance, if the focus of the company is societal concerns, it will assess the requirements/needs of the community and make investments accordingly. However, if the focus is on securing financial returns without other considerations the organisation may for example, provide infrastructural support on which a charge commensurate to its ROI may be levied.

The leadership team's concept of 'walk the talk' heralds involvement at all levels within the organisation. The nurturant values, philosophy and vision of the company and the leaders, become the guiding post for motivating all employees. There is no law which explicitly states that, in addition to the responsibilities entrusted by the organisation, an additional enabling role of CSR should be thrust on the employees. Organisations need to devise methods (reward and recognition) where the division between CSR and 'duty' blurs and the two become indistinguishable and inseparable. This will happen only when the responsibility of success is entrusted to employees and the larger community.

CSR as Part of Duty: My Kartavya

At a time when companies are grappling with strategies to engage employees in their CSR activities, My Kartavya (duty), a NASSCOM initiative, has created an industry-wide network of employees who volunteer with various NGOs to aid the development and progress of communities all around the globe. Its uniqueness lies in the fact that it connects employees to a broad range of volunteering opportunities, and also helps them to manage and evaluate their efforts, promising a sense of satisfaction, new skills and value-addition to their profiles. Several IT majors as MphasiS Ltd., Aegis Computers, Cactus and Octaware Technologies Pvt. Ltd., to name a few, support My Kartavya.[34]

At the third level of influencers we have the employees or the individuals. An interesting question which emerges at this level is: why should individuals involve themselves in activities promoted by the organisation? In the previous paragraphs, we have discussed the approach to be adopted by organisations for success in societal investments. The same needs to be also considered at the level of implementers. Three factors govern the choice of possible involvement. The values espoused by the company should ideally align with the individual values. Do I, as an important stakeholder within the organisation, connect with ethics, honesty and simplicity in approach or do they look good only on paper and are not significant for me? Without doubt, developing a connect with values and issues helps in securing commitment. For example, personal focus on education versus organisational commitment to women empowerment may secure interest, but not following.

Identifying with organisational commitments and winning approval through rewards and recognition are other determining factors for individual involvement. The best strategy, of course, is one in which employees are able to connect personal and organisational goals. A good example is IBM where the company acts as a force multiplier, providing employees with a platform to continue with their personal interests in contributing to society. Every year, at IBM India, volunteers are recognised on a global platform. Regions nominate individuals for the Chairman's Excellence Award for exemplary work in the community, and winners receive a certificate personally signed by the global CEO.[35]

The ripple effect of CSR initiatives on reputational quotient may be difficult to measure but can be assessed by the ability to attract and retain talent, customer trust in products and investor confidence. Considering the tangible and intangible benefits, it is no surprise that CSR has become a strategic imperative for sustenance in the competitive landscape.

Commitment through Connect: Maruti Suzuki India Ltd. (MSIL)

Maruti Suzuki India Ltd.'s volunteer programme, called e-Parivartan (the 'e' stands for employee and Partivartan for change) attempts to align company values with individual ones to secure commitment for social and community work. The e-Parivartan programme identifies NGOs across the National Capital Region (NCR) where employees can go and volunteer on Sunday mornings across a range of activities—mentoring, teaching, community development, raising environment awareness and organising health camps. Started in 2011, e-Parivartan enabled MSIL employees to put in over 3,200 hours of active volunteering within one year of its inception.[36]

As Fig. 7.1 shows, CSR influencers and actors operate at three levels: institutional, organisational and individual. At the institutional level, society, regulatory bodies and stakeholders influence CSR activities and priorities of the company. At the organisational level, the leadership team plays a crucial role in determining the direction and scope of CSR through its vision, mission, values and responsibility. Additionally, the extent of stakeholder engagement and the potential financial returns impact choice of CSR activities. At the individual level, it is important to align individual with organisational values, connect with issues and create a sense of identification with the organisation. These influencers and actors together determine the level, scope, direction and type of CSR activities, which yield multiple financial (increased financial performance and enhanced investor confidence) and non-financial benefits (customer satisfaction, ability to attract

Figure 7.1   Levels of Initiation and Outcome

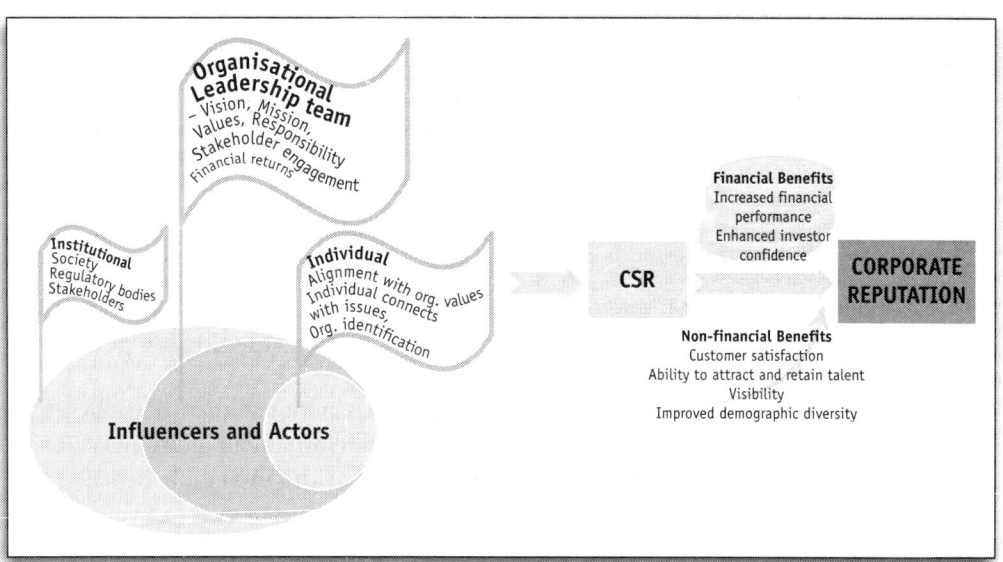

and retain talent, visibility and improved demographic diversity). It is the combined effect of tangible and intangible benefits that helps build corporate reputation.

IS CSR A STRATEGIC IMPERATIVE?

Companies still thinking about the environment as a social responsibility rather than a business imperative are living in the dark ages.

—Carter Roberts[37]

Yes, today CSR has become a strategic imperative, and reputation is an outcome of the strategic choices made by companies. Why should companies be socially responsible? How is CSR woven in the overall strategy of the company? Who drives these initiatives? The link between business and society (discussed above) is actually an exploration of their interdependence. If the two operate in isolation, making sporadic attempts to connect with each other, all efforts at creating a strategic design for CSR and its functioning will prove futile.

How should companies decide on the areas of societal investments? By creating a social priority list in which 'generic social issues, value chain impacts and social dimensions of competitive context'[38] are scripted. Generic social issues earn 'good citizenship' for the company. However, they do not directly impact company operations. CSR along the value chain (e.g. ITC Ltd. and Nestle India Ltd.) create stakeholder commitment by transforming social activities to societal benefit and mitigating harm along the value chain. 'Social dimensions of competitive context' suggest environmental/social concerns in areas around operations which provide a competitive advantage to the company. In this strategic CSR, organisational capabilities are leveraged to create societal capital. The choices made by the leadership team in selecting CSR initiatives and driving the agenda are important for success. Executives who understand the competitive landscape are able to present and project strategic imperatives within the framework of company values and are most suited as drivers for change. Introducing an initiative which concerns both business and society requires long-term and careful planning. Not all initiatives require commitment; some may also be in response to monetary support. Companies must selectively choose areas in which they can contribute by leveraging capabilities and make a substantial difference.

'Saanjhapan': Creating Shared Value at Nestle India Ltd. (Nestle)

Since 1961, Nestle India Ltd. (Nestle) has taken CSR one step further by focussing on creating shared value. Its 50-year journey that began with dairy farming in Moga village in Punjab has now spread to various other links in its value chain. Instead of establishing company-owned milk farms, Nestle preferred to create a model of equipping local farmers with technology and know-how, enabling them to increase their milk output hygienically and reduce wastage in the process. This approach lets farmers improve their returns, and relieves Nestle of the burden of heavy investment. Today, the company follows the same concept for sourcing all its raw materials, be it milk or chicory beans.

Additionally, it creates value for consumers through initiatives as the Nutritional Compass, Stay Healthy educational campaign and science-based product innovation and renovation. It enriches the communities it operates in, through its nutrition and water awareness programmes, clean drinking water projects and energy conservation initiatives.[39] According to Nestle India's Chairman and MD, Mr Antonio Helio Waszyk, 'Saanjhapan' or creating value for all stakeholders and the community it operates in, is now ingrained in the way the company does business.[40] The company has been reporting its value creation through its annual Creating Shared Value (CSV) report since 2010.

In making a strategic choice on creating shared value, the involvement of the leadership team in conceptualising, initiating programmes and securing support of the executives becomes an important enabler. Should they introduce mandates for the teams to adhere to CSR guidelines or promote volunteerism? In the first case, it may be difficult to secure sustained commitment from the employees/teams recruited for CSR. Results can only be positive and sustained if the top management, through creative endeavours, introduces a culture of volunteerism, where excitement and desire to contribute become propelling factors. For instance, IBM, in its corporate citizenship initiatives encourages volunteerism by:

* Involvement of team in strategising and designing initiatives
* Rewards and recognitions
* Narratives of successful volunteers[41]

The zeal to contribute is fuelled by motivating factors as facilitation and recognition by top management. Creative endeavours, as the flash mob (IBM), in which volunteers perform in public spaces, help in creating a desired image in the minds of stakeholders.

Another creative method for inspiring employees is used by the Mahindra Group. Through a programme called Employee Social Options Programme (ESOP), employees are encouraged to take up volunteering projects that address the health, education and environment needs of underprivileged communities in their immediate vicinity. Involvement is high, as every step, right from generating ideas, planning annual activities, implementing and monitoring results, is executed by employees themselves. Funding for these initiatives comes in the form of contributions (targeted at 0.5 per cent of profit after tax) from each company sector to the central CSR fund and the ESOPs.

How Does CSR Impact the Reputation of a Company?

The answer to the above question is embedded in early definitions which assign 'competitive advantage' to companies with a high reputational quotient. Reputation, interestingly, has also been considered as a long-term assessment of external stakeholders about the organisation, its ability to adhere to its commitments, match stakeholder expectations and its effectiveness in managing its performance with its socio-political environment.[42] Reputation building and managing is important for businesses as their actions and behaviour predict support from stakeholders. Companies need to develop their 'value priorities',[43] which, at a later stage, become the foundation/base for reputation enhancement. However, there are no defined criteria for assessing the nature of CSR initiatives and expected returns.

HOW IS CSR COMMUNICATED?

People are going to want, and be able, to find out about the citizenship of a brand, whether it is doing the right things socially, economically and environmentally.

—MIKE CLASPER[44]

In the earlier sections we have discussed the concept of 'societal consent'. For legitimacy in operations, 'communicating' is as important as 'doing'. Objectives for communication should be defined in terms of the emergent issues to the three different types of stakeholders, viz. clients/consumers, employees and shareholders. These issues should relate to a host of topics as values, vision, mission, workplace climate, environment, ethics, etc.

While most organisations are involved in CSR of some form or the other, the communication or reporting provides information to all stakeholders concerning social and environmental issues. Providing this information is critical in mitigating risks, being included in indices and satisfying behavioural standards. In this domain of social responsibility, a public-information model should be created to inform the public of all responsible behaviour and also account for lapses, if any. This will provide organisations with a strategy to legitimise their activities.

Undoubtedly, communicating CSR in different ways takes a major toll on company resources. Then why communicate CSR activities? It is the commitment of organisations to different stakeholders as government agencies, non-governmental organisations (NGOs), employees, investment firms, investors and the general public, who, both demand and seek information concerning company policy on governance, environmental issues, social programmes and community involvement.

Notably, a major concern for corporate communication practitioners is to strategise CSR communication. What could be the purpose of the same? Stakeholder involvement and engagement is secured when tools are adopted to keep them informed and involved. Consumers, for instance, want companies to behave ethically and responsibly. The need is to assess if company operations meet expectations of consumer standards. Both these perspectives—creating engagement and reporting—are crucial and companies are toying with innovative techniques and tools to secure stakeholder engagement and confidence.

Research points towards three CSR communication strategies: stakeholder information, response and involvement (Table 7.2).

Table 7.2 CSR Communication Strategies[45]

Strategy	Focus	Objective	Task	Tools
Stakeholder information	One-way communication from organisation to stakeholders	Disseminating information/data; sense-giving	Ensuring effective communication of CSR actions	Active media relations programmes
Stakeholder response	Two-way asymmetric communication	Improving stakeholder understanding of CSR efforts; sense-making	Attempting to engage stakeholders and obtain external endorsement	Opinion polls/market surveys to gauge understanding and acceptance of CSR activities
Stakeholder involvement	Two-way symmetric communication	Influencing and seeking to be influenced by stakeholders; iterations of sense-giving and sense-making	Engaging in frequent and systematic dialogue with stakeholders	CSR programmes integrating CSR concerns of organisation and external stakeholders

Communication of CSR is also based on the relationship shared with the stakeholder. For instance, CSR communication with consumers focusses on building reputation, differentiating products, securing customer loyalty, projecting social and environmental responsibility. Studies point to multiple benefits from CSR engagement. For instance, a positive disposition towards a product and increase in reputational quotient is seen if a company is involved in extensive CSR.[46] Further, companies engaged in CSR can charge a premium price as they can attract loyalty from customers, who also consider products to be better and more trustworthy.

Communicating CSR to employees is equally important. The objective for this communication is to create a positive image in the minds of internal stakeholders; enhance employee satisfaction and commitment; make the company more appealing to prospective employees and, reduce employee turnover. Researchers[47] state that 85 per cent of employees are more likely to engage in spontaneous word-of-mouth promotion if they are engaged in CSR initiatives and 65 per cent if they are informed of the same. Employees like to be associated with a company which has a track record of being ethical. Employee turnover is considerably reduced when CSR communication is aligned with personal goals and objectives and commitment levels are high. Similarly, prospective applicants are attracted to companies high on ethical and social quotient as association with company values and philosophy that are integrated in the culture of the organisation makes it an attractive place to work in.

The objectives of CSR communication with shareholders focus on increasing awareness about social investments and the tangible benefits accruing from CSR strategies. While there is considerable debate in research circles concerning the financial returns from socially responsible behaviour, it has been concluded that CSR-friendly companies indicate less volatility in their earnings.[48]

CSR Communication

While there is clarity on the objectives, goals and benefits of CSR, the actual mode of communication is open to various interpretations. For most companies, CSR communication means an annual sustainability report, which may be either separately published or be a part of the annual report itself. Companies use these vehicles to provide information about various CSR initiatives undertaken, playing out the stakeholder information strategy. For example, Indian Oil Corporation Ltd. (IOCL) highlights its environmental, economic and social performance in addition to outlining business risks, materiality issues, modes of stakeholder engagement and sustainable development. Tata Consultancy Services Ltd. (TCS), a company with a number of CSR-related awards to its credit, follows the stakeholder involvement strategy for CSR reporting. A series of continuous, monthly or quarterly interactions with varied stakeholder groups as customers, employees, shareholders, academic institutions, staffing firms and other suppliers, industry bodies, governments, NGOs and local communities throw up a large list of topics that each group considers important. These topics range from fair customer practices, employee career development, dividend payouts, internship opportunities, ethical behaviour, support for developmental programmes to environmental impact. A materiality filter is applied to the entire list of topics and after evaluation by a team of senior managers, the key sustainability topics, to be covered in the CSR report, are determined.

Intense and well-structured CSR communication has multiple advantages as impacting reputation, evoking trust and signalling product and company quality. At the same time, communication of CSR initiatives is not without its own set of challenges (refer Fig. 7.2).

Simply communicating sustainability efforts may not translate into more positive reputation for an organisation. Some researchers have suggested that high levels of CSR communication may invite critical stakeholder attention,[49] or even put off stakeholders who do not like conspicuous announcements about the good work done. It may lead to doubts about the company's intentions (is this self-serving CSR?), its self-complacency (is CSR a substitute for performance?) or even its transparency (is the company hiding something?).[50] The key is to be able to have effective CSR communication that engages stakeholders.

CSR communication can be both persuasive and informative. In the first category, the customer purchase decisions are influenced by creating a psychological drive associated with volunteering for the society in general. A good example of the same would be CSR campaigns designed to influence purchase decisions. Informative CSR simply provides information on the best practices in CSR. Companies use plain tactics of informing to influence in the long term. Annual reports and sustainability reports of companies are examples of this form of communication.

CSR communication thus is

a process of anticipating stakeholders' expectations, articulation of CSR policy and managing of different organization communication tools designed to provide true and transparent information about a company's or a brand's integration of its business operations, social and environmental concerns, and interactions with stakeholders.[51]

Figure 7.2 CSR Communication

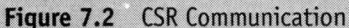

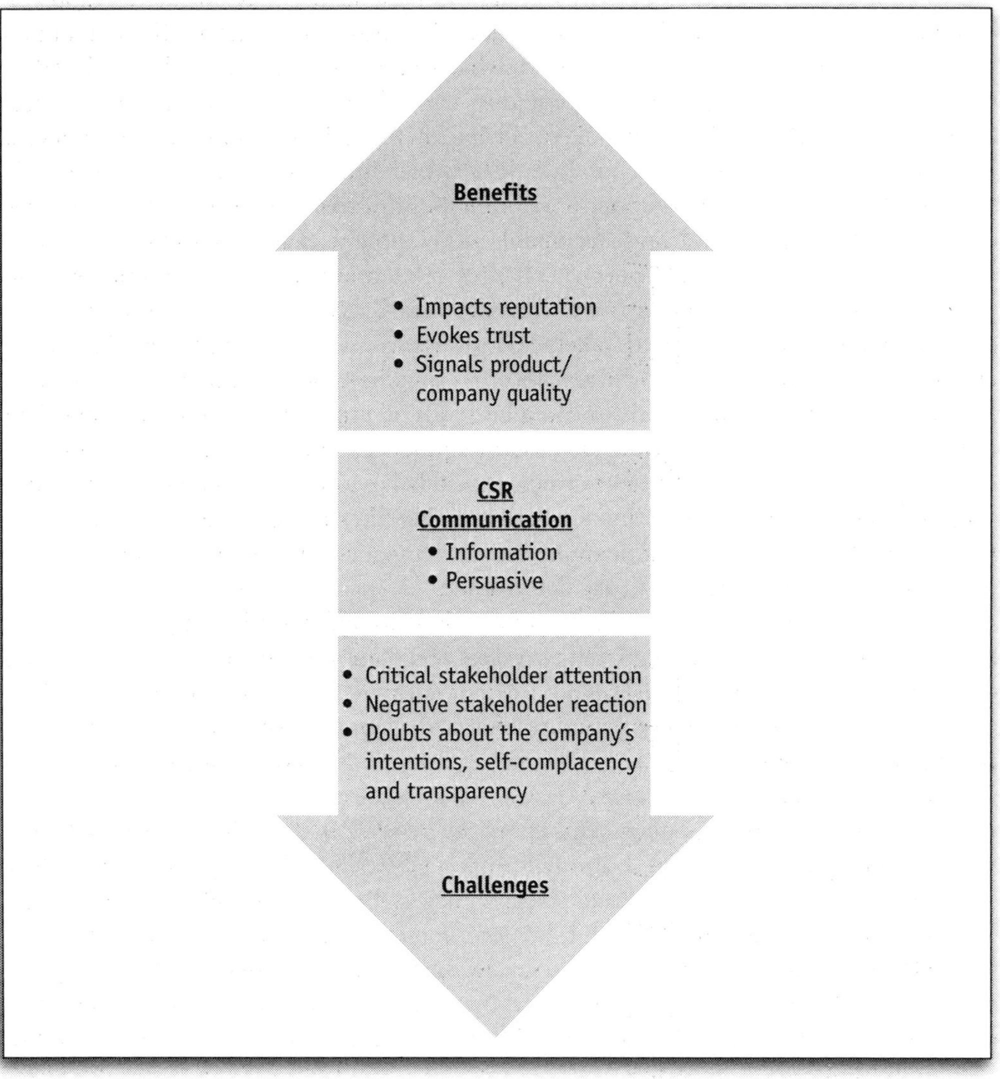

Benefits

- Impacts reputation
- Evokes trust
- Signals product/ company quality

CSR Communication
- Information
- Persuasive

- Critical stakeholder attention
- Negative stakeholder reaction
- Doubts about the company's intentions, self-complacency and transparency

Challenges

Persuading Consumers: Procter & Gamble India's Project Shiksha

In 2005, Procter & Gamble India (P&G) launched a national consumer programme called Project Shiksha (education) in partnership with Child Rights and You (CRY), and Sony Entertainment Television. It involved participation of consumers in a nation-wide campaign aimed at supporting the education of needy Indian children by purchasing large packs of major P&G brands as Tide, Ariel, Pantene, to name a few. The programme emphasised the contribution of the consumer in enabling a child's right to education, by making certain brand choices.

In 2007, the company launched the 'Shiksha' song on all national music channels as a form of persuasive communication, highlighting the plight of underprivileged children and persuading consumers to support their cause by buying P&G products.

In 2010, sensing some apathy towards the cause from urban consumers, P&G used a unique mode of persuasive communication to motivate consumers to contribute to the campaign. Some of the most popular websites carried gibberish on their home pages instead of the regular text, 'placing the elite, educated Indian consumer in the shoes of an illiterate child',[52] and jolting them into realising the plight of the uneducated. After this campaign, awareness about the Shiksha programme increased. Additionally, sales of products that were part of the campaign rose dramatically. Celebrating its innovation, this campaign was 'long-listed' for the 2012 Warc Prize in communication.[53]

CSR Reporting

Companies follow different formats for reporting which can be mandatory, solicited or voluntary. In India, as stated earlier, for the top 100 listed companies (in terms of market capitalisation at the BSE and NSE) CSR reporting is mandatory. Solicited reporting is still in its nascent stage and is usually a response to demand for information by a particular stakeholder group. More conversational in nature, this form of reporting enables stakeholders to obtain richer and better information and is based on a two-way symmetric model of communication. There is an underlying emphasis on dialogue and consulting with the community, in the values and processes of organisations which emphasise social responsibility.[54] The third form of reporting, viz. voluntary, is the most widely recognised form and, as per KPMG 2005 international survey, has witnessed a steep incline since 2002. Companies adopt this style of reporting to project a favourable image (Table 7.3).

Table 7.3 Forms of Voluntary Reporting

Forms	Purpose
Global Reporting Initiative (GRI) developed in collaboration with the United Nations Environment Programme	To develop and disseminate globally applicable Sustainability Reporting Guidelines for voluntary reporting on social, environmental and economic dimensions. 660 companies across 50 countries have adopted the reporting guidelines
Accountability AA1000 assurance standard	Focusses on the importance of engagement with stakeholders
OECD Guidelines, ILO declaration	Defines standards of corporate behaviour
SA8000 and ISO14000	Offers frameworks for implementation of socially responsible practices
Dow Jones Sustainability Index and FTSE4Good	Provides basis for responsible investing and comparing companies
GRI has included elements of other standards (specified above) in its reporting guidelines which indicate a need and desire for a globally acceptable uniform standard of reporting.	

Scoring on Sustainability Reporting: Reliance Industries Ltd.

GRI gave Reliance Industries Ltd. (RIL an A+ level for its Sustainability Report for the seventh consecutive year. RIL submitted the report to GRI, Amsterdam, the Netherlands for application-level check, as per the New GRI 3.1 Guidelines. RIL's report follows the guidelines of the American Petroleum Institute and the International Petroleum Industry Environmental Conservation Association. It also incorporates the Ministry of Corporate Affairs, Government of India's National Voluntary Guidelines for Social, Environmental and Economic Responsibilities of Business.[55]

Indian Sustainability Reporting Goes Global: Tata Index for Sustainable Human Development

The Tata Group developed the Tata Index for Sustainable Human Development in 2003, with an aim of correctly estimating the value or impact of its sustainability activities, through its central agency Tata Council for Community Initiatives (TCCI).

The Tata Index provides a method of putting in place, objective co-ordinates on a comprehensive scale. It enables the user company to direct, measure and enhance its community work. Currently, the top 16 companies of the Tata Group, with 95 per cent of the group's revenue and employee size, are using this index.

The Tata Index is now poised to be used on a global level. TCCI has recently collaborated with eXtensible Business Reporting Language (XBRL) International to add value to the existing form of XBRL by creating a social and environmental dimension. It has submitted its classification containing 334 elements to XBRL for review. After going through the mandated review process XBRL International may 'acknowledge' it, making the Tata Index the only international standard for sustainability reporting.[56]

CSR reporting is also contingent upon country, type and size of industry, and social expectations. Development of global guidelines can have a neutral impact on region and country-specific initiatives. Having stated this, we would like to propose that global guidelines would be typically suitable for multinational companies that operate in multiple markets than companies whose stakeholder expectations are limited to national and local levels.

WHAT ARE THE TOOLS FOR CSR COMMUNICATION?

Creating a strong business and building a better world are not conflicting goals—they are both essential ingredients for long-term success.

—WILLIAM CLAY FORD JR.[57]

What channels do companies use for communicating CSR? Annual reports, sustainability reports, websites, booklets are some of the most popular examples. Other channels include social and thematic reports, codes of conduct, websites, stakeholder consultations, internal channels, prizes and events, cause-related marketing, product packaging, interventions in the press and on TV and points of sale. The most prominent of these are the social reports, websites and advertising.

The overall approach to communicating CSR is contingent on factors as location, size and departmental origin of the communicative behaviour.[58] Definition of methodology has been sought by researchers and they have proposed a model with economic, legal and ethical responsibilities.[59] Stemming from this model of communication, CSR may include descriptions as citizenship, environmental sustainability, stewardship, community, human rights, volunteerism and ethics, which may be communicated by the leader or the scripted organisational policies and norms.

As discussed earlier in the chapter, reporting is mandatory only for companies in a specific economic range. However, several companies have begun the process of providing social and environment information with the intention of reflecting transparency in processes and procedures by providing a window into social strategy and performance.

A large number of organisations have begun using annual and social reports as a medium of communicating citizenship efforts, focussing on CSR evaluations and environmental performance. One of the reasons for this is that Indian stakeholders are not yet looking proactively for information on corporate CSR and hence, there is room for embedding these messages in the mainstream communication. Annual reports undoubtedly, even today, improve the company's accountability to the external stakeholders, whose investing decisions may, to a certain extent, be influenced by citizenship initiatives of the company. Social reports communicate 'the social and environmental effect of organisations' economic actions to particular interest groups within society and to society at large'[60] and build an ongoing relationship with the stakeholders.

Do I want the shareholders on my side? Individual leaders/CEOs need to take a call and relate their personal values with adoption and implementation of CSR. In addition to financial presentations and interviews, the letter to shareholders is also used by corporate honchos to rationalise events and make future predictions.

Companies have begun participating in environment and CSR alliances dedicated to public policy and systematic social issues. Greenpeace and World Business Council for Sustainable Development are a few bodies which enable companies to adopt a more proactive approach.

With the growth of the Internet, corporate websites provide ample room for projection and advocacy of CSR projects. Advertising is also used to communicate themes of social responsibility. The impact of these media, though, still needs to be ascertained.

CONCLUSION

Goodness is the only investment that never fails.

—HENRY DAVID THOREAU[61]

The Sir Ratan Tata Trust, Infosys Foundation and Azim Premji Foundation are some examples of social initiatives by industrialists which have brought about a paradigmatic shift in stakeholders. Many companies have been engaged in similar pursuits of giving 'back to society'. However, what gives these companies the differentiating edge is the intent of these activities—philanthropy or business. In the first case, the giving is without any expectation of returns; in the second, it is a business imperative.

As a business case, CSR has become mandatory for companies operating in a sensitive global scenario where success is measured by reputation. Hence, societal investments in the name of CSR, through voluntary or 'reluctant' measures are being developed as part of the corporate strategy to secure higher returns while mitigating risk and addressing stakeholder concerns. Over the years, it is this strategic intent of demonstrating and showcasing responsible leadership which has helped companies acquire reputational capital and gain competitive edge.

What can and what should companies do to improve their ranking in the societal commitment index?

- Assess level of CSR engagement
- Determine nature of CSR spend
- Identify geographies and communities for implementation
- Communicate with and engage internal stakeholders in CSR processes
- Devise methods for CSR communication
- Select tools for CSR communication

Key Points

- CSR is a blend of performance, transparency and societal concerns creating an organic link between business and society. It encompasses the economic, legal, ethical and discretionary expectations of society for the company.
- CSR helps companies and organisations build stakeholder and societal appreciation leading to increase in reputational capital.
- CSR initiatives, aligned with the corporate strategy and leadership vision, can help boost the reputation of an organisation, and resurrect inadvertent loss of reputation. In addition to profits, CSR entails compliance, caring, being synergistic and holistic.
- The license to operate or societal consent germinates from the concept of socially responsible and ethical investing based on stakeholder expectations, environmental scanning and arena of operations.
- A framework of shared values is the most appropriate for CSR ventures.
- CSR should create value for the company in terms of enhanced performance, risk mitigation and societal consent.
- Influencers and actors for implementing social investments are at three levels: institutional, organisational and individual.
- Institutional level comprises stakeholders, society and regulative measures.
- At the organisational level, we have the leadership team, values, vision and mission of the company.

- The individual level comprises the ability to see the link between personal values and organisational objectives, and organisational identification.
- Companies can select their initiatives from the social priority list comprising generic social issues, value chain impacts and social dimensions of competitive context.
- Communication of CSR is with three types of stakeholders: clients/consumers, employees and shareholders.
- Objectives of communication relate to topics as values, vision, mission, workplace climate, environment, ethics, etc.
- Intense and well-structured CSR communication will impact reputation, evoke trust and signal product and company quality.
- CSR communication can be both persuasive and informative.
- Styles of reporting CSR can be mandatory, solicited or voluntary.
- The three most prominent channels of reporting are social reports, websites and advertising.

END NOTES

1. 'The BodyShop: Social responsibility or sustained greenwashing?', website http://www.icmrindia.org/casestudies/catalogue/Business%20Ethics/The%20Body%20Shop-Social%20Responsibility%20or%20Sustained%20Greenwashing.htm (accessed 12 April 2013).
2. 'Quotations from business and thought leaders on ethics and CSR', website http://www.interpraxis.com/quotes.htm (accessed 12 April 2013).
3. PTI, 'Companies Bill 2011: Key provisions affecting mergers and acquisitions—A compilation', website http://www/shbathiya.com/FC4.pdf (accessed 14 August 2012).
4. 'Cabinet approves amendments to the Companies Bill, 2011', website http://pib.nic.in/newsite/erelease.aspx?relid=88156 (accessed 14 August 2012).
5. 'Parliamentary panel for mandatory CSR', *Business Standard*, website http://www.business-standard.com/india/news/parliamentary-panel-for-mandatory-csr/483237/ (accessed 14 August 2012).
6. A. Sheth and M. Singhal, 'India Philanthropy Report 2011', website http://www.bain.com/Images/Bain_Philanthropy_Report_2011.pdf (accessed 10 August 2012).
7. M. E. Porter, 'Corporate philanthropy: Taking the high ground', *Foundation Strategy Group* (2003), 1–12.
8. G. P. Lantos, 'The ethicality of altruistic corporate social responsibility', *Journal of Consumer Marketing* (2002), 19(3), 205–230.
9. A. Sheth and M. Singhal, 'India Philanthropy Report 2011', website http://www.bain.com/Images/Bain_Philanthropy_Report_2011.pdf (accessed 10 August 2012).
10. M. E. Porter and M. R. Kramer, 'Strategy and society: The link between competitive advantage and corporate social responsibility', *Harvard Business Review*, website http://hbr.org/2006/12/strategy-and-society-the-link-between-competitive-advantage-and-corporate-social-responsibility/ar/1 (accessed 14 August 2013).
11. C. M. Genest, 'Cultures, organizations and philanthropy', *Corporate Communication: An International Journal* (2005), 10(4), 315–327.
12. A. B. Carroll, 'A history of corporate social responsibility: Concepts and practices', in A. Crane, A. McWilliams, D. Matten, J. Moon and D. Seigel (eds), *The Oxford Handbook on Corporate Social Responsibility*, (pp. 19-46), Oxford: Oxford University Press (2008).
13. 'Quotations from business and thought leaders on ethics and CSR', website http://www.interpraxis.com/quotes.htm (accessed 12 April 2013).
14. G. S. Dhanesh, 'Better stay single? Public relations and CSR leadership in India', *Public Relations Review* (2012), 38(1), 141–143.

15. M. B. E. Clarkson, 'A stakeholder framework for analyzing and evaluating corporate social performance', *The Academy of Management Review* (1995), 20(1), 92–117, p. 98.

16. D. Votaw, 'Genius becomes rare: A comment on the doctrine of social responsibility Pt. 1', *California Management Review* (1972), 15(2), 25–31, p. 25.

17. A. B. Carroll, 'A three-dimensional conceptual model of corporate performance', *The Academy of Management Review* (1979), 4(4), 497–505, p. 500.

18. D. A. Whetten, G. Rands and P. Godfrey, 'What are the responsibilities of business to society?', in A. Pettigrew, H. Thomas and R. Whittington (eds), *Handbook of Strategy and Management* (pp. 373–409), London: SAGE Publications (2002), p. 374.

19. R. Levy, *Give and Take.* Cambridge, MA: Harvard Business School Press (1999).

20. M. Friedman, 'The social responsibility of business is to increase its profits', *New York Times Magazine* (13 September 1970), 122–126 p. 122.

21. M. Friedman, *Capitalism and Freedom.* Chicago, IL: University of Chicago Press (1962), p. 133.

22. Tata Group, 'Tata index for sustainability', website http://www.tata.com/ourcommitment/articles/inside.aspx?artid=4k1011ilySU= (accessed 14 August 2013).

23. Ibid.

24. M. V. Marrewijk, 'Concepts and definitions of CSR and corporate sustainability: Between agency and communion', *Journal of Business Ethics* (2003), 44(2/3), 95–105.

25. M. M. Singh, 'Ten point social charter', Excerpt from speech at inaugural session of Confederation of Indian Industry's annual summit', 24 May 2007.

26. M. R. Ahlgreen, 'When the business of business became everybody's business', *The Magazine for International Business and Diplomacy*, 2, website http://ibde.org/component/content/article/114-when-the-business-of-business-became-everybodys-business.html (accessed 12 April 2013).

27. E. C. Kurucz, B. A. Colbert and D. Wheeler, 'The business case for CSR', in A. Crane, A. McWilliams, D. Matten, J. Moon and D. Seigel (eds), *The Oxford Handbook on Corporate Social Responsibility* (pp. 83–112), Oxford: Oxford University Press (2008), p. 84.

28. Ibid.

29. IFC, 'FVTool: Cairn India', website http://fvtool.com/page.php?node=aWQ9Nw (accessed 24 October 2012).

30. Delloitte India. (2011), 'Public sector enterprises in India: Pursuing the triple bottom line', website http://www.deloitte.com/assets/Dcom-India/Local%20Assets/Documents/Public_sector_enterprises_in_India1.pdf (accessed 12 August 2013).

31. GAIAMlife, 'Stream of consciousness', website http://blog.gaiam.com/quotes/authors/john-mackey (accessed 12 April 2013).

32. H. Aguinis and A. Glavas, 'What we know and don't know about corporate social responsibility: A review and research agenda', *Journal of Management* (2012), 38(4), 932–968.

33. ITC Ltd., 'ITC CSR booklet' (2012), website http://www.itcportal.com/sustainability/images/ITC-CSR-Booklet-PDF.pdf (accessed 13 August 2012).

34. MphasiS Ltd., 'Community Initiatives', website http://www.mphasis.com/about-us/corporate-social-responsibility/community-initiatives.asp (accessed 13 August 2012).

35. V. Chaudhri and A. Kaul, 'Beyond 'social' responsibility: Corporate citizenship at IBM India', Unpublished Case, Indian Institute of Management, Ahmedabad.

36. 'Maruti Suzuki's CSR initiatives', *The Economic Times*, website http://articles.economictimes.indiatimes.com/2012-06-03/news/32033323_1_ppp-model-itis-skill-development (accessed 13 August 2012).

37. A. Neilsen, 'Environmental challenges are profit opportunities, says Roberts of World Wildlife Fund', Stanford Graduate School of Business, website https://www.gsb.stanford.edu/news/headlines/VonGugel_Roberts.html (accessed 12 April 2013).

38. M. E. Porter and M. R. Kramer, 'Strategy and society: The link between competitive advantage and corporate social responsibility', *Harvard Business Review* (2006), 84(12), 4–17, p. 6.

39. Nestle India, 'Nestle creating Shared Value Report 2010', website http://www.nestle.in/asset-libraries/Documents/Creating%20Shared%20Value/CSV_Publication_2010.pdf (accessed 14 August 2012).

40. S. Bhan, 'Nestle: Redefining corporate social responsibility concept', website http://www.moneycontrol.com/news/business/nestle-redefining-corporate-social-responsibility-concept_463610.html (accessed 14 August 2012).

41. V. Chaudhri and A. Kaul, 'Beyond 'social' responsibility: Corporate citizenship at IBM India', Unpublished Case, Indian Institute of Management, Ahmedabad.

42. T. J. Brown and J. M. Logsdon, 'Corporate reputation and organization identity as constructs for business and society research', in D. Woods and D. Windsor (eds.), *Proceedings of the Tenth Annual Meeting of the International Association for Business and Society* (1999), Paris, France, 168–173.

43. S. Schwartz, 'A theory of cultural values and some implications for work', *Applied Psychology: An International Review* (1999), 48(1), 23–47, p. 23.

44. G. Menon, 'The role of business in society: Delivering sustainable development'. *PricewaterhouseCoopers Board Agenda Series*, website http://www.pwc.com/en_ID/id/energy-utilities-mining/assets/delivering-sustainable-development.pdf (accessed 12 April 2013).

45. M. Morsing and M. Schultz, 'Corporate social responsibility communication: stakeholder information, response and involvement strategies', *Business Ethics: A European Review* (2006), 15(4), 323–338.

46. A. McWilliams and D. Siegel, 'Corporate social responsibility: A theory of the firm perspective', *The Academy of Management Review* (2001), 26(1), 117–127.

47. J. Dawkins and S. Lewis, 'CSR in stakeholder expectations: And their implication for company strategy', *Journal of Business Ethics* 44(2/3), 185–193.

48. M. Mainelli, 'Ethical volatility: How CSR ratings and returns might be changing the world of risk', *Balance Sheet* (2004), 12(1), 42–45.

49. B. E. Ashforth and B. W. Gibbs, 'The double edge of organisational legitimation', *Organization Science* (1990), 1(2), 177–194.

50. M. Morsing, 'Communicating responsibility', *Business Strategy Review* (Special report: Corporate social responsibility) (2005), 84–88.

51. K. Podnar, Guest Editorial: 'Communicating corporate social responsibility', *Journal of Marketing Communications* (2008), 14(2), 75–81, p. 75.

52. WARC, 'Procter & Gamble shiksha: Unlearning to educate', website http://www.warc.com/Pages/TopicsAndTrends/Features/Feature.aspx (accessed 13 August 2012).

53. Ibid.

54. D. J. Wood, 'Corporate social performance revisited', *The Academy of Management Review* (1991), 16(4), 691–718.

55. 'GRI A+ rating for RIL's corporate sustainability report', website http://www.indiacsr.in/en/?p=7313 (accessed 14 August 2012).

56. Tata Group, 'A scale for excellence', website http://www.tata.com/article.aspx?artid=F3m1FKzl1DU= (accessed 14 August 2012).

57. T. Smith, 'How businesses view sustainability and CSR reporting', http://www.csr-company.com/csr-resources-quotes.php?nPage=102 (accessed 12 April 2013).

58. M. E. Porter and M. R. Kramer, 'Strategy and society: The link between competitive advantage and corporate social responsibility', *Harvard Business Review* (2006), 84(12), 4–17.

59. M. S. Schwartz and A. B. Carroll, 'Corporate social responsibility: A three-domain approach', *Business Ethics Quarterly* (2003), 13(4), 503–530.

60. R. H. Gray, D. Owen and K. T. Maunders, *Corporate Social Reporting: Accounting and Accountability.* UK: Prentice-Hall (1987), p. ix.

61. B. Azhar, 'Why CSR: 12 quotes to help build your argument', Good Business Sense, website http://www.gbsense.com/2012/01/12/why-csr-12-quotes-to-help-build-your-argument/ (accessed 20 January 2014).

8

Choreographing the Organisation–Media Tango: Managing Media Relations

Journalists have long carried the reputation of being the watchdogs for citizens, monitoring the government and corporate giants for power abuse.

—SHARI VEIL[1]

Objectives:

- Understand the relationship between organisation and media
- Explain concepts of framing and inverted pyramid
- Identify strategies for securing media attention
- Assess Return On Investment (ROI) of media interactions
- Recognise the role of media in building organisational and leader reputation

INTRODUCTION

Journalism is printing what someone else does not want printed; everything else is PR.

—GEORGE ORWELL[2]

Media is a carrier of institutional logic, generally agreed-to beliefs, assumptions, values concerning organisational behaviour with the task of disseminating information which accords with these values. As a social arbiter and gatekeeper, media focusses on influencing and providing a legitimate platform for assessing individuals and organisations and shaping and reshaping perceptions of social reality, the veracity of which, is rarely, if ever questioned or disputed. Reality for organisations is defined by journalists, also referred to as 'image makers' and 'spin doctors', through a process called enactment, which is an act of framing through inclusion, exclusion and emphasis.[3] Framing is critical

Key Words

- Agenda building
- Agenda setting
- Crisis
- Crowdsourcing
- Fourth estate
- Framing
- Image makers
- Inverted pyramid
- Journalists
- Leadership
- Media
- Media buy-in
- Media catching
- Media effects
- Media engagement
- Media exposure
- Media system dependency theory
- Narratives
- 'New news'
- Online press rooms
- Public relations
- Reputation
- Return on investment (ROI)
- Social media
- Spin doctors
- Stories
- Tools of framing
- Virtual press rooms
- Watchdog
- Website
- WikiLeaks

Media Helps ICICI Bank Ltd. Clarify Its Stand

One of India's leading banks, ICICI Bank Ltd., was plagued with rumours of financial distress in the wake of the US financial crisis in September 2008. There were unusually large withdrawals of cash from the bank's branches and Automated Teller Machines (ATMs) by customers concerned about the bank's stability. Managing Director and CEO Mr K. V. Kamath and Joint MD and CEO Ms Chanda Kochhar issued statements about the robustness of the bank's capitalisation to restore confidence. The Finance Ministry too came out in support of the bank.

Throughout this storm of 'baseless and malicious'[4] rumours, ICICI Bank Ltd. received very good media support. Apart from the statements of senior bank officials, leading newspapers carried stories explaining how ICICI Bank Ltd. was properly capitalised, had sufficient liquidity and the fact that it had the backing of the Finance Ministry and the Reserve Bank of India. Newspapers as *The Times of India* even responded favourably to the numerous calls from readers inquiring about the bank's situation and whether they should withdraw their money.

ICICI Bank Ltd.'s careful cultivation of media relations helped it to tide over what could have ballooned into a major crisis. The positive tone of media reports helped build up investor and customer confidence, and ensured that it emerged from the episode with an intact reputation.

in establishing and maintaining mutually beneficial relationships with organisations and the audiences.

This organisation–media tango is a complex dance in which the two entities are locked together, where neither can do without the other. The complexity increases when we begin to consider the third entity, the public, which is both influenced and sensationalised through the media's reporting of organisational news. Some questions as what do the media report? who is the protagonist in the story? why is it being scripted? where and when is it being written? and what is the tone? are of major concern to organisations partnering with the media in information dissemination. An answer to many of these questions ascertains the nature of reporting which may be positive or negative. Interestingly, the impact of controversial stories bordering on negativity, by far, surpass interest in positive narrations as mergers and acquisitions, joint ventures, introduction of new product, appointment of new CEO, etc.

How does media shape audience perceptions? What is the role of organisations in providing content to the media? To create captive readership, there is a keenness in journalists to recount stories as fire, employee strike, dismissal of CEO, fraud, etc. with emotionally charged syntactical structures, which shape and reshape audience perceptions. The desired effect may boomerang if there is incorrect understanding of events by journalists or reporters which may excite the audiences, but damage organisational reputation.

The objectives of media and organisations are more often than not in contradiction. While the media focus is on increasing readership or Target Rating Points (TRPs), the organisational emphasis is on building reputation and increasing performance. A wrong statement made inadvertently by the company representative or an incorrect assessment of a situation by the journalist can have long-lasting repercussions on the carefully built organisational reputation. Is there a solution to this problem? Beginning with an understanding that both media and organisations need one another for sustenance, healthy connects, based on trust and transparency, can form the foundation for building the edifice of relationships.

Companies can build good media relations and develop trust through constantly monitoring journalist interest and providing required stories and narratives, either through email exchange or direct face-to-face interaction. The newsworthiness of a story depends on the quantum of transparent facts shared by the company and its response to follow-up queries. This dictum would hold true even in moments of crisis when the media is clamouring for information. Shying away from journalist questions in today's fast moving world of technology, is not always the best strategy. Journalists, in their desire to create a sensational frame for their readers, may present a 'half-baked' story collated from material gathered from not-so-reliable sources. More so in the current era of social media, a shift in the traditional communication patterns has led to 'media catching'[5] becoming common practice, through which journalists ask for specific information for stories on the Internet. Some of the examples are use of Facebook, Twitter and Listserv where journalists appeal to a larger pool of practitioners for practical inputs on a storyline not necessarily initiated by the company.

'New News' ... The Fourth Estate

Can news be old? Undoubtedly not! However, the transformational nature of news reporting over the years and the convergence between various channels is what assigns a 'new' category to it. The convergence of media content over the digital platform has changed the relationship with audiences. With the onslaught of digital media, conventional news channels are being threatened by new players (e.g. Google), social media, new kind of news sources (bloggers) and wholesale information supplier (WikiLeaks).[6] 'News traditionally has emphasised storytelling, but now confronts new possibilities and imperatives to shape information for a participatory, networked and digital environment.'[7]

The story of WikiLeaks is the most interesting. WikiLeaks has been declared as the 'world's first stateless news organisation'[8] which is 'everywhere' and does not produce news, implying that the news it carries is complete in all respects and yet, not structured enough to be referred to as a 'news item'. While the definition is intriguing, it definitely provides a comprehensive understanding of WikiLeaks, which is a database with raw information on an event/sequence of events. It captures all the information on a particular incident and places it on its website in no particular order. Traditional media or people interested in this information then carve out a story as per their understanding and perceived readers' interest.

Also termed as 'cultural chaos',[9] WikiLeaks is an example of growing dissent and openness in reporting news through provision of multiple data points. While online reporting has become the norm, collaborations with newspapers and magazines provide credence and authority. In isolation, WikiLeaks lacks credibility and authenticity, and needs support from established media networks. An example which illustrates this is the WikiLeaks reporting of three major news events in the year 2010: Afghan war, occupation of Iraq and transcripts of diplomatic cables sent from more than 250 US embassies. The reporting on these three incidents was in collaboration with three major Western news publications: *The Guardian*, *The New York Times* and *Der Spiegel*. Building on the reach, editorial contacts and distribution resources of these newspapers, WikiLeaks was able to capture attention which may not have been possible if unedited data was posted on its website. 'What WikiLeaks anticipates, but so far has been unable to organise, is the "crowdsourcing" of the interpretation of its leaked documents. The work, oddly, is left to the few remaining staff journalists of selected "quality" news media.'[10]

Closer home, WikiLeaks' posting of confidential US embassy cables sent in December 1976, disclosed the determination of the Indira Gandhi family to remove Mr S. S. Ray from the post of West Bengal Chief Minister. The information that the 'prestige of Sanjay Gandhi has been placed on the line in this affair, and for Ray to remain in office indefinitely would be a serious loss of face for him',[11] was able to draw the attention of the larger public only after one of India's leading newspapers, *Hindustan Times* carried this story.

Journalists, accustomed to thinking of themselves as the fourth estate, are compelled to sift through online information, make sense and craft a story according to their understanding and interest. When raw data with multiple points of entry and access is provided online, journalists develop cause-and-effect relationships. Each reporting entity decides upon the entry and exit points of news reporting based on economic, cultural, social, technological and organisational requirements.

Given the power that media unleashes, organisations develop an agenda for building healthy connects with the media.

Agenda Building and Setting

Agenda building and setting begins with a realisation that simple messages and their media placement can hugely impact the image of a company. Both factors—building and setting—are required to make media engagement strategies more focussed. The first level of agenda building emphasises techniques for influencing multiple groups and shaping public opinion of policy makers, interest groups and companies. The second level of agenda setting is linked to the concept of framing which suggests that publics can be influenced through a news item by selecting and placing emphasis on certain attributes linked to the message and ignoring others. It has been found that discussing or concentrating on agenda building and setting can help enunciate the relationship between news media content, Public Relations (PR), reputation and performance, and provide the required visibility to organisations (Table 8.1).

Visibility in and through the media helps allay fears or apprehensions in the mind of stakeholders and audiences. To be visible, organisations should get coverage or remain in the news for all the right reasons, at least once or twice a month. They can convey their point of view to internal and external stakeholders. Once the agenda is designed, organisations begin the process of securing media attention and buy-in.

Media representatives, on the other hand, strategise on writing styles to deliver news. In this process of sharing stories and information, framing of message by the media and

Table 8.1   Agenda Building and Setting

Level	Objective	Tools	Focus
Building[12]	Influencing multiple groups and shaping public opinion of policy makers, interest groups and corporations	News conferences (together with news releases), interviews, PR programmes and campaigns with a high degree of emphasis on political news, public relation activities and programmes	Anecdotal reference of what the organisation has done to achieve laurels
Setting[13]	Framing: influencing organisation's publics through a news item by selecting and placing emphasis on attributes linked to the message and ignoring others	Stories on corporate vision, leadership and social responsibility	Impact of attributes on product and services, financial performance, workplace environment, social responsibility, vision and leadership and emotional appeal

the organisation deserves due consideration. Later in this chapter, we discuss the ROI of media relations and reputation quotient developed with the help of positive and negative reporting. Some strategies followed by organisations in developing media connect are further presented.

HOW DO ORGANISATIONS BUILD RELATIONSHIP WITH MEDIA?

> *It is always a risk to speak to the press: They are likely to report what you say.*
>
> —Hubert H. Humphrey[14]

Practitioner–journalist relationship can be built by honesty and transparency, accuracy of information, responsiveness and timeliness, reliability and consistency and, preparedness.[15] In this list, the most important is honesty in organisational handling of media. The dominant correlate in building an honest relationship is that both entities should comprehend and respect the significance of this mutually beneficial relationship, which is one of give and take for survival and sustenance.[16] Both entities should secure support and involvement of the leadership team and be cautious of sacrificing interests which are fundamental to their existence.

Capitalising on the growing focus on the Internet, organisations make extensive use of their websites to influence the public either directly or through journalist visits and revisits. The design of the website together with its content structure and positioning is critical. A dynamic webpage rather than a static one, well-crafted details on company publications, news releases, advertisements and promotional material are initial points of consideration. The design of the website should be such that one part of the information flows intuitively and logically into the other, making it simplistic and convenient for users. Going overboard with animations or 'dynamic' information may not prove to be a very good strategy. To make the website user-friendly, the homepage should be easy to navigate and lend itself to conveniently accessible information on happenings, company information, Frequently Asked Questions (FAQs) and contacts.

There are multiple ways in which different types of news can be uploaded. For instance, informative documents can be uploaded on the website as .pdf files. Speeches, high-quality graphics and annual reports can be documented with links on the main webpage to enable journalists to get an objective view of the story. The website should ideally include:

- News release links in reverse chronological order with timelines
- Speeches with situations, timelines, graphic images of the speakers
- Annual reports as html and .pdf files
- Fact sheets with organisation and product information, which could be clearly demarcated into product, employee and investor information categories
- Contact information for PR staff[17]

Additional data as links to recent stories, keyword search engines, online demonstration of products and searchable news archives are also useful. The nature of the content provides value to online visitors and an opportunity to stakeholders to assimilate useful and trustworthy information.

For disseminating knowledge and information, some organisations also provide links to other websites. However, there are contradictory views concerning the value addition of the same. While one school of thought emphasises enhanced organisational credibility when external website links are provided, enabling users to cross-check information,[18] another school posits that such links can distract visitors. A personal touch to the website can be provided by initiating an honest dialogue by positing a statement of intent, a counter statement or a statement of action which can intensify relationships with journalists and the public. If for some reason, the process is subverted for organisational benefits due to manipulation or exclusion, dialogue will be impregnated with suspicion and mistrust.

Another strategy adopted by organisations for media engagement is the use of virtual press rooms for sharing information, responding to queries to improve sales, enhancing reputation or providing information to various stakeholders.[19] This strategy is based on the concept of 'power of influencing' in which participants talk with one another instead of one person talking to others. This focussed communication stems from a network of relationships between companies and their stakeholders.

Virtually Everything for the Press at the Virtual Press Room: Microsoft India

Microsoft India uses a virtual press room as an information resource. Much more advanced than the routinely found 'Press' sections of corporate websites, this virtual press room is a huge storehouse of information about the company, its products and relevant issues.

It has different sections as press releases, image gallery, video gallery and even a comprehensive compendium of articles written by Microsoft India leaders and employees on various issues. Between the first three sections, every major piece of information about the company, its products and services, employees, CSR initiatives and innovations, is covered. Its well-designed search function enables journalists or any other interested person looking for specific information to easily search for it, with subject and date filters. A handy 'leadership profile' section provides brief profiles of all key management personnel which can be printed with one click, along with their downloadable pictures. A 'global news centre' link connects the visitor to the Microsoft global press room, providing quick and easy access to news and press-related information about Microsoft worldwide.[20]

Organisations attempt reciprocity on the Internet through stable and legitimate dialogue which emphasises co-operation, collaboration and co-ordination.[21] Stability in dialogue helps achieve orderly and reliable patterns and legitimacy aids improved inter-organisational relationships based on existent norms and beliefs. In this process of initiation and response, dialogue with media and stakeholders is more important than one-way message framing by the media.

WHAT IS FRAMING?

The questions don't do the damage. Only the answers do.

—SAM DONALDSON[22]

Framing is a process through which media draws out key themes from the content through '… repetition of certain words and phrases across the life of a story [which] shapes meaning by telling readers what the important story elements are and how to think about them'.[23] In other words, framing means sequencing of events and issues, which are similarly or differently understood by media professionals and stakeholders. Frames can be created around four topics: communicators, texts, receivers and culture.[24] Together with rhetorical focus on framing, there is an emphasis on the implicit psychological processes of the audiences through which they examine information, make judgements and draw inferences. Hence, establishing emotional connect is crucial in reaching out to the publics.

Media creates frames through well-crafted stories by organising and providing meaning to a series of events. Information on 'perceived reality' is sequentially arranged giving prominence to certain facts, which validate perceptions and interpretations of the journalists covering the story. While framing a message, positive or negative connotations are attributed to the 'framed' entity, and responsibility assigned to the afflicted and/or afflicting parties. 'Framing essentially involves selection and salience. To frame is to select some aspects of a perceived reality and make them more salient in communicating a text, in such a way as to promote a particular problem definition, causal interpretation, moral evaluation and/or treatment recommendation for the item described.'[25] The desired attitude and perceptual change is brought about by the packaging of information together with the message source, reference points and numerical or oral presentation.[26]

To bring about attitudinal change, consistency in messages is required while sharing information, as readers rely on existing beliefs and expectations which help them to pronounce judgement on organisations. Frames analyse the causes, try and locate issues that may have created problems, make ethical judgements and recommend suggestions justifying the cause of action. The framing intention of the journalist may or may not receive identical response from the receiver. The dominant message has to be reinforced through repetitions which will help audiences to select, highlight, agree, disagree to the argument constructs, evaluate and make suggestions. Organisations can help the media design their frames by being consistent in information sharing and delegating the task of media interaction to any one individual/team who structures the message, and has clarity on the 'what' and the 'how' to be said.

Frames highlight some information and follow it up by appropriate placement, and linkage with culturally similar symbols. Their effectiveness is characterised by the content they include or omit, creating a positive or negative effect on the receiver's perception and information processing mode. Hence, both exclusion and inclusion of facts and interpretations determine the extent of influence. What should, then, be the content which should go into framing? Journalists present the story based on their assessment of the presence or absence of salient words, facts, images, new stories, press releases and organisational communication. The criterion for selecting a story is based on the premise that frame generators, by encapsulating a series of events as per their understanding, will secure a similar response from the audience, which notably, is not always possible.

Organisations find it difficult to control information accessed by the media through various sources. However, they can work against odds by structuring information and frequently sharing the same with the media, thus obliterating the need to refer to other unreliable sources which may lead the audience astray.

With a change in technology the audience has also become receptive to news exchange over the Internet. It is at this point that traditional media has to exercise caution while framing news, for the impact should be cascading rather than top-down. A beginning point for doing this is an analysis of the five Ws and the one H: 'what, when, where, why, who and how'. An illustrative example of the same is as follows:

CEO informs the stakeholders about their new CSR initiative. The message is iterated by the CSR and corporate communication team members who inform the employees and media of the new initiative. The media presents the story using a frame with appropriate words and images to influence public perception. The message reaches the audience/ stakeholders who assimilate the information for further intervention or action. In the developed frame, the focus of the journalist is on: what led to the development of the CEO message? What is the rationale behind this venture? What are the predictors of success? When was the decision taken? When do they intend implementing the same? Why was this decision taken? Is there a history of similar events or linked events? In case of the last question, the journalist will be keen to learn if any attempt, e.g. reducing carbon footprints has been adopted earlier by the organisation which gives credibility and relevance to the venture. Who will initiate and who will be the beneficiary? How will this venture be implemented?

Framing can be done in seven ways: situations, attributes, choices, actions, issues, responsibility and news. These address relationships between individuals in varying situations; accentuate characteristics of people and objects; propose alternative decisions in situations of uncertainty; alternative actions to be taken by an individual with either positive or negative elaboration; explanation of social problems and issues in varying terms; assigning responsibility based on individual attribution to events arising from either internal or external factors and reporting of news with familiar, culturally appropriate themes.[27]

The structuring of information is done with use of syntactical devices (arranging of words and phrases); script structures (developing events in the text in a predictable manner); thematic constructs (developing content as per the themes) based on stated propositions with words as 'because', 'so', etc. and rhetorical structures as metaphors, similes, etc. No matter what the model, the audience, through association and expectation, is able to make inferences about the sequence of events which may not necessarily gel with the reporter's intentions.

WHAT IS THE INVERTED PYRAMID STYLE OF WRITING?

The inverted pyramid remains the Dracula of journalism. It keeps rising from its coffin and sneaking into the paper.

—Bruce DeSilva[28]

In the course of journalism, the most investigated genre is 'hard news' which focusses on 'selectivity of expression'[29] and presentation. Breaking away from the conventional style of news reporting is the inverted pyramid style of writing, defined as a 'top heavy form' in which the crucial information is followed by other content in decreasing order of importance. The structuring of the news items is to place the most important information at the head of the news and summarise by a key sentence which should answer at least four of the five W questions, i.e. what, who, where, when, why and be of interest to the reader. The rest of the information which follows the lead question can be treated as redundant by the reader.

Inverted pyramid style of writing news is different from the conventional form which begins with the lead issue or an outline of the story and is followed by the body detailing the points mentioned in the lead.[30] In written news, media text with descriptions aims to prove existing facts which can be strictly verified. However, the aim of the inverted pyramid goes a step beyond, to identify verifiable facts as who (protagonist) and what (involvement of people and the happenings around them) in the news item. The 'where' and the 'when' though important, are only secondary pieces of information and do not contribute to the cohesion of the news item. Ideally, in the inverted news pyramid, it is the event or the action which is important. The value of this style of writing can be gauged by its potential to reach the audience in spite of the nature of news which can be interesting, uninteresting, desired or undesired.

The inverted pyramid is a good strategy for reporting in newspapers, as readers can stop at any point and still get the key points of the article. Using this style on the web has proven to be of extreme value for readers who need not scroll the entire length of the message but can get the key message by focussing on the main point. While this approach is uncreative and stilted, it manages to capture audience attention through intensity in presentation of media content (refer Fig. 8.1).

Media Content and Effects

The form or content of media message system influences the 'study of how to control, enhance or mitigate the impact of the mass media on individuals and society'[31] by understanding the audience and impact of influence which can be social, cultural and psychological.[32]

Inverted pyramid and chronological presentation are two ways of structuring narrative content which can be presented in a linear or non-linear fashion. The selection of the method or a mix is an outcome of media channel analysis for communicating the message.

Figure 8.1   Inverted Pyramid Style of Writing

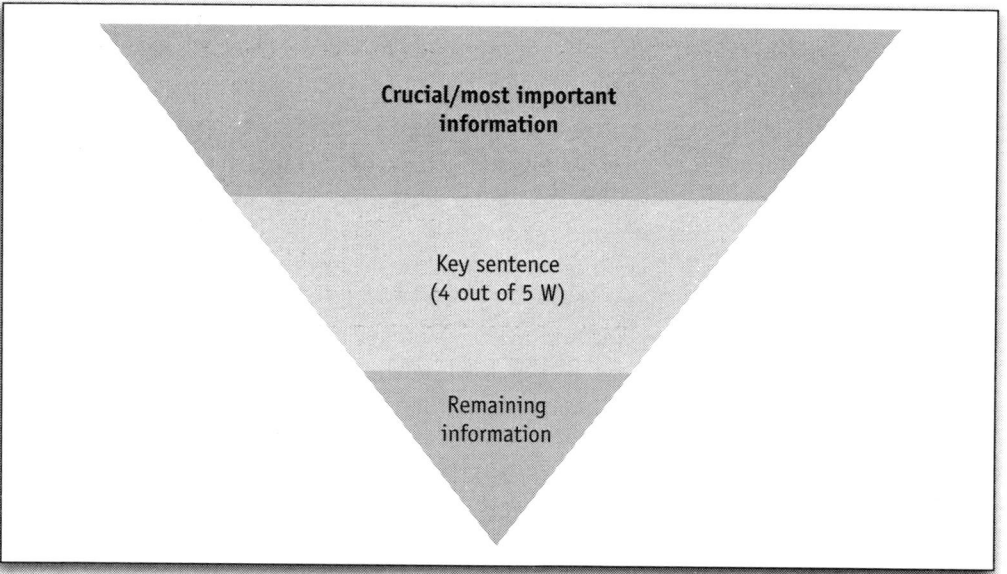

The Inverted Pyramid Style: Key Points First

The following is an excerpt of a news item from *The Economic Times*, 7 May 2008:

ONGC has little to show after 4 years of oil hunt
Largest Oil Producer Missed Leads In Over 20 Wells: D&M Audit
—Rajeev Jayaswal, New Delhi

ONGC, the largest oil producer in the country, may have to face some tough questions on its explorations. At a time when private oil majors, like RIL, are striking oil and gas in every new well, ONGC appears to have missed leads in as many as 20 wells drilled between 2002 and 2005. These are the findings of petroleum consulting firm DeGolyer and McNaughton (D&M), which audited 350 wells.

In a typical representation of the inverted pyramid style of reporting, the first paragraph provides the crux of the entire message, including the 'who' and the 'what'. In this example, we have the who, the why, the where and what clearly specified. The rest of the paragraphs develop the key ideas presented in paragraph one.

For instance, presentation of messages in newspapers is mostly in the inverted pyramid form whereas television (TV) news follows a chronological pattern. While reporting on TV, there is a strong connection between the voiceover and the images. Documentation

shifts to narration of a new event which is validated through the 'news style'[33] characterised by the formalised information and intonation provided by the reader. This reflects
the shift from traditional style of reporting which provides information by emphasising
and analysing factual content to communicating, which is engaging and easy to understand. The transition from traditional to modern style of reporting is, as on date, not
complete. On many occasions there is a clash in news priorities between informing and
communicating. The constant attempt is to provide a glimpse of reality with the power
of the narrative to grip the attention of the readers or viewers.

News is organised into 'beats' indicating arrangement and presentation of interesting and newsworthy items. The idea is to capture an audience for the product.
Media possesses the capacity to show the same images and ideas at varying platforms
through different forms and channels by selecting an attribute or mix of attributes.
These media messages can be visual, audio or textual with explicit or implicit meaning, that is, some part of the message may be naturally or explicitly stated, while
some may contain implicit suggestions. The catch in these presentations, normally
of a controversial nature, is that the text may be read differently by the audiences,
some of who may subscribe to the presented views, while others may not. In such
situations, both the diverse effect and impact of the media content can spark the
issue with an increase in readers or viewers.

Media content is influenced by levels within a communication setting which are individual, routine, organisational, social/institutional and ideological.[34] To elaborate, the
individual level covers factors close to the news reporter; under the routine category, fall
the structured practices followed by media workers as inter-media agenda setting (pack
journalism); organisational takes into account market intelligence; social comprises cultural
dimensions and, ethical factors fall under the ideological category.

There are four ways by which media can capture the attention of the audience:

- Reputation management, which lies behind all kinds of investments made by ad-
  vertisers, sponsors, etc.
- Content management, which comprises handling the editorial section
- Team cohesion and common purpose, i.e. experienced identity, which is a result
  of cohesion of values which are professed and followed
- Management of forms, i.e. projected identity which leverages brand management[35]

The newsworthiness of the story results from media effects which are an interplay
of a wide set of attributes. Crucial among this set is the interactivity in the news item
which indicates that communication should be fed on and responded to. This form of
interactivity is common in the Internet news websites. The extent of control provided to
the user, that is, the amount of time taken to read the story, the order in which it is viewed
and read, together with the quantum of information, helps in creating the impact. The
relative weight assigned to the channel associated with communicating the message, for
instance visual, audio or both creates the desired media effect.

WHAT IS THE ROI OF MEDIA INTERACTION?

What you do speaks so loud that I cannot hear what you say.

—Ralph Waldo Emerson[36]

Organisations measure ROI on media interaction as an aggregate of expenses incurred on a communication activity and the benefits derived therein, expressed in terms of revenue generation, cost reduction and avoidance by risk mitigation.[37] ROI can also be measured as an aggregate of impressions created by the media with the ultimate objective of behaviour change or reinforcement. The goal is to embed a message or create a set number of impressions for generating awareness about the organisation. This model follows a linear progression from message generation, to transmitter receipt, to purchase and may not always hold true.

Can the impact of media be analysed? Assessing media impact requires minute scrutiny of the sentiment or tone of media coverage. Two common practices followed by organisations for the same are: latent and manifest analysis. Latent analysis considers the entire article and assesses the whole, based on the overall tone. Under manifest analysis, the process followed is an assessment of sentences, paragraphs, judging each by the tone, adding the total number of positives and negatives to obtain a final score.

In addition to these two types, there is a third approach which advocates analysing the story on the basis of pre-determined messages (positive and negative) which are present in the article. Is there quality in the news item? What is the content placement? Is the positioning visually prominent? Additional questions assessed and measured are: Who is the spokesperson? What is the frequency of including quotes from spokespersons? How frequently is the organisation or programme the dominant subject within the news item as compared to competitors?

Measuring Media Favourability

'Media coverage can serve as a proxy for public perception and is relatively inexpensive and accessible. PR professionals apply media analysis to help demonstrate the value of public relations, provide insights to make better decisions, improve performance, understand issues and anticipate change.'[38] What measures can be used for media analysis? Some standards which are normally observed for analysis are: getting agreement from all concerned parties, being transparent and consistent in the analysis. The number of people who get an Opportunity To See (OTS) is the total audited circulation and its receptivity. Measures for assessing different media vary across types. For instance, in the print media, the assessment is based on the circulation of copies of publication (as contrasted with read) and impressions created through earned media as opposed to paid media. In online media, calculations are based on impressions or daily views posted on the Unique Resource Locator (URL) or subdomain (as www.google.com compared to marketinggoogle.com) which are divided by the number of unique visitors per month.

Table 8.2 Parameters for Measuring ROI of Media Relations[39]

Counting Media Placements	Tracking Coverage in Mainstream or First-tier Publications
Assessing quality	Assessing whether media placements will impact behaviour and attitudes of readers
Viral impact	Measuring number of mentions; number, tone and sentiment of influencers for online media coverage
Behavioural impact	Measuring increase in inquiries, recommendations and sales of product/service
Growth	Monitoring customer retention and revenue growth

The result is then multiplied by the number of days in a month. Finally for the broadcast media, the numbers are provided by the broadcast monitoring service. Various metrics are used to measure the ROI made in media relations (Table 8.2).

What items count as a 'hit' and can be used for analysis? Only those which pass the test of being run through the editorial filter, become a differentiator between validated information and simple assertions. The interest of audiences in the narrative is validated by the reprints for different readership and updation of the same story in online media several times in one day.

Quality checks are important for practitioners focussing on measurement techniques for analysing media content; for instance, incorporation of visuals—photo, chart, logo; placement and prominence accorded to the news item—front page, first column, etc.; message penetration—how many items include the key message; spokesperson—per cent of items which include a quote of the chief organisational spokesperson; third party—per cent of items which include third party endorsement of the organisation item being reported; shared/sole mention—per cent of items where the organisation has sole presence in the media column as compared to the space being shared by competitors.

Media favourability translates to audience acceptance which finally affects organisational reputation.

CAN ORGANISATIONAL REPUTATION BE BUILT BY MEDIA?

There is only one thing in the world worse than being talked about, and that is not being talked about.

—Oscar Wilde[40]

Organisational reputation can be built or marred by statements made deliberately or inadvertently in the media. Not only coverage but 'no coverage' can also impact reputation, more specifically in the case of unpaid media which assesses or measures media coverage 'in print, broadcast and internet channels devoted to a particular channel or topic which would be analysed to determine what per cent of output is devoted to a client or product'.[41]

The definition provided above helps in assessing the competitive landscape. However, it is limited as it focusses on clip impressions rather than tone, message, etc. To counter negative impact organisations should ideally:

- State their goals, objectives and tactics
- Focus on positive note and strategic messages that have a long lasting impact
- Maintain pressure

Constant monitoring, realigning and resetting agenda for securing media coverage and maintaining share of discussion are required. For an organisation there are five rules: maintain and build relationship with journalists; be honest and ethical; provide enabling environment; do not force particular stories or frames—share both positive and negative stories and send appropriate material which is relevant and newsworthy.[42] In short, for organisation–media tango to reflect vibrancy, organisations should send stories which are newsworthy, interesting, timely, and in a form that can be used.

The richness of media information is assessed by the capacity of immediate feedback, personalisation and language variety. If however, the media is lean and static, it will not provide additional information. The efficiency of communication through media is measured by the ability to facilitate exchange of information. Gaining attention in the public media 'involves infusing the [organisation] story with either news or entertainment value (or both) and, thereby making the story or idea attractive to media producers'.[43]

Media system dependency theory[44] suggests that there is a relationship among media, audience and a larger social and economic system. Organisations are dependent on the media for conveying their message to the stakeholders. If the message is communicated directly through the organisation, its credibility is not as high as when transmitted through the media. Previous experience with the channel, communication partner and topic influence the perception of stakeholders regarding the credibility and richness of the media channel.[45]

The reputation of an organisation is dependent on media interplay with the culture of the targeted group and organisational identity. Culture can be defined as 'a pattern of shared basic assumptions that was learnt by a group as it solved its problems of external adaptations and internal integrations'.[46] Organisational identity can be communicated through any of the five representations: actual, communicated, conceived, ideal and desired identities.[47] The media define themselves through the identity of the organisation. A mismatch in the interplay among the three entities: media, organisation and audience culture may tarnish organisational reputation.

For the match to be as per the desired objective, organisations adhere to the following rules:

- Be proactive
- Make the story meaningful

- Keep it short and simple
- Be truthful
- Do not exaggerate

In today's world of technology, with enhanced diversity and far-reaching influence from media and other online channels, organisations have begun to actively listen to media for reputation enhancement. Organisations, with their PR teams, are constantly on the move to build relationships for media effectiveness, through consistent message alignment and provision of accurate data. While media credibility in providing information is much higher than that of the organisation, the good news is that within the country, credibility of news media is not as high as it would be otherwise due to 'cash for news coverage'.[48]

How can media be used to build corporate reputation? Through media interaction strategies where the company shares stories and information through its website or virtual press room, or during direct interactions as press conferences and interviews. The media and the company itself, both give frames to this information using any of the seven models: situations, attributes, choices, actions, issues, responsibilities and news. The framing process creates company and CEO visibility, which ultimately contributes to corporate reputation. Additionally, the company measures the ROI of these interactions on a regular basis, so that it can realign and reset agenda for optimising media relations (refer Fig. 8.2).

Figure 8.2 Furthering Reputation through Media Relations

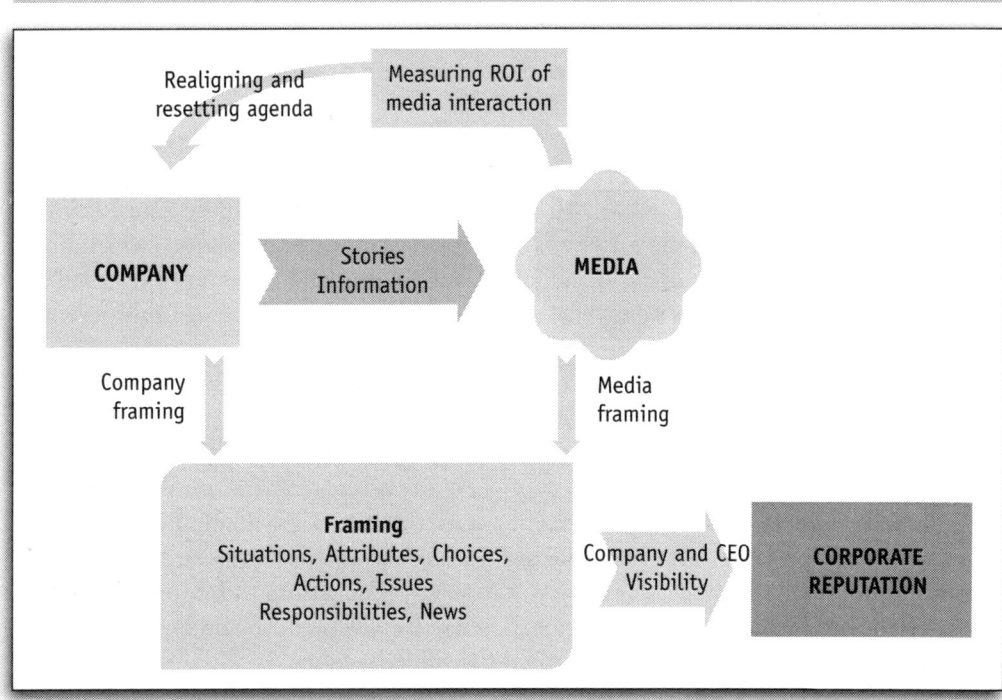

What Is the Power of Media Reporting?

The power of media reporting cannot, and should not, be underestimated. Media reports shape the social processes through which leader images are constructed. Repeated positive coverage can assign a CEO celebrity status, increase earning power and career opportunities whereas negative coverage can have a reverse effect. Additionally, media reporting exercises corporate control by exerting pressure on organisations to either reform their existing policies, or even change their board or CEO in response to low financial performance.[49] Thus, media plays the role of a 'watchdog of business and information asymmetry between management and external constituencies'.[50] In other words, it throws light on certain issues which force decision makers to take actions which can reinforce or amend existing norms and policies. Hence, media response becomes consequential for the organisations, as their subsequent actions are determined by media reporting.

Media Impact on Leader Reputation

It has not been incorrectly stated that leaders and CEOs are created by the media. To assess the success of a leader, it may be interesting to take a look at the media coverage that a CEO receives in relation to organisational coverage. CEO visibility and reputation are directly proportional to the organisational media coverage. However, it cannot be categorically stated that a rise in one leads to a corresponding increase in the other. For instance, with an upsurge in controversial news, there is a corresponding increase in media coverage of the CEO and the organisation. However, the same does not hold true in case of positive news.

Additionally, organisational and leader reputation are dependent on the media interaction skills of the CEO, through which a clear and consistent corporate vision is projected. Hence, maintaining a good relationship with journalists is a good strategy to remain in the news for all the right reasons. Providing a formal, structured pattern may not be one of the best ways to get media buy-in. How should we then approach the issue? Prior to reporting or a news telecast, the questions are provided to the organisations which helps them prepare a response reflective of a 'halo effect'. This may not be possible on all occasions. To counter rough terrains, leaders often try to divert attention from potential controversies. While they maintain the appearance of being spontaneous in their press interaction, they are well-armed to focus on the key message and persuade reporters to accept what they consider to be 'real headline'.[51]

During media broadcast, leaders select inclusive language and appeal to ideals that evoke shared meaning among diverse groups. While addressing the audience through TV channels, leaders normally demonstrate good oratory skills, maintain eye contact, place hands on the table with palms facing upwards and maintain a straight spine to communicate confidence and assertiveness. Emphatic hand gestures to emphasise the key point, use of impersonal words, slow speech, select words, rhetoric and gestures project their clear vision, confidence and control on the subject matter.

The image of the CEO through extensive media coverage, organisation reputation, and enunciation of concrete activities, determines organisational success in building relationships with multiple stakeholders. Though it is the responsibility of the PR department to project the activities of the organisation positively by managing a good image, it is not always the case. Public, when exposed to negative information, reflect greater attitudinal change.[52] For instance, many crisis situations have been attributed to negative coverage which reflects difficulty in building good media relationships. As information placed in the public domain by the media is considered to be believable and credible, it is more influential than any other form of market-driven communication. Hence, it is important that a series of positive assertions and appearances of the CEO be made through media channels so that public response is positive and customer relationship strengthened. In the current scenario, new/social media is being used extensively to increase the reach and spread of the target audience.

Assessing CEO Visibility: Mint Influencers Index

The Mint Influencers Index tracks media visibility of corporate and political figures in global and Indian media, assigning ranks for both. This monthly measure tracks the volume of media citations of these leaders in an attempt to assess visibility and share of voice. It is based on media analysis by Factiva.

The methodology consists of using text mining and visualisation technologies to scrutinise around 10,000 global sources, which include *Dow Jones*, *Reuters* and *The Associated Press* newswires, and coverage in *The Wall Street Journal*, *The New York Times*, *Washington Post*, *The Globe and Mail* and other major international newspapers. For the Indian rankings, 50 major domestic newspapers and wire services are used. Both, the global and Indian rankings, do not consider routine news items and company announcements.

Among corporate personalities, the February 2012 list figured Mr Anil Ambani (Reliance ADAG) at fourth position with 331 media citations and Mr Ratan Tata (Tata Group) at fifth with 198 citations. The other corporate leaders who made it in the top 10 list were Mr Anand Mahindra (Mahindra Group), Mr Mukesh Ambani (Reliance Industries Ltd.), Mr Sunil Mittal (Bharti Group), Mr Kumar Mangalam Birla (Aditya Birla Group), Mr N. Chandrasekaran (Tata Consultancy Services), Mr Deepak Parekh (HDFC), Mr Y. C. Deveshwar (ITC Ltd.), Mr A. M. Naik (L&T Ltd.), Ms Chanda Kochchar (ICICI Bank Ltd.), Mr Aditya Puri (HDFC Bank), Mr Azim Premji (Wipro Ltd.), Mr S. Gopalakrishnan (Infosys Ltd.) and Mr O. P. Bhatt (State Bank of India).[53]

Organisation Handling of Media

Organisations develop partnerships for 'collaborative advantage'[54] with all stakeholders including media, by maintaining good relationships and being transparent in communication. The relationship established is important for transference of information, energy or resources. These partnerships also create a protocol for communication and allow a smooth process of interaction during crisis situations.

Organisations normally have a PR cell which addresses all issues related to building and maintaining media relationships. It is important for the PR cell to view the media and journalists as collaborators for developing their image and transmitting a single message to the audience. Historically, media has 'repetitively' traced and presented to the readers and viewers content provided to them by PR practitioners.

Print media has seven categories for the use of PR, 'distraction, disaster, challenge, hype, merely war and schmooze'.[55] Most of the references to the organisations have been found to be negative or unfavourable, with maximum citations falling under the categories of distraction, disaster and challenge. However, when it is a question of positive news as reporting CSR, media has been found to use positive terms which are fair and objective, speak highly of corporate achievements, express community and social expectations and spin on corporate reputation.[56] This would indicate that media is more tolerant of positive than negative news items. Their role is critical as they tend to construct a dramatised version of the negative news (as in the case of crisis) and amplify risks so as to secure eyeballs. These narrative accounts are elaborated and the spun version of organisational reality is sufficient to damage reputation.

The question before us is why does media focus on negative news more frequently than good news? Because it attracts attention of the audience and impacts brand perception. As long as the crisis remains within the precincts of the organisation, leaders have the freedom to operate and normalise the situation in a manner they deem fit. However, when it reaches the media, the problem and risks are amplified with the consequence that consumers rapidly change their perception about the brand and organisation, leading to a steep decline in trust. Media can construct and project claims as well as set the social agenda.[57] The complexity and technicality of the issue makes it difficult for consumers to understand the processes independently. Hence, when messages are drafted in simple language which deconstruct the complex problem, the credibility is higher and faith in information steeper. Different media channels attempt to project the story in multiple ways with differing storylines so that readership and viewership is higher than that of competitors.

WHAT STRATEGIES DO ORGANISATIONS FOLLOW FOR MEDIA BUY-IN?

If it's going to come out eventually, better have it come out immediately.

—HENRY KISSINGER[58]

For making a story interesting, meaningful and relevant to the audiences organisations should:

- Communicate with print media, generate online content and build relationships with other journalists.
- Use CEO reputation to generate and monitor media tonality.
- Adopt proactive measures by developing an interesting and compelling story.
- Give shape and meaning to the story from the perspective of the audience.

- 'Pitch' the story to the reporters without waiting for the interview slots. Keep the pitch simple, with one or two main ideas and a one-page write-up.
- Focus on the media outlet audience. Is it consumer or business oriented?
- Follow the KISS principle of communication—keep it short and simple.
- Keep the recency effect in mind. A story provided after the event is over, will have little significance to either the media or the public.
- Reinforce ideas and story by sending in brief write-ups every fortnight or month.[59]
- Search for innovative methods to provide the news.
- Double check on the accuracy of information and contact.
- Help journalists find sources for information.
- Respond to inquiries related to professional expertise without considering immediate benefits.

CONCLUSION

I fear three newspapers more than a hundred thousand bayonets.

—Napolean Bonaparte[60]

The 2G scam, Nira Radia case, Anna Hazare-led movement, etc. are some examples of how media can shape audience perceptions by sharing glimpses of reality. Media exposure of organisational activities is an important factor which can be related to changes in corporate reputation. The newsworthiness of company activities together with reality of performance, diversity of responses, communication effort, time and memory recall, suggests that media exposure can bring about a major shift in reputational focus.

Media exposure or 'the aggregated news reports relating to a specific company within a prescribed period'[61] refers to news coverage of any one company within a defined period. The media serves as a vehicle reflecting personality and expectation of company leader and stakeholders. Individuals have limited capacity to perceive processes or store, retrieve and infer data. Hence, this information is provided by the media to shape reality and force perceptions which will help them judge and understand the impact of the message.

Two factors which impact perceptions are tone and 'recency effects' of media messages. Negative tone will have a higher impact than a positive one, and recency effect will help garner stakeholders' interest. From the perspective of the stakeholder, selective perception and persuasiveness helps in assimilating information. Stakeholders use the media to both form and voice their expectations. Organisations, on the one hand, can attain the ideal situation by giving careful attention to the expectations of stakeholders. On the other hand, they may decide to ignore stakeholders and fight for their rights as intensity of common voice increases in the media.

In this love–hate relationship between the organisation and media, neither can ignore the other. The most prudent step then, is to nurture the relationship through partnerships in which presented information is credible, honest and helps project a positive organisational image.

> ### Key Points
>
> - Media acts as a carrier of institutional logic, a social arbiter and gatekeeper.
> - Media focusses on influencing and providing a legitimate platform for assessment of individuals and organisations.
> - It shapes and reshapes perceptions on social reality.
> - Media sensationalises and influences the public through positive and negative reporting. The impact of negative stories surpasses the interest in positive narrations.
> - Media relations and trust can be developed through constantly monitoring media interests and providing them with the required stories and narratives.
> - Agenda setting and building are required to make media engagement strategies more focussed.
> - Practitioner–journalist relationship can be built by honesty and openness; accuracy of information; responsiveness and timeliness; reliability and consistency and preparedness.
> - Support and involvement of the leadership team is important in handling media.
> - Organisations have begun to make extensive use of their websites to influence the public either directly or through media visits and revisits to their webpages.
> - Framing is the scripting of events and issues, which are similarly or differently understood by media professionals and stakeholders.
> - Frames can be created around four topics: communicators, texts, receivers and culture.
> - Frames emphasise the psychological processes of the audiences through which they examine information, make judgements and draw inferences.
> - Framing is done in seven ways: situations, attributes, choices, actions, issues, responsibility and news.
> - In inverted pyramid, the most important information is placed at the head of the news and the content then summarised by key sentence which answers at least four of five of the W questions, i.e. what, who, where, when, why, and is of interest to the reader.
> - Media effect is the comprehension of the wide variety of attributes which make for the newsworthiness of the message.
> - Organisations measure media ROI which is an aggregate of expenses incurred on a communication activity and the benefits derived therein.
> - Assessing media impact requires analysis of the sentiment or tone of media coverage. Two common practices followed by organisations are: latent and manifest analysis.
> - Organisational reputation can be built or marred by statements made deliberately or inadvertently in the media. Not only coverage but 'no coverage' can also impact reputation.
> - Organisations adhere to the following rules while interacting with media: be proactive, make the story meaningful and keep it short and simple.
> - Media exposure refers to the aggregated news reports relating to a specific company within a prescribed period.
> - Tone and recency of media messages impact audience perceptions.

END NOTES

1. S. Veil, 'Friend vs. foe: Viewing the media as a partner in crisis response', website http://www.institute-forpr.org/iprwp/wp-content/uploads/FriendvFoe.pdf (accessed 22 April 2013).

2. 'George Orwell quotes', GoodReads, website http://www.goodreads.com/quotes/77244-journalism-is-printing-what-someone-else-does-not-want-printed (accessed 22 April 2013).

3. R. M. Entman, 'Framing: Toward clarification of a fractured paradigm', *Journal of Communication* (1993), 43(4), 51–58.

4. 'ICICI Bank rallies, says depositors' money safe', *The Times of India*, website http://articles.timesofindia.indiatimes.com/2008-09-30/india-business/27900889_1_icici-bank-managing-director-private-sector-bank-rumours (accessed 13 March 2013).

5. R. D. Waters, N. T. J. Tindall and T. S. Morton, 'Media catching and the journalist–public relations practitioner relationship: How social media are changing the practice of media relations', *Journal of Public Relations Research* (2010), 22(3), 241–264, p. 241.

6. G. Meikle, 'Continuity and transformation in convergent news: The case of WikiLeaks', *Media International Australia* (2012), 144, 52–59.

7. Ibid., p. 53.

8. J. Rosen, 'The Afghanistan war logs released by WikiLeaks, the world's first stateless news organization', website http://archive.pressthink.org/2010/07/26/wikileaks_afghan.html (accessed 2 May 2013).

9. B. McNair, *Cultural Chaos: Journalism, and Power in a Globalised World.* New York: Routledge (2006), p. 49.

10. G. Lovink and P. Riemens, 'Twelve theses on WikiLeaks', in B. Brevini, A. Hintz and P. McCurdy (eds), *Beyond Wikileaks: Implications for the Future of Communications, Journalism and Society* (pp. 2450–253), Hampshire, UK: Palgrave Macmillan (2013), p. 248.

11. 'Wikileaks: 'Sanjay Gandhi plotted to oust Cong CM', *The Hindustan Times*, website http://www.hindustantimes.com/India-news/NewDelhi/Wikileaks-Sanjay-Gandhi-enjoyed-exalted-status-among-Indira-s-advisors/Article1-1040064.aspx (accessed 9 April 2013).

12. B. Blyskal and M. Blyskal, *PR: How the Public Relations Industry Writes the News.* New York, Morrow (1985).

13. S. Kiousis, C. Popescu and M. Mitrook, 'Understanding influence on corporate reputation: An examination of public relations efforts, media coverage, public opinion, and financial performance from an agenda-building and agenda-setting perspective', *Journal of Public Relations Research* (2007), 19(2), 147–165.

14. D. Philips, '20 quotes to inspire PR professionals', website http://www.prdaily.com/Main/Articles/20_quotes_to_inspire_PR_professionals_11380.aspx (accessed 22 April 2013).

15. E. Battenberg, 'Managing a media frenzy', *Public Relations Tactics* (2002), 9(12), 1–2.

16. S. E. Desiere and B. L. Sha, 'Exploring the development of an organizational approach to media relationships', *Public Relations Review* (2007), 33(1), 96–98.

17. M. L. Kent and M. Taylor, 'Maximizing media relations: A website checklist', *Public Relations Quarterly* (2003), 48(1), 14–18.

18. J. L. Horton, *Online Public Relations: A Handbook for Practitioners.* Westport, CT: Greenwood (2001).

19. J. E. Pettigrew and B. H. Reber, 'The new dynamic in corporate media relations: How Fortune 500 companies are using virtual press rooms to engage the press', *Journal of Public Relations Research* (2010), 22(4), 404–428.

20. Microsoft India, Press Room, website http://www.microsoft.com/india/msindia/msindia_pressroom.aspx

21. G. M. Broom, S. Casey and J. Ritchey, 'Concept and theory of organization–public relationships', in J. A. Ledingham and S. D. Bruning (eds), *Public Relations as Relationship Management: A Relational Approach to the Study and Practice of Public Relations* (pp. 3–22), Mahwah, NJ: Lawrence Earlbaum Associates (2000).

22. Brainy quote, website http://www.brainyquote.com/quotes/quotes/s/samdonalds162209.html (accessed 22 April 2013).

23. D. L. Dickerson, 'Framing 'political correctness': The New York Times' tale of two professors', in S. D. Reese, O. H. Gandy, Jr. and A. E. Garnt (eds), *Framing Public Life: Perspectives on Media and Our Understanding of the Social World* (pp. 163–174). Mahwah, NJ: Lawrence Erlbaum Associates (2001), p. 168.

24. R. M. Entman, 'Framing: Toward clarification of a fractured paradigm', *Journal of Communication* (1993), 43(4), 51–58.

25. R. M. Entman, `Framing: Toward clarification of a fractured paradigm', *Journal of Communication* (1993), 43(4), 52.

26. J. A. Ruth and A. York, 'Framing information to enhance corporate reputation: The impact of message source, information type, and reference point', *Journal of Business Research* (2004), 57(1), 14–20.

27. K. Hallahan, 'Seven models of framing: Implications for public relations', *Journal of Public Relations Research* (1999), 11(3), 205–242.

28. C. Scanlan, 'Writing from the top down: Pros and cons of the inverted pyramid', website http://www. poynter.org/how-tos/newsgathering-storytelling/chip-on-your-shoulder/12754/writing-from-the-top-down-pros-and-cons-of-the-inverted-pyramid/ (accessed 23 April 2013).

29. H. Pottker, 'News and its communicative quality: the inverted pyramid-when and why did it appear?', *Journalism Studies* (2003), 4(4), 501–511, p. 501.

30. G. F. Mott, *New Survey of Journalism*. New York: Barnes & Noble (1950).

31. E.M. Perse, *Media Effects and Society*. Mahwah, NJ: Lawrence Erlbaum Associates (2001), p. 9.

32. G. Gerbner, L. Gross, M. Morgan, N. Signorielli and J. Shanahan, 'Growing up with television: cultivation processes', in J. Bryant and D. Zillmann (eds), *Perspectives on Media Effects* (pp. 43–67). Hillsdale, NJ: Lawrence Erlbaum Associates (2nd ed.), (2002)..

33. T. A. van Dijk, *News as Discourse*. Hillsdale, NJ: Lawrence Erlbaum Associates (1988), p. 75.

34. S. A. Park, M. E. Len-Ríos and A. Hinnant, 'How intrinsic and extrinsic news factors affect health journalists' cognitive and behavioural attitudes toward media relations', *PRism* (2010), 7(1), 1–14.

35. G. Soenen and B. Moingeon, 'The five facets of collective identities. Integrating corporate and organizational identity', in B. Moingeon and G. Soenen (eds), *Corporate and Organizational Identities: Integrating Strategy, Marketing, Communication, and Organizational Perspectives* (pp. 13-34). London: Routledge (2002).

36. Quote investigator, website http://quoteinvestigator.com/2011/01/27/what-you-do-speaks/ (accessed 27 January 2011).

37. F. Likely, D. Rockland and M. Weiner, 'Perspectives on the ROI of media relations publicity efforts', *Institute for Public Relations* (2006), 2–10.

38. M. Eisenmann, D. Geddes, K. Paine, R. Pestana, F. Walton and M. Weiner, 'Proposed interim standards for metrics in traditional media analysis', *Institute for Public Relations* (2012), website http://www.instituteforpr.org/topics/proposed-interim-standards-for-metrics-in-traditional-media-analysis/ (accessed 15 March 2013).

39. M. L. Butler, '10 ways to measure the ROI of public relations', website http://everything-pr.com/roi-public-relations/241033/ (accessed 13 March 2013).

40. Quotations book, website http://quotationsbook.com/quote/17569/#sthash.H4axIR2f.dpbs (accessed 23 April 2013).

41. 'The dictionary for public relations measurement and research' cited in A. Jeffrey, D. Michaelson and D. Stacks, 'Exploring the link between share of media coverage and business outcomes', *Institute for Public Relations* (2007), website http://www.instituteforpr.org/iprwp/wp-content/uploads/MediaCoverageAndVolume.pdf (accessed 15 March 2013).

42. G. M. Broom, *Cutlip & Center's Effective Public Relations*. Upper Saddle River, NJ: Prentice-Hall (2008).

43. K. Hallahan, 'Strategic media planning: Toward an integrated public relations media model', in R. L. Heath (ed.), *Handbook of Public Relations* (pp. 461–470). London: SAGE Publications (2001), p. 465.

44. S. J. Ball-Rokeach and M. L. DeFleur, 'A dependency model of mass-media effects', *Communication Research* (1976), 3(1), 3–21.

45. J. R. Carlson and R. W. Zmud, 'Channel expansion theory and the experiential nature of media richness perceptions', *Academy of Management Journal* (1999), 42(2), 153–170.

46. E. H. Schein, *Organizational Culture and Leadership* (3rd ed.). San Francisco, CA: Jossey-bass (1985), p. 17.

47. G. Deslandes, 'Corporate culture versus organizational identity: Implications for media management', *Journal of Media Business Studies* (2011), 8(4), 23–36.

48. M. Daniels and A. Jeffrey, 'International media analysis made simple', *Institute of Public Relations* (2012), website http://www.instituteforpr.org/topics/international-media-analysis-made-simple/ p. 7 (accessed 15 March 2013).

49. J. D. Westphal, S. H. Park, M. L. McDonald and M. L. A. Hayward, 'Helping other CEOs avoid bad press: Social exchange and impression management support among CEOs in communications with journalists', *Administrative Science Quarterly* (2012), 57(2), 217–268.

50. M. K. Bednar, 'Watchdog or lapdog? A behavioral view of the media as a corporate governance mechanism', *Academy of Management Journal* (2012), 55(1), 131–150, p. 133.

51. F. D. Roosevelt, 'Excerpts from the press conference', *The American Presidency Project*, website http://www.presidency.ucsb.edu (accessed 11 February 2009).

52. R. Ahluwalia, R. E. Burnkrant and R. H. Unnava, 'Consumer response to negative publicity: The moderating role of commitment', *Journal of Marketing Research* (2000), 37(2), 203–214.

53. 'Raja gains the most in Feb', website http://newsle.com/article/0/15017703/ (accessed 29 January 2012).

54. C. Huxham, 'Collaboration and collaborative advantage', in C. Huxham (ed.), *Creating Collaborative Advantage* (pp. 1–18), London: SAGE Publications (1998), p. 7.

55. C. H. Spicer, 'Image of public relations in print media', *Journal of Public Relations Research* (1993), 5(1), 47–61, p. 47.

56. J. Zhang and D. Swanson, 'Analysis of news media's representation of corporate social responsibility (CSR)', *Public Relations Quarterly* (2006), 51(2), 13–17.

57. D. McQuail, *McQuail's Mass Communication Theory* (6th ed.). London: SAGE Publications (2010).

58. Brainy quote, website http://www.brainyquote.com/quotes/quotes/h/henryakis153478.html (accessed 22 April 2013).

59. M. Daks, 'Media relations are key to repairing banking's image: You may not have been the problem, but you can be the solution', *New Jersey Banker* (Winter 2013), 18–19.

60. WARC, Quotebank: Media, website http://www.warc.com/Pages/NewsAndOpinion/Quotebank.aspx?Category=Media (accessed 29 June 2013).

61. S. L. Wartick, 'The relationship between intense media exposure and change in corporate reputation', *Business and Society* (1992), 31(1), 33–49, p. 34.

9

Understanding the 'Tweet. Post. Call. Comment' Affair: Managing Reputation through Social Media

We don't have a choice on whether we DO social media, the question is how well we DO it.

—Erik Qualman[1]

Objectives:

- Study the history of social media
- Outline objectives of social media
- Explain strategies for initiating the social media process
- Identify platforms of social media
- Assess ROI of social media
- Establish link between social media and corporate reputation

INTRODUCTION

If you make customers unhappy in the physical world, they might each tell 6 friends.
If you make customers unhappy on the Internet, they can each tell 6000 friends.

—Jeff Bezos[2]

Social Media (SM) is an online/electronic form of communication to share information, converse, form groups, establish associations, develop relationships, build awareness, shape opinions and attitudes, modify user-generated content, influence purchase decisions, stimulate post purchase communication and evaluation of products. Also referred to as consumer-generated media, SM 'describes a variety of new sources of online information that are created, initiated, circulated and used by consumers intent on educating each other about products, brands, services, personalities and issues'.[3]

A summary look at the box below capturing the usage trends in 2013, points to the clear fascination with and use of SM. The ease, volume, reach and speed of this form of communication has made it the most preferred style in today's fast-changing consumer-driven world.

Key Words

- Awareness
- Blogs
- Communication
- Consideration
- Crowdsource
- Cyberspace
- Facebook
- Forums
- Generation C
- Internet
- LinkedIn
- Loyalty
- Microblogging
- Preference
- Reach
- Second life
- Seeding strategy
- Social analytics
- Social media
- Social networking
- Speed
- Technical evangelists
- User-generated content
- Viral diffusion
- Viral marketing
- Volume
- Webcast
- Weblog
- Wired generation
- YouTube

Social Media Usage Trends in India 2013[4]

- Social media is used by 95.7 per cent Indian organisations to build communities.
- 76.1 per cent Indian organisations use social media to highlight brand news.
- The most popular platforms for engaging customers are Facebook, Twitter, YouTube and blogging.
- Popular practices for engaging with social communities include:

  ○ Posting generic updates instead of brand updates
  ○ Posting multiple updates a day
  ○ Organising frequent picture contests/promotions, usually on a monthly basis

- A majority of tech-savvy Indian companies have guidelines in place for governing and monitoring social media, including online monitoring programmes and response management for listening to conversations in the cyber space.
- Less than 50 per cent of Indian organisations have crisis manuals for social media.
- Almost 50 per cent of social media-using Indian organisations have conducted research for obtaining customer feedback and better understanding of customer behaviour.
- 50 per cent of the social media-savvy Indian organisations have already created mobile phone apps and 25 per cent are planning to do so.
- Most social media-savvy organisations claim to respond to queries within half an hour to an hour on Twitter and within 30 minutes to a few hours on Facebook.

Organisations are competing with one another to increase their stakeholder base by wooing them through innovative techniques, messages and technologies. Clearly, the perceived benefits are many: direct and open communication between management and employees, management and customers, management and shareholders; promotion of content through techniques as webcast and videos which have a more lasting impact than plain text; receiving feedback through online communities; creating technical evangelists; viral marketing programmes; promoting relationships; improving the creation and synthesis of knowledge; better filtering of information; quick strike in lobbying effect, etc. SM provides a platform to organisations to talk and converse directly with their consumers; and, consumers to engage in dialogue with one another. The medium has accorded huge powers in the hands of the consumers who can, with little effort and a click of the mouse, initiate simultaneous talk, and in no time, influence hundreds and thousands of other consumers.

The advantages and disadvantages associated with this media are well pronounced. If used appropriately, SM can help organisations secure a loyal following with minimal cost, time and effort. However, with inappropriate application the effect can boomerang and damage the reputation of the company. Within a matter of a few seconds a wrong word or an incorrect statement can become viral and tarnish the image of the company. Hence, when SM is used as a tool for projecting organisational views, or promoting products and services it is important that users be sufficiently trained in social networking etiquette so that maximum benefits can be reaped.

A term frequently used by marketing area is Word-Of-Mouth (WOM) which acts as an important medium for influencing purchase decisions. It provides leeway to marketers to experiment and innovate in reaching out to consumers as it is more appealing than advertising and more suited for making psychologically and financially taxing decisions. Keeping this in mind, large organisations have created dedicated teams to monitor and manage SM campaigns. Accurate assessment of the conversations helps them decide which of the following strategies they should employ: maintain silence, stop, control damage through litigation, reinvigorate or boost.[5]

Use of SM for Organisational Benefit

Social recruiting, or the process of sourcing or recruiting candidates by using social platforms, is gaining ground among Indian companies. Many Indian companies now prefer Internet sourcing for candidate data and information by surfing through SM profiles, blogs and online communities.

Chief among these sources is LinkedIn for posting job descriptions, required skills and experience, which can be viewed by the contact list of the HR personnel and forwarded to other people. This is not limited to large companies. On the contrary, smaller companies with limited HR budgets and from smaller/non-metro cities find this a very cost-effective method of recruitment. Some companies as QX Ltd., a UK-based BPO firm with an office in Ahmedabad, Gujarat and Cybersurf India Pvt. Ltd., Ahmedabad, Gujarat have used this practice to their advantage.

Organisational vision and mission can also be communicated through SM. For example, YouTube is being used to communicate organisational vision and mission.

> ### Communicating Vision, Mission and Much More via YouTube: Tata Group
>
> The Tata Group, which can boast of three companies in the top 10 at *Fortune* 'India's Most Admired Companies 2012' list, has embraced social media for communicating one of the cornerstones of its business—its vision and mission, and much more.
>   Tata Group has its own YouTube channel at http://www.youtube.com/user/TataCompanies, where it has posted more than 145 videos across eight different playlists covering diverse areas as corporate introductions, CSR events, business excellence, group initiatives, leadership thoughts and careers. There are videos that cover the entire scope of the group's business activities and its impact on the country's development, one that traces the legacy of the Tata Group from the time of its founder. Videos sharing exemplary leadership and business practices and ones that play out entire functions of Tata's 'Building India' school essay writing competitions, have been neatly archived since 2009–10.

Interestingly, organisations have begun to employ SM to improve engagement levels of employees. Most of these employees, who are also consumers of various products, fall in the Generation Y category, also referred to as the 'wired generation'.[6] This current generation with its focus on making informed decisions about an organisation, product or a service is dependent on peer opinion and digital referrals. Hence, the need to reinvent the wheel and provide a platform for conversations which, if carefully listened to and enacted upon, can create multitude of followers conversing and tweeting favourably about the company or its products. Generation X is also educating itself in the use of SM. Generation Z, the youngest and the most tech-savvy of the lot still has time to refine its understanding of SM before it picks up jobs in the corporate world.

Given the newness, benefits and challenges associated with this form of communication, it is important to consider its history before we proceed to a discussion of the objectives for initiating or joining the SM movement, how to begin the process, platforms for use of SM, its Return On Investment (ROI) and techniques of building reputation with the help of SM.

HOW DID THE CONCEPT OF SM EVOLVE?

*There is a fundamental shift that social media necessitates in business today—
the need to transition from 'Me First' to 'We First' thinking.*

—Simon Mainwaring[7]

Emails were introduced in the 1960s and were supposedly the first form of Internet connectivity. It was only after 1991 that they were made available to the public. Originally emails were introduced with the explicit purpose of sharing and exchanging messages from one computer to another which required both computers to be online. Gradually with passage of time the scope and function of email communication expanded. Users could store messages on the server which could be accessed at a convenient time. In the 1970s, with further development of technology, users were able to experience multiuser dungeon/dimension/domain with role-playing games, fiction and online chat. Towards the second half of the 1970s, users could log in to download or upload software, read news and exchange messages through the bulletin board system. In 1980, consumers began to use Usernet for posting articles or news. However, Usernet was different from bulletin board system. It did not have a central server or devoted administrator. All messages were forwarded through the newsfeed. Around the same time, the term 'weblog' was used which later got truncated to 'blog' when one of the users jokingly used it to state 'we blog'.[8]

The 1990s saw the advent of many social networking sites as Six Degrees, Black Planet, Asian Avenue and MoveOn, and some blogging services as Bloggers and Epinions. In the next 10 years, many other sites, similar to these, popped up and connected people with a similar interest in different spheres as sports, politics, music, education, etc.

With rise in number of users and widespread high-speed Internet access, social networking sites as MySpace (2003) and Facebook (2004) were created. Gradually 'virtual worlds' and computer-based simulated environments came to the fore.

Paradigmatic Shift

Historically, organisations played a critical role in controlling information which was passed on to the consumers and public at large. However, with the advent of SM and social networking sites, organisational intervention shifted to observation with little or no control on what was being said and shared. This transformation in the role of organisations and the control they exercised stemmed from the nature of the social platform which made conversation and communication two-way, easy for all to initiate, join and/or follow.

With an increased hype around SM, all companies have increased their technological pace and seem to be in a rush to join the bandwagon. To align with the changing technology patterns, companies are redefining their strategy by laying emphasis on social analytics, an analysis of the dialogue in cyberspace, which helps them work out a more personalised and real-time approach. This, however, is a challenge as the world of SM is dynamic, keeps changing with few or no repetitive processes.

Companies are targeting a new Generation C,[9] which defies age boundaries and likes to remain 'connected', is rich in terms of cultural capital, desirous of status recognition in the cyberspace and possesses the capacity to give shape and credence to online dialogue.

Generation C: Shaping Social Media Trends

An online survey of more than 2,000 Indian YouTube users conducted by Google, resulted in the categorisation of 'Generation C (Gen C)' consumers, defined not on the basis of age but on the viewership traits of 'creation, community, curation and connection'. The survey also revealed that Gen C moves between devices as many as 27 times a day, and Indian users watch nearly 30 per cent of their total number of YouTube videos on their mobiles. Smartphone owners were found spending 25 per cent of their YouTube time on mobile, and tablet owners about 20 per cent of the same on their mobile phones.

According to Ms Danielle Tiedt, Vice President, Marketing, YouTube, 'If brands create videos that Gen C loves to share, they will. If you create communities around your brand, Gen C will join and participate.'[10]

SM, Social Networking Sites, Apps and Virtual Worlds

SM and Social Networking Sites: Many a time, SM and social networking sites are spoken of in the same breath. However, there are several differences between the two. SM refers to channels of communication between two or more parties. Social networking is the process of engagement in which people with similar interests 'associate together and build relationships through community'.[11] There is a further difference in communication styles between the two. SM is only a channel through which messages are transmitted. However, social networking is a two-way communication process through which associations are developed and relationships established. SM operates more on the basis of 'telling' rather than 'conversing', as is the case with social networking sites. SM messages are direct and prompt and do not give access to the users to comment, correct or use for personal or business benefits.

SM provides consumers an opportunity to network with people with similar interests and desires, thus aiding organisations to target specific communities. Through social networking sites, content communities can also be created for sharing information. From the organisational perspective, this can prove to be dangerous as copyrighted material may also be shared. Though there are stringent rules about use of this kind of material which can be banned if found to be illegally posted, it is not always easy to do so considering the reach and volume of SM.

On a positive note, SM can also help organisations in devising product development strategies, engaging customers, providing online polling opportunities, etc. which will increase a sense of involvement and enhance ownership. For instance, consumers like giving feedback to organisations, which, if appropriately managed, can help in improving product offerings and enhancing engagement with the company. The online information on a product and the ensuing dialogue by the consumers provides the online community a security network and expedites purchase decisions.

Using Social Media to Boost a New Marketing Campaign: Revlon India

Revlon India, a leading cosmetics company, in a series of polls on the Revlon India Facebook page, tried to understand the beauty habits of Indian women. Leveraging the power of social media, the company wished to begin a new campaign. Over a two-week period, women were asked questions about their usage pattern of a foundation cream. Almost 75,000 women responded to the questionnaire. The responses were collected and used to tailor the campaign. Revlon's ColorStay Whipped Crème foundation was then illustrated as an answer to the prevailing preferences, and projected to be the perfect solution which matched with majority of the responses.

Social networking sites as MySpace and Facebook allow users to invite friends and acquaintances to be privy to personal information. Organisations have begun to use social networking sites for marketing research and creation of brand communities.[12] Facebook is also being used as a distribution channel to give virtual gifts and bouquets.

Attracting Customers through SM: Lays in India

In a bid to attract more customers and increase sales, Lays India has created a strategy for SM use which aims at creating an online community around Lays chips, engaging it, building brand affinity through greater presence and promoting ongoing campaigns.

Using a combination of Facebook, Twitter and YouTube, the company has been able to constantly interact with its online community. Along with regular posts (one or two daily) on varied content including creatives, trivia, puzzles, anagrams and contests, it has successfully used presence management, information management, engagement and monitoring.[13] One of its most popular contests was the 'Guess whose Flavour' campaign involving six popular cricketers in April 2012.[14]

A proactive approach to community building and engagement, with about 550 wall posts in a six-month period in 2011, resulted in around a million interactions and almost 50,000 total conversations on its Facebook page[15]—a creditable success.

Apps: With the recent rise in the use of apps, defined as application programmes designed for a particular purpose on a computer or mobile phone operating system, SM has received another boost. The global apps business is estimated to reach $17 billion by the end of 2012.[16]

The number of smartphone users in India touching 40 million in 2012[17] is a sharp indication of the strong potential for companies that use apps to reach out to its customers, in one way or another. The average smartphone user spends 82 per cent of his mobile time on apps, and only 18 per cent with web browsers, downloading around 40 apps and regularly using around 15 of them.[18]

Out of the five apps categories (games, SM, utilities, discovery and brands), the major preferences for apps remain games, chat, instant messaging and live music streaming. The use and impact of SM is only compounded by apps, as most social networking sites have their mobile apps, and customers prefer using them for their convenience and mobility. Similar to the use of social networking sites for marketing research and creation of brand communities, companies are now using SM apps as tools for marketing and strengthening their corporate reputation.

Virtual Worlds: Virtual worlds are of two types: game worlds and social worlds. Virtual game worlds have scripted rules for users to behave in multiplayer online role-playing games. With a high multitude of users across the globe, self-presentation and self-disclosure are limited, though the association of players with game characters is so deep that they begin to resemble the personality of the individual. Virtual social worlds are more accommodating in the sense that they allow inhabitants to live a virtual life which closely resembles reality. There are multiple opportunities for self-disclosure which makes 'living virtual' a second life, closely mirroring real-life actions and behaviour.

Gojiyo: Godrej Industries Ltd.'s Virtual World

Realising the need to establish an identity in the online medium, Godrej Industries Ltd. launched India's first online virtual world, Gojiyo (meaning—go and live life to the full) on 21 March 2010.

Targeted at young Indians, Gojiyo is a 3D platform with six worlds, each with a set of activities, where users can interact with one another by creating personalised avatars and can befriend 'like-minded' strangers. The launch of this virtual world was supported by an SM marketing strategy using Facebook to increase the circle of influence and Twitter to engage customers and answer queries. YouTube and Flickr were used to supplement these efforts.

The company's innovative effort has paid off. Gojiyo reached a strength of more than 550,000 registered members in 15 months of its launch and the company found that intention-to-purchase levels for Godrej products rose from an average of 70 per cent to an average of 80 per cent in the same time frame.[19]

WHAT ARE THE OBJECTIVES OF SM USE?

The goal of social media is to turn customers into your personal evangelists.

—SHANE BARKER[20]

Today, almost all organisations are using SM with differing objectives to reach out to the consumers and public at large and secure for themselves the first-mover advantage. Some of these are creative and innovative and are able to sustain the onslaught of peer pressure while some die a natural death. Clearly, the consequences of appropriate application of strategy to SM cannot be denied.

The objective of organisations using SM is to secure eyeballs, build awareness, consideration and preference, stimulate action and generate loyalty.[21] Micromedia is used for securing eyeballs and building awareness. Digital referrals and peer influence, consideration and preference is developed through online discussions via blogs. Organisations, with the help of bloggers and active blogging, are engaging and educating consumers about products and services, and generating loyalty with two clear goals: to spread the message and get other users to talk about the message and to measure the success of the endeavour.

Using Social Media to Make Heroes: Greenpeace India

Greenpeace India, over the last 12 years, has been campaigning on national environment issues. It has been one of the frontrunners in using social media. In October 2012, Social Bakers rated Greenpeace India's Facebook page as second in India in terms of user engagement. For an NGO funded only by individual donors in India, surpassing top Indian corporate brands in this area was a remarkable achievement.[22]

One of its more interesting modes of engagement is a Facebook application called Forest Hero. It requires the user to give access to his/her Facebook account and upload a picture, after which it merges the user image within the video and shows it in different parts of the film displaying him/her as a forest hero. The user can share the video on social media, thus sending the message that anyone can defend forests through small, simple steps. According to social media analysts, the entire process of being part of such a customised video inculcates a sense of identity among users, while the personalised visual content provides room for engagement.

Greenpeace India also launched Greenpeace Extra, (GPx) a free online petition site, on 14 March 2013. This is a people-powered website that enables starting, running and winning campaigns about local issues affecting their community. Featured campaigns on GPx are provided with required resources and a strategy to make them more impactful. Campaign trainings and skill development for individuals and communities are also organised to help win local campaigns.

Petitions are a starting point for activists, who can then go on to lobby and create different strategies for winning campaigns. For example, Mr Umang Choudary, an activist from Jharkhand, started a petition on GPx and challenged a company for illegally dumping toxic waste in his village, located in an eco-sensitive area. His efforts, along with the support of locals, have forced the company to stop the illegal dumping and a court order is pending on the compensation required from the company for damages caused. According to him, 'GPx helped me connect my campaign to people worldwide and 120 people have registered their support for this cause till date. This gave me the confidence to challenge the company which is both financially and politically strong.'[23]

Table 9.1   SM Objectives and Measurement[24]

	SM Objectives	Measurement Techniques
1	Generating awareness	Analysis of web traffic Web traffic referrals Share of voice Volume of conversation and trends
2	Enhancing sales	Web traffic Time spent Repeat visits Content acceptance rate Followers Share of voice
3	Developing customer loyalty	Web traffic Time spent Repeat visits Content acceptance rate Followers Share of voice Repeated social mentions Recommendations and reviews Social connectivity among buyers

Why do organisations use SM? As discussed earlier, for generating awareness, enhancing sales and developing customer loyalty. The success of the initiatives is measured through different techniques (refer Table 9.1).

While considering the objectives and related metrics of SM, we need to bear in mind that the medium is, at the same time, both robust and frail. Robust, for it has the strength to garner immediate support, and frail, because it can be easily abused causing immense damage to the reputation of the company. Freedom to express together with speed of transmission and volumes of reach can be both a blessing and a curse for the organisation. To avoid negative repercussions, a set of specific guidelines are crafted for employees designated as official influencers in cyberspace. To avoid any controversy stemming from inadvertent statements made by these influencers, all comments and posts carry a line clearly specifying that the views in the post/message are 'those of the author' and the organisation does not necessarily subscribe to the same.

To create an image in cyberspace, organisations follow some common guidelines (also referred to as 'netiquette') as:

- Show respect to communicators
- Avoid mentioning competing organisation policies
- Do not denigrate to gain an upper hand

- Avoid cyber abuse
- Do not plunge into a 'save my company' war in case of negative comments about the organisation or products
- Do not post confidential information about colleagues or other employees
- Adhere to organisational norms
- Be transparent[25]

Organisational Role in Championing SM

Based on the desired projection of image, an organisation may decide to adopt any one of the following four strategies:[26]

1. Predictive practitioner: This will require focus on any one distinctive usage for example, customer service. Organisations with definite goals and keen to provide specific and measureable results, normally adopt this approach. They form groups with the intention to be more 'social'. Results for this strategy are almost immediate.
2. Creative experimenter: Organisations use this approach when they wish to explore uncertain terrains by listening to customer and employee voice on Twitter and Facebook. Similar to the strategy of predictive practitioner, this strategy too produces significant and immediate results.
3. SM champion: This strategy helps the organisation to enlist internal and external supporters who are similarly enthused about the initiatives. The role involves initiatives which are large in scope and have predictable results.
4. SM transformer: When organisations decide to take on the role of being a transformer, large scale initiatives have to be adopted which are new and can improve ways for conducting business. This strategy transforms the organisational processes and impacts almost all functions and stakeholders.

HOW TO BEGIN THE PROCESS OF SOCIAL NETWORKING?

One of the greatest challenges companies face in adjusting to the impact of social media, is knowing where to start.

—Simon Mainwaring[27]

The process of social networking begins with a seeding strategy[28] which requires organisations to plan on the target segment. What should be the number and type of consumers? Selecting prudently the customer base (seed), is the first step in the process of viral diffusion. This customer base then draws other members into the company's fold by transmitting the required information. The selection of the 'seeds' is critical and is based on an assessment of their online standing, credibility, ability and willingness

to initiate the viral effect, develop relationships with online communities and generate message characteristics.

Seeding a Fan Frenzy: Mumbai Indians at Indian Premier League 5

Mumbai Indians used an innovative video seeding strategy to drive up the level of engagement on its Facebook page during Indian Premier League (IPL) 5 in 2012. One of the most popular fan pages for any Indian sports brand, the Mumbai Indians Facebook page introduced personalised interactions with team players in a campaign termed 'Players become Friends'. The team management asked cricketers to actively respond to their fans and send messages directly from their hotel rooms, to give fans an idea of what was going on inside the team dressing room.

In order to drive traffic to this Facebook page, Mumbai Indians used a seeding strategy of creating and uploading videos from cricketers like Sachin Tendulkar, Harbhajan Singh, Rohit Sharma and Lasith Malinga on its YouTube channel for more than a month before the actual campaign. The main objective of these personalised videos was to increase engagement and interaction on the Facebook fan page.

The seeding strategy is relevant for cases where the organisation chooses to either train employees in the process of implementation or hire external experts as advisors or consultants. However, there can also be instances where the viral diffusion process is begun by the consumers or communities. This process may be either positive or negative. The impact of these conversations varies with the authenticity of the message initiator in cyberspace. Organisations may decide to join these groups to validate the conversations, respond to them or correct impressions. Entry into this invisible space can be through listening to tweets, reading Facebook posts and product rating entries; filtering information through assessment of entry sentiments (positive, negative or neutral) and aggregating this information; focussing on the chain reaction of each SM and comprehending relevance of the topics.

What do the online communities have to say about the organisation, product and services? SM teams are being formed with specific mandates to promote visibility in the online community. Clear guidelines have been spelled out so that all speak the language of accuracy and transparency and demonstrate ethical conduct. Though directives have been laid down for online behaviour and conduct, there can be aberrations for which the online representative is accountable.

Organisations can establish a compelling presence by monitoring and engaging groups and people and increasing reach and share of voice. Though stated simplistically, developing a presence is a long and tedious process in which organisations listen and respond to concerns, admit mistakes, if any, and selectively engage the target audience (refer Fig. 9.1).

Figure 9.1   The Process of Social Networking

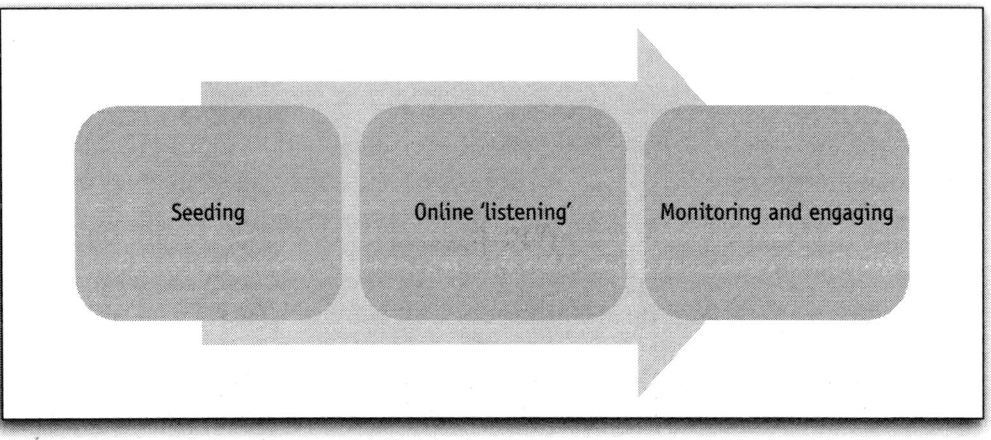

Seeding   Online 'listening'   Monitoring and engaging

WHAT ARE SOME OF THE PLATFORMS OF SM?

The qualities that make Twitter seem insane and half-baked are what makes it so powerful.

—JONATHAN ZITTRAIN[29]

Organisations have begun setting up 'mission control' centres where social activity can be construed, observed, monitored, analysed and shared. The question is how should organisations proceed with mission control? They can do it by following the 4C approach: cognise, congruity, curate and chase.[30] Cognise entails recognising and comprehending the SM landscape, collecting information on competitors, their presence and strategies in cyberspace. Congruity implies developing strategies which are appropriate to the objective of the organisation. For instance, depending on the conversation about a product or a service, the volume, reach and velocity, strategies can be chalked out to build awareness or promote sales or develop relationships. The process of 'curating' content and information in SM involves developing a clear understanding of ongoing conversation and the need and time to interject. Assigning the task of chiming in at appropriate junctures is important. The selection should involve a person who possesses the capability to listen, to create content which is both logically and emotionally appealing and divert cyber traffic. Rules and guidelines are drawn up to reflect the core values and philosophy of the organisation. The last of the 4Cs, viz. 'chase' is important for the organisation to remain visible in the invisible space. Organisations need to chase the velocity and volume of conversations and information flow carefully and meticulously, and then devise their own strategies and select appropriate platforms which will give them an edge over existing conversations.

Which platform should be used for conveying information? For a comprehension of the most appropriate platform for decision making, organisations can focus on either half-life of information or depth of information.[31] The half-life of information relates to the content and medium which appears on screen and its acceptance or longevity. Depth of information pertains to the richness, diversity and complexity. Microblogs, as Twitter, contain half-life of information as the focus is on building awareness and keeping the customers informed on short topics. Other platforms which require greater depth of information, and more details than Twitter are blogs, forums, etc.

The decision on the choice of SM platform depends on how the problem is defined. Does the problem relate to awareness, complexity or accessibility? Viral videos are the most suited to addressing awareness problems; blogs for complexity issues and, accessibility can be addressed by either beginning online communities or joining already existing ones through forums or social networking.

Viral Videos

A video posted on the website by an organisation or an individual goes viral because of the nature of the content. It is instantly shared through SM, networking or emails. For a video to go viral, the design of the content is important. It can be either intensely humorous or compellingly depressive. Extreme emotions are used to capture attention. Sometimes a video is designed by organisations to go viral and sometimes the nature of the content helps it achieve that position.

As viral videos are by nature temporary, they have a short shelf life. Organisations attempt to make the video unforgettable by designing content which has mass appeal and which is focussed on the macro rather than micro. For instance, issues addressed in these videos can be age, gender, life and death which are used to highlight some attribute of the product. Choice of issues is critical in providing longevity to the video. Consumers need to discuss on a topic which is not commonplace and cannot be easily forgotten.

The beginning point for organisations is to take cognisance of the seven crucial elements of viral videos which are:

- Engage the customers by grabbing their attention
- Enlighten them by providing good content
- Create an unforgettable experience
- Remain focussed
- Entertain through content and stylisation
- Touch the core by introducing content which has universal appeal
- Prompt to take action[32]

The ideas proposed should have both substance as well as possess the capacity to entertain.

Being able to state a controversial or debatable issue with creativity can be a beginning point for the big leap. In this process, it is important to remember that for a video to go viral, it should be short and present ideas and concepts in an entertaining and creative manner without making an attempt to sell. If the idea is appealing, customers themselves will flock to their fold.

Using Viral Video for a Cause: Lifebuoy

Lifebuoy created a unique social campaign titled 'Help a child reach five' in February 2013, to create awareness on the disturbingly high level of diarrhoea that leads to the death of 2 million children under the age of five every year.

A 3.17-minute ad film highlighting this fact went viral on YouTube with over 1.4 million views in just three weeks since its release.[33] The YouTube page directs viewers to the Facebook application on the click of 'Pledge on Facebook' where they must like the page to be able to pledge their support. The pre-framed pledge can then be shared on the viewer's Facebook wall as well as on Twitter through the hashtag '#helpachildreach5'.

By end of March 2013, the campaign was able to garner over 3.5 million views for the video, over 2 million likes on the Facebook page and more than 76,000 pledges.[34]

Blogs

The earliest form of SM was the blogs which became a critical way of connecting and sharing public opinion in a 'blogosphere'. Blogs have been somewhat similar to personal diary pages, where entries are displayed in reverse chronological order. A single individual operates them. This individual may be writing self-generated content or may be hired as a technical evangelist to write about products or services. Blogs can become interactive by inviting readers to post comments on the content and its nature. Organisations have begun to use blogs to keep internal and external customers updated on developments. Customers, dissatisfied with products or services of a company, may decide to create an online community by blogging. These virtual grievances captured at one spot create a highly positive or negative image of the company.

The classic example of what bloggers and blogging can do to the image of an organisation is that of Jeff Jarvis and his BuzzMachine. In 2005, Jeff's dissatisfaction with his Dell purchase and indifference of the Dell service centre made him create 'Dell Hell' which was soon joined by other readers. The immense negativity impacted sales and generated negative online conversation. Dell created Direct2Dell blog to communicate with consumers and followed it up in 2007 with IdeaStorm as an online suggestion box where consumers could post their suggestions and ideas on the products and services.

Why do organisations use blogs? To convey information about a product, enhance knowledge and seek responses through 'reply' or 'comments'. Various perspectives are posted on blogs making it easy for the reader to gather a holistic view. The social objective of creating a blog is to promote evangelism. Technical evangelists, who are subject matter experts, are designated the task of generating cyber traffic and communicating with online communities. These evangelists take on the role of opinion leaders shaping the views of followers.

Writing a blog for an organisation is not simple. Equal efforts are required on the part of the organisation and the blogger to make it a success. Some techniques to be followed

for the blogging process are: listening, determining the goal, estimating the ROI, developing a plan and an editorial process for sanity checks, designing the blog and connecting it to the company website. For it to gain popularity it should be hosted with a well-designed marketing plan which will help people find the blog and post their honest comments.

The returns are almost immediate: upgradation in the virtual social standing of the organisation and the blogger, generation of belief in the competencies and skills of the blogger and development of faith in the product and the services.

Forums

Forums have increased the interactivity between readers in the online community. Readers interested in a particular issue, and with prior knowledge on the same join the forum. The ensuing discussions have coherence, and follow a linear progression. As they are platforms for exchange of views and opinions, they are not dominated by specialists. Hence, problems associated with one-way communication, as not listening or unwillingness to listen, are obliterated creating a healthy intellectual arena for discourse which aims at knowledge enhancement rather than product promotion.

Microblogging

Microblogging focusses on providing real-time updates instantaneously to a group of friends from multiple devices as phones, emails and texts (SMS). With an enhanced presence in the social networking space, microblogs are being used to share information and details, opinions, and actions and reactions about businesses, people, products and services. The growth of this form of SM is based on the premise of trust and social relationships. People tend to trust the opinions of a close-knit circle of friends and associates. With organisations and brands vying to compete for attention, this medium has, by far, become the most popular form of information sharing in an 'attention economy'.[35]

Twitter, a form of microblogging, was created in 2006. This platform, consisting of 140-character-long messages, rapidly gained popularity with a record number of 15 million users in India in 2012, which is approximately 3 per cent of Twitter's global total.[36] With tweets, users describe areas of interest, talk about small events in their life and show attitude through small posts. As only 140 characters can be used, the tweets have to be viewed in entirety and not individually. Sense on the collated text will emerge when a series of tweets are combined. When used by individuals, tweets help share or seek information or talk about small events in the lives of the users. Organisations also use Twitter for brand promotion. The immediacy-effect associated with microblogging and its potential application to the growing number of consumers has made it the most sought-after form of online WOM promotional technique.

In June 2012, a new mobile application called Vine was launched to help transference of short, six-second videos with the objective of strengthening brand relationships with followers and consumers. Acquired by Twitter in October 2012, Vine can be used on multiple social networking sites. It was made a free iOS application on the iPhone and iPod Touch in January 2013. While Twitter uses 140 characters to communicate, Vine uses 30-second films to capture, record and share video content or illustrate a point.

With a growing number of mobile users, marketing-savvy organisations have prudently begun using Vine to connect with their potential consumers. Vines have shifted Twitter focus from text-based information sharing to visual presentations using intriguing videos which allow organisations to capture consumer attention and possess the required content for going viral. As defined by BBC it is a 'stop motion animation' and has well captured the attention of advertisers and organisations, alike.

However, this form of SM is not without its disadvantages and can be inappropriately used by teenagers for their own benefit. Realising this, Twitter, on 5 February 2013, increased the age bar from 12 to 17 years for downloading and using the application. This mandate was in response to a request made by Apple following a controversy in which pornographic content was uploaded using Vine.

CAN THE ROI FOR SM BE MEASURED?

Quit counting fans, followers and blog subscribers like bottle caps. Think, instead, about what you're hoping to achieve with and through the community that actually cares about what you're doing.

—Amber Naslund[37]

Organisations have begun to look for measurement techniques to validate their SM spend. For some the ROI is measured in tangible or financial terms as costs involved in creating an interactive website, while for others, it is intangible as customer behaviour, measured in terms of clicks, visits, time spent and number of updates. These can be used to measure the growth in awareness of a product and the liking for the brand. Online prediction markets are being set up to crowdsource new ideas and mine online information through forums where consumers comment on products and services.

Conversation, engagement and evangelism are three intangible returns on SM investments. For example, if we were to consider the validity of the investment, we can study the conversation on a product or a service. It is a 'relationship-based currency, a social currency',[38] invested in building relationships, which though truthfully debited from the organisational account, is credited back with returns. Another technique is creating technical evangelists who, because of their authenticity and credibility in the social space, are able to draw traffic. The focus of the spend is on building communities through conversations, finding evangelists who have a high influence on the followers and employing promotional techniques as contests, etc.

Engaging with Customers

Once the right platform has been selected, involvement and engagement of customers has to be planned and strategised for securing attention and subsequent buy-in. Hence, online communication about products and services should be fun-filled, exclusive, highly visible and carry talking points. Pandering to the emotions of the users with appropriate stories which are memorable and evoke a sense of empathy can be used. Additionally, if organisations, in their stories, can project involvement in a cause close to the consumer community as, education, empowerment of women, health, etc. they can evoke emotional engagement.

As the content in SM is user generated, organisations have begun to study the four key parameters of motivating consumers: connections, creation, consumption and control.[39] These active investments by the consumers in building associations through creation and sharing of controlled content are part of the ROI recognised by the organisation as a beginning of a long-term relationship.

Using Emotional Engagement: Hero MotoCorp Ltd.

Hero MotoCorp Ltd. designed a unique emotional engagement programme using its 'Hum Mein Hai Hero' song that had already become one of the most popular advertising jingles in 2011. In January 2012, the company invited consumers to sing the Hero song, shoot their video and upload it to heromotocorp.com. The chance was provided to them to create and innovate content in the video, which could become part of the company's next ad film.

Mr Anil Dua, Senior Vice President—Marketing and Sales, Hero MotoCorp Ltd., described how the tremendous response and large number of spontaneous uses to the A. R. Rahman song prompted the company to explore the option of creating content for the next film by consumers themselves.

The engagement programme was further boosted by social media. It began with a set of television commercials created by Hero, where everyone was singing with the 'Hero' song, and simultaneously inviting others to join in.

Mr Anil Nair, CEO, Law & Kenneth Communications (I) Pvt. Ltd., the firm that designed the campaign explained the rationale for the concept as: 'The era of communication where brands tell people what to do is long over. Now the consumer has to be at the centre of everything. They have to be engaged in a manner that completely makes them in sync with the brand's philosophies and ethos.'[40]

In this process of engagement, consistency in messages and singleness of purpose deserve due consideration. All messages, no matter how diverse, should finally converge to the values, vision and mission of the organisation.

SM Aggregators

SM aggregators are a reflection of the increasing demand of users for content unification. Hootsuite is the most comprehensive tool for measuring various SM accounts and their effectiveness allowing clients to send and reschedule their updates. To measure the 'airtraffic control for Twitter' Tweetdeck can be used which allows for following messages, feeds and postings. Sproutsocial allows business owners to read SM campaign results from simple charts and graphs. All outlets are consolidated into one portal which

Table 9.2   Social Media Aggregators and Their Functions[41]

SM Aggregators	Functions
Rebelmouse.com (personal media)	Categorises personal social media 'front page'
Glos.si (personal media)	Provides automated organisation of personal social media life
Memolane.com (personal media)	Provides a chronological look at personal social media activity
Sulia.com	Provides subject-based social network assessment
CircleMe.com	Follows people and/or topics
Storylane.com	Provides collaborative curation
CheckThis.com	Provides social poster editor facilities
Tackk.com	Similar to CheckThis but with some added features
Pixlr.com/express	Collages, filters and frames at the touch of a button
PicMonkey.com	Provides powerful and easy-to-use photo editing
Listgeeks.com	Provides a 'lists hub' featuring contributions that range from the very useful to the very inane
Listango.com	Provides a basic bookmarking service that makes it easier to categorise favourite sites and resources
Spread.us	Helps tweet curated content on behalf of colleagues, friends and fans (essentially a mailing list for Twitter)
Wanelo.com	Provides a universal catalogue of products organised by users of the site

makes it simple to post and read results. Vertical Response provides a central location to marketers for managing different types of campaigns across many platforms. All updates across the different platforms are synced and aggregators presented at one central location (Table 9.2).

Tools to Measure Online Listening

Why and how do organisations listen to and measure online conversation? Based on the platform on which conversation is to happen, organisations are using and devising tools to measure the tone, sentimentality, reach and volume. Twendz, through assessment of positive, negative or neutral tweets, helps assess the public sentiment about a brand or a topic. Twitter search application also helps find conversations. Organisations or individuals can also subscribe to RSS feed without an account and gather information about real-time microchat. Blogs which carry public or organisation opinion, information about a product or service can be tracked through Technocrati or Google Blog Search. With increasing competition and competitors trying to outdo one another in wooing customers, success stories can be collated at one point, bookmarked with the help of Delicious or Diigo for reference, at a later date. Website and Blog Graders are used for analysis of the site and visits per site vis-à-vis competitors.

Additionally, organisations have also started using web analytics through which they are able to track most frequented sites, corporate websites and blogs. It helps develop close relationships with bloggers, and internal and external customers. The challenge before them is to be right first time with the right person and right time, that is, the situation, the person and the timing should be correct. Number of diggs, number of blogs on Technocrati, tracking dashboard are just some of the techniques to capture trends related to content published over a specified timeframe on the site and consumer preferences.

With over 400 tools to track conversations, organisations may choose to study the sites and select the most appropriate one for their use. http://delicious.com/lldoolj2/twitter+tools provides a list of tools which can be used with ease. Though organisations make a huge attempt to garner followers on the Internet or gather support, it in no way impacts their immediate performance. These followers who join in the conversation are/may also be part of other Internet social groups and act as influencers possessing higher credibility than organisations. Simply joining SM as a fad is not sufficient. Targeting the right group with the right message is mandatory to build trust, as these followers will later take on the role of advocates and champion the cause of the organisation and its products.

Measuring SM Attributes

The measurable attributes of SM are activity, tone (sentiment), velocity (spread over time), attention (duration on site), participation (comments), qualitative attributes as comments, what was said, etc.[42] On many occasions it may be difficult to measure ROI but increased satisfaction and improved retention through quick responses to customer queries helps develop connections on participatory platforms and secures the buy-in of customers. The results of the same are long-term and more rewarding than a quick financial ROI as building social goodwill, which though difficult to measure, is beneficial in the long run. For instance, measurement of SM is in the form of:

- Understanding and measuring the conversation—increase and decrease
- Getting to know what consumers are talking about
- Developing capabilities to participate
- Assessing the buying pattern
- Measuring the buying cycle, developing efficiencies in product development based on consumer feedback
- Minimising damage to brand through monitoring unsolicited conversations

---

Measuring Success in SM: Myntra.com

Mr Manu Prasad, Head, SM at Myntra.com explains how his organisation has not treated SM as a silo by creating specific objectives exclusively for it. On the contrary, the company objectives for using SM are to make it an enabler and amplifier of various functions, augmenting efforts in marketing, customer care, acquisition and sales, and retention.

> In terms of the success rate of various SM options, the company has found Facebook to be a particularly effective channel to drive sales. Facebook's targeting options coupled with new innovations like Facebook offers, news feed ads and custom audiences has delivered results that are very competitive, in terms of ROI, when compared to search ads.
>
> In tracking the ROI of social media, Myntra.com tracks platform-specific metrics as increase in likes/followers and People Talking About This (PTAT) as well as other function-relevant parameters as number of issues resolved and turnaround time on customer care, number of transactions via SM for sales, reach in marketing and so on.[43]

Organisations have also come up with metrics for understanding the effectiveness of SM which have been broken up into three main categories: sites, blogs and widgets. For websites, the ROI can be measured by unique visitors, cost per unique visitor, visits, return visits, time spent, video installed, actions taken, positive press, increased YouTube views, retweets, positive WOM, social mentions and increased number of Facebook friends and twitter followers; blogs: nature, size, relevance, author credibility; widgets and SM applications: installs, active users, audience profile, growth influence.[44]

A study of the business impact of SM has been proposed in terms of financial, digital, brand and risk management (refer Table 9.3).

Table 9.3   Understanding Business Impact: Balanced Scorecard Model[45]

Financial	Digital	Brand	Risk Management
Increase/decrease in profits and costs	Creation of digital assets	Measurement of customer favourability to the brand and generation of awareness	Preparedness to address risks related to reputation management

HOW CAN REPUTATION BE BUILT WITH SM?

... one witty tweet, one clever blog post, one devastating video—forwarded to hundreds of friends at the click of a mouse—can snowball and kill a product or damage a company's share price.

—TIM WEBER[46]

It cannot be denied that reputations are built over decades with concentrated effort at doing good, perceived to be doing well and creating social good. Organisations need to manage right—the medium, the audience and the message—by creating online platforms which safeguard reputation by 'building trust, promoting quality, improving collaboration and instilling loyalty'.[47]

Within the online community, where almost everyone is connected in the digital space, managing reputation is tougher than otherwise as connections are built and broken over conversations, connections are formed and associations discovered within fractions of seconds. In this scenario to build trust through 'correct' behaviour, and ensure that quality standards are met with respect to content, it is important to keep contributors who share similar interests and passions in a coterie comprising loyal followers. These followers are the ones who will be most tolerant of *faux pas*, and crisis, if any.

Building a set of loyal followers entails tracking the users, their purchase decisions, behaviours, and actions. This can be done by using metrics created for this purpose and tracking the feedback provided by others on the assessed user. Assessment should be based on both numbers and qualitative commenting. Organisations need to be careful when using purely number-centric metrics which could present a lop-sided picture. While a study of the raw statistics and data can make the assessment objective and unbiased, it robs the conclusion of the 'human touch' which cannot be quantified, but has to be studied and interpreted.

Building a Strong Social Media Platform for Employees: Asian Paints Ltd.

India's largest paint company, Asian Paints Ltd. found that its traditional email platform and internal web-conferencing had become obsolete when its employees began using Facebook to collaborate within the organisation.

The company came up with 'Huddle', a social media-enabled collaboration platform. The aim was creating a better and faster employee association. It provided users the facility to share files, blogs and encouraged participation in discussions.

'In addition to personal peer-to-peer sharing, a lot of team activities and employee communication have been rolled out on the platform. This has substantially improved our visibility and transparency', says Mr Manish Choksi, Chief—Corporate Strategy and CIO, Asian Paints Ltd.[48] The project bagged the CIO100 Innovation award.

The objectives of the company for using SM (which may be awareness, sales or loyalty) influence the strategy adopted by it (predictive practitioner, creative explorer, SM champion or SM transformer). Both of these influence the choice of SM platform (blogs, viral videos, microblogging or forums), which contribute to reputational capital by creating customer engagement. Companies can measure online conversation using various tools to comprehend the tone, sentimentality, reach and volume of its SM activity. This provides feedback that can be used to calculate the ROI of SM use. On the basis of the ROI, the company's SM strategy can be re-examined (refer Fig. 9.2).

Building Blocks for Enhancing Reputation

Much work is being done by organisations to understand and manage SM activities, how relationships are to be developed and appropriate strategies to be adopted for understanding the audience and their engagement needs.

Figure 9.2   Building Reputation through Social Media

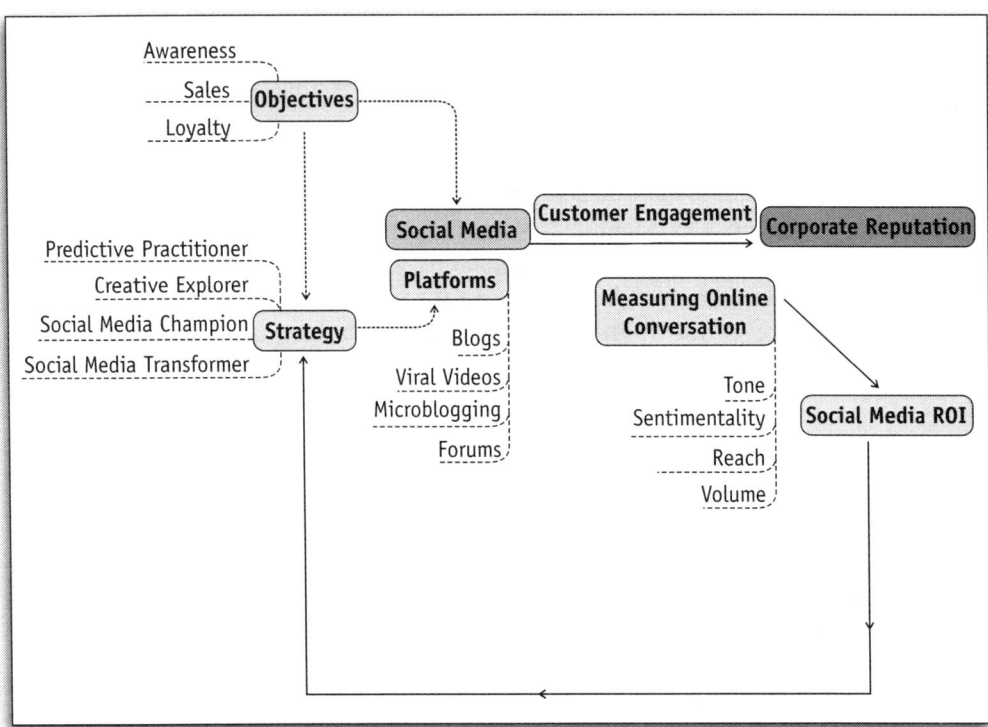

There are seven building blocks[49] for managing SM activities: identity, conversations, sharing, presence, relationships, reputation and groups. These are neither exclusive nor necessarily present in all SM activities. They allow organisations latitude in shaping their communication by clearly understanding SM functionality. The identity of the user or organisation can be revealed through a conscious/unconscious presentation of subjective information as attitudes, feelings, likes, dislikes and personality or brand traits. Some may however, want to use their real names and self-promote, while others may want to be known by their nicknames, also referred to as 'handles'. The choice of revealing the identity is core to selection of media tools, for a wrong mix can lead to bullying or unhappy commenting in cyberspace.

Conversing in Cyberspace

Conversations refer to the extent to which users or organisations wish to communicate with other users. While some may use the SM platform to offload, build friendships, others may decide to espouse larger causes as environment, health, etc. The diversity of conversations is determined by the nature of the medium. For instance, Twitter is all about sharing real-time information through 140 characters; while blogs define opinions,

urging readers to respond, and engage in lengthy conversations on a topic of mutual interest. The 'conversation velocity'[50] which determines the rate of conversations over a period of time and direction of change in continuity and discontinuity spells out the favourable or otherwise disposition of the conversationalists towards the product and the organisation. Competencies on understanding conversations and knowing when to join and when not to join are required to gain the winning edge.

Sharing constitutes willingness of users to share, exchange and disseminate information and knowledge. The question before us is: does sharing lead users develop a need to further converse in cyberspace? Organisations willing to share information should ideally work around devising strategies to increase sociability in SM. This can be done by attempting mediation to find out commonalities between customers and areas on which sociability can be developed.

The presence of users in SM is indicated by 'available' or 'not available/hidden' indicating their desire to contribute to the dialogue at a given point in time. The geographical location of the user in the real world helps connect the real with the virtual. For instance, in Foursquare, the exact physical location can be deciphered if the user so wishes to share this information, thus, bridging the gap between the real and the virtual. Through presence, organisations can trace user availability and location.

Building Reputation

Users are able to relate to the company and its products by building connects, sharing sociability and establishing ties and developing associations. These relationships may be varied: formal, informal, structured and unstructured. A good example is LinkedIn which indicates the level of connection and association between users, introduces a chain of connects, reflects the number of connections and the strength of relationship in this network of ties. Organisations feed on this 'relationship' which has a cascading effect in the 'influencing chain'.

Individuals and organisations build their reputation by the strength of connections, positioning in the context. Reputation can be built by endorsements, nature and authenticity of posted content. The view counts, the likes, dislikes, ratings help add to the dimension of reputation. Filtering of information by users of common interest through a 'thumbs up' or a 'thumbs down' sign can help organisations figure out commonalities among users.

Groups formed by individuals sharing similar likes and dislikes create communities and subcommunities. The size of these communities is directly proportional to the nature of the network: the more 'social' it gets, the higher is the group size than in lesser 'social' networks. One hundred and fifty individuals have been found to be the optimum size of a group to have stable and steady social relationships.[51] Groups can be self-created, that is, individuals with common interests come together to form a group or it may be open to wanderers in the digital space, with approval or invitation. The focus on granting permission for joining these groups and filtering is important, considering the need to monitor the high traffic in the space.

Tread Cautiously!

As discussed in the earlier sections, SM can threaten the existence and reputation of an organisation. The reason may or may not be justified, for critics of organisations and organisational conduct are many and do not need institutional support to make their voice heard. They may anonymously hurl charges which again, may be partially true and not logical. Organisations may or may not have prior intimation of the onslaught. In most cases they are not in the loop and hence have no control over the unfolding of events which may gain mammoth proportions. But what is sure is that if quick and timely action is not taken in case of negative commenting, it can jeopardise the reputation of an organisation, leaving it floundering in a quagmire of accusations and incorrect or partial information. Even with the best of intentions, an organisation, if not alert to SM onslaught, may realise that it has become embroiled in a warfare from which there is no escape.

Trouble Brewing on Twitter: Cafe Coffee Day

An incident where a group of friends lingering over coffee and snacks at Cafe Coffee Day (CCD) were allegedly asked to pay cover charges or leave the restaurant by the manager, snowballed into a huge online tirade against the company.

On 4 February 2010, the group posted its first negative post on Twitter with the hashtag #ccdsucks. By the second day, there were a large number of conversations around the episode, with more than 650 posts. The group also began showing resentment against the manager's behaviour, and writing posts about bad customer service and coffee. In short, the grievances against the brand were all posted.

Some people highlighted the fact that the company had already issued an apology over its Twitter page by mentioning explicitly that they did not have a cover charge policy and that they were willing to resolve the issue. The subject proved to be the most trending in the week from 4 February to 11 February 2010. During the same week a Facebook group, ccdsucks and an anonymous Twitter account @ccdsucks became active.[52]

After three days, the issue gradually started diminishing with CCD's apology message. This found widespread mention. There was also a growing sentiment in the public that the brand was too harshly penalised for an individual representative's mistake. Though the incident was short-lived, it did create a reputational risk for the company.

In the last few decades, the rules of engagement with stakeholders were very different from what have now emerged with SM. However, organisations have devised strategies to enhance engagement and combat threats, if any, to their reputation.

Strategies Adopted by Companies to Intercept or Combat the SM Threat

- Listen to dialogue and be alert to minor changes in sentiment of conversations
- Avoid erroneous or disputable statements. If these statements have been inadvertently made, be quick to apologise

- Ensure timely and speedy intervention
- Empower a group of employees to immediately address the issues
- Adopt ethical stand which benefits the community at large
- Use existing reputation to assertively and aggressively champion the cause

SM has changed corporate rules for communicating with stakeholders. Earlier organisations could afford to be silent over customer queries or even be abrasive in response. Today, the rules of the game are different. Collaboration with, and timely response to customers is the key to success. Any unthought or untoward strategy can antagonise customers and create a ripple effect in the online communities to which he/she belongs. This could turn the tide leading to real-time losses in terms of plummeting sales following customer exodus to competitor products and services. However, if an error of judgement does happen which creates a negative impression in customer perception, organisations should be proactive, apologise and seek community forgiveness. Undoubtedly, past history of erroneous online conversation, actions and reputation will determine the extent to which customers are willing to 'forgive and forget'.

A Step in Time: PepsiCo India

PepsiCo India provides a good example of a company that acted swiftly in the face of a threat to its reputation from its SM activities.

Mr Akshar Pathak, the minimalistic designer of Minimal Bollywood Posters, has an enviable 30,000 fans on his Facebook page. One Friday in February 2013, PepsiCo India posted a content featuring Mr Pathak's original art work, asking fans about their weekend plans, without perhaps realising its error in taking original content from a highly popular SM personality.

Mr Pathak posted the content on Facebook and Twitter, pointing out the similarity between his work and the PepsiCo post, leading to quick reactions from the online community in the form of shares, likes and conversations.

However, the company was quick to swing into action. It deleted the content, contacted Mr Akshar Pathak personally and also wrote an apology. The entire episode was over within an hour and showed the company's intent to resolve the matter as soon as possible. The steps taken by the company to resolve the matter were posted by Mr Akshar Pathak himself, who updated his Facebook page and showed his pleasure at the company taking copyright infringement seriously.[53]

Success of SM technology is contingent on the user profile. For instance, if the product caters to Generation Y, which is actively engaged in SM, then effort and time can be invested in building awareness through SM. A quick peek into what is already there in cyberspace and its favourability can help organisations craft their strategy and its interactivity within online communities for gaining similar approval. It is important for organisations to ensure a flat communication process and remember that they are talking with the customers and not talking to them.

Developing online communities is critical to the success of a product. Organisations should only venture forth to create communities if they are confident that they will be able to support them through new content, features and redesigns. These carefully built communities can be successful if they focus around customer passions or pain points.

CONCLUSION

What happens in Vegas stays in Vegas; what happens on Twitter stays on Google forever!

—Jure Klepic[54]

SM makes use of many collaborative projects which are created by end users with the basic objective that these will yield much better results than could possibly be achieved through individual endeavours. However, this does not ascertain truth or reliability of information though the veracity of the information is never questioned. For instance, when an organisation is under duress and partial or incorrect information is perceived to be 'the truth', the impact on the reputation can be damaging and difficult to recover from. Hence, as an ongoing process, SM can be used to leverage position in the market by:

- Gaining insight into a company's own and competitor strategies
- Taking action based on negative conversation in cyber space
- Conversing directly with customers and gaining insight into their preferences
- Learning how to manage and influence online community
- Garnering larger community support through rapport-building
- Implementing new strategies based on customer feedback
- Finding the most appropriate solution with stakeholder collaboration and consensus

Key Points

- Social media (SM) is an online/electronic form of communication to share information, converse, form groups, establish associations, develop relationships, build awareness, shape opinions and attitudes, modify user-generated content, influence purchase decisions, stimulate post purchase communication and evaluate products.
- The ease, volume, reach and speed of SM has made it the most preferred style in today's fast-changing consumer-driven world.
- SM can help organisations secure a loyal following with minimal cost, time and effort.
- Inappropriate use of SM can boomerang and damage the reputation of the company.
- Organisations have begun to employ SM to recruit as well as improve engagement levels of employees.
- The target audience for SM is the new Generation C, which is connected, rich in terms of cultural capital, desirous of status recognition in the cyberspace and possesses the capacity to give shape and credence to online dialogue.

- Social networking is the process of engagement through which people with similar interests associate and build relationships.
- SM operates more on the basis of telling rather than conversing, as is the case with social networking sites.
- Virtual worlds are of two forms: virtual game worlds and virtual social worlds.
- Virtual game worlds have scripted rules for users to behave in multiplayer online role-playing games.
- Objectives of SM use are to secure eyeballs, build awareness, consideration and preference, stimulate action and generate loyalty.
- Based on the desired projection of the image, an organisation may decide to adopt to be a predictive practitioner, creative experimenter, SM champion or SM transformer.
- Viral diffusion is done through a seeding strategy in which organisations decide on the number and types of consumers (seeds) they need to target in the initial phase.
- Organisations have begun 'mission control' centres where social activity can be construed, observed, monitored, analysed and shared.
- Mission control can be achieved by following the 4C strategy of cognise, congruity, curate and chase.
- The ROI of SM can be both tangible as well as intangible.
- The business impact can be measured by a Balanced Scorecard model which measures financial, digital, brand and risk management.
- Seven building blocks for managing SM activities are identity, conversations, sharing, presence, relationships, reputation and groups.

END NOTES

1. E. Qualman, 'Socialnomics: How social media transforms the way we live and do business', website http://www.socialnomics.net/2010/05/05/social-media-revolution-2-refresh/ (accessed 20 March 2013).
2. H. Guzman, 'If social media isn't transforming your business, you're doing it wrong', website http://www.hugoguzman.com/2011/09/if-social-media-isnt-transforming-your-business-youre-doing-it-wrong/ (accessed 20 March 2013).
3. P. Blackshaw and M. Nazzaro, 'Consumer-generated media (CGM) 101: Word-of-mouth in the age of the web-fortified consumer', website http://www.nielsenbuzzmetrics.com/whitepapers (accessed 13 March 2013).
4. Ernst & Young, 'Social media marketing: India trends study 2013', website http://www.ey.com/IN/en/Services/Advisory/Social-Media-Marketing-India-Trends-Study-2013 (accessed 15 May 2013).
5. M. Corstjens and A. Umblijs, 'The power of evil: The damage of negative social media strongly outweigh positive contributions,' *Journal of Advertising Research* (2013), 52(4), 433–449.
6. S. Rai, 'Engaging young employees (Gen Y) in a social media dominated world—Review and retrospection', *Procedia—Social and Behavioural Sciences* (2012), 37, 257–266, p. 262.
7. Social media quotes, website http://www.brainyquote.com/quotes/keywords/social_media.html (accessed 20 March 2013).
8. A. M. Kaplan and M. Haenlein, 'Users of the world, unite! The challenges and opportunities of social media', *Business Horizons* (2010), 53(1), 59–68, p. 60.
9. B. Solis, 'Meet Generation C: The connected customer', *Social Media Today*, website http://socialmediatoday.com/node/488295 (accessed 10 March 2013).

10. J. Krishnamurthy, 'If brands create videos that Gen C loves to share, they will', *Campaign India*, website http://www.campaignindia.in/Article/333132,8216if-brands-create-videos-that-gen-c-loves-to-share-they-will8217.aspx (accessed 13 February 2013).

11. S. Hartshorn, '5 Differences between social media and social networking', *Social Media Today*, website http://www.socialmediatoday.com/SMC/194754 (accessed 4 May 2010).

12. R. V. Kozinets, 'The field behind the screen: Using netnography for marketing research in online communities', *Journal of Marketing Research* (2002), 39(1), 61–72.

13. 'Lays India social media marketing', website http://www.slideshare.net/shackcompanis/lays-india-social-media-marketing (accessed 4 April 2013).

14. S. Naidu, 'Lay's India guess whose flavour social media campaign', Lighthouse Insights, website http://lighthouseinsights.in/lays-india-guess-whose-flavour-social-media-campaign.htm (accessed 25 April 2012).

15. 'Lays India social media marketing', website http://www.slideshare.net/shackcompanis/lays-india-social-media-marketing (accessed 4 April 2013).

16. R. Vaidyanathan, 'India's appetite for apps grows as mobile users surge', *BBC*, website http://www.bbc.co.uk/news/business-16607844 (accessed 18 January 2012).

17. '50 per cent of smartphone users in India are under 25 years: Nielsen survey', *The Economic Times*, website http://articles.economictimes.indiatimes.com/2013-02-12/news/37059018_1_smartphone-owners-android-ios-devices (accessed 12 February 2013).

18. S. Gupta, 'For mobile devices, think apps not ads', *Harvard Business Review* (2013), 71–75.

19. GoJiyo, 'Delivering delight in a virtual social world for REAL' [Case Study], *India Social*, website http://www.indiasocial.in/case-study-gojiyodelivering-delight-in-a-virtual-social-world-for-real/ (accessed 4 April 2013).

20. S. Barker, '15 Great social media quotes', website http://shanebarker.com/15-great-social-media-quotes/ (accessed 20 March 2013).

21. C. Li and J. Bernoff, *Groundswell: Winning in a World Transformed by Social Technologies*. Boston, MA: Harvard Business School Press (2008).

22. I. Thekaekara, 'Become a forest hero with greenpeace', Greenpeace India website http://m.greenpeace.org/india/en/high/news/Become-a-Forest-Hero-with-Greenpeace/ (accessed 15 March 2013).

23. 'Greenpeace India brings people powered campaigns to its 10 lakh supporters', website http://in.news.yahoo.com/greenpeace-india-brings-people-powered-campaigns-to-its-10-lakh-supporters-063402717.html (accessed 15 March 2013).

24. J. Baer, 'Why before how: The keys to developing a social media strategy in 7 steps', website http://www.slideshare.net/jaybaer/developing-a-social-media-strategy-in-7-steps (accessed 20 March 2013).

25. J. Dobrian, 'Social media maze: Find your way', *Journal of Property Management* (2013), 78(1), 54–59.

26. H. J. Wilson, P. J. Guinan, S. Parise and B. D. Weinberg, 'What's your social media strategy?', *Harvard Business Review* (2011), 23–25.

27. Social media quotes, website http://www.brainyquote.com/quotes/keywords/social_media.html (accessed 20 March 2013).

28. Y. Liu-Thompkins, 'Seeding viral content: The role of message and network factors', *Journal of Advertising Research* (2012), 52(4), 465–478.

29. N. Cohen, 'Twitter on the barricades: Six lessons learned', *The New York Times*, website http://www.nytimes.com/2009/06/21/weekinreview/21cohenweb.html?_r=0 (accessed 20 March 2013).

30. J. H. Kietzmann, K. Hermkens, I. P. McCarthy and B. S. Silvestre, 'Social media? Get serious! Understanding the functional building blocks of social media', *Business Horizons* (2011), 54(3), 241–251.

31. B. D. Weinberg and E. Pehlivan, 'Social spending: Managing the social media mix', *Business Horizons* (2011), 54(3), 275–282.

32. J. Bader, 'The 7 elements of a viral video campaign', website http://www.brandchannel.com/images/papers/434_Viral_Marketing_v5.pdf (accessed 4 April 2013)

33. V. Naidu, 'With 1.17 million views, Lifebuoy's 'Help a child reach 5' goes viral', Lighthouse Insights website http://lighthouseinsights.in/lifebuoy-help-a-child-reach-5-social-media-campaign.html (accessed 11 March 2013).

34. S. Tillway, 'Social media campaign review: Help a child reach 5 by Lifebuoy', Social Samosa, website http://www.socialsamosa.com/2013/03/social-media-campaign-review-lifebuoy/ (accessed 29 March 2013).

35. T. H. Davenport and J. C. Beck, *The Attention Economy: Understanding the New Economy of Business.* Cambridge, MA: Harvard Business Press (2001), p. 205.

36. S. Kemp 'Social digital and mobile in India', We Are Social, website http://wearesocial.net/blog/2012/11/social-digital-mobile-india-2/ (accessed 11 March 2013).

37. A. Nashund, '10 Ways to get serious about social media', *Social Media Today*, website socialmediatoday.com/index.php?q=SMC/161834 (accessed 20 March 2013).

38. B. D. Weinberg and E. Pehlivan, 'Social spending: Managing the social media mix', *Business Horizons.* 54(3), 275–282, p. 278.

39. T. P. Novak and D. L. Hoffman, 'Roles and goals: consumer motivations to use the social web', Paper presented at the INFORMS Marketing Science Conference, Cologne, Germany (19 June 2010).

40. N. Dewan, 'Hero MotoCorp gives new identity to their anthem by asking people to be a part of their ad', *The Economic Times*, website http://articles.economictimes.indiatimes.com/2012-01-06/news/30597643_1_videos-rebranding-campaign-television-commercials (accessed 6 January 2012).

41. A. Vincenzini, '15 Interesting (and new) social media tools from 2012', website http://www.comms-corner.co (accessed 11 March 2013).

42. J. Owyang, 'Web strategy: How to measure your social media program', website http://www.web-strategist.com/blog/2007/06/07/web-strategy-how-to-measure-your-social-mediaprogram/ (accessed 15 March 2013).

43. R. Kumar, 'Understanding Myntra's social media strategy', Social Samosa, website http://www.social-samosa.com/category/interviews/ (accessed 11 March 2013).

44. IAB, 'IAB brings clarity and definition to social media advertising metrics', website http://www.iab.net/about_the_iab/recent_press_releases/press_release_archive/press_release/pr-050509 (accessed 11 March 2013).

45. R. S. Kaplan and D. P. Norton, *The Balanced Scorecard: Translating Strategy into Action.* Cambridge, MA: Harvard Business School Press (1996).

46. I. McCarthy, 'Understanding the social media ecology: A honeycomb framework', It depends–Ian McCarthy's blog website http://itdepends4.blogspot.in/2011_04_30_archive.html (accessed 20 March 2013).

47. C. Dellarocas, 'Online reputation systems: How to design one that does what you need', *MIT Sloan Management Review* (2010), 51(3), 33–38, p. 34.

48. M. Choksi, website http://www.cio.in/cio100-2011/manish-choksi-chief-corporate-strategy-cio-asian-paints (accessed 26 February 2013).

49. J. H. Kietzmann, K. Hermkens, I. P. McCarthy and B. S. Silvestre, 'Social media? Get serious! Understanding the functional building blocks of social media', *Business Horizons* (2011)., 54(3), 241–251.

50. Ibid., p. 244.

51. L. Gaines-Ross, 'Reputation warfare: Six strategies every company should use to defend itself against small but fierce attackers', *Harvard Business Review* (2010), 88(12), 70–77.

52. A. Malhotra 'Café Coffee Day—A lot can happen over Twitter', India Social, website http://www.indiasocial.in/ccd/ (accessed 16 February 2010).

53. P. Naidu, 'How Pepsi India saved itself from a social media blunder', Lighthouse Insights, website http://lighthouseinsights.in/how-pepsi-india-saved-itself-from-a-social-media-blunder.html (accessed 18 March 2013).

54. Materia Bloga, 'The philosopher's spoon blog: Last likes', website http://blog.philosophersspoon.com/2013/04/05/last-likes.aspx (accessed 20 June 2013).

10

Restoring Confidence and Re-engineering Stakeholder Frames in 'The Eye of the Storm': Crisis Management

My reputation grows with every failure.

—GEORGE BERNARD SHAW[1]

Objectives:

- Understand crisis
- Recognise symptoms of crisis
- Comprehend crisis communication strategies
- Define leadership role and communication in crisis
- Examine link between crisis and reputation

INTRODUCTION

When written in Chinese, the word 'crisis' is composed of two characters.
One represents danger and the other represents opportunity.

—JOHN F. KENNEDY[2]

A crisis, a 'unique moment' in the lifecycle of an organisation is an accidental, unpleasant perilous moment that disturbs the normal performance of a system and stops it from moving ahead as per its planned trajectory.[3] Crises can be global, economic, national and corporate. Though the aggregate of problems leading to a crisis situation is large, our focus in this chapter is primarily on corporate crises resulting from surprise, threat and short reaction time. Some of the factors contributing to the crisis can be macro and external as global economic recession or micro and internal as work processes, management, resources, etc. The end result in

Key Words

- Apology
- Attribution theory
- Bolstering
- Care
- Consideration
- Corrective action
- Crisis
- Damage containment
- Delay
- Denial
- Diminish
- Framing
- Image repair
- Leadership
- Learning
- Model of decline
- Mortification
- Perceptions
- Prevention
- Probing
- Rebuild
- Recovery
- Reputation
- Reviewing
- Signal detection
- Sincerity
- Situational crisis communication theory
- Traps

One Crisis—Varying Effects on Reputation

The 2G scam in India, rated second in *Time* magazine's all-time 'Top 10 Abuses of Power' list, shocked the entire nation and had major reputational repercussions for many of India's top corporate groups. Reliance Communications Ltd. (formerly Reliance Telecom, from the Reliance ADAG group) and the Essar Group were among those named by the Comptroller and Auditor General (CAG) to have received licences at favourable rates from then telecom minister Mr A. Raja. Idea Cellular Ltd. (Aditya Birla Group) and Tata Teleservices (Maharashtra) Ltd. (Tata Group) were among those whose licences were cancelled by the Supreme Court of India.

A MD and two senior vice-presidents of Reliance ADAG were taken into Central Bureau of Investigation custody in April 2011 under the Prevention of Corruption Act and granted bail in November 2011,[4] while the promoters of the Essar Group were summoned in court.[5]

Reliance ADAG issued a statement through its senior advocate to the effect that the group, its promoters or executives had not committed any offence. It denied allegations of the group or any associated individual with any beneficial interest in the 2G license issued in January 2008.[6] The Essar Group made an official statement that it had not violated any laws in its holding of Loop Telecom and that it would do everything in its power to protect its reputation.[7]

Both Tata Teleservices (Maharashtra) Ltd. and Idea Cellular Ltd. clarified that they had applied for licences in 2006, which were delayed and granted to them in 2008, making their case different from those of the other companies whose licences were cancelled. Both suffered revenue losses as a result of the Court's decision.

This crisis, which shook the nation by its sheer magnitude, had varying effects on the reputations of each of the companies involved. While some could emerge unscathed due to their strong pre-crisis reputation, some saw a substantial loss of reputational capital.

both situations impacts competitiveness, profitability and performance. In such situations, changes are required which purge the organisation of inefficiencies, if any, address shortcomings and provide a renewed perspective.

How does an organisation respond to this challenge? Through quick and timely intervention by the senior leadership team; and, creation of organisation frames emphasising values, success and satisfaction measures in the past. These tactics which reduce the severity of damage may not be able to address issues related to reputational loss. While it is difficult to assign a direct linkage between crisis and loss-of-face for the organisation, it is certain that negative impact on organisational reputation is steeper when the crisis is severe, as in the case of death or injury, than when it is minor as problems with resource management.[8]

Does the prior reputation of the organisation have a buffering or boomerang effect?[9] Crisis scholarship is divided on this question. On one hand, a good prior reputation builds tolerance in stakeholders, while on the other, the dissonance between the existing reputation perception and loss-of-face generates negativity.

What strategies, then, should be crafted to manage stakeholder perception in a crisis situation? Companies need to devise and employ redemptive measures for restoring faith and confidence in their products and services. To abet the effect of crises, organisations normally adopt a four-step crisis communication strategy: managing uncertainty, responding, resolving and learning.[10]

Corporate crisis management teams are formed to address the following questions:

- How does one identify a crisis before it is too late?
- What strategies should be adopted to overcome the crisis?
- What is the role of the top management during a crisis?
- How should stakeholder perceptions be redefined?
- How can crisis management turn into a learning experience for the company?

Organisations are of the view that if they operate with caution they can avert dangers associated with reputational loss as drop in profitability and market confidence, and may be even threat to survival.[11] There is no one defined strategy for addressing crisis situation. Strategies defining the correct approach to handling crisis are varied as perception, duration, intensity and consequence of each situation is different. Therefore, it is important to understand the causal link between crises, framing and organisational response for protecting image and reputation.

In this chapter, we discuss what is a crisis; what factors embroil an organisation in a crisis: related internal and external causes, traps/mistakes made by organisations; framing—media and company; how do organisations defend their reputation through an understanding of the attributional theory, image repair theory, situational crisis communication theory; how do companies demonstrate leadership traits during a crisis and what are the strategies adopted for crisis management.

WHAT IS A CRISIS?

When is a crisis reached? When questions arise that can't be answered.

—RYSZARD KAPUSCINSKI[12]

A crisis is a deviant situation from the normal, a destabilisation process involving multiple stakeholders and stakes, with multiple consequences, which fall outside the organisational framework and possess the capability to destabilise the existing framework.[13] A crisis can be defined as 'a specific, unexpected and non-routine event or series of events that create high levels of uncertainty and threat or perceived threat to an organisation's high priority goals',[14] and possesses the potential of financial and reputational damage. However, crisis may not be an unexpected isolated event. It could also be an aggregate of failures or iterations of wrong decisions made by the management which have escaped notice and attention.

The good news is that crises can be arrested. All such situations if intercepted in a timely manner can be addressed through a five-step cyclical process: signal detection—when organisations are cautious about warning signals, and are able to detect and prevent the same; probing and prevention—when organisations work towards identification of risk factors and attempt to mitigate the impact; damage containment—at the onset of the crisis, organisations work hard to limit the baneful impact; recovery—how soon are organisations able to recover from the crisis impact and learning—reviewing the process[15] (refer Fig. 10.1).

Figure 10.1 Five-stage Process of Crisis

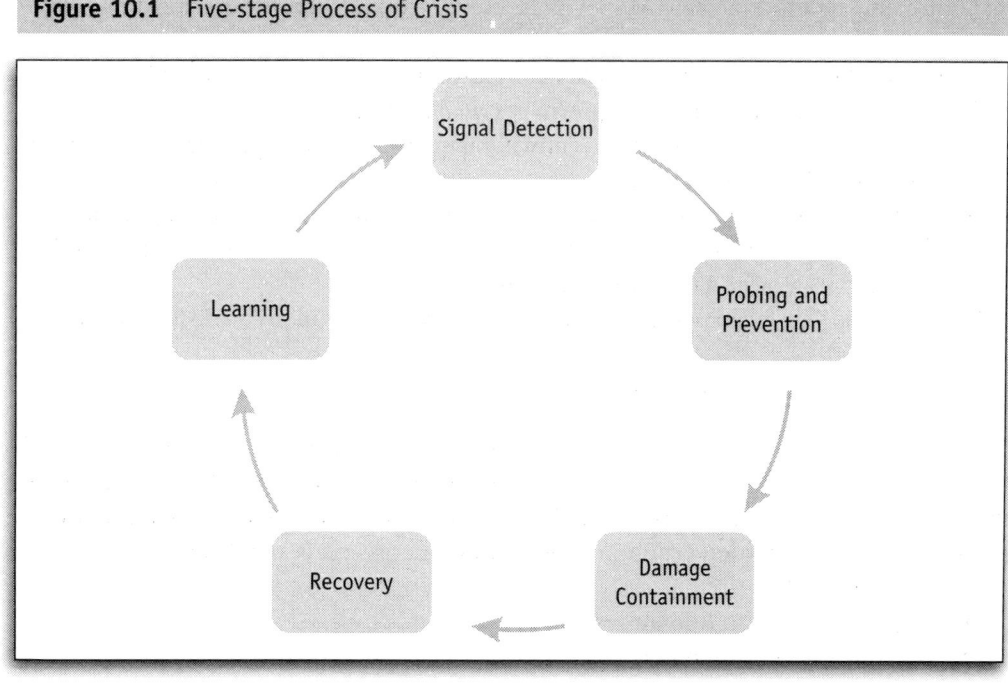

Corporate crisis management is a three-dimensional problem.[16] Organisations often limit themselves to correcting the symptoms rather than addressing the problem at the root cause. As a result, the link between the causes and consequences, essential for overcoming the crisis, is not well identified. Ignoring signs and signals which herald the onslaught of an 'untoward incident' till it gains mammoth size and appearance is a major problem faced by crisis managers. Organisations begin the process of fire-fighting which involves taking quick actions for immediate results. The carefully delineated roles for addressing the crisis, beginning with the top management are obscured in the process. As not all crises are accidental, environmental or technical, it is important to address the behavioural and political dimensions as employees, hierarchies, etc. while keeping the strategic perspective and outcome in view.

WHAT FACTORS EMBROIL AN ORGANISATION IN A CRISIS?

The easiest period in a crisis situation is actually the battle itself. The most difficult is the period of indecision—whether to fight or run away. And the most dangerous period is the aftermath. It is then, with all his resources spent and his guard down, that an individual must watch out for dulled reactions and faulty judgment.

—RICHARD M. NIXON[17]

Why is it that an organisation in a crisis situation finds it difficult to restore its lost performance and reputation? The Model of Decline[18] explains the reasons for the same:

- *Blinded:* Moving ahead with blinkers, organisations are unable to identify the problems which threaten their long-term survival and sustenance.
- *Inaction:* Senior leadership team is unwilling to take action despite clear signals from internal and external sources.
- *Faulty action:* Incorrect and inappropriate decisions which are not timed appropriately.
- *Crisis:* As a result of the three stages mentioned above, when crisis hits radical changes are required in strategy and structure.
- *Dissolution:* The fall in market is inevitable and the organisation can do little to recover.

Internal and External Factors

There are multiple internal and external factors which contribute to a crisis. Internal factors relate to employees, organisation, senior management and policies. Intrinsic to the organisation, many of the problematic issues may not either have been addressed or created a problem. Sudden eruption which causes a crisis may stem from:

- Problems related to human resource
- Incompetent management
- High production costs

- Poor performance
- Inefficient/outmoded systems
- Falling market position, etc.

External causes refer to those environmental changes which have gone unrecognised and have not been addressed in a timely and appropriate fashion.

Some of the external causes of crises are:

- Market changes as competition, price increase or decrease, change in consumer behaviour and preferences, suppliers, regulations, etc.
- Sectoral changes as takeovers, sector crisis, changed relationships between sectors
- Economic crisis as decreased investments, decrease in economic growth, decrease in exchange rates, etc.
- Changes in technology
- Natural and environmental calamities as cases of organisational or environmental force majeure, hurricanes, typhoons
- Political changes
- Socio pathological phenomena as abductions, extortions, sabotage, etc.
- Macro-economic indicators as cost of obtaining finance, exchange rates, custom duties, increase of taxation and welfare burdens on organisations, agreements, etc.

Kingfisher Airlines Ltd.: Good Times Gone Bad

Kingfisher Airlines Ltd., once a popular Indian domestic airline, has been grounded since October 2012 after its staff went on strike and refused to operate, citing lack of pay for eight months. Its debts are estimated at $2.5 billion, which include bank loans, trade debts and other short-term liabilities.[19] Promoter Mr Vijay Mallya has repeatedly expressed interest in resurrecting the airline, which is also what the lending banks are looking forward to, in order to avoid completely writing off their exposure of $1.5 billion.[20]

Kingfisher's decline began when the balance sheet did not reflect expected returns. The problem intensified with the company's inability to pay fuel dues and repeated strikes by pilots due to non-payment of salaries. Losses were further aggravated after its acquisition of Air Deccan. The subsequent suspension by Directorate General of Civil Aviation led to the airline slipping from number two position to last in the industry.[21] In February 2013, International Air Transport Association clearing house-suspended Kingfisher Airlines, putting on hold its proposed participation to the Oneworld Airlines Alliance. Subsequently, the Government of India announced the withdrawal of its domestic and international flight entitlements.

Understandably, there has been a complete loss of stakeholder confidence, with analysts predicting that even if Kingfisher is resurrected, its operations will be scaled down from its peak of 66 aircrafts to seven planes, and eventually expanded to around 20.[22]

Traps/Mistakes Made by Organisations

Consideration of the internal and external causes for crisis reveals that there are traps[23] or mistakes made by organisations which escalate the situation. Traps are as follows:

- The trap of paralysis: while dangers have been identified, no appropriate measures are being taken.
- The trap of escape: top management is not willing to take responsibility.
- The trap of selective perception: events which are favourable to the sustenance of the organisation are perceived and it is believed that the cause for the current situation rests somewhere else.
- The trap of embellishment: trying to deceive self and the other.
- The trap of inappropriate orientation: while the management is cognisant of the fact that their focus on business issues is not appropriate, they are unable to bring in the right orientation.
- The trap of 'coat cleaning': indecisiveness and fear of making mistakes (indecision and fear of the consequences of mistakes).
- The trap of protection: protecting unprofitable turf.
- The trap of correction: providing a short-term response to crisis due to a myopic view; relying on the possibility of corrections.

Maruti Suzuki India Ltd.'s Manesar Plant Crisis: Trapped in Several Traps

The crisis at Maruti Suzuki India Ltd.'s (MSIL) Manesar plant began in October 2011 with a 14-day-long strike by workers. It was finally called off after tripartite agreements were made between the management, workers and the Haryana government. Car production at the plant had been hampered thrice since June 2011 due to discontent among workers, leading up to ₹1,600 crores in lost revenues.[24] While management believed that all issues with workers were settled, they obviously were not.

In July 2012, a seemingly small altercation between a worker and a supervisor escalated into an episode of violence with a mob of workers taking management hostage and setting fire to offices, leaving one senior HR official dead and around 100 injured.

Analysts claim that the root of the crisis lay in two factors—the dissatisfaction among workers regarding their pay scale, which they felt was not commensurate with industry standards and company profits; and cultural slights—a casteist slur from a supervisor to a Jat-Dalit worker, that incensed the already volatile workforce.[25] Was this a trap?

WHAT IS FRAMING?

The media's the most powerful entity on earth They have the power to make the innocent guilty and to make the guilty innocent, and that's power. Because they control the minds of the masses.

—Malcom X[26]

Organisational response to a crisis is based on the perceptions created in the minds of the stakeholders by the media. News workers operate as agents who (de)construct social reality[27] as per the governing social constructs/frames, by sequentially arranging random pieces of information into a meaningful story. This narrative or framing revolves round a key or central idea and is easily and willingly interpreted by the audience.

Frames, thus, 'define problems—determine what a causal agent is doing and costs and benefits, usually measured in terms of cultural values; diagnose causes—identify the forces creating the problem; make moral judgements—evaluate causal agents and their effects and suggest remedies—offer and justify treatments for the problem and predict their likely effects.'[28] Additionally, frames provide an interpretation to the audience and help them to 'locate, perceive, identify and label'[29] issues, which form the substance round which public opinion is shaped. Interpretations of the same vary across groups and stakeholders and are often determined by the interpretative frames provided by the media and the organisations. During a crisis situation, there is involvement of a wide set of stakeholders, both as an aggrieved party and an afflicted bystander. Hence, framing news by the media and organisation has to be comprehensive and focussed on situation, attribute, action, issue and responsibility. The narrative can be inclusive or exclusive of events and activities, emphasising select information.[30]

Organisations embroiled in crisis need to present issues related to the unexpected and maybe unprecedented turn of events, emphasise or de-emphasise attributes related to the event (maybe framed by the media). They should suggest a modus operandi that addresses issues and elaborates on the responsibility associated with it.

Media and organisations use framing as a technique for presenting information that often creates a cognitive bias in the mind of the recipient. By providing contextual cues, the decision-making processes of the stakeholders are influenced. Both positive as well as negative frames are used for guiding decisions in situations, more specifically, of uncertainty or risk.[31] In such situations, there is greater weight assigned to negative information[32] for it possesses higher capacity to draw attention and leads to higher levels of involvement and desired behavioural patterns.[33]

Given the dynamic nature of framing by the media to relate issues to audience in a fashion that appeals and creates meaning, organisations have begun to use the same by framing actions, persuading consumers, providing justification, achieving co-operation and securing compliance. This is highly relevant in a situation where expectations have to be managed, justifications provided and negative mindsets changed to positive.

Trial by Media: Coca-Cola India and PepsiCo India

International soft drink giants Coca-Cola India and PepsiCo India faced a second round of allegations of pesticide contamination in 2006. The news hit the headlines when accusations were made by the Centre for Science and Environment (CSE), New Delhi, that these soft drinks contained pesticides at more than 24 times the safe limits. Within no time, both the companies were embroiled in a crisis situation.

While both companies were still working on legal and PR issues, and commissioning laboratory tests to formulate a detailed official response, media frenzy spiralled the crisis into a national scandal and a political controversy. Coca-Cola India and PepsiCo India failed to realise the speed of media and news in modern India and were caught unawares. The crisis deepened when newspapers carried photographs of Coke and Pepsi cans with captions saying 'toxic cocktail'. Images of protesters making donkeys drink Coke were aired on as many as 36 news channels.[34]

The non-stop press coverage raised angst levels among consumers, and had political repercussions as well—Gujarat and Madhya Pradesh banned the drinks at schools and government offices and Kerala imposed bans on their sale and manufacture. One of the leading political parties demanded a national ban on Pepsi and Coke and their party workers broke bottles and organised mock funerals in protest.[35]

Company executives felt that their task of reinstating consumer confidence was all the more difficult because the subject was complex. There was agreement on standards for safe pesticide levels in drinks in India, but no legal requirement for the same. Some experts believed that the high level of contamination of ground water in India led to pesticide residue in a majority of food products. Mr Asim Parekh, VP, Coca-Cola India and Mr Rajeev Bakshi, PepsiCo India Head, admitted that communicating their companies' stand on the level of pesticides was very difficult. Any defence would involve technical terminology and hence become confusing for a layperson.[36]

In spite of communicating facts and figures about the level of pesticides found, giving full-page ads proclaiming the safety of their drinks, directing reporters to positive blogs and public interest groups, tendering open invitations for plant visits to the public and questioning the scientific credentials of their accusers, both soft drink giants realised that the problem was not about facts, but about perception; a clear example of how framing influences stakeholders even more than hard facts.

HOW DO ORGANISATIONS DEFEND THEIR REPUTATION?

Your reputation can be your biggest asset or your biggest liability.

—REBECCA MADEIRA[37]

The concept of reputation in the context of crisis and its management is important as it creates negative perceptions that can affect the organisational profitability, growth and position in market. The greater the reputation of an organisation, the higher is the impact of crisis. A major threat to organisational reputation is that while attempts are made to shape stakeholder perceptions, there are other influencers (positive and negative) acting simultaneously to provide stimulus for existing perceptions. Each of these influencers has different concerns, interests and goals. In a crisis, the manager's task is to prioritise the audience and frame messages which address audience concerns.

As discussed in the earlier part of the chapter, one of the most important influencers in forming public opinion is the media, which can act as a threat to corporate reputation. Media assessment of the situation also plays an important role, for it is considered more relevant than actual glimpses into reality. Based on a combination of media frames and prior reputation in the market, stakeholders develop perceptions, assess and attribute organisational responsibility. Perceptions, assessments and attributes are shaped by crisis history of an organisation or similar incidents in the past together with the treatment meted out to the stakeholders. A positive and favourable or negative and unfavourable treatment will solicit a reciprocal response from the stakeholders. Hence, the response patterns of organisations to crisis situations are geared towards moulding stakeholder attributions, changing perceptions and minimising negativity.[38]

The attack to the image is applicable only if the organisation is considered responsible for the act, which in itself is considered offensive.[39] Responsibility is determined by the extent to which the organisation allows, orders, performs and encourages the act. In case it is found that the organisation is not responsible for the act or is not considered offensive in the eyes of the stakeholder, the image is not threatened. The critical point is management of perception, which is shaped by organisation and media, detailing acts of commission and omission, which are considered more important than reality.

Hindustan Unilever Ltd.: Surviving an Attack for 12 Years

Hindustan Unilever Ltd. (HUL), ranked second in *Fortune* 'India's Most Admired Companies' in 2012, is generally known for its various sustainability initiatives. Its Sustainable Living Plan is committed to taking responsibility not just for the company's own direct operations but for its suppliers, distributors and also for how its consumers use the company's brands.[40] However, in 2012, the company was compelled to provide explanations for an episode of alleged irresponsibility which happened 12 years ago. In March 2001, Greenpeace India and other NGOs accused HUL of dumping more than 5.3 tonnes of mercury waste from its mercury thermometer factory at a local scrap yard in the Indian tourist town of Kodaikanal. It was alleged that just before its shutdown, the factory released toxic mercury fumes into the air and contaminated streams and soil in its immediate vicinity.[41]

HUL was faced with allegations of failure to disclose operations as 'dangerous' to the Factories Inspectorate, inform the workers/community of its hazardous operations, specify the amount of mercury emitted into the environment and operate safety protocols/practices. On its part, the company argued that it had comprehensive occupational health and safety systems including employee training and awareness, use of personal protective equipment and adherence to safety procedures.[42]

Twelve years on, the matter is still under consideration by the Tamil Nadu Pollution Control Board, and HUL has a five-page 'position paper' on the erstwhile Kodaikanal factory case, where it categorically denies dumping mercury waste or causing adverse impact on the health of its employees or the environment and only admits to a sale of scrap to a local scrap-dealer in violation of its guidelines. It also details the steps taken for remediation of the soil surrounding its erstwhile factory.

One of the possible reasons why HUL successfully survived the negative media and NGO onslaught was its strong reputation, its history of commitment towards sustainability and its skill in establishing that it was not responsible for the environment and health damage as alleged.

Crises impact both the organisation and its reputation. The nature of the response to the situation and media framing helps in restoring stakeholder faith in the organisation, leadership, products and services. The intensity and duration of a reputation crisis can be best addressed by understanding the organisational response. A quick and appropriate response, as per the expectations and perceptions of the stakeholders reduces the effect of the crisis. Delays or inappropriate responses have related costs as drop in sales, share prices, customer loyalty and reputational capital. Arguably, the first step forward for organisations facing crisis is to develop a response strategy which can restore their image. What then, is the image restoration dialogue adopted by the organisation in response to the crisis?

Attributing Blame and Image Repair

Within organisations, the element of risk is always high and is affected by a host of factors as trust, familiarity, media, dread, catastrophic potential, scientific uncertainty, controllability, impact on children, receptivity, voluntariness of exposure, reversibility and attribution.[43] Hence, forming, managing and building reputation is always a difficult task.

Organisations develop their reputation through the information which stakeholders gather through media, press releases, website, online resources or word-of-mouth. The most important of these is the media which helps shape or distort organisational reputation through total or partial reports, framing of information and news. As reputations are evaluative, stakeholders compare the existing information with similar data from other organisations. The comparison is based on a standard which is socially or cognitively accepted. Expectations are built around this information and inability to meet the same creates a gap which organisations find difficult to bridge.

Hence, it is important for organisations to develop a stable reputation which often acts as a 'reservoir of good will' from which they can feed in turbulent times.[44] How well has the organisation managed its reputation is what provides the cushion to absorb negativity.

Attributional Theory

When a crisis occurs, the stakeholders search for causes, try to assign responsibilities and attribute blame. The intensity of the crisis situations and how organisations address them are perceived by the stakeholders on a continuum of organisational control (weak to strong) and choice of strategy. For instance, defensive strategies are suitable in weak control situations as environmental crisis. Accommodative strategies are best suited in strong personal control situations as accidents or acts in which the organisation is held responsible. In case the organisation is attributed responsibility, the public develops a negative attitude which is reflected in a drop in sales and market confidence.

A critical issue for organisations is to change public perceptions of the crisis. One strategy adopted is to show sincerity to the public and stakeholders in all their communication. For instance, while tendering an apology, if the leader demonstrates sincerity, stakeholders are more tolerant of the wrongdoing. In addition to sincerity, care and consideration for the victims or the environment should also be reflected in the communication. Involvement in earlier acts of corporate social responsibility is a good example of moving up the ladder of sentiments—negative to positive. For instance, if an organisation has been involved in providing education to children in the area of operations, the local community will be more tolerant of company action in a crisis situation.

Positive reputational equity can insulate an organisation against risks of crises or the perceived impact can be minimal. Similarly, earned social equity through generation of shared value can be beneficial in face-saving during crisis and will reduce the impact of attribution.

Image Repair Theory

Leaders have to walk the tightrope while zeroing in on the appropriate strategy. For instance, if they acknowledge guilt and the organisational contribution, it would lead to reputation loss and heavy litigation costs. They may be able to secure a short-term win but it may jeopardise their long-term financial viability by negative response from the investor community. In such situations, shareholders would prefer a defensive strategy which protects their financial interests, whereas victims would welcome an accommodative strategy which protects their personal interests.[45] At the end of the day image repair strategies will need to be adopted. Crisis scholarship suggests five image repair strategies as shown in Table 10.1.

An interesting example is of Air India in which the company was found evading responsibility.

Table 10.1 Image Repair Strategies[46]

Strategy	Action
Denial	Denying performance of the act or shifting responsibility to some other entity
Evasion of responsibility	Stressing involvement of other entities in provoking; arguing in favour of lack of information or emphasising the event being an accident with coincidental involvement of the company
Reducing offensiveness	Stressing on good deeds in the past (bolstering); presenting the act as, not so serious as projected (minimisation); emphasising that the act is not as offensive as similar acts in industry (differentiation); stressing more important facts under consideration (transcendence); attacking the person or organisation which has levelled allegations and/or compensating victimised parties
Corrective action	Offering a plan or a solution to address the problem
Mortification	Apologising, admitting to guilt and expressing remorse and concern

Air India: Evading Responsibility

The 2012 pilots' strike at Air India (AI) was the longest in its history and the most hard-hitting. It caused revenue losses of more than ₹610 crores, grounded an entire fleet of Boeing 777s, leading to idle human resources and closure of services along important routes. All of these repercussions adversely affected the airlines' chances of overcoming the financial problems it faced post its merger with Indian Airlines. The strike also dealt a severe blow to AI's international operations by stranding thousands of passengers set to fly to East Asia and the Middle East, further adding to reputational loss.[47]

The striking pilots under the Indian Pilots Guild (IPG) blamed the airlines' decision to send Indian Airline pilots for the Dreamliner aircraft training as the cause of the dispute, as this issue had raised concerns among AI pilots about their own career progression. In this situation, Civil Aviation Minister Mr Ajit Singh used the strategy of evading responsibility by blaming the merger as the reason behind the current crisis, stating it should not have been done, or due diligence should have been carried out before the deal was completed.[48]

Image repair strategies are often used in combination. When a combination of strategies as bolstering, shifting blame and/or corrective action is used, the organisation normally has strong personal control over the situation or crisis.

Organisations which are perceived to be responsible for a crisis require use of accommodative strategies which increase in proportion to increase in crisis responsibility and reputational damage. This indicates a direct relationship between responsibility and reputation in the crisis situation.[49] As organisations become more accommodative in the strategies they use, there is a proportionate increase in costs for the company.

Situational Crisis Communication Theory

There exists a close link between types of crisis and choice of response strategy. Situational Crisis Communication Theory (SCCT) is a response strategy designed by managers to address the reputational damage which challenges their position and credibility in the market. SCCT compartmentalises crises into three clusters: victim cluster, in which organisational responsibility is weak; accidental cluster, with low organisational responsibility and preventable cluster with high perceived organisational responsibility.[50] The reputational damage depends on the crisis type and the perceived responsibility. Damage to organisational reputation is minimum in case of victim cluster and maximum in case of preventable cluster. Undoubtedly, the organisational reputation and history of crisis management have a bearing on current perceptions.

SCCT recognises the importance of identifying, communicating and influencing publics and their perceptions on facts and policies which can give rise to dispute It is followed by risk communication which has to do more with allaying fears and building long-term relationships with stakeholders. The nature of response to the crisis affects perceptions and protects the organisational image and reputation.

Based on the nature of the crisis three response strategies can be adopted by organisations: deny, diminish and rebuild. As the name specifies, when organisations adopt 'deny' strategy, they rest their claims on the fact that they are in no way to be held responsible for the untoward incident.

Tata Steel Ltd.: Denying Illegal Mining

When global steel giant and India's 'Most Admired Company', Tata Steel Ltd. was believed to have been fined about ₹6,000 crores for its alleged 'illegal and excess mining' at its captive mines in Odisha by Deputy Director of Mines of Joda mining circle, the company denied any illegal mining. Acknowledging that it had received 'two–three notices',[51] the company representative said that their case could be considered as excessive mining but definitely not illegal mining.

Tata Steel Ltd. also emphasised their commitment to ethical behaviour by reiterating that they have always engaged in mining in Odisha and other states in absolute conformity with the existing laws.[52]

Under 'diminish' category, organisations minimise their responsibility.

Nokia: Reducing the Scare by Diminishing Responsibility

In 2007, Nokia issued a product advisory regarding 46 million BL-5C batteries used in a range of its handsets which were at risk of overheating during charging. While offering to replace all faulty batteries for free, the company also played down customer fears by mentioning that only about 100 cases of overheating had been reported globally, and none in India, without any serious injuries or property damage. The company's strategy of attempting to diminish responsibility paid off, as it was able to avert panic and avoid reputational loss.[53]

'Rebuild' strategies focus on offering compensation to the victims or apologising.

Rebuilding to Emerge from a Crisis: Ford India P. Ltd.

Ford India P. Ltd. found itself in the eye of the storm when three advertisements created by JWT India, a division of WPP, one of the world's largest advertising agencies, went viral in March 2013. The drawings, aiming to emphasise the ample rear storage space of the Ford Figo car, depicted three bound and gagged women in the boot of Silvio Berlusconi's car, socialite Paris Hilton abducting the Kardashian sisters and Michael Schumacher kidnapping his rivals, with the tagline 'Leave your worries behind with Figo's extra large boot'.[54]

At a time when there is widespread concern over womens' safety in India, the ads were seen as insensitive and led to public outcry, especially among womens' groups.

Although Ford India had not officially approved or released these ads, it issued a formal apology in a statement to *The Hindu*: 'We deeply regret this incident and agree with our agency partners that it should have never happened. The posters are contrary to the standards of professionalism and decency within Ford and our agency partners.'[55] The company also promised to review its approval and oversight processes to avoid repetition of such an incident.

In addition to this strategy of 'rebuilding', the company also clarified who was to blame. JWT South Asia CEO Mr Colvyn Harris explained that the posters were not actually released or published and did not have an official endorsement from Ford. He clarified that they had been independently uploaded by team members 'with inappropriate judgement and without proper oversight or authorisation'.[56]

Which strategy is most suited is dependent on the assessment of the situation and the stand organisations decide to take. It has been found that deny is most appropriate for victim crisis, diminish for accidental crisis and rebuild for preventable crisis.[57]

Figure 10.2 presents an interesting link between crisis and corporate reputation, the impact of crisis on a company's reputation, media and company framing post the crisis,

Figure 10.2   Crisis and Corporate Reputation

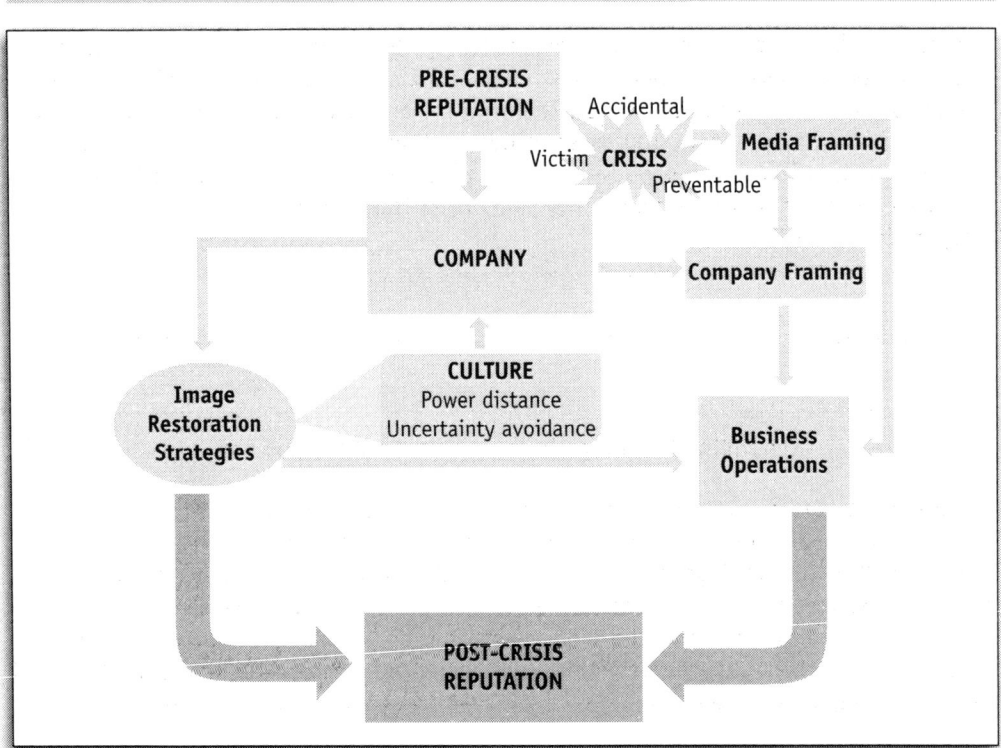

the country culture, the image restoration strategies, all of which collectively shape the post crisis corporate reputation.

HOW ARE LEADERSHIP TRAITS DEMONSTRATED DURING A CRISIS?

You never let a serious crisis go to waste. And what I mean by that it's an opportunity to do things you think you could not do before.

—Rahm Emanuel[58]

When is the leader most under duress? When faced with a crisis! The involvement is not only at the assessment and procedural levels but also at the point of establishing contact with the people directly or indirectly affected. The leader in such situations needs to show concern and be visible to the public. To a great extent it helps abet the intensity of the situation. Additionally, the leader has to take measures to restructure and re-engineer existing policies for which employee support is critical and crucial. The challenge is to motivate and align the internal stakeholders to newer systems and policies.

When a crisis hits an organisation, all eyes are riveted to the leader. How should a leader behave and respond are some questions that the leadership team often grapples with. The decisions and their implementation have to be 'right first time' and timely, as there is little or no room to make amends. The stance of the leaders ascertains the confidence in the stakeholders.

In periods of upheaval, workers want concrete evidence that top management views their distress as one of the organisation's key concerns. Written statements have their place, but oral statements and the sound of empathetic human voice communicate sincerity. And if the voice belongs to an organisation leader, the listener has reason to think that the full weight of the organisation stands behind whatever promises or assurances are being made.[59]

The key words for the leader in such instances are 'being vigilant'. Being present on the scene, listening to employees, sifting through the information, addressing key stakeholders, ensuring that the priorities of the organisation are met, responding to media queries, acting in the best interest of the organisation and the stakeholders are some key measures to be adopted by leaders. Slackness in attitude or behaviour will sooner or later boomerang and find reflection in the balance sheet of the organisation. Effective leaders carefully scan the environment, study the issues which led to the crisis situation, assess the present situation and finally prepare a roadmap for the stage of recovery. During the crisis it is critical for the leader to take on complete responsibility, assure that situation can be amended, form teams which will look into the situation and carefully select the right option for recovery, which is based on criteria that prioritise organisational benefits. Hence, as an effective strategy, organisations need to outline a broad value-based strategy which is well supported by a vision and a mission. As it is near impossible to predict all situations, favourable or otherwise, organisation-developed framework of values acts as a guiding post for leaders to resolve crisis situations.

What should be the leadership style during a crisis? This point has been extensively debated and some argue in favour of an authoritarian style while others emphasise a participative style. Both these styles are found wanting in an extreme situation, which requires a combination of authoritarian and democratic or participative leadership style. Someone will have to take the lead and show the way. For large numbers to follow, discussions are required. However, in situations where immediate action has to be taken, as in the case of fire or accident, a 'command and obey' style is the most suited.

The reputational threat stemming from a crisis is a result of three factors: initial crisis responsibility, crisis history and prior relational reputation.[60] In the lifecycle of a crisis, the post crisis handling is the most important. Leaders should be seen as reflecting on changes required to quell a repeat of the crisis situation. How an organisation implements the learning is important from the point of view of stakeholders. Leaders should be seen as implementers of change, possessing the capability to restore faith and trust in the organisation. This role is critical as perceptions on the intensity of the crisis will be varied. For instance, when an organisation has been working for a social cause, allegations of crisis may be toned down. The organisation may also refrain from commenting on the situation. This 'no comment' strategy will hold good only in situations where the source of accusations has low credibility and when the intensity of the crisis is low. Eastern societies more than Western societies are tolerant of this strategy which points to the cultural perception of crisis and choice of image repair strategies.[61] The advantage of this strategy over a defensive one is that it keeps the leader out of news coverage and does not provide information which can give rise to speculation and distrust of organisational acts and intentions.

Addressing Stakeholder Apprehensions and Fears

Leaders strive to build trust in the minds of the stakeholders. This helps negate the impact of negative information and news which carries more weight in shaping perceptions, is more visible and perceived as credible and raises the important question of ethical frameworks created by leaders to address the situation. Should economic or rational theory gain precedence over stakeholder welfare or should the reverse hold true? There are arguments in favour of both sides. An 'economic' or rational perspective may help the leader gain credence in the eyes of the shareholders but it can damage reputation and earn for the leader a long-lasting resentment and disapproval of other stakeholders.

Believing in the virtue of trust, leaders can adopt a virtue ethics, ethic of justice or ethic of care.[62] The leader's position and credibility in the organisation together with intentions of doing good will reflect virtue ethics. The ethic of justice will focus on impartiality, use of objective standards and reciprocity.[63] Ethic of care emphasises on building and strengthening relationships, respecting commitment and fulfilling responsibilities.[64] It is important to demonstrate through actions and disposition 'I/We care' to win support and forgiveness. For this a triple A approach—acknowledge, apologise and act—can be followed.[65] Undoubtedly, application of the ethic of care will have a more positive outcome in winning a favourable response from all concerned stakeholders than the ethic of justice.

Leaders need to keep in perspective the following six points of successful crisis management:

- Effective leader management which has the approval and support of the teams
- Strict yet relaxed leadership
- Motivated employees with good team spirit
- Good conflict management team
- Back-up of banks and financial organisations
- A realistic restructuring plan with sufficient room to address strategic, operational and liquidity issues[66]

WHAT ARE THE STRATEGIES FOR CRISIS MANAGEMENT?

The secret of crisis management is not good vs. bad, it's preventing the bad from getting worse.

—ANDY GILMAN[67]

Leaders and their expert advice are important in moments of crisis. For this, leaders can either hire experts or use their prior experience to:

- Understand the nature of crises that can hit the organisation
- Shift focus from commercial concerns to media monitoring
- Identify the organisation's past, present and future activities which are subject to scrutiny from external sources
- Plan in advance for responses to the situation
- Focus on response priorities
- Choose the right message—specific message to media and individuals
- Emphasise situation, understand cause, assign responsibility, assess relative harm and adopt remedial measures
- Determine the optimal timing
- Exert control measures and provide guidance and recommendations for collective and personal responses
- Redefine stakeholder perceptions
- Communicate, communicate and communicate!

CONCLUSION

Crises and deadlocks when they occur have atleast this advantage that they force us to think.

—JAWAHARLAL NEHRU[68]

A crisis is an unexpected state of events, which if inappropriately addressed, can lead to reputational loss. Though organisations are always on the vigil to protect themselves from these unwarranted incidents, there are various factors outside their control. For instance, environmental hazards, financial downturn, etc. can create turbulence in the entire company and lead to loss of stakeholder confidence. While it is given that a crisis will hit an organisation in its lifecycle, what is not given is the redemptive strategy which will help abet the intensity of the situation.

Some measures which an organisation can adopt on a continuous basis to maintain stakeholder confidence and keep them appeased, that will help minimise if not nullify the negative impact of the crisis are:

- Work on past crisis situations and use the learning to avoid a repeat of the same
- Maintain a high profile in terms of ethics and care
- Create positive frames for stakeholders
- Ensure visibility of the leader
- Keep employees engaged and motivated

Key Points

- Crises impact both the organisation and its reputation.
- The greater the reputation of an organisation, the higher is the impact of the crisis.
- Positive reputational equity can insulate an organisation against risk of crises or the perceived impact can be minimal.
- The threat to reputation arising from a crisis is a result of three factors: initial crisis responsibility, crisis history and prior relational reputation.
- The impact on organisational reputation is steeper when the crisis is severe as in the case of death or injury than when it is minor as resource management.
- Crisis can be intercepted and arrested through following a five-step cyclical process: signal detection, probing and prevention, damage containment, recovery and learning.
- Inability to address crises can be explained by The Model of Decline which specifies five reasons: being blinded, inaction, faulty action, inability to understand crisis and dissolution.
- Organisations often fall into traps or make mistakes which escalate the crises as trap of paralysis, escape, selective perception, embellishment, inappropriate orientation, 'coat cleaning', protection and correction.
- Media and organisations use framing as a technique for presenting information that often creates a cognitive bias in the mind of the recipient.
- Framing focusses on the situation, attribute, action, issue and responsibility. Framing can be inclusive or exclusive of events and activities, emphasising select information.
- The response patterns of organisations to crisis situations are geared towards moulding stakeholder attributions, changing perceptions and minimising the negativity.
- The nature of the response to the situation and media framing helps in restoring stakeholder faith in the organisation, leadership, products and services.
- It is important for organisations to develop a stable reputation which often acts as a 'reservoir of good will' from which the organisation can feed in turbulent times.

- All strategies adopted during crisis to mollify the stakeholders should have an underlying tone of sincerity, care and consideration.
- There are five image repair strategies: denial, evasion of responsibility, reducing offensiveness, corrective action and mortification.
- SCCT compartmentalises crises into three clusters: victim cluster; accidental cluster and preventable cluster.
- Based on the nature of the crisis there are three responses strategies which can be adopted by the organisation: deny, diminish and rebuild.
- The leadership during a crisis has to secure co-operation and motivation of employees through a style which is appropriate to addressing the situation and enhancing the management perspective and possesses the ability to undertake restructuring and re-engineering measures.
- During a crisis a leader should adopt a style which lies between authoritarian and democratic.
- Building on the virtue of trust, leaders can adopt virtue ethics, ethic of justice and ethic of care.
- To be on the path of ethical behaviour, leaders acknowledge, apologise and act.

END NOTES

1. Brainy quote, website http://www.brainyquote.com/quotes/quotes/g/georgebern163471.html (accessed 13 April 201 3).
2. Brainy quote, website http://www.brainyquote.com/quotes/quotes/j/johnfkenn103820.html (accessed 13 April 2013).
3. K. Kromeyer-Hauschildt and K. Zellner, 'Trends in overweight and obesity and changes in the distribution of mass index in school children of Jena, East Germany', *European Journal of Clinical Nutrition* (2007), 61(3), 404–411.
4. 2G scam: 'Charges against Raja & others', *NDTV*, website http://www.ndtv.com/article/india/2g-scam-charges-against-raja-others-143384 (accessed 22 October 2012).
5. '2G scam: Court summons Essar Group directors, Loop Telecom promoters', *The Indian Express*, website http://www.indianexpress.com/news/2g-scam-court-summons-essar-group-directors-loop-telecom-promoters/890401/ (accessed 22 October 2012).
6. J. Venkatesan, 'No offence committed, says Reliance ADAG', *The Hindu*, website http://www.thehindu.com/business/no-offence-committed-says-reliance-ada/article2500512.ece (accessed 30 September 2012).
7. 2G scam: Essar denies violation of cross-holding norms', *NDTV Profit*, website http://profit.ndtv.com/news/corporates/article-2g-scam-essar-denies-violation-of-cross-holding-norms-294322 (accessed 17 December 2012).
8. W. T. Coombs and S. J. Holladay, 'Helping crisis managers protect reputational assets: Initial tests of the situational crisis communication theory', *Management Communication Quarterly* (2002), 16(2), 165–186.
9. Y. J. Sohn and R.W. Lariscy, 'A "Buffer" or "Boomerang?": The role of corporate reputation in bad times', website http://crx.sagepub.com/content/early/2012/11/19/0093650212466891 (accessed 24 November 2012).
10. R. R. Ulmer, T. L. Sellnow and M.W. Seeger, *Effective Crisis Communication: Moving from Crisis to Opportunity.* Thousand Oaks, CA: SAGE Publications (2011).
11. W. T. Coombs, 'Protecting organization reputations during a crisis: The development and application of situational crisis communication theory', *Corporate Reputation Review* (2007), 10(3), 163–176.

12. Search quotes, website http://www.searchquotes.com/quotation/When_is_a_crisis_reached%3F_When_questions_arise_that_can't_be_answered./87853/ (accessed 13 April 2013).

13. D. I. Tănase, 'Procedural and systematic crisis approach and crisis management', *Theoretical and Applied Economics* (2012), 19(5), 177–184.

14. M. W. Seeger, T. L. Sellnow and R. R. Ulmer, 'Communication, organisation and crisis', in M. E. Roloff (ed.), *Communication Yearbook* 21 (pp. 231–275), Thousand Oaks, CA: SAGE Publications (1998), p. 233.

15. I. I. Mitroff, 'Crisis management and environmentalism: A natural fit', *California Management Review* (1994), 36(2), 101–113.

16. R. Muller, 'Corporate crisis management', *Long Range Planning* (1985), 8(5), 38–48.

17. Quotations book, website http://quotationsbook.com/quote/9227/#sthash.XUGtZJjs.dpbs (accessed 13 April 2013).

18. W. Weitzel and E. Jonsson, 'Decline in organizations: A literature integration and extension', *Administrative Science Quarterly* (1989), 34(1), 91–109.

19. Kazmin, 'Grounded Kingfisher hopes for reprieve', *Financial Times*, website http://www.ft.com/intl/cms/s/0/cd19e64a-70f7-11e2-9d5c-00144feab49a.html#axzz2KaBg81Qd (accessed 10 February 2013).

20. Ibid.

21. Wikipedia, 'Kingfisher Airlines', website http://en.wikipedia.org/wiki/Kingfisher_Airlines_financial_crisis#Financial_difficulties (accessed 6 March 2013).

22. Kazmin, 'Grounded Kingfisher hopes for reprieve', *Financial Times*, website http://www.ft.com/intl/cms/s/0/cd19e64a-70f7-11e2-9d5c-00144feab49a.html#axzz2KaBg81Qd (accessed 10 February 2013).

23. P. Faulhaber and N. Landwehr, *Turnaround – Management in der Praxis*, Frankfurt: Campus (2001).

24. V. Dhoot and C. P. Chauhan, 'Maruti strike: Trade union leader Sonu Gujjar quits with ₹40 lakh payout', *The Economic Times*, website http://articles.economictimes.indiatimes.com/2011-11-04/news/30359568_1_manesar-plant-maruti-s-manesar-maruti-suzuki-labour-unrest (accessed 4 November 2012).

25. A. Mishra, 'Manesar: Class struggle of the 21st century', *The Times of India*, website http://blogs.timesofindia.indiatimes.com/the-mainstream-maverick/entry/manesar-class-struggle-of-the-21st-century (accessed 4 November 2012).

26. Goodreads, website http://www.goodreads.com/quotes/74430-the-media-s-the-most-powerful-entity-on-earth-they-have (accessed 20 April 2013).

27. G. Tuchman, *Making News: A Study in the Construction of Social Reality*. New York: Free Press (1978).

28. R. M. Entman, 'Framing: Toward a clarification of a fractured paradigm', *Journal of Communication* (1993), 43(4), 51–58, p. 52.

29. E. Goffman, *Frame Analysis: An Essay on the Organization of Experience*. New York: Harper & Row (1974), p. 21.

30. K. Hallahan, 'Seven models of framing: Implications for public relations', *Journal of Public Relations Research* (1999), 11(3), 205–242.

31. D. Kahneman and A. Tversky, 'Prospect theory: An analysis of decision under risk', *Econometrica* (1979), 47(2), 263–291.

32. D. L. Hamilton and M. P. Zanna, 'Differential weighting of favourable and unfavourable attributes in impressions of personality', *Journal of Experimental Research in Personality* (1972), 6, 204–212.

33. C. S. Elliott and D. M. Hayward, 'The expanding definition of framing and its particular impact on economic experimentation', *Journal of Socio-Economics* (1998), 27(2), 229–243.

34. A. Gentleman, 'Pesticide allegations trip up Coke and Pepsi', *The New York Times*, website http://www.nytimes.com/2006/08/22/business/worldbusiness/22iht-coke.2562750.html?pagewanted=all (accessed 7 March 2013).

35. B. Bremner and N. Lakshman, 'India: Pesticide claims shake up Coke and Pepsi', *Bloomberg Business Week*, website http://www.businessweek.com/stories/2006-08-09/india-pesticide-claims-shake-up-coke-and-pepsi (accessed 7 March 2013).

36. A. Gentleman, 'Pesticide allegations trip up Coke and Pepsi', *The New York Times*, website http://www.nytimes.com/2006/08/22/business/worldbusiness/22iht-coke.2562750.html?pagewanted=all (accessed 7 March 2013).

37. M. Morley, *How to Manage Your Global Reputation*. Basingstoke, UK: MacMillan (1998), p. 16.

38. W. T. Coombs, 'Choosing the right words: The development of guidelines for the selection of the "appropriate" crisis response strategies', *Management Communication Quarterly* (1995), 8(4), 447–476.

39. W. L. Benoit, 'Image repair discourse and crisis communication', *Public Relations Review* (1997), 23(2), 177–186.

40. Unilever, 'Unilever sustainable living plan', website http://www.hul.co.in/sustainable-living/uslp/ (accessed 7 March 2013).

41. Greenpeace, 'Unilever admits to dumping of mercury in Indian tourist town', website http://www.greenpeace.org.uk/media/press-releases/unilever-admits-to-dumping-of-mercury-in-indian-tourist-town (accessed 22 March 2001).

42. HUL, 'Update on Kodai for online sustainability report for Unilever.com', website http://www.hul.co.in/Images/Update_on_Erstwhile_Kodaikanal_Factory_tcm114-195572.pdf (accessed 12 April 2013).

43. V. T. Covello and M. W. Merkhofer, *Risk Assessment Methods: Approaches for Assessing Health and Environmental Risks*. New York: Plenum Publishing Corporation (1993).

44. M. Morley, *How to Manage Your Global Reputation*. Basingstoke, UK: MacMillan (1998).

45. A. A. Marcus and R. S. Goodman, 'Victims and shareholders: The dilemmas of presenting corporate policy during a crisis', *Academy of Management Journal* (1991), 34(2), 281–305.

46. 'Air India strike', *The Times of India*, 1 July 2012.

47. IANS, 'The reason behind Air India despair', Bihar Prabha, website http://news.biharprabha.com/2012/05/the-reason-behind-air-india-despair/ (accessed 13 May 2012).

48. W. L. Benoit, 'Image repair discourse and crisis communication', *Public Relations Review* (1997), 23(2), 177–186.

49. W. T. Coombs and L. Schmidt, 'An empirical analysis of image restoration: Texaco's racism crisis', *Journal of Public Relations Research* (2000), 12(2), 163–178.

50. W. T. Coombs and S. J. Holladay, 'Helping crisis managers protect reputational assets: Initial tests of the situational crisis communication theory', *Management Communication Quarterly* 16(2), 165–186.

51. PTI, 'Rs. 6,000-cr fine on Tata Steel for illegal mining: sources', *Hindustan Times*, website http://www.hindustantimes.com/India-news/NewDelhi/Rs-6-000-cr-fine-on-Tata-Steel-for-illegal-mining-sources/Article1-955324.aspx (accessed 5 November 2012).

52. Ibid.

53. PTI, 'Customers throng Nokia centres seeking battery replacement', *The Economic Times*, website http://articles.economictimes.indiatimes.com/2007-08-16/news/28417316_1_bl-5c-faulty-batteries-devinder-kishore (accessed 16 August 2007).

54. R. Mackey, 'Indian car ad goes viral, not in a good way', *The New York Times*, website http://thelede.blogs.nytimes.com/2013/03/25/indian-car-ad-goes-viral-not-in-a-good-way/ (accessed 13 October 2013).

55. A. Srivas, 'Italy seethes at Ford's Indian job', *The Hindu*, website http://www.thehindu.com/business/Industry/italy-seethes-at-fords-indian-job/article4541960.ece (accessed 13 October 2013).

56. 'Why Ford Figo's "unapproved" JWT ads have created a rage', *The Economic Times*, website http://economictimes.indiatimes.com/slideshows/advertising-marketing/why-ford-figos-unapproved-jwt-ads-have-created-a-rage/official-apologies-have-been-issued/slideshow/19187157.cms (accessed 13 October 2013).

57. A. Claeys, V. Cauberghe and P. Vyncke, 'Restoring reputations in times of crisis: An experimental study of the Situational Crisis Communication Theory and the moderating effects of locus of control', *Public Relations Review* (2010), 36(3), 256–262.

58. Brainy quote, website http://www.brainyquote.com/quotes/quotes/r/rahmemanue409199.html (accessed 13 April 2013).

59. P. Argenti, 'Crisis communication: Lessons from 9/11', website http://hbr.org/web/special-collections/insight/communication/crisis-communication-lessons-from-9-11 (accessed 12 January 2013).

60. W. T. Coombs, 'Protecting organisation reputations during a crisis: The development and application of situational crisis communication theory', *Corporate Reputation Review* (2007), 10(3), 163–176.

61. B. T. Lee, 'Audience-oriented approach to crisis communication: A study of Hong Kong consumers' evaluation of an organizational crisis', *Communication Research* (2004), 31(5), 600–618.

62. D. C. Bauman, 'Evaluating ethical approaches to crisis leadership: Insights from unintentional harm research', *Journal of Business Ethics* (2011), 98(2), 281–295.

63. S. Simola, 'Ethics of justice and care in corporate crisis management', *Journal of Business Ethics* (2003), 46(4), 351–361.

64. Ibid.

65. D. C. Bauman, 'Evaluating ethical approaches to crisis leadership: Insights from unintentional harm research', *Journal of Business Ethics* (2011), 98(2), 281–295.

66. R. Muller, 'Corporate crisis management', *Long Range Planning* (1985), 8(5), 38–48.

67. M. Agnes, '8 great crisis management quotes from the pros', Melissa Agnes Crisis Management, website http://www.melissaagnescrisismanagement.com/8-great-crisis-management-quotes-from-the-pros/ (accessed 20 January 2014).

68. Quotes for crisis, website http://www.slideshare.net/oma/quotes-for-crisis (accessed 13 April 2013).

Strategising Corporate Reputation

11

'Walk the Talk' and 'Talk the Walk': Strategising Corporate Reputation

However much of time, labor, or other means it takes to establish a reputation, it frequently happens that it requires nearly as much to maintain it.

—Christian Nestell Bovee[1]

Objectives:

- Strategise building and maintaining corporate reputation
- Develop a corporate vision
- Build organisation–stakeholder relationship
- Learn techniques of developing narratives
- Acquire skills in crafting a communication plan

INTRODUCTION

It is easier to add to a great reputation than to get it.

—Publilius Syrus[2]

A quick search on Google for the word 'reputation' throws up an astronomical figure of 575,000,000 in 0.28 seconds.[3] What is the reason for this emphasis on reputation, more specifically corporate reputation? Which of the following can be an answer to this question—enhanced diversity, environmental uncertainty or information asymmetry? Possibly one or maybe a combination of all these factors. Small wonder then, companies endeavour to fabricate a reputational shield to protect in adverse moments, help in differentiating from competitors and reaffirm trust and faith of stakeholders. No two shields are similar. Each company has a unique formula for creating and strengthening this shield. What is common is the structuring process comprising actions, capabilities and strategic intent.

Once reputation is formed, can it be developed as an asset, albeit intangible? Undoubtedly yes, provided the company aligns its goals with reputational

---

A Robust Reputation—Built or Acquired? Infosys Ltd.

The story of seven young middle-class engineers pooling their savings to set up a software company in 1981, with a dream of making it world-class, is known to every Indian today. Thirty-two years later, this incredible tale of determination and entrepreneurship combined with strong values is what most of us identify Infosys Ltd. with. Over the years, Infosys Ltd. has had its share of ups and downs, but has been able to consistently maintain its reputation as an organisation that places values as trust, integrity and honesty above everything else. The company always figures high on the list in reputation rankings as *Businessworld*'s 'India's Most Respected Companies' or *Fortune India*'s 'Most Admired Companies'. It has a slew of awards to its credit in areas ranging from corporate governance, investor relations, CSR, customer satisfaction and leadership.

Is this reputation built or acquired? It appears to be a combination of having a compelling vision and powerful leadership, engaging meaningfully with stakeholder groups and aligning their goals with those of the organisation, creating and sustaining a culture of transparency with media, investors and regulatory authorities and ensuring the highest quality of offering for customers.

The company has proven how taking stakeholders along can yield superior financial and non-financial benefits, and, as Mr Narayana Murthy, Executive Chairman, states, '... it is possible to be world-class from India'.[4] While financial performance, leadership and governance have played their part, the management's focus on creating an 'Infosys story' and making it known, definitely seems to have paid off in terms of reputational gain.

quotient strategically built into the company DNA. To achieve this purpose companies craft a reputation plan based on the 'normative, economic or competitive logic of the organisation'[5] which aligns the internal (core business model, purpose and values of the company) and external (company engagement with the environment) to the business philosophy. Reputations are thus built into the company strategy keeping in view the goals, economic logic, customers and value created and derived from the product. The philosophy behind strategising corporate reputation however, may vary across companies as only focus on earning profits, or creating value for society, etc. Such 'built in'[6] reputations are different from 'bolted on'[7] which use tactical initiatives as indulging in CSR, which is unrelated to company philosophy or cheque book philanthropy, to earn reputational capital. Should companies build in or bolt on reputation? The answer to the question lies in the definition of corporate reputation which is 'a perceptual representation of a company's past actions and future prospects that describes the firm's overall appeal to all of its key constituents when compared with other leading rivals'.[8] Based on this definition, we discuss the three most important points which help build a reputation: perceptions of stakeholders; past performance and future projections and competitive advantage. The critical issue before companies is to assess measures applicable for changing perceptions of internal and external stakeholders and securing their support.

Stakeholders develop perceptions based on company history, what it has done and what it could not do in moments of rest and crisis. Values and vision, involvement with the community and stakeholders, governance practices and ethical code of conduct help a company increase its stakeholder base and gain respect and admiration. Notably, the past performance of the company is an important factor for developing a specific or overall reputational quotient. To elaborate further, when we discuss 'specific' reputation our focus is only on any one company attribute as position in the market, product, etc. 'Overall' on the other hand, connotes an aggregate of factors as product and services, leadership and workplace, performance, innovation, citizenship, governance.[9] Overall reputation is a composite of specific reputation emphasising single company attributes. For instance, specific reputations may be 'Best Employer', 'Best HR practices', etc.

The Alignment Factors

A strategic structuring of reputation hinges on alignment of four factors: economic logic, goals and objectives, values, vision and mission, and environment. Economic logic refers to areas on which the company focusses and cost leadership. The economic logic is part of the strategic consideration for operations and is applicable across industries emphasising the who, what and how of building reputation. Who or what will the company target? Would it be the customer, the employees or the culture? Based on prioritisation of the target, leader stories are crafted, resources allocated and committed to various entities for managing reputation. These may take on the role of non-core activities as CSR, which act as a defence mechanism or act as a social safety net.[10]

Can companies operationalise their processes which extend beyond focussing on shareholder returns? The answer to the question rests in the purpose of building or strategising reputation which is lost when financial returns become the focal point in strategy design. The ROI on reputational capital is positive when the goal in strategy formulation reflects stakeholder concerns, needs, expectations and perceptions. An overarching goal which can help a company build 360 degree trust and credibility lays emphasis on all stakeholders instead of just investors and shareholders.

Closely aligned with objectives are the values that a company espouses, the vision and mission. Corporate values are normally reflected in the vision statement which guides employees towards a common target and reassures stakeholders of company intent. A narrowly defined vision statement with focus on the next five or 10 years makes it limited and excites the question 'What then?' A well-defined vision statement, while considering the macro issues, also presents flexibility in approach and helps in preparation of a mission statement which managers can use to navigate changes in environment. To illustrate, ITC's vision: 'Sustain ITC's position as one of India's most valuable corporations through world class performance, creating growing value for the Indian economy and the Company's stakeholders',[11] is flexible in its description of performance and value. This enables development of its mission, 'To enhance the wealth generating capability of the enterprise in a globalising environment, delivering superior and sustainable stakeholder value',[12] which facilitates the company in pursuing its chosen objectives in a dynamic global environment.

Environmental concerns can be internal as well as external. Companies follow different approaches to internal environmental hazards which can, to a great extent, be anticipated ahead of time, and provisions made to combat through well-defined crisis management plans. Comparatively, the approach to addressing external environment issues is simple. The most sustainable approach is one which considers and embeds concern for environment in the company strategy framework and philosophy. Some companies as oil and gas, mining, etc., because of the nature of their business, feature high on the hit-list of the media. Their activities concern activists, NGOs and the public at large. How do these companies respond to environmental concerns? By launching risk mitigation programmes, bolting on CSR activities into operations or building in CSR into the business model as part of the core philosophy? Let us consider the last six years where there have been radical changes in the environment as economic recession, frauds, natural disasters, etc. Some companies have withstood the test of time while others have buckled under the pressure. On the reputation index, some companies have scored a higher per cent, some have remained constant and some have taken a dip. Wading through these volatile environmental changes requires quick assessment of situation, appropriate actions, constancy in purpose, transparent systems, good governance practices and employee support. Greater the belief in the relationship between reputation and competitive advantage, higher is the focus on crafting strategies which are built in rather than bolted on.

Figure 11.1 explains how the alignment factors affect corporate reputation. The economic logic determines the company's priorities and in turn, resource allocation for reputation management. The values, vision and mission espoused by the leader influence

Figure 11.1 The Interplay of Aligning Factors

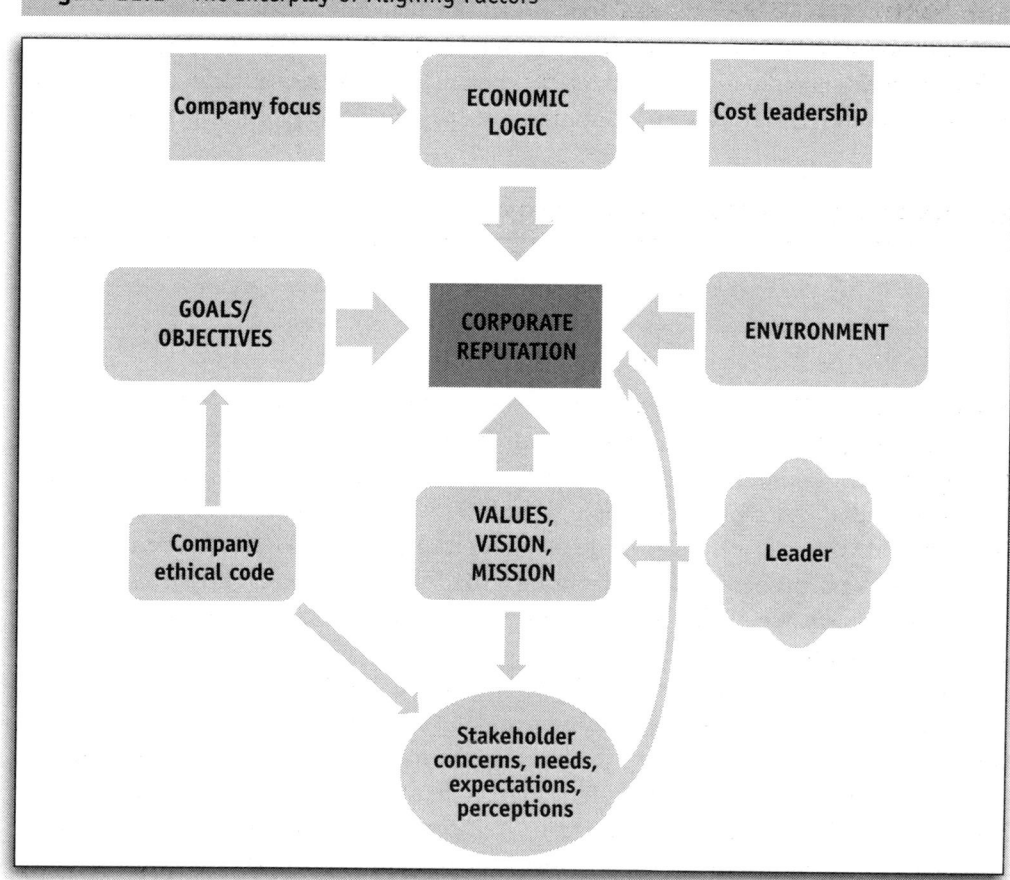

reputation directly, as well as through their effect on stakeholder concerns, needs, expectations and perceptions. These are also impacted by the organisation's ethical code of conduct, and they in turn affect its goals and objectives. The internal and external environment hazards, as well as the organisation's history of dealing with them, also influence corporate reputation.

Studies by the Corporate Executive Board and the Economic Intelligence Unit[13] have defined four reputation building tactics. Moving from a tactical to a strategic base, the first strategy is developed post crisis and is reactive. The second stems from literature on stakeholder relationship management, where perceptions of key stakeholders are targeted and managed. The third lists reputation management as a key line manager's responsibility and the fourth views it as a branding issue under the domain of the marketing team. In all four strategies the onus of maintaining reputation rests with different people within the organisation. The stemming question then is who is the 'reputation keeper' or who should ideally be assigned that role within the company? Undoubtedly, the leader best manages reputation by building it in the company strategy, embedding it in the culture and developing narratives espousing values and vision which are told and retold across the board to all concerned stakeholders.

Strategising corporate reputation is all about developing and constructing a vision, relating it to building reputational quotient, developing and strategising stories and designing a communication plan to address reputational issues at the strategic and operational level.

HOW DO COMPANIES CONSTRUCT A VISION?

If you don't know where you are going, any road will take you there.

—Lewis Caroll[14]

What is a vision? Why is it important to develop a compelling vision? What are the advantages associated with developing a good vision? A vision is an attempt to articulate the future of the company. It can be likened to '… an organisational dream—it stretches the imagination and motivates people to rethink what is possible'.[15] A vision has two fundamental parts: 'one is to provide a conceptual framework for understanding the organisation's purpose—the vision includes a roadmap. The second important element is the emotional appeal; the part of the vision that has motivational pull with which people can identify.'[16]

Though a considerable amount of time is spent on developing the vision, building a visionary company requires only '1% vision and 99% alignment'.[17] At the time of crafting and executing a company strategy, the first and the most important stage is developing a strategic vision which provides long-term direction, describes the company purpose and provides a set of core values to be pursued. Well-conceived vision statements are distinctive and specific to the company and provide direction by conveying the future path for the company. These statements provide a reference point for managers to take strategic decisions and prepare a future plan for the company.

A vision is a guiding post towards which companies move. Developing a winning or compelling vision is not a straightforward process. If the objective is to get the buy-in of all stakeholders and deliver results, then a concrete plan is to be drafted, with minimal abstractions. It is 'conservation'[18] rather than 'revelation'.[19] Structured, logical, creative and action oriented, the vision is aligned with the product, company policy, market and competitors. A vision which looks good on paper but is not grounded in reality, which has grandiose terminology but cannot be put to practice, is of no use. A vision should reflect structured thinking and be the outcome of stakeholder participation rather than stray or functional thinking limited to silos or groups.

What is the starting point for vision engineering? It is much more than looking internally at products, employees or competitors. The foundation, based on facts and knowledge of various trends and how they impact the company progress and future, provides a map for strategic design and development. For companies to draw up a long-lasting vision, they should study the changing economic, environmental and technological changes and then craft a statement which will sell to all stakeholders. Senior leadership team should possess the capability to persuade employees to expand their horizon and view the changing environment with a shared understanding on how it will affect company growth. Drawing on employee support can help the company progress beyond functional issues and converge to a common goal in which all are aligned.

Vision Engineering at Larsen & Toubro Ltd.

Larsen & Toubro Ltd. (L&T) has developed its vision statement in a manner that has ensured complete employee buy-in. The company's vision statement is the result of a large-scale collaborative process that involved employees at every level, throughout the world. It is not surprising, then, that apart from customer satisfaction and shareholder value, the vision statement expresses the values expected of the employee team and the company's commitment to ensuring an encouraging organisational culture.
This is what it states:

L&T shall be a professionally-managed Indian multinational, committed to ensuring total customer satisfaction and enhancing shareholder value. L&T-ites shall be an innovative, entrepreneurial and empowered team constantly creating value and attaining global benchmarks. L&T shall foster a culture of caring, trust and continuous learning while meeting expectations of employees, stakeholders and society.[20]

The most effective technique of vision engineering is a process called 'slamming'[21] in which an understanding of the environment or the externalities is superimposed on the existing value chain. This forced collision often results in constructive and creative outpourings essential for vision engineering.

Core Ideology and Envisioned Future

A vision comprises a core ideology and envisioned future.[22] Core ideology refers to the reason for existence and envisioned future implies what the company hopes to achieve or aspire for, which will require change and progress. How are core ideologies developed? Definitely not by looking at the external environment, but by looking inwards, by comprehending what the company passionately espouses and the employees nurture and remain committed to. The core ideology can be broken up into core values and the core purpose of the company. Visionary companies develop a core ideology which guides them in their lifecycle.

The core values are a set of guiding principles and core purpose is the reason for existence of the company which transcends beyond the market, the product and the competition. It is the 'glue that holds the organisation together through time'.[23] Which core values should be adopted? There is no set of right or wrong values. Each company has a set of three to five values that are intrinsic and do not change with the changing times or market scenario.

The core purpose defines what the company stands for. The 'soul'[24] of the company is captured through a definition of the core purpose that is different from the specific business goal or strategy. Historically, it has been found that this core purpose is always much larger than maximising shareholder returns. The lifespan of the core purpose of existence of a company should be a minimum of 100 years and should not be easily achievable for the simple reason that companies will constantly be on the move to achieve their 'core purpose'. If the core purpose is important to company growth, the process of engineering needs some thought. The strategy of defining and developing the core purpose begins with the process of raising queries on the importance of the product or the services. A repeat of this exercise helps in zeroing in on the core purpose.

The concept of envisioned future has a long-term goal (a 10–30-year achievement frame) and a vivid description of the final picture of the company post goal realisation. Developing a goal that is loud in statement but not able to secure commitment lacks specificity and is not steeped in company ideology. Aiming for 100 per cent success is a misnomer. Even if companies are able to realise 70–80 per cent of their envisioned future plan, we can categorically state that they have been successful in pursuing the right direction.

Often companies confuse between the core purpose and the envisioned future. The major differentiating factor between the two is that the first is a process of discovery and can rarely, if ever be achieved. The objective is that all continuously strive to achieve the purpose. The second possesses the capacity of being realised in the next 10–30 years and is creative.

'Reiterating the basis for the new direction [new strategic vision], addressing employee concerns head-on, calming fears, lifting spirits and providing updates and progress reports as events unfold all become part of the task in mobilising support for the vision and winning commitment to needed actions.'[25] While creating a vision, companies should provide a focussed graphic description of their position and the direction in which they are moving and make sure that the journey is feasible, memorable and makes good business sense.[26] There are five common themes in powerful visions: 'they have broad, widely shared appeal; they help organisations deal with change; they encourage faith and hope for the future; they reflect high ideals and they define both the organisation's destination and the basic rules to get there.'[27]

A brief vision statement, written in simple language, which can be explained in easy terminology, arouses interest, garners support, motivates to move in a common direction and is well scripted, is the most appropriate. A well-crafted vision captures the eye and is retained just as a catchy slogan. There are three important criteria for scripting a good vision statement:

> 'A quantified success indicator
> A definition of a niche
> A timeline for execution'[28]

For instance one can script a vision as, 'Ranked as the leading pharmaceutical company, with cutting edge research in the next 50 years'.

Often there is confusion concerning the vision and mission of the company. The vision describes the strategic course of action and mission, the current position: 'who we are, what we do and why we are here.'[29] The company vision focusses on beliefs, traits that are characteristic of a company. They relate to higher issues as fair treatment, ethical practices, corporate stewardship, community service, etc. Mission provides a definition to the company identity with respect to product and services, market, customers/consumers. For example, while Tata Steel's vision: 'We aspire to be the global steel industry benchmark for Value Creation and Corporate Citizenship'[30] focusses on its commitment to value creation and citizenship, its mission statement deals with the more practical aspects: 'Consistent with the vision and values of the founder Jamsetji Tata, Tata Steel strives to strengthen India's industrial base through the effective utilisation of staff and materials. The means envisaged to achieve this are high technology and productivity, consistent with modern management practices.'[31]

Leadership Vision

The role of the leader in carving out the vision and linking it to strategic action is important. It is critical for the leader to own the vision and provide direction through strategy formulation and implementation. Additionally, the leader also has the responsibility of gaining control and transforming or changing the company to a desired state by creating an environment of creativity that fosters stability. Also referred to as 'core paradox',[32] this leadership vision is able to bring about the desired change.

These compelling visions inspire and motivate the employees—by being realistic, believable and with a promise of moving in a strategically focussed direction in which all employees move ahead at the same pace and in the same path. In this process of vision creation and implementation, the leader's contribution is important. The vision serves to act as a beacon of change by guiding, helping leaders share beliefs and values, building ownership and making the company culture more inclusive and pervasive.

Figure 11.2 describes how the strategic vision of an organisation can be developed. With economic, environmental and technological changes in the backdrop, the company decides upon its core values and purpose that determine its core ideology. This, in conjunction with its envisioned future, helps develop the strategic vision. The core paradox or the vision of the company's leader also contributes greatly to the strategic vision.

While leaders help develop vision, they also set an example by following strategies which demonstrate commitment through words and actions. Leaders are committed to the vision and 'walk the talk' by indicating their consistency in statement, intention and action. How does a vision grab the attention of the people? People like to be associated with something which is larger than their career, their family and highlights the contrast between today's reality and tomorrow's promise.

Developing a vision is critical and fundamental in helping a company visualise its future. This is more specifically applicable in situations where change is the order of the day. Providing a direction makes the change almost indispensable. Good visions are: 'clear

Figure 11.2   How to Develop a Vision

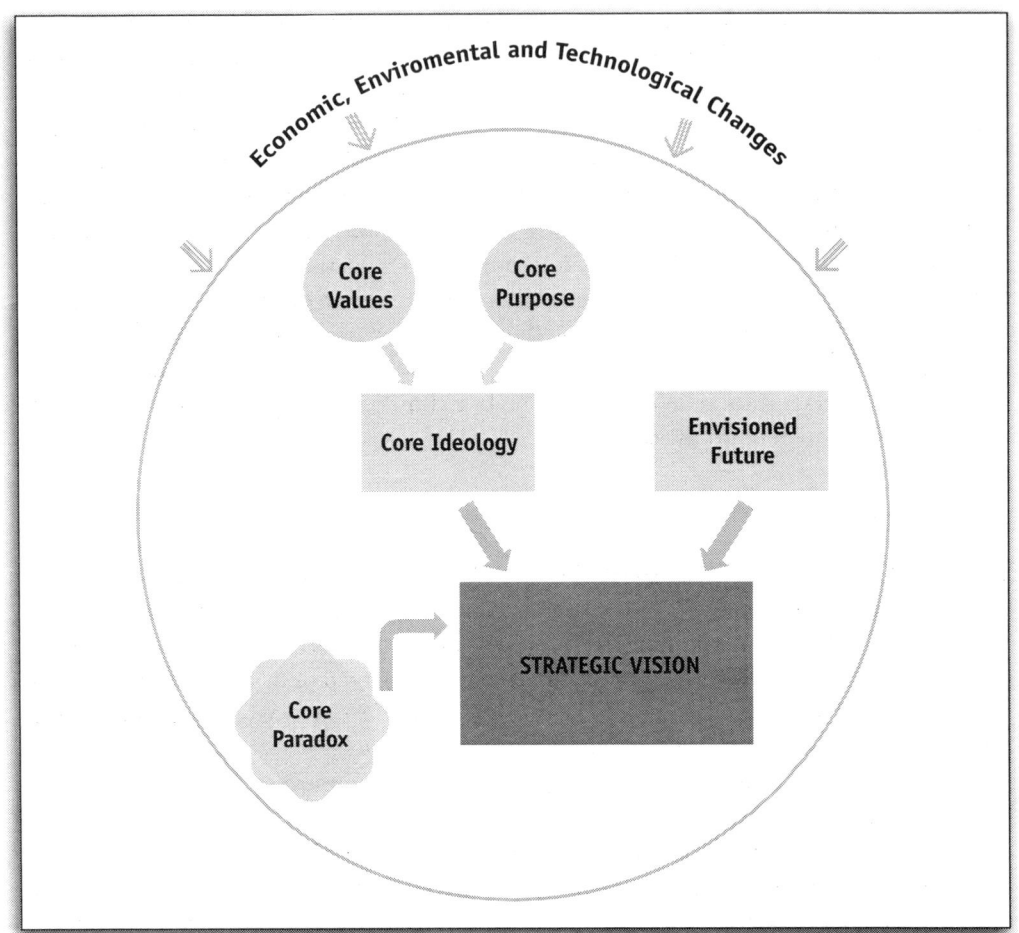

Dhirubhai's Vision Driving Reliance Communications Ltd.

In 1999, Mr Dhirubhai Ambani set forth his vision: 'Make a phone call cheaper than a postcard and you will usher in a revolutionary transformation in the lives of millions of Indians.'[33] It was his conviction that communication technology could radically transform every sphere of commercial and personal life. This vision was the force behind Reliance Communications Ltd. (earlier Reliance InfoComm) venturing into low-cost communication offerings.

Work on laying fibre optics totalling 60,000 km began three years after Dhirubhai articulated his vision. Today, Reliance Communications Ltd. has developed a high-capacity digital network that includes wireless and wireline voice, data and video services for commercial and individual use.[34]

and concise; memorable; exciting and inspiring; challenging; excellence-centered; stable but flexible; implementable and tangible'.[35]

Is it sufficient for a leader to only craft a vision? Developing vision receptivity in the minds of stakeholders is the next step. Leaders and the senior leadership team move ahead with zeal and enthusiasm, sharing concern and developing a purpose. In the process, the organisations bond with all constituencies.

WHAT STRATEGIES ARE DEPLOYED FOR BUILDING REPUTATION WITH STAKEHOLDERS?

Corporate executives need to re-frame their responsibilities to include the interests of all the stakeholders in society at large; not just shareholders, but also employees, the citizens of our communities, and those who care about the environment.

—SIMON MAINWARING[36]

Business is about creating value for stakeholders who fall into four groups: definitive, expectant, latent and non-stakeholders.[37] Definitive are owners and customers, expectant are personnel and management, latent—industry area and suppliers and non-stakeholders are potential customers. The relationship with stakeholders keeps evolving and changing over time. Leaders and managers pay more attention to those stakeholders who are viewed as powerful and have legitimate claims. They attempt to create value for this group by learning their objectives; sharing company history; enhancing interaction patterns; developing platforms for information sharing and building trust and, understanding their potential to learn.[38]

The exchange between the company and the stakeholders is more relational than transactional. Has a company been successful in implementing a relational model? The criteria for measuring success in implementation are co-operation, collaboration and networking. In other words, is there a one-to-one correspondence between stakeholder wants and their contributions to company growth?[39]

Addressing the issue of the relational model has gained immense importance with the advent of social media, also referred to as the 'virtual atlas',[40] where the company is being constantly monitored for communicated commitment, human voice, dialogue and feedback. Open dialogue and interaction have begun to be emphasised for building trust, commitment, mutual influence and satisfaction[41] and creating shared meanings that 'enable people in human interaction to be open, creative and constructive'.[42] The social media not only enhances the organisation–stakeholder relationship making it public and visible, but also makes certain concepts as relational system, common interest and mutual orientation, tangible and measurable.[43]

The concept of building relationship with stakeholders is not new but has been in existence since early 2000. Initially, the emphasis was on maintenance strategies as positivity, openness, shared tasks, networking and assurances of legitimacy.[44] With passage of time these relationships (positive or negative, proactive or reactive, intentional or unintentional) moved beyond purchase decisions to 'strategic alliances, networks and vertical integration'[45] focussing on mutual interest. They comprised a set of stakes bordering on varied shared interests in each relationship.

From a communication viewpoint, researchers have identified the specific dialogue forms that can help an organisation achieve the optimum level of communication with various stakeholder groups, as shown in Table 11.1.

Table 11.1   Stakes and Dialogue Forms for Major Stakeholders[46]

Stakeholder	Stake/Interest	Form of Dialogue
Consumers	Good quality and differentiated products/services, 'licence to consume'	Networking
Investors	High returns, minimised risk and responsible investing	Mutual consultation
Employees	Safe working environment, job satisfaction and recognition	Involvement
NGOs	Influence, awareness, control and legitimacy	Negotiation
Suppliers	Long-lasting association, commitment and inclusion	Exchange

Broadly, stakeholders can be categorised as internal and external. The internal stakeholders or the employees within a company are more important than external as they can communicate internal issues to the outside world which may enhance or damage company reputation. Each company has a unique method of addressing concerns of this group which can vary from engagement methods to formulation of employee-friendly policies to empowerment of the minority groups. External stakeholders comprise end consumers, investors, activists, government, media, local communities, etc. Appeasing and engaging a wide range of external stakeholders is difficult. An understanding of the 'how' of engagement often helps to get all on board. Building engagement can be through active listening, anticipating concerns through previous interactions and taking action. Companies develop a process of institutional listening and gathering feedback through well-designed studies aimed at documenting important stakeholder perceptions through interviews or in open forums. This data is later analysed by the leadership team. Annual general meetings are also a good forum for listening to important stakeholders and their concerns and presenting the company story.

In the fast-changing and educated consumer-driven market, listening to concerns and promptly acting upon it has shown positive results. Being part of the dialogue rather than playing the role of the orator can help companies speak the same language as the stakeholders, develop co-operative relationships and influence strategically. However, there are some associated caveats:

- Company image in the market: Its past actions and redressal techniques
- Company governance structures: Transparency and openness in reporting ethical detours

- Company policies: Institutionalising policies which prevent repeat of offensive behaviour, if any

Some techniques through which stakeholder commitment can be assessed are:

- Commitment from customers and employees
- Support from local communities, vendors, channel partners
- Objective treatment from media[47]

From a long-term perspective, a company may secure positive visibility, cost reduction, enhanced reputation, employee motivation, improved and synergised relationship network, increased commitment and trust.[48]

The impact of different groups of stakeholders on company performance and competition, their perception and assessment of company culture and behaviour which is directly and indirectly impacted by their perception, interest and voice should definitely be underscored. For addressing stakeholder concerns companies create a core message, which reverberates internally and forms the basis of company identity.[49] Notably, the 'one voice, one look'[50] strategy has been proposed by integrated management communication scholarship to project one image and one key message for all stakeholders.[51] With passage of time and conflicting interests, this view has been dispelled in favour of different messages. For instance, under the overarching umbrella of a vision statement, companies may wish to craft messages for internal stakeholders, end consumers and investors which are different and yet converge under the vision statement.

Stakeholders are selective in their approval of proposed actions by the company which promotes their agenda. Can ambiguity in defining mission be the answer to the problem? A strategy of ambiguity in defining messages is often followed by companies. Ambiguous messages with emotional overtures have the advantage of promoting authenticity while providing room for multiple interpretations and thus, minimising stakeholder conflict.[52] For instance, some of the words used are 'honesty', 'authenticity', 'sincerity', 'caring', 'nurturing', etc., which may lend themselves to varied interpretations. Reputation management, through such messages, allows stakeholders to ascribe their own understanding, empathise with the company and assign a local hue which, while being local, is actually conceived and conceptualised at the strategic level.

A Stakeholder Approach to Business: Tata Steel Ltd.

Tata Steel Ltd. uses the dictum 'excellence for common good' to explain its approach to stakeholder engagement. The company uses a detailed map to identify its most important stakeholders. Going beyond mere listing, the Tata Steel Ltd. stakeholder engagement map shows the interface between internal and external stakeholders. For example, it clearly depicts the direct relationship between the MD, Board of Directors, vice-presidents of long- and flat-products, chiefs of marketing and sales and the customers. In this manner, the relationship between each set of stakeholders as employees, suppliers, investors, regulatory bodies, community, government and NGOs is mapped with the relevant top management personnel. This approach gives a crystal-clear idea about the degree of inter-relationship between groups, and enables management to formulate the correct strategy of engaging with each.

The advantage of using this method is obvious. The company has been able to tailor specific engagement programmes with each group of stakeholders. To illustrate, it has launched a Supplier Relationship Management Programme to nine out of its 43 'strategic partner' suppliers under various buying categories. Customer/distributor meets and satisfaction surveys are used to find out customer needs. Investor interaction is carried out on a quarterly and annual basis through analyst meets, press meets, annual general meetings and road shows. For each community that it operates in, Tata Steel Ltd. responds to community aspirations through its social strategy. It has developed a resettlement and rehabilitation programme called Tata Parivar (Tata family) aimed at improving quality of life at all its greenfield sites. Members of the senior management regularly interact with leaders of indigenous communities in Jharkhand, Odisha and Chhattisgarh where Tata Steel Ltd. operates, in an attempt to integrate them within the company's social strategy. Media interactions by top management are frequent, ensuring information sharing. The company's association with NGOs and institutions (promoted by Tata Steel Ltd. or supported by it) goes beyond material support. Top management volunteers time and skills towards these activities, leading to knowledge partnerships, best practices, consultancy and research opportunities. In order to address government and regulatory bodies, Tata Steel Ltd. engages with committees and government ministries directly and through industry associations. By providing its own views on policies as import duties, mineral exploration, land acquisition and rehabilitation, coal allocation and distribution, the company attempts to promote common good through policy advocation.[53]

This in-depth stakeholder identification and engagement process has definitely contributed to the company's reputational capital. Tata Steel topped *Fortune India*'s 'Most Admired Companies' list in 2012.[54]

CAN STORIES BE CRAFTED FOR REPUTATIONAL GAIN?

Those in leadership positions who fail to grasp or use the power of stories risk failure for their companies and for themselves.

—John Kotter[55]

What has your company done? What is it doing? What does it plan to do? Stakeholders are always keen to get answers to these questions. Constant communication with all stakeholders satisfies their queries, validates and revalidates the company position. Selling through talking or corporate communication about company initiatives and contributions to society, definitely helps secure their trust, support and attention, if not the buy-in. Corporate communication raises awareness, generates interest and understanding about company initiatives; informs and reinforces company vision, values and mission and, finally, defends or provides explanations for a company's behaviour, if controversial.[56]

Stakeholders by gaining insight into company values are able to judge the trustworthiness of a company.[57] Stories focussing on values and vision are thus, developed by companies which revolve around two basic questions: identity (who are we) and offering (this is what we offer) which proceed to detail the past achievements, current behaviour and provide the stakeholders a platform to build on 'What the company has in store for us.' In other words, the stories defend and extend the core philosophy, build on company growth possibilities and exploit new opportunities.[58] Company proclamations about business ethics, short-term wins, corporate governance and stakeholder concerns, or enhancing social value and acquiring long-term wins[59] help in embedding stories in the right context.

For the stories to achieve the desired result, alignment among the mission, morality and behaviour should be perfect. A dissonance may lead to stakeholders' ignoring, contesting, disbelieving or ridiculing the story.[60] Manufacturing credibility[61] is a well-known persuasion tactic used by companies, as in the case of big oil majors or mining industries which promote their cause for the environment. A sub-plot of the stories builds on dialogue initiated by the company to engage with stakeholders asking them to share their concerns. The advantage of these sub-plots is that companies implicitly try and convert stakeholders to allies in the corporate journey.

Adding Credibility to Growth: ITC Ltd.

ITC Chairman Mr Y. C. Deveshwar, ranked seventh by *Harvard Business Review* among the world's best-performing CEOs in its January–February 2013 issue,[62] is adept at the art of using storytelling to enlist stakeholders as allies. Whether it is a letter to shareholders in the annual report, or a speech at the Annual General Meeting (AGM), Mr Deveshwar presents financial performance statistics along with a recurring theme of sustainable and inclusive growth.

He emphasises the 'deeply Indian character'[63] of the company that focusses on aligning its strategy to national priorities. For example, while discussing ITC's contribution to foreign exchange earnings, he presents how 65 per cent has been agriculture-based exports, thus underlining the company's commitment to developing the rural economy.

He assures shareholders that they can feel confident about their financial progress which has been achieved on a 'strong foundation of trust'[64] that Indian farmers have reposed in ITC. By repeating the message of rural partnerships and trust, Mr Deveshwar ensures that the credibility of the company's sustainability efforts is maintained.

What Content Should Go in the Story?

Developing a corporate story is similar to any other story writing process. There has to be a protagonist who narrates the healthy development of the corporate life. This is followed by the entry of a demon who, in the case of a corporate story, is represented by an unexpected sequence of events which bring disrepute or throw the company out of gear. The climax or high point in the story is the strategy adopted by the protagonist to bring the company back on track. The elements of truth and accuracy in the narrative capture attention and stakeholder empathy. The turns and twists in the story, contrary to the expectations of the stakeholders, are important. If narration is as per expectations, the narrator misses out on a golden opportunity of generating interest, where the audience perforce asks the question: 'What then?' The next step in the story revolves round the reputation platform, which for the protagonist becomes an important criterion for making the right choice.

'Springboard'[65] is another story-developing technique in which the narration emphasises the company mission without ornamentation. The future or end-point is deliberately kept vague, providing the listener an opportunity to construe the remaining part of the story as per personal interests, beliefs and faith in company operations.

Another form of storytelling is narration of corporate brand stories based on promises made to the customer often using the CEO as a gatekeeper of company character. A corporate branding story matches the aspirations or lifestyle of the stakeholders, helps them associate and relate and has a distinct identity. While stories of this nature are appealing, they are short lived. For a story to have longevity, it should be based on the moral compass of the company, be overboard and possess the capability of countering attacks, if any, by the local communities or activists.[66]

The Story of a Promise Fulfilled: Tata Nano

The story of the genesis of Tata Nano is quite well known. Mr Ratan Tata, then Chairman, Tata Group, first talked about the story behind it at the car's launch on 10 January 2008. He described how the Nano story began with his observation of Indian families travelling on two wheelers, with the father driving, a young kid standing in front of him, the wife sitting behind holding a baby. The need for a safe, affordable, all-weather transportation for such families led to the quest for a car that would be low-cost and yet meet all safety, pollution-control and fuel efficiency standards. This was how the Nano was conceptualised.[67]

By talking about this project as a dream for himself, a challenge for the company and a promise to the customer, Mr Ratan Tata used the storytelling technique most effectively. There was massive interest generated in the product, not only in India, but worldwide.

Can one story hold good for all stakeholders? It is difficult to answer this question. Some parts of the story can remain constant, as those which advocate mission and ethical conduct. The rest, which focus on behaviour can be restructured and customised to achieve the desired objective.

Functions of a Story

Stories have multiple functions which are guided by what the company has set out to achieve or what is its vision and mission. Research[68] has identified four such types of companies: altruistic which focus on stakeholder interests; excellent companies with the primary objective of being the best in whatever they do; discovery companies which are still in the explorative mode, and focus on the creative and the innovative and hero companies, determined to lead, demonstrate and challenge bigger fish in the pond.

Lauding the Hero: Reliance Group

The Reliance Group uses the storytelling technique to document its rise from a single textile unit to a multibillion dollar conglomerate, in a classic example of a 'hero' company determined to lead and challenge the big fish in the pond. Stories of the founder Mr Dhirubhai Ambani working at a petrol pump in Yemen while trading in commodities at night; his foresight in anticipating the potential of polyester and taking the corporate giants of the day head on; his vision in areas as varied as agri-businesses, petrochemicals and telecommunications; his unique philosophy for shareholder value; his superior people skills and the now iconic 1985 AGM at Cooperage Football Ground, flagging off their practice of hosting AGMs in stadiums; have been featured in numerous articles, books and have even inspired a Hindi film.[69]

Stories are crafted based on the primary objective with which companies operate. The objectives can be varied as profits, social commitment, products and services, etc. Stories can:

- Influence the concerned parties by their emotional and intuitive appeal.
- Convey the good, the ethical and the aspirational.
- Generate enthusiasm about the projected actions.[70]
- Reaffirm and update beliefs of the stakeholders.

Storytelling to Reiterate Excellence: Larsen & Toubro Ltd.

Mr A. M. Naik, CEO, Larsen & Toubro Ltd. (L&T), uses the storytelling technique in most of his interviews, to emphasise the culture of excellence that prevails at L&T. For him personally, it is a driving force.

His role model is his father, a principal at a village school, and he frequently tells the story of his father's untiring efforts for the upliftment of the village community and their children. Citing the example of his father who would devote long hours in teaching and mentoring, he emphasises the need for leaders to be good role models.

Another favourite story of Mr Naik is that of a Hong Kong–based head-hunter who contacted him soon after he took over as CEO in 1999. He gleefully recounts the story of how he invited the head-hunter to Mumbai, even requesting him to help out in recruitments for L&T—an effective way of reiterating his unwavering commitment towards L&T, and inspiring others to inculcate the same.[71]

The stories thus developed and narrated by leaders, attempt to influence and persuade. Appropriately crafted stories serve to help stakeholders change their mindsets, excite emotions and reinforce trust and confidence in the leader and company.[72] The success of a company story is gauged by the media coverage in terms of 'themed messaging'[73] which implies the tone of reporting—positive, negative or neutral; the image the company wishes to project; the main message themes and presentation of contradictory messages, if any.[74]

Stories should carry both the qualitative as well as quantitative details. To give credence to the story both positive as well as negative numbers should be added unfolding the yesterday, today and tomorrow. When stories project the tomorrow, the scripting is vague and lacks specificity which helps listeners assess and be part of the solution and the direction. This is an extremely good technique for employee engagement as it helps them develop a sense of contributing to the future. When scripting stories, companies must take proactive steps to project expertise, sincerity, likeability and powerful characteristics which help foster trust, esteem and interest.[75] Additionally, personalisation of message, acknowledgement of strengths and weaknesses can provide value to the lifecycle of a company[76] by adding a personal touch of comprehension which cannot be achieved by statistics alone.[77]

The Story of Altruism—Words Stronger than Numbers Alone: Aditya Birla Group

Mrs Rajshree Birla, Chairperson, Aditya Birla Centre for Community Initiatives and Rural Development, and Director on the board of all major Aditya Birla Group companies, uses storytelling in an interesting manner to describe the group's altruistic activities.

She often narrates the story of how Mahatma Gandhi was the inspiration behind the group's philanthropic activities, due to his close bond with the late G. D. Birla.

Apart from this history, she also uses storytelling to talk about the various initiatives of her foundation and their profound impact on people and communities.

Instead of merely presenting facts and figures about their 18 hospitals catering to more than five lakh poor people, Mrs Birla uses storytelling to add a human element. Her interesting description of Vishnu, a 20-year-old girl from Madhya Pradesh, illustrates the impact of reconstructive surgery for polio patients sponsored by the Aditya Birla Group. One can almost picturise Vishnu, singing 'like a lark' in fields with swaying golden shoots of wheat as she helps her parents in farming.

Another story she shares is of Shakuntala, a mother of five from a water-scarce area of Uttar Pradesh, who used to believe that rural women are children of a lesser God. The Aditya Birla Group, in collaboration with UNICEF, installed hand pumps for every 10 houses in 110 villages, providing water to over 100,000 people. Shakuntala does not have to walk kilometers for a few pots of water now. She is a qualified hand pump mechanic, earning around ₹28,000 in the summer months and even training 80 other women. Mrs Birla's engaging style of storytelling drives home the changes brought about by the group's women empowerment initiatives that have helped 45,000 women in 4,500 self-help groups across India.[78]

Across interviews and articles, in public forums and private ones, Mrs Birla's style of using stories to add life to statistics has enabled her to generate enormous interest and respect for the work done by her foundation.

While the impact of stories cannot be undermined, it is important to consider them as only one of the tools for securing stakeholder faith. This tool is further sharpened by good communication skills, leader credibility and conviction. Part of the responsibility of crafting a story falls in the domain of the corporate communication team which develops a plan detailing communication responsibility for corporate reputation.

HOW IS A STRATEGIC COMMUNICATION PLAN DEVELOPED?

Plans are only good intentions unless they immediately degenerate into hard work.

—PETER DRUCKER[79]

Reputation management through communication is not a new discipline. However, in recent times, with growing emphasis on traditional and new communication media, it has been accorded immense importance. In the last few decades, the responsibility of building company reputation by interacting with multiple stakeholders fell in the domain of the leader or the CEO. Today, with the changing scenario the rules of this corporate game of building reputation have been rewritten. Some of the causative factors for this required change are growing number of educated and well-informed stakeholders, Internet and social media and speed of message transmission. Messages are today drafted post review and measurement of competitor impact and reputation; and stakeholder assessment. An erroneous or incorrectly worded message which may hurt the sentiments of a group of stakeholders can damage reputation leading to poor performance and drop in sales. Thus, drawing up a strategic communication plan for building and managing corporate reputation is an imperative. Dynamic in nature, the plan frames media messages, communicates to internal and external stakeholders, sets company priorities, targets audiences and allocates resources for different company activities.

The communication plan details the process of communicating messages to key constituencies through various sources as online media, interviews, press releases, advertisements, etc. A team of PR specialists are often hired for the exercise, who give due consideration to the context (environmental scanning), objectives, stakeholders, messages, budget, timeframe and evaluation. Though a designated team draws up the communication plan, the attempt of the company is to secure involvement of maximum number of people, which to a large extent, ascertains accountability and commitment.

Building on the history of the company is the first step in strategic planning. Following steps are a response to questions as: What was the initial position of the company? Where does it stand today? Who are the competitors? What does the media report? What have been the key success factors? Has the company faced a crisis situation and how has it dealt with the same? These are some of the initial questions which help in conducting an environmental scan and assessing the general health and well-being of the company. A good beginning point is either a PEST (Political, Economic, Social and

Technological or SWOT (Strengths, Weaknesses, Opportunities and Threats Analysis). Post the environmental scanning begins the process of defining the objectives. Some questions essential for providing definition are: What is the company focus? What does it hope to achieve? What is its target/goal? The defined objectives from this exercise should be relevant to company operations and be Specific, Measurable, Achievable and Realistic within a Timeframe (SMART).[80] Following the objective definition is an assessment of all stakeholders which helps a company formulate a set of messages, some of which may be common and some targeted to a specific group. Different target audiences will have different needs. Hence, the content, order and quantum of messages for them will vary. Fewer and specific messages help in reaching out to the targeted group/groups. It is at this point of analysis that the stated vision and mission of the company become relevant. A four to 10-word message of what the company stands for can be repeatedly used to ensure consistency in message transmission. Selection of messages, spokesperson for different stakeholders and choice of medium to transmit the message, become important components in the design of the communication plan.

Companies normally allocate a separate budget for implementation of the communication plan. For instance, a company may decide to build schools for children of local communities as a means of developing relationship with a group of stakeholders. This may be a one-off activity or part of a group of activities. A separate budget will be drawn up for this activity designed to be completed within a specified timeframe. Some activities may not need a separate budget, whereas others may need a dedicated budget to meet expenses related to extra manpower, development of communication material, etc. Defining the timeframe with respect to anticipated environmental changes, competitor initiatives, internal competencies and potential negative reactions of stakeholders has to be well documented.

The most important component in the communication plan is the evaluation methodology which is company-specific. Evaluation entails assessing the success or impact of the communication objectives. Both quantitative as well as qualitative techniques are adopted for impact assessment. Evaluation techniques consider quantum of media coverage, tonality, nature of messages, quotations; interactivity generated as in social media—visits, revisits, hits; reactions of stakeholders; public inquiries in the form of letters, emails, calls, etc.

Once the plan is drafted, the responsibility of successful implementation rests with the CEO and the leadership team. The design and implementation requires strategies to be brainstormed, reviewed, prioritised and then implemented, keeping in perspective the urgency and allocated resources.

Below we provide a sample of part of the communication plan designed for a PSU, and the manner in which it can be crafted. It is worthwhile to notice that specific messages to be transmitted to stakeholders have not been scripted. Consistency in message transmission is ensured when there is one spokesperson for interacting with a wide array of stakeholders.

Table 11.2 Sample Execution Plan for the Corporate Communication Team[81]

Board Level Responsibilities

Central Theme	Execution	Execution Responsibility	Timeline	Recurrence
CC Team structure	Entrust CC Team with responsibility of managing and building company reputation. Appoint a single Head to run all the functions of the CC Team and divide the responsibilities across smaller teams as per the following functions: 1. Media management team 2. Print publication team 3. Advertising team 4. Web publication team (website management—company reports, etc.) 5. Events management team 6. Creative team 7. Corporate CC office management 8. Office management and order processing	Board of Directors	Six months	–
Mass media communication exercise	Appoint CC as the single-point window for all external and internal branding exercises as per corporate brand manual	Board of Directors	Three months	–
	Policy decision on making payment systems should be made more flexible for jobs executed by CC	Senior management	Three months	–
	Launching a mass media campaign for revolving around the central theme of 'Service to the country'	Board of Directors	Six months	Once every two years
	Creation of the Identity Manual for procedural norms for company-branded stationery (envelopes, letterheads, file covers, etc.) To be reviewed every two years by a three-member committee (E-7 level) constituted by CMD from CC, corporate planning and HR, so that the Identity Manual covers all stationery used at all locations of the company	CMD-recommended committee from CC, HR and planning departments	Six months	Every two years
	Sanctioning of empanelment of event managers or advertising agencies for all big events (above value of ₹5 lakhs in small towns and ₹10 lakhs in big cities)	Board of Directors	Six months	–

(Table 11.2 Continued)

(Table 11.2 Continued)

Corporate Level Responsibilities

Central Theme	Execution	Execution Responsibility	Timeline	Recurrence
CC Team structure	Ensure that systemic procedures are in place and tasks are assigned based on the skill set of the individuals. CC Team should advocate regions as strong and sensitive centres for image building	CC Team	Six months	–
CSR promotions	Develop a focussed CSR plan on one of the eight Millennium Development Goals	CSR department	12 months	–
Triple bottom line reporting	Conduct an external audit on social and environmental impact of company	CC Team	From the next financial year	Every financial year
Employer branding	Sponsoring events and competitions in prominent engineering and business schools	CC Team	Six months	Annually, a month before the recruitment season
PR exercises—investor relations	Organise investor meets and ensure attendance by Ministry officials	Investor relations team	From the last quarter in the financial year 2009–10	Once every quarter
PR exercises—media relations	Formulate corporate communication policy	CC Team	Two months	Update as and when required
Synergy with local community	Open and transparent information sharing with the community	CC Team	Continuous process	Continuous process
	Sponsoring festive events of villages near site of operations	CC Team	Three months	Two to three major festivals in one year
Open-book reporting	Develop transparent reporting standards	CC Team	Six months	Every financial year
Website improvement—external portal	Audit of website quality by CC team	CC Team	Two months	Continuous process
Website improvement—internal portal	Audit of website quality by CC team	CC Team	Two months	Continuous process
Employee communications	Communicating policy changes and their impact on employees to CC team	HR department	12 months	Update as required

(Table 11.2 Continued)

(Table 11.2 Continued)

Central Theme	Execution	Execution Responsibility	Timeline	Recurrence
	Communication of hiring of more youngsters at site of operations to CC team	HR department	36 months	
	Communication of internal rewards that have been given out to the CC team	HR department	Three months	Monthly recognitions
	Utilise social events of company to brainstorm new ideas and communicate any significant ideas to the CC team	HR department	Three months	
	Streamline the procedure to get a job done and communicate the changes to CC team	HR department	Six months	
	Introduce employee referral pro- grammes for new job recruitments and communicate to CC team	HR department	Three months	
	Organise social and cultural meets for employees and communicate to CC team	HR department	Three months	Every two months
Skill enhancement of CC team	Organise training programmes for CC team on: 1. Written communication (writing of media releases, interesting articles and understanding of content for brochures) 2. Precise writing, summarising and creative catch-line writing skills 3. Interpersonal communication skills: a. Listening b. Feedback c. Motivational communication d. Public speaking e. Gender communication f. Inter-cultural communica- tion 4. Understanding communication aesthetics—designing of bro- chures, pamphlets, banners, annual reports, etc. 5. Public speaking 6. Negotiation and persuasive skills	HR department	Three months	Every quarter, one training programme of five working days by a field expert

(Table 11.2 Continued)

(Table 11.2 Continued)

Operational Responsibilities

Central Theme	Execution	Execution Responsibility	Timeline	Recurrence
Mass media communication exercise	Design a mass media campaign for company revolving around the central theme of 'Service to the country'	CC Team	Six months	Once every two years
	Set up a panel of three CC persons to assess the capabilities and empanel at least three film makers for the company genre of films at each region	CC Team	Six months	Once every two years
Employer branding	Organise case study competitions	CC Team	Three months	Annually
PR exercises— investor relations	Create database of all analysts and investors of the company	CC Team	Six months	Update every six months
	Send out invitations to analysts for company anniversaries	CC Team	End of last quarter of 2009–10	Regular invitations for important company events
	Send out regular mails and updates to investors	CC Team	Three months	Monthly updates
PR exercises— media relations	Create a database of internal contact points for information to the CC team	CC Team	Two months	Update every six months
	Create a database of journalists and reporters for the sector the company operates in	CC Team	Three months	Update every six months
	Send pre-emptive communication to network of media personnel in case of special incidents/crises	CC Team	Three months	Regular communication
	Create a centralised media filter for local communications	CC Team	Three months	Regular filtering
	Provide regular media updates	CC Team	Three months	Regular updates
	Engage in regular interaction with media	CC Team	Three months	Regular interaction
	Organise regular press meets	CC Team	Starting April 2010	Every quarter
	Promotion of CSR activities at media meets	CC Team	Three months	Every quarter

(Table 11.2 Continued)

(Table 11.2 Continued)

Central Theme	Execution	Execution Responsibility	Timeline	Recurrence
PR exercises— other relations	Organise for corporate gifts to be given to district authorities like Deputy Commissioners, Additional Deputy Commissioners, Sub-Divisional Officers, etc. as well as local senior officials	CC Team	Three months	Twice a year— Diwali and New Year
Website improvement— external portal	Implementing the content and layout suggestions in the recommendations section	Web portal team of the company	Two months	Every three months
Website improvement— internal portal	Updation and enhancement of website quality	Web team	Two months	Every three months
External press releases	Implementing the content and layout suggestions in the recommendations sections	CC Team	Two months	
Tender advertising	Tender advertisements in Hindi newspapers should be given. Negotiate rates on a yearly basis with annual space assurance	CC Team	Two months	Every year
Employee communications	Send out employee communication focussing on hiring of more youngsters at site of operations	CC Team	36 months	
	Send out employee communication focussing on internal rewards given out	CC Team	Three months	Monthly recognitions
	Send out employee communication focussing on new ideas generated during social events	CC Team	Three months	
	Send out employee communication focussing on method of implementation of streamlining of procedures	CC Team	Six months	
	Send out employee communications focussing on employee referral programme on internal communication media	CC Team	Three months	
	Send out employee communication focussing on various social and cultural meets organised for employees	CC Team	Three months	Every two months

In Table 11.2, we have made an attempt to share board and corporate level responsibilities. Following these two sections are the operational responsibilities. In drawing up this plan it is important to allocate task to functional heads or their counterparts, have clarity in mentioning the timeframe and the recurrence of the activity. The plan ensures involvement, engagement and accountability of all concerned in building reputation.

CONCLUSION

You can't build a reputation on what you are going to do.

—HENRY FORD[82]

Corporate reputation management is both an art and a science. Creativity in crafting a vision, narrating a story and managing stakeholders requires a very high order of expertise and skill set. However, the entire process of managing reputation is steeped in three principles: tailwind, headwind and banana skins.[83] Tailwind principle elaborates on the things a company does well and can build on to enhance reputation. Headwind principle discusses issues that stall the company progress as stringent government rules and regulations. Banana skins are unforeseen incidents in the lifecycle of a company which tarnish the reputation, as a crisis. Planning in advance for crisis management is important to reduce the impact of the incident.

Though each company has a different method of building and managing its reputation infrastructure, some basic steps to be followed for creation of a unique plan are as follows:

- Understanding stakeholders and influencers
- Listening to stakeholder concerns and mapping them with overall company objectives
- Developing a culture in which all are engaged in communicating a similar corporate message
- Employing a reputation manager who overlooks all reputation issues and directly reports to the CEO
- Engaging in dialogue
- Donning the role of thought and action leaders

Additionally, if reputation is built as part of a company strategy, there are three distinct advantages:

- Reflects effective company strategy and compels consumers to view company policies and market behaviour favourably
- Creates links and enhances culture of the company by weaving all internal stakeholders with a common thread
- Makes company behaviour and response more predictable to stakeholders[84]

Key Points

- Each company has a unique formula for creating a reputational shield through a series of actions linked to intention, which showcase their capabilities and strategic intent.
- Reputation can be built in the corporate strategy or bolted on through tactical initiatives.
- A strategic structuring of reputation hinges on alignment of four factors: economic logic, goals and objectives, values, vision and mission and environment.
- There are four reputation building tactics: being reactive post crisis, targeting and managing perceptions of key stakeholders, enlisting key line managers as responsible for building reputation and a branding issue under the domain of the marketing team.
- A vision is an attempt to articulate the future of the company by providing long-term direction, describing the company purpose and providing a set of core values.
- A vision consists of two parts: core ideology and envisioned future.
- Mission provides a definition to the company identity with respect to product and services, market, customers/consumers.
- Business is about creating value for stakeholders who fall under four groups: definitive, expectant, latent and non-stakeholders.
- Stories develop on the moral high ground adopted by companies which could be short-term wins, corporate governance and stakeholder concern or enhancing social value and acquiring long-term wins.
- Companies persuade stakeholders by use of the technique of 'manufacturing credibility'.
- There are different forms of narration: simple, springboard, corporate-branding stories.
- The success of a company story is gauged by the media coverage in terms of themed messaging.
- Companies must take proactive steps to project expertise, sincerity, likeability and powerful characteristics in their stories which help foster trust, esteem and interest.
- Communication plan is dynamic in nature and frames media messages, communicates to internal and external stakeholders, sets company priorities, targets audiences and allocates resources for different company activities.
- The communication plan details the process of communicating messages to key constituencies through various sources as online media, interviews, press releases, advertisements, etc.
- Reputation can be managed by adhering to three principles: tailwind, headwind and banana skins.

END NOTES

1. Notable quotes, website http://www.notable-quotes.com/r/reputation_quotes.html (accessed 30 June 2013).
2. Notable quotes, website http://www.notable-quotes.com/r/reputation_quotes.html (accessed 30 June 2013).
3. Website, http://www.google.co.in/search?client=safari&rls=en&q=reputation&ie=UTF-8&oe=UTF-8&redir_esc=&ei=1RmrUZu4N8LqrQeyooGAAQ (accessed 2 June 2013).
4. R. Mahapatra, 'At 25, Infosys an Indian success story', website http://www.tholons.com/pdfs/at25_infosys_anindiansuccessstory.pdf (accessed 12 June 2013).

5. G. Dowling and P. Moran, 'Corporation reputations: Built in or bolted on?', *California Management Review* (2012), 54(2), 25–42, p. 26.

6. Ibid.

7. Ibid.

8. C. J. Fombrun, *Reputation: Realizing Value from the Corporate Image*. Boston, MA: Harvard Business School Press (1996), p. 72.

9. Reputation Institute, 'Global Rep Trak Pulse Study', Website, http://www.reputationinstitute.com/global-reptrak-pulse (accessed 2 June 2013).

10. C. J. Fombrun, N. A. Gardberg and M. L. Barnett, 'Opportunity platforms and safety nets: Corporate citizenship and reputational risk', *Business and Society Review* (2000), 105(1), 85–106.

11. ITC Ltd., 'The ITC vision', website http://www.itcportal.com/about-itc/values/vision-mission.aspx (accessed 30 April 2013).

12. Ibid.

13. EIU, Reputation: Risk of risks, *Economist Intelligence Unit* (2005).

14. Philosiblog, website http://philosiblog.com/2011/07/13/if-you-dont-know-where-youre-going/ (accessed 30 April 2013).

15. W. P. Belgard, K. K. Fisher and S. R. Rayner, 'Vision, opportunity, and tenacity: Three informal processes that influence formal transformation', in R. H. Kilmann and T. J. Covin (eds), *Corporate Transformation: Revitalizing Organizations for a Competitive World* (pp. 131–151). San Fransisco: Josey-Bass (1988), p. 135.

16. N. M. Tichy and M. A. Devanna, *The Transformational Leader.* New York: John Wiley & Sons (1986), p. 130.

17. J. C. Collins and J. I. Porras, 'Building your company's vision', *Harvard Business Review* (1996), 65–77, p. 77.

18. B. Frisch, 'Strategic thinking: A pragmatic approach to vision', *Journal of Business Strategy* (1998), 19(4), 12–15, p. 13.

19. Ibid.

20. L&T Ltd., 'Vision', website http://www.larsentoubro.com/lntcorporate/common/ui_templates/HtmlContainer.aspx?res=P_CORP_AABT_ACOM_CVIS (accessed 6 June 2013).

21. B. Frisch, Strategic thinking: 'A pragmatic approach to vision', *Journal of Business Strategy* (1998), 19(4), 12–15, p. 15.

22. J. C. Collins and J. I. Porras, 'Building your company's vision', *Harvard Business Review* (1996), 74(5), 65–77.

23. Ibid., p. 66.

24. Ibid., p. 68.

25. 'Charting a company's direction: Vision and mission, objectives, and strategy', in A. A. Thompson Jr., A. J. Strickland and J. E. Gamble, Concepts and Techniques for Crafting and Executing Strategy, New York: McGraw Hill, website http://highered.mcgraw-hill.com/sites/dl/free/0078112729/898107/Chapter02.pdf (accessed 6 June 2013), p. 23.

26. Ibid.

27. R. L. Daft, *Leadership: Theory and Practice*. Fort Worth: The Dryden Press (1999), p. 130.

28. R. S. Kaplan, D. P. Norton and E. A. Barrows, Jr., 'Developing the strategy: Vision, value gaps and analysis', *Balanced Scorecard Report* (2008), 10(1), 3–7 p. 4.

29. 'Charting a company's direction: Vision and mission, objectives, and strategy', in A. A. Thompson Jr., A. J. Strickland and J. E. Gamble, Concepts and Techniques for Crafting and Executing Strategy, New York: McGraw Hill, website http://highered.mcgraw-hill.com/sites/dl/free/0078112729/898107/Chapter02.pdf (accessed 6 June 2013), p. 27.

30. Tata Steel Ltd., 'Vision and mission', website http://www.tatasteelindia.com/corporate/vision-and-strategy.asp (accessed 2 July 2013).

31. Ibid.

32. T. Peters, *Thriving on Chaos: Handbook for a Management Revolution*. New York: Harper & Row (1987), p. 395.

33. Reliance Communications Ltd., 'Milestones', website http://www.rcom.co.in/Rcom/aboutus/over-view/overview_milestones.html# (accessed 2 July 2013).

34. Reliance Communication Ltd., 'A dream come true', website http://www.rcom.co.in/Rcom/aboutus/overview/overview_ourfounder.html (accessed 2 July 2013).

35. T. D. Jick, 'The vision thing', *Harvard Business School Case*. Boston, MA: Harvard Business School Press (1989), 1–7, p. 2.

36. Brainy quote, website http://www.brainyquote.com/quotes/quotes/s/simonmainw493958. html#VjWbM82qBcgJjEYs.99.

37. R. K. Mitchell, B. R. Agle and D. J. Wood, 'Toward a theory of stakeholder identification and salience: Defining the principle of who and what really counts', *The Academy of Management Review* (1997), 22(4), 853–886.

38. P. Myllykangas, J. Kujala and H. Lehtima ki, 'Analyzing the essence of stakeholder relationship: What do we need in addition to power, legitimacy, and urgency?', *Journal of Business Ethics* (2010), 96(1 Supplement), 65–72.

39. R. E. Freeman, J. S. Harrison and A. C. Wicks, *Managing for Stakeholders. Survival, Reputation, and Success*. New Haven: Yale University Press (2007).

40. B. G. Smith, 'Public relations identity and the stakeholder–organization relationship: A revised theoretical position for public relations scholarship', *Public Relations Review* (2012), 38(5), 838–845, p. 842.

41. S. Yang and J. E. Grunig, 'Decomposing organizational reputation: The effects of organization–public relationship outcomes on cognitive representations of organizations and evaluations of organizational performance', *Journal of Communication Management* (2005), 9(4), 305–325.

42. K. N. Dervitsiotis, 'Beyond stakeholder satisfaction: Aiming for a new frontier of sustainable stakeholder trust', *Total Quality Management & Business Excellence* (2003), 14(5), 515–528, p. 518.

43. B. G. Smith, 'Public relations identity and the stakeholder–organization relationship: A revised theoretical position for public relations scholarship', *Public Relation Review* (2012), 38(5), 838–845.

44. J. E. Grunig and Y. H. Huang, 'From organizational effectiveness to relationship indicators: Antecedents of relationships, public relations strategies and relationship outcomes', in J. A. Ledingham and S. D. Bruning (eds), *Public Relations as Relationship Management: A Relational Approach to the Study and Practice of Public Relations* (pp. 23–53). Mahwah, NJ: Lawrence Erlbaum Associates (2000).

45. F. Cownie, 'Relationship marketing', in P. J. Kitchen (ed.), *Marketing Communications: Principles and Practice* (pp.403-421). London: Thomson Business Press (1999), p. 418.

46. T. S. Johansen and A. E. Nielsen, 'Strategic stakeholder dialogues: A discursive perspective on relationship building', *Corporate Communications: An International Journal* (2011), 16(3), 204–217.

47. D. Susniene, 'Synergy and strategic value of organization–stakeholder relationships', *Economics and Management* (2008), 13, 842–847.

48. Ibid.

49. J. M. T. Balmer and S. A. Greyser, 'Corporate marketing: Integrating corporate identity, corporate branding, corporate communications, corporate image and corporate reputation', *European Journal of Marketing* (2006), 40(7/8), 730–741.

50. S. Dickinson-Delaporte, M. Beverland and A. Lindgreen, 'Building corporate reputation with stakeholders: Exploring the role of message ambiguity for social marketers', *European Journal of Marketing* (2010), 44(11/12), 1856–1874, p. 1858.

51. M. B. Beverland and S. Luxton, 'Managing integrated marketing communications (IMC) through strategic decoupling: How luxury wine firms retain brand leadership while appearing to be wedded to the past', *Journal of Advertising* (2005), 34(4), 103–116.

52. S. Dickinson-Delaporte, M. Beverland and A. Lindgreen, 'Building corporate reputation with stakeholders: Exploring the role of message ambiguity for social marketers', *European Journal of Marketing* (2010), 44(11/12), 1856–1874.

53. Tata Steel Ltd., 'A stakeholder approach to business', 12th Corporate Sustainability Report 2011–12, website http://www.tatasteelindia.com/sustainability/2012/stakeholder-Approach-to-business01.asp (accessed 14 June 2013).

54. PTI, 'Tata Steel India's most admired company: Fortune', *Business Today*, website http://businesstoday. intoday.in/story/tata-steel-indias-best-company-fortune-magazine-ranking/1/22947.html (accessed 3 July 2013).

55. Storytelling quotes, website http://storytellingquotes.tumblr.com/ (accessed 30 June 2013).

56. G. R. Dowling, 'Communicating corporate reputation through stories', *California Management Review* (2006), 49(1), 82–100.

57. G. R. Dowling, 'Corporate reputations: Should you compete on yours?', *California Management Review* (2004), 46(3), 19–36.

58. G. Shaw, R. Brown and P. Bromiley, 'Strategic stories: How 3M is rewriting business planning', *Harvard Business Review* (1998), 76(3), 41–50.

59. K. T. Jackson, *Building Reputational Capital: Strategies for Integrity and Fair Play that Improve the Bottom Line*. Oxford: Oxford University Press (2004).

60. G. R. Dowling, 'Communicating corporate reputation through stories', *California Management Review* (2006), 49(1), 82–100.

61. A. Pratkanis and E. Aronson, *Age of Propaganda: The Everyday Use and Abuse of Persuasion*. New York: W. H. Freeman & Company (2001).

62. M. T. Hansen, H. Ibarra and U. Peyer, 'The best performing CEOs in the world', *Harvard Business Review* (January–February 2013), website http://hbr.org/2013/01/the-best-performing-ceos-in-the-world (accessed 24 August 2013).

63. Y. C. Deveshwar, 'Making markets work for CSR', Speech at 96th AGM on 27 July 2007, website http://www.itcportal.com/about-itc/ChairmanSpeakContent.aspx?id=104&type=B&news=chairm an2007 (accessed 12 June 2013).

64. Ibid.

65. S. Denning, *The Leader's Guide to Storytelling: Mastering the Art and Discipline of Business Narrative*. CA: Jossey-Bass, (2005), p. vii.

66. G. R. Dowling, 'Communicating corporate reputation through stories', *California Management Review* (2006), 49(1), 82–100.

67. 'A promise is a promise', Ratan Tata's speech at Nano launch, website http://www.funonthenet.in/ forums/index.php?topic=81793.0;wap2_(accessed14 June 2013).

68. N. Mourkogiannis, 'The realist's guide to moral purpose', *Strategy + Business*, website http://www. strategy-business.com/article/05405?pg=all (accessed 3 July 2013).

69. R. Dubey, '39th AGM of Reliance: Jiyo as life moves on', website https://www.sptulsian.com/ article/74809 (accessed 3 July 2013).

70. H. Gardner, *Changing Minds: The Art and Science of Changing Our Own and Other People's Minds*. Boston: Harvard Business School Press (2006).

71. S. Layak, 'A M Naik on what lies ahead for Larsen and Toubro' (2012), *Business Today*, website http:// businesstoday.intoday.in/story/a.m.-naik-of-larsen-and-toubro-interview/1/21729.html (accessed 12 June 2013).

72. S. Denning, *The Springboard: How Storytelling Ignites Action in Knowledge-era Organizations*. New York: Routledge (2011).

73. G. R. Dowling, 'Communicating corporate reputation through stories', *California Management Review* (2006), 49(1), 82–100, p. 96.

74. Ibid.

75. J. R. Rossiter and S. Bellman, *Marketing Communications*. Sydney: Pearson Prentice-Hall (2005).

76. R. McKee, 'Storytelling that moves people', *Harvard Business Review* (2003), 5–8.

77. K. Hansen, 'Organisational storytelling', *CPA Australia Exchange* (2008), 78(5), 42–45.

78. R. Birla, 'The role of business in alleviating poverty', *Quality Times*, October 2010, website http://www. adityabirla.com/CSR/business-in-alleviating-poverty (accessed 12 June 2013).

79. The quotations page, website http://www.quotationspage.com/quote/1990.html (accessed 30 April 2013).

80. D. Fleet, 'Strategic communications planning', (Ebook), website http://davefleet.com/wp-content/uploads/2008/08/comm-plan-ebook.pdf (accessed 6 June 2013).
81. A. Kaul and V. Singh, Unpublished document created for a PSU. The name of the company has been removed to maintain confidentiality.
82. Brainy quotes, website http://www.brainyquote.com/quotes/keywords/reputation.html (accessed 30 June 2013).
83. G. Peters, *Waltzing with the Raptors: A Practical Roadmap to Protecting your Company's Reputation*. USA: John Wiley & Sons (1999).
84. G. Dowling and P. Moran, 'Corporation reputations: Built in or bolted on?', *California Management Review* (2012), 54(2), 25–42.

Index I

Companies, Regulatory Bodies and Institutes

Index II

People

About the Authors

Asha Kaul is Professor in the Communication Area, Indian Institute of Management, Ahmedabad. She obtained her doctorate in stylistics from the Indian Institute of Technology, Kanpur in 1990. She is the author of *Effective Business Communication* (2000), *The Effective Presentation: Talk Your Way to Success* (2005), *Business Communication* (2nd edition, 2009) and is the co-editor of two books: *Management Communication: Trends and Strategies* (2006) and *New Paradigms for Gender Inclusivity* (2013).

Her current areas of interest include genderlect, politeness, managerial, corporate and digital communication. Currently she is working on Indian cases to comprehend the intricacies involved in corporate decision making for enhancing reputation.

Avani Desai holds a PhD in Investor Relations from Dharmsinh Desai University, Nadiad and an MBA in Finance from Gujarat University. She is a visiting faculty at Indian Institute of Management (IIM), Ahmedabad in the areas of communication and investor relations. She is Director at N R Institute of Business Administration, Gujarat University.

Her areas of interest are investor relations, corporate reputation and corporate communication, especially financial communication.